THE DESCENT OF IDEAS

To the editors and friends, past and present, of the *Journal of the History of Ideas*

The Descent of Ideas
The History of Intellectual History

DONALD R. KELLEY

Ashgate

© Donald R. Kelley 2002

Published by
Ashgate Publishing Limited
Gower House
Croft Road
Aldershot
Hants GU11 3HR
England

Ashgate Publishing Company
131 Main Street
Burlington VT 05401–5600 USA

Ashgate website: http://www.ashgate.com

British Library Cataloguing in Publication Data
Kelley, Donald R. (Donald Reed), 1931–
    The Descent of Ideas: The History of Intellectual History.
    1. Intellectual life—Historiography. 2. Knowledge, Theory of.
    I. Title
    001'.09

Library of Congress Control Number: 2001099660

ISBN 0 7546 0776 3

Typeset by Manton Typesetters, Louth, Lincolnshire, UK.
Printed and bound in Great Britain by MPG Books Ltd, Bodmin, Cornwall

Contents

Acknowledgments

This book is at least indirectly the product of my seventeen-year experience as editor of the *Journal of the History of Ideas*; but the debts I owe go back to my undergraduate and graduate mentors, especially to the late Paul Oskar Kristeller, Felix Gilbert, J. H. Hexter, Hans Baron, John Herman Randall, Jr, Marjorie Hope Nicolson, and Harry Levin – all of whom have served on the editorial board of this journal (except for Baron, who was a contributor). To this list I add the names of scholars who have added in many ways to my understanding of intellectual history, especially Hans Aarsleff, the late Lewis White Beck, Constance Blackwell, Ann Blair, Michael Carhart, Marcia Colish, William Connell, Julian Franklin, Anthony Grafton, Knud Haakonssen, Sarah Hanley, Maryanne Cline Horowitz, J. Paul Hunter, Joel and Karen Kupperman, I. Leonard Leeb, Joseph M. Levine, Edward Mahoney, Alan Megill, Dean Miller, Peter Miller, Martin Mulsow, Steve Nadler, Anthony Pagden, Peter Paret, Kathleen Parrow, John Pocock, Timothy Reiss, David Harris Sacks, J. H. M. Salmon, Wilhelm Schmidt-Biggemann, the late Charles B. Schmitt, J. B. Schneewind, Ulrich Schneider, Gordon Schochet, Jerrold Seigel, Quentin Skinner, Bonnie Smith, Donald Verene, Françoise Waquet, Daniel Woolf, John Yolton, and Perez Zagorin – many presently on the board of editors of the *Journal*. I have no doubt that they all support my project in our common field, whether or not they approve of my eccentric routes.

Much of the writing was done during a year at the Institute for Advanced Study in Princeton, that modern counterpart, for scholars, of the Abbaye de Thelème, and an extraordinary haven for me at several points in my life. I have also profited much from support by the Folger Shakespeare Library, Woodrow Wilson Center, and Rutgers University, and from my association with the International Society for Intellectual History. Closer to home I have been sustained and improved in many ways by Bonnie, Patrick, and Patience Smith, John Kelley, and Robin Ladrach, who keep me in touch with so many important things besides and beyond the life of the mind.

D. R. Kelley

Introduction:
What was the History of Ideas?

> We have a duty to think of
> the dead. It is the only way
> to remain in communion with them.
> Novalis

'What we call the history of ideas itself has a history,' wrote Joseph Mazzeo, referring to classical and Christian precedents.[1] Under various labels – the history of wisdom, the history of thought, the history of the human spirit, and so on – this field of study has had a place on the map of human knowledge for over two centuries, and in more particular aspects – the histories of art, literature, science, and above all philosophy – for a much longer time. Most directly and nominally, the history of ideas is a legacy of the eighteenth century, the pious German *Aufklärung* even more than the French *lumières* or the English Enlightenment. From J. J. Brucker, Vico borrowed the phrase 'history of ideas' to designate one aspect of his 'new science';[2] and thereafter the concept and term had a rich *fortuna* in European thought through the French eclectic school of the nineteenth century down to the time of the American philosopher Arthur O. Lovejoy and various contemporaries.

Ideas begin in the heaven of contemplation and end, for students of the human condition, in the sublunar realm of historical experience. Philosophers try to preserve the transcendent vision of Plato and the dialectical wisdom of Aristotle, but historians have discovered that they must remain in the cave of human discourse in which words and not ideas provide the medium of exchange and targets of inquiry. 'An idea, in the highest sense of that word', Coleridge

---

[1] 'Some Interpretations of the History of Ideas', *Journal of the History of Ideas*, 33 (1972), 379; repr. in *The History of Ideas: Canon and Variations*, ed. D. R. Kelley (Rochester, 1990), 92.

[2] *Scienza nuova*, para. 347, citing Brucker, *Historia philosophica doctrinae de ideis* (Augsburg, 1723), an earlier version appearing as *Testamen de historia de ideis* (Jena, 1718).

1

remarked, 'cannot be conveyed but by a symbol.'[3] The history of ideas may seem to bridge the gap between the ideal and the real, but this is an illusion to the extent that these ideas are already ('always already') incarnate in conventional language. This is one reason for the recent shift from 'history of ideas' to 'intellectual history' – and one reason why I speak of the 'descent of ideas'. Darwin's famous question in *The Descent of Man* was 'whether man ... is descended from some preexisting form', and this study follows an analogous line of inquiry into the early ancestry of intellectual history – except that, like modern revisions of Darwin, the story is not one of simple linear evolution.

The one constant in the writing of intellectual history has been an opposition, implicit or explicit, between an interest in creations of human thought and ingenuity and concerns with war, politics, and public institutions. The libraries are filled with histories of sieges and battles, complained J.-F. Montucla, the eighteenth-century historian of mathematics; it was time to look at the more positive side of human history, for here was revealed the 'human spirit' itself.[4] And as Lord Acton wrote in 1861,

> There is nothing which so favorably distinguishes modern from ancient historians as the importance they allow to the immaterial metaphysical agents in human affairs, and the attempts to trace the progress of ideas, as well as the succession of events, and the reaction of one upon the other.[5]

Intellectual history is closely related to cultural history, being analogous to the polar modes of inquiry commonly known as internalist and externalist – or the 'intellectualist' (or even 'spiritualist') and 'contextualist' – approaches. The first of these methods is located in individual psychology and mental phenomena, the second in collective behavior, inherited or learned practice, and cultural surroundings. For history this takes two forms. One is the habit of tracing ideas in terms of an inner dynamic, or familiar logic, similar to what the eighteenth century called 'reasoned' or 'conjectural' history.[6] The

---

[3] *Biographia Literaria*, I, 9.

[4] *Histoire des mathematiques* (4 vols; Paris, 1758–1802²), 42–3, and Noel Swerdlow, 'Montucla's Legacy: The History of the Exact Sciences', *Journal of the History of Ideas*, 54 (1993), 315; also Jean Dagen, *Histoire de l'esprit humain dans la pensée française de Fontenelle à Condorcet* (Paris, 1977).

[5] 'Expectation of the French Revolution', in *Essays in the Study and Writing of History*, ed. J. Rufus Fears (Indianapolis, 1985), 38; and for a collection of manuscript musings on 'Ideas as Historical Forces', see *Essays in Religion, Politics, and Morality*, ed. Fears (Indianapolis, 1989), 643–7.

[6] See, for example, the analytical approach of Mark Bevir, *The Logic of the History of Ideas* (Cambridge, 1999), and Carl Page, *Philosophical Historicism and the Betrayal of First Philosophy* (University Park, PA, 1995).

second tries to set ideas in the context of their own particular time, place, and environment, without assuming any spiritual continuities over time.[7]

Think of this polarity as complementary forms of inquiry undertaken within a horizon-structure of experience.[8] The center of this intellectual space locates the historical subject (conscious, intentional, or even unconscious), or perhaps a single act of discovery, creation, or conceptualization – a pure spiritual or phenomenological moment that becomes a target of historical inquiry. The surrounding space encompasses the contexts of the central subject – the preconditions, influences, possibilities, resonances, connections, and effects involving other fields of cultural activity, states of disciplinary questions, and 'climates of opinion' – the 'past' being represented by residues in the present signifying otherwise inaccessible bygone experience. Beyond the circle of experience, beyond perhaps even the resources of language, we may imagine a transition from intellectual and cultural history to philosophical speculation and metahistorical criticism. In any case this is one way of imagining the problem from the standpoint of the human agent: intellectual history is the inside of cultural history, cultural history the outside of intellectual history; but in both cases 'ideas' must be brought down to a human level.

Writing intellectual and cultural history was and still is central to the 'Enlightenment project';[9] and it is in this context that the 'history of ideas', the 'history of civilization', and the 'history of culture' have been defined as particular fields of study and represented by vast outpourings of books, articles, and learned exchanges. In the nineteenth century these fields became distinguishable genres and disciplines, with codes of practice and theoretical justifications that were celebrated and subjected to critical and historical examination. In European universities, in the larger intelligentsia once defined as the Republic of Letters, and in a wider literate public, intellectual and cultural history found a base, a following, and a succession of schools and subdisciplines that struggled over this legacy.

Romanticism also gave an impulse to intellectual history through its various obsessions with the cultural past. 'The human being continues to live and be active only in the realm of ideas … ,' Novalis wrote, and his conclusion was in effect a motto for the post-Enlightenment view of the history of ideas: 'Therefore we have a duty to think of the dead. It is the only way to remain in

---

[7] For an older view, see the work of Lovejoy's colleague, George Boas, *The History of Ideas* (New York, 1969), and Kelley, ed., *The History of Ideas*.

[8] Guenther Buck, 'The Structure of Hermeneutic Experience and the Problem of Tradition', *New Literary History*, 10 (1978), 31–47.

[9] See D. R. Kelley, 'Intellectual and Cultural History: The Inside and the Outside', *History of the Human Sciences* 9 (2002).

communion with them.'[10] As for social meanings of intellectual creations, they were defined most famously by Bonald's oft-repeated formula, 'Literature is an expression of society.'[11]

The tap root of intellectual history, especially in the earlier form of the 'history of ideas', is the history of philosophy, 'the common seed-plot', said Lovejoy, 'of the greater number of the more fundamental and pervasive ideas, ... which manifest themselves in other regions of intellectual history'.[12] According to the seventeenth-century polyhistor Johann Alsted, philosophy was the 'knowledge of everything intelligible',[13] and so its history encompassed the whole range of human intellectual effort. The history of philosophy (*historia philosophica*) emerged at this time as a distinct discipline and was endowed with a more or less official canon by J. J. Brucker's *Critical History of Philosophy* (1742–44), a cornerstone of the eclectic school of philosophy, which took history rather than metaphysics as 'first philosophy'.

In the later eighteenth century, however, especially under the influence of Kant, philosophy narrowed its focus and sought a status as a 'rigorous science', in the words of the Kantian Tennemann, anticipating those of Husserl a century later.[14] The Cartesian *Cogito* and the Kantian transcendental subject – the first-person, thinking subject without memory, passion, gender, race, nationality, or class – captured the minds of many thinkers who sought a philosophy purged of contingency, human qualities, and so of history. The upshot was a growing divergence between the 'critical' advocates of pure reason like Kant, and learned and 'metacritical' defectors like Herder who, following the descent of ideas into the medium of language, strayed off into what came to be known as cultural history.

In a longer perspective this opposition between purists and culturalists reproduced the old distinction between philosophy 'itself' and doxography – between ideas and the 'lives and opinions' of the philosophers, which treated

---

[10] *Philosophical Writings*, trans. Margaret Mahony Stoljar (Albany, 1997), 29.

[11] *Législation primitif* (Paris, 1829), II, 223.

[12] *Essays in the History of Ideas* (Baltimore, 1948), 8. Lovejoy's first usage of the phrase 'history of ideas' occurred in 1919 (*Modern Language Notes*, 34, 305), according to Gladys Gordon-Bournique, *Arthur O. Lovejoy et l'histoire des idées* (Ph.D. dissertation, Paris, 1974).

[13] Johann Heinrich Alsted, *Philosophia digne restituta libros quatuor* (Herborn, 1615), 10: 'philosophia est omnis scibilis cognitio'; and see also his *Scientiarum omnium Encyclopedia* (Lyon, 1649), *Panacea Philosophica* (Herborn, 1610), and *Theatrum scholasticum* (Herborn, 1620).

[14] Edmund Husserl, 'Philosophie als strenge Wissenschaft', *Logos*, 1 (1910); and W. G. Tennemann, *Geschichte der Philosophie* (8 vols; Leipzig, 1798), I, viii, 'ein strenge wissenschaftliches System'.

the human condition of philosophizing, including anecdotal insights, the classical model being the work of Diogenes Laertius (third century AD), which has been continued down to the present in surveys of western philosophy.[15] On a higher and more critical level, this view of philosophy demanded awareness of the larger cultural context and what the skeptic Joseph Glanvill called 'climates of opinion'.[16] Turning from philosophical foreground to cultural background, eighteenth-century German historians of philosophy like C. A. Heumann studied the influence of climate, environment, race, nationality, psychology, physiology, gender, and historical periods.[17] More recently such 'old ways of thinking' echo in the no-nonsense criticisms of pragmatism – William James declaring, for instance, that 'The history of philosophy is to a great extent that of a clash of human temperaments.'[18] On many levels philosophy was a human effort and not above human criticism.

'This is an age of criticism,' declared Kant, but in fact it was an age of many 'criticisms', not all of them very 'critical' from a modern standpoint.[19] On the one hand there was the traditional art of criticism (*ars critica*), which focused, sometimes carpingly, on literary and philological matters – the tradition extending from Valla and Poliziano to Kant and Herder's contemporary, F. A. Wolf – and on the other hand the 'critical' stance of Brucker's history of philosophy, which, in keeping with eclectic method, professed to distinguish truth from error (and especially Lutheran truth from pagan and Catholic errors). Then there was Kant's own project, which identified criticism with the free play of reason and in his view offered a transcendental foundation for knowledge beyond language and experience.

But this transcendental space, too, was an arena of endless controversy. Disagreement about the meaning of philosophy – a process of reasoning aimed at scientific certainty or a common-sense pursuit carried out within the limitations of the human condition? – locates the point where the canon of philosophy and the trajectory of ideas diverges from its larger literary history, including auxiliary disciplines like philology and aesthetics. There was a deep conceptual divide – a *Methodenstreit* – between Kant's 'apriori history of philosophy' and the irrelevant 'archeology' (Kant's pejorative term; Hegel's was 'pedantry') of a Brucker or a

---

[15] Diogenes Laertius, *Lives of Eminent Philosophers*; and see below, Chapter 2.

[16] *Vanity of Dogmatizing* (London, 1661), 227.

[17] *Acta Philosophorum, Gründl. Nachrichten aus der Historia Philosophica*, ed. C. A. Heumann (Halle, 1715–21), I, 567ff.; and see below, Chapter 5.

[18] *Pragmatism, a New Name for Some Old Ways of Thinking* (New York, 1907), 6.

[19] Jean Jehasse, *La Renaissance de la critique: l'essor de l'humanisme érudit de 1560 à 1614* (Saint-Etienne, 1976); and see below, Chapter 3.

Tennemann, and the endless accumulation of 'the literature' of the subject and questions of psychology, environment, mythology, and 'culture'.[20]

This brings us to an even larger context of these issues, which is the history of literature – literature in the similarly traditional sense of the total accumulation of humanity's written remains. This was the view taken by scholars like Alsted, Morhof, and Vossius, for whom philosophy itself, especially in an age of print culture, was in the first instance a form of literature. But 'literature' itself of course covered many other creations of the human spirit, and its history (*historia literaria*) cut another channel that converged with the history of philosophy and with the study of culture in a more general sense. As one scholar puts it, 'What Vossius called "literary history", was really what would now be called cultural history.'[21]

While philosophy involves thought, however, literature is confined to written expression; and here language becomes of central concern. The first question is whether language is an obstacle to ideas, whether God-given or rendered clear and distinct by human conceptualizing, or whether ideas are constituted by human language. This issue, which was debated furiously by early modern authors, lies at the heart, too, of the practice and theory of intellectual and cultural history. Philosophy may rise above language in its premises and goals, but can historians also make a leap of faith beyond written discourse and between the lines of textual remains? This dilemma marks the point of divergence not only between the history of philosophy and of literature but also between the history of ideas and the history of culture.

Yet this issue has also bound these intellectual traditions together over many generations. The significant point here is that any effort to understand the more remote background of these areas of inquiry must follow the trail of the history of literature in general and of philosophy in particular; and this is just the strategy adopted in this book.[22] What I offer on this journey is a series of mappings and soundings in the large, and largely uncharted, fields of the practice and theory, *ante litteram*, primarily of intellectual and secondarily of cultural history.

---

[20] Lutz Geldsetzer, *Die Philosophie der Philosophiegeschichte* (Meisenheim, 1968), with further references.

[21] Nicholas Wickenden, *G. J. Vossius and the Humanist Concept of History* (Assen, 1993), 73; see also C. S. M. Rademaker, *Life and Works of Gerardus Joannes Vossius (1577–1649)* (Assen, 1981), 55.

[22] D. R. Kelley, 'What is Happening to the History of Ideas?', *Journal of the History of Ideas*, 51 (1990), 3–25, and 'Horizons of Intellectual History: Retrospect, Circumspect, Prospect', ibid., 48 (1987), 143–69, repr. in *The History of Ideas*, ed. Kelley; and for some recent bibliography in a vast literature see Robert F. Berkofer, Jr, *Beyond the Great Story: History and Text and Discourse* (Cambridge, MA, 1995).

I begin with the seminal period of early nineteenth-century France because it is here, and specifically in the 'eclectic philosophy' of Victor Cousin, that the history of philosophy found a rationale and that the 'history of ideas' found theoretical as well as nominal and practical expression. Although its purpose was philosophical, eclecticism depended in the most fundamental way on historical understanding and selection and on the history of ideas; and in his historical approach Cousin himself was building on the foundations of the Enlightenment as well as the history of western philosophy in its encyclopedic sense, going back, via Descartes and Abelard, to Plato, Aristotle, and their followers.

My exploration traces eclecticism from its Greek beginnings, when the succession of philosophical schools set the pattern for the history of doctrines; through the medieval and early modern periods, when the history of ideas was in effect defined by Christian commentators on and humanist revivers of these doctrines, and sometimes of the 'barbarian' prehistory of philosophy before its Greek inception; the seventeenth-century 'way of ideas' and the challenge from the standpoint of language and history; and then back to the German and French eclectics of the eighteenth and nineteenth centuries, when the history of philosophy acquired disciplinary and professional status and produced an autonomous offshoot in the form of 'cultural history', and when the 'history of ideas' itself assumed quasi-disciplinary form. In the following chapters I survey a number of nineteenth- and twentieth-century practitioners of the history of ideas, who, working within the disciplines of literature, science, the human sciences, and philosophy, have contributed to intellectual and cultural history.

Finally, what about the current state of the common ground shared by these fields of inquiry and intellectual history? Despite the temptations to invoke millennialist rhetoric, a historical perspective prevents banal talk about decadence, revival, crisis, or utter novelty. Yet change there is; and I seem to detect, among historians, a significant turn away from the spiritual world of ideas to the human condition of language, interpretation, communication, and cultural construction. As Whitehead remarked, 'Ideas won't keep.'[23] For twenty-four centuries 'ideas' have served to locate the elements of human experience and reflection (and indeed still serve as a useful shorthand), but successive waves of skepticism have cast shadows over the bright and avowedly 'real' world of Plato's devising. For Nietzsche this is illusory, if not mendacious; for in his view humanity has remained confined to the cave, and the dream of

[23] *Dialogues of Alfred North Whitehead* (New York, 1953), 100.

escaping into a spiritual world belongs to the hope of religion and philosophy, not the experience of history.

A conjectural or reasoned history of the question of 'ideas' would begin with the Platonic formulation, which was associated with the basically religious, or mythical, conception of the soul, its divinity, its immortality, and its transcendent substance, and with Aristotle's philosophical reformulation of ideas as forms. The fortunes of ideas involved massive commentaries and elaborations in other religious traditions, Greek and Islamic, as well as Latin and vernacular, and revivals in Renaissance Neoplatonism and the 'way of ideas' in seventeenth-century philosophy. The other (Nietzschean) side of this history was the anti-philosophical, or at least anti-spiritualist, critique of this spiritual world beyond nature and human experience, a critique which began with the sophists and which included philologists, rhetoricians, and skeptics, whose arguments underlay the linguistic and cultural turns of the Enlightenment and more recent times. In this highly generalized account the practice and theory of the 'history of ideas' has shifted from the speculative task of intuiting the thoughts of past authors to the scholarly project of examining historically the linguistic traces and expressions of this putative and mediated tradition of thought.

The story is one not so much of evolution or even inheritance, however, as of incarnation, the descent of the dove, or perhaps of Icarus, of Dante's pilgrimage taken in reverse, from the height of spiritual belief down to the world and netherworld of human experience, of the death of Socrates without the hope of immortality, of the return to the Platonic cave without a transcendent vision of a spiritual reality, or even a return to the realm of myth before this vision. This time, however, the return to earth, or to myth, represents a critical advance beyond the aspirations of a higher reality and a life beyond life. This counter-creed is hardly sufficient for religious, philosophical, or perhaps even political convictions, but for historians it is an invigorating challenge – and moreover a perspective that cannot be transcended in this life.

In any case these are some of the issues taken up in the last chapter, which has been written in the spirit of this line of criticism. The premise is that intellectual historians must be resigned to carry on their work in a world which is accessible only in its cultural – written or material – manifestations, a world in which ideas descend from the heights of philosophical reflection to the heuristic and interpretative level of intellectual and cultural history.

Chapter 1

Prelude:
The New Philosophy of Victor Cousin

> In our eyes Eclecticism is the true
> historical method, and for us it has all
> the importance of the history of philosophy.
> Victor Cousin

The 'history of ideas' had a nominal existence in the Enlightenment, but it was in nineteenth-century France that it emerged most conspicuously as an independent practice. It was still associated with philosophy, to be sure, but it also became recognizable as a branch of historical scholarship distinct from the old conventions of 'doing philosophy'. Or rather, it was joined to a particular way of doing philosophy, a so-called 'eclectic' way, in which history in effect took precedence over unassisted and unencumbered reason and became 'first philosophy'. The modern philosophy of eclecticism appeared in France in the early nineteenth century. Eclecticism had important antecedents in early modern Germany and in antiquity; but it was Victor Cousin, student of philosophical schools from Plato and Proclus to Descartes and Kant, who revived the term, established his own school, and found a rationale for this conception which incarnated the history of philosophy and that more particularized pursuit which he called *l'histoire des idées*.[1] So it is Cousin's work that marks the point of entry for this study of the backgrounds of the history of ideas.

1. French Eclecticism

In December 1815, in the first year both of the Restoration Monarchy and of his own teaching at the Ecole Normale Supérieure, Victor Cousin was lecturing

---

[1] *Manuel de l'histoire de la philosophie de Tennemann* (Paris, 1829), I, 36, 'Histoire des idées, de principes, de doctrines particulières', such as the idea of God, atheism, pantheism, fate, liberty, soul, association of ideas, and so on. Tennemann, *Geschichte der Philosophie* (Leipzig, 1798), I, xli, also uses the term 'Philosopheme'.

on the history of philosophy. In post-Revolutionary France this was a field in great disarray, and Cousin harked back to the great schools of the Enlightenment, commending three of these in particular – the French, the Scottish, and the German traditions, which were represented respectively by Condillac, Reid, and Kant. 'It would be an interesting and instructive study', he told his enthusiastic young students, 'to examine the weaknesses of these schools by engaging one with another and by selecting their various merits in the context of a great eclecticism which would contain and surpass all three.'[2]

Over his next five years of lecturing, before being dismissed in 1820, Cousin had established his own doctrinal school, an Eclectic (capital E) philosophy – whose name he 'first stammered' in 1816 – which purported to draw on and to transcend these earlier systems.[3] Thereafter French eclecticism was publicized by Cousin's many scholarly publications, the lectures he gave after returning to his chair of philosophy in 1828, his international contacts, his many disciples, and his public career as minister of education. For a half-century before his death in 1867 Cousin had an unparalleled influence as virtually the 'official philosopher' in France, with his version of eclecticism being widely regarded as a 'state philosophy';[4] and translations of his works extended his renown also into Germany, Italy, and the Anglophone world.

Cousin's eclecticism was in part a search for his own intellectual forebears – literally an ego trip, following the fashionable *Ich*- and *Moi*-centered idealism

[2] *Premiers essais de philosophie* (Paris, 1862; 4th edn), 280. See especially the recent comprehensive work by Patrice Vermeren, *Victor Cousin* (Paris, 1994) and Ulrich Johannes Schneider, *Philosophie und Universität: Historisierung der Vernunft im 19. Jahrhundert* (Hamburg, 1998), 180–212. Important earlier studies are by followers, especially Jules Barthélemy-Saint-Hilaire, *M. Victor Cousin, sa vie et sa correspondance* (3 vols; Paris, 1895), the major life and times, with many letters; Jules Simon, *Victor Cousin* (Paris, 1897); and Paul Janet, *Victor Cousin et son œuvre* (Paris, 1865). See also the collection edited by Vermeren, *Victor Cousin, suivi de la correspondance Schelling–Cousin*, Corpus, 18–19 (1991), and *Catalogue des manuscrits des bibliothèques publiques de Paris. Université de Paris* (Paris, 1918), and the *Supplement. Bibliothèque de la Sorbonne* (Paris, 1989).
[3] *Course of the History of Modern Philosophy* (New York, 1960), I, 272. Paul Janet, *La Philosophie française* (Paris, 1879), 8, calls Cousin's school 'la philosophie nouvelle'. See also Sainte-Beuve's articles, collected in *Les grands écrivains français: XIXe siècle, Philosophes et essayistes*, ed. Maurice Allem (Paris, 1930); Augustin Thierry, *Dix ans d'études historiques* (Paris, 1835), 203; Hippolyte Taine, *Les Philosophes classiques du XIX siècle en France* (Paris, 1888), 79ff.; J. E. Alaux, *La Philosophie de M. Cousin* (Paris, 1864); and Saphary, *L'Ecole éclectique et l'école française* (Paris, 1844); also Frederick Copleston, *A History of Philosophy*, IX (London, 1975), 37–50, and Martial Gueroult, *Histoire de l'histoire de la philosophie*, III (Paris, 1988), 707ff.
[4] See Stéphanie Donailler et al., *La Philosophie saisie par l'état* (Paris, 1988), 149ff.

of Kant, Hegel, Fichte, and Maine de Biran – and a way of locating himself in philosophical tradition. The link with antiquity was established especially through Plato and Proclus, whose works he edited. The Neoplatonist Proclus, who stood precariously between paganism and Christianity, was the last in the line of ancient philosophers before Justinian closed the Greek schools in 529. For Proclus Platonic ideas had originated with Pythagoras and (contradicting sectarian opinion) were preserved by Aristotle. As Cousin's disciple Jules Simon wrote, 'All the Alexandrines are eclectics, but Proclus is the most eclectic of all'; and so indeed he was represented by Cousin.[5] To Plato's pure insight Proclus added the precious gift of Hellenistic erudition.

The great chain of ideas linking Cousin with Plato and Proclus was continued in the twelfth century, when philosophy came to center on Paris. The originator of this French tradition was Peter Abelard, who had created an 'intermediary system' in 'the great quarrel of the time, which was that between the Realists and the Nominalists'.[6] Five centuries later Descartes, who was Abelard's only peer, also became his nemesis as the 'destroyer' of Abelard's scholastic system and, thereby, 'father of modern philosophy'. There were other links in the chain, but the philosophical canon and Cousin's own culminating posture, seven centuries after Abelard and two centuries after Descartes, seems clear. Obviously Cousin, editor of the works of both of these predecessors, was claiming a place in this philosophical genealogy by adapting and combining their ideas in the higher mediation of eclecticism.

In assembling his eclectic system Cousin ranged as widely in space as he did in time, his appetite for foreign ideas being displayed not only in his courses but also in his translations and in his role in bringing the works of Kant, Hegel, Herder, and Vico to the attention of the French intelligentsia. 'I congratulate myself', he wrote later in his famous textbook, 'upon having encouraged my two young friends, MM. Michelet and Quinet, to give to France Vico and Herder.'[7] Yet against the principles of his own school and in the face of a long tradition of eclecticism by no means unknown to French scholars, Cousin claimed an absolute originality and a unique truth-value for his derivative ideas. Eclecticism had not been drawn from German sources, he protested in 1855. 'It was born spontaneously in our own spirit [*notre esprit*] from the spectacle of the resounding conflicts and the hidden harmonies

---

[5] *Procli philosophici platonici opera*, Latin trans. Victor Cousin (Paris, 1820); and see Simon, *Histoire de l'école d'Alexandrie* (Paris, 1845), II, 397.

[6] Introduction to *Ouvrages inédits d'Abelard pour servir à l'histoire de la philosophie scholastique en France*, ed. Victor Cousin (Paris, 1836), ii, iv.

[7] *Course of the History of Modern Philosophy*, I, 225.

of the three great philosophical schools of the eighteenth century', he declared. 'Thus', he concluded, 'eclecticism is a French doctrine and peculiar to us.'[8]

Nothing, historically speaking, could be further from the truth – or indeed from the premises of the eclectic tradition. The defining characteristic of his philosophy was its dependence not only on the three schools he recognized in his early years, but on the whole history of philosophy from its Greek and especially Platonic beginnings, to which Cousin himself devoted much of his historical scholarship. Rejecting 'that blind syncretism which destroyed the school of Alexandria', he shared the premises accepted by German eclectics for over a century that the history of philosophy, including its errors as well as its truths, was inseparable from and indeed an essential part of philosophy itself. (This was the message of Hegel, too, in his lectures, begun in October 1816 and known to Cousin, on the history of philosophy.) 'What I recommend', Cousin declared in 1817, 'is an enlightened eclecticism which, judging with equity, and even with benevolence, all schools, borrows from them what they possess of the true and neglects what in them is false.'[9]

Eclecticism was a philosophy for post-Revolutionary and Restoration times – for the 'new generation' of 1815 it was, in the words of Alfred Musset, 'notre goût'.[10] In many circles eighteenth-century philosophy had worn out its welcome. The Jacobin and subsequently Bonapartist views – 'abuses of the philosophical spirit', in the phrase of one critic, writing out of exile experience[11] – called out for a reevaluation of intellectual tradition; and Cousin was among the first to ride the wave of this philosophical revisionism, based on an inventory of philosophically correct ideas culled from the history of philosophy. The most obvious approach to Cousinian eclecticism is therefore a kind of critical *Quellenforschung*, a chronicle of 'influences' – or record of plagiarisms – native and foreign, which, if exhaustively carried, would turn out to be a review of the whole history of philosophy, to which Cousin indeed devoted much of his scholarly life.

In fact Cousin was anticipated even in France in the quest for a renewed philosophy based on an examination of its history. In 1804 Baron M.-J.

---

[8] Cousin, *Premiers essais*.

[9] *Lectures on the True, the Good and the Beautiful*, trans. O. W. Wight (New York, 1872), 9. On the distinction between 'true' eclecticism and 'false' eclecticism (that is, syncretism), see Jacques Matter, *Essai historique sur l'école d'Alexandrie* (Paris, 1820), II, 253; cf. I, 297.

[10] Cited by Alfred Cornelius, *Die Geschichtslehre Victor Cousins unter besonderer Berücksichtung hegelschen Einflusses* (Genestre, 1958), 19. The phrase 'nouvelle generation' is Sainte-Beuve's (*Les grands écrivains*, 221).

[11] J. E. M. Portalis, *De l'usage et de l'abus de l'Esprit philosophique durant le dix-huitième siècle* (Paris, 1827).

Degérando had published his *Comparative History of the Systems of Philosophy with regard to the Principles of Human Knowledge* (1804), written after the experience of exile and under the influence of 'Idéologie' – that 'science of ideas' which Napoleon so despised. Like Cousin after him and Tennemann and Brucker before him, Degérando believed that philosophy was inseparable from its history. According to Degérando, the earliest systems, established in Ionia, represented a victory over myth and idolatry and the beginning of 'slow progress' toward enlightenment. The sophists were not really philosophers at all; the impact of the skeptics was largely negative; the ancient eclectics offered only a 'mélange of sects'; and medieval philosophy, including the Arabs, made the unpardonable mistake of confusing logic and reality. More significant were the new, 'original', and 'happier' systems of authors like Bruno, Ramus, Campanella, and especially Condillac. For Degérando the true beginning of 'modern' philosophy, however, was in the work of Bacon – in the 'positive' and 'natural' way to the 'advancement of learning' and to what Degérando called a 'revolution in ideas'.[12] In a later edition (1842) he added a notice about the 'new eclecticism in Germany' which he recognized as preceding the 'regeneration' of philosophy in Britain, Italy, and France.[13] In this connection Degérando quoted Kant's friend and critic Garve's celebration of the history of philosophy as 'not only the tableau of the ideas and opinions of different philosophers ... [but also] the description and explanation of the various revolutions which human knowledge [*la science humaine*] has experienced from the origins to the present'.[14] In Degérando's comparative study one may catch a glimpse of the epistemological foundations of the amorphous field which Cousin, shifting from individual psychology to collective humanity, called the 'history of ideas'.

The chief characters of Degérando's story were not individual philosophers but their more or less ingeniously devised 'systems', the constituent parts of which were particular 'ideas', which 'formed a body and an ensemble through the connection they have in the mind of the one who conceived them'.[15] In particular Degérando recognized, after the 'reformation' of philosophy begun by Bacon, individual schools of idealism, dogmatism, rational or speculative philosophy, modern skepticism, empiricism, Scottish philosophy, and criticism (that is, Kant) – not to mention 'modern eclectics' such as J. F. Buddeus and Diderot.[16] This discussion was surely significant in turning his own mind

---

12 *Comparative History*, I, 17.
13 Ibid., IV, 33.
14 Ibid., IV, 128–9.
15 Ibid., II, 486.
16 See below, Chapter 5.

toward these German antecedents, though he never connected it with his own methodological innovations. The ultimate purpose of Degérando, like that of Cousin, was 'by studying the history of different sects, their birth, development, successions, conflicts, and mutual relations, to seize upon their true points of divergence, the causes of their oppositions, and the origins of their disputes', and so to judge their utility for modern problems. It was above all in post-Baconian 'experimental philosophy' that these systems and ideas, critically understood, were to be 'reconciled and mediated' and in this way to find their 'harmony' and fulfillment. In his investigations into the history of the 'human spirit', what Degérando offered, then, was an elaborate theory of intellectual 'progress' based on a 'philosophy of experience' – and of course on a more correct understanding of the past of philosophy. This was the foundation on which Cousin, along with many colleagues and epigones, was also building.

2.   Cousin's Way

Born in 1792, Cousin, the future tsar of higher education in France, was educated during a period of doldrums in French intellectual life, with only the school of 'Idéologie' exerting much influence and 'Romanticism' being still largely a foreign menace. In 1810, having made a clean sweep of the available academic prizes, Cousin entered the first class of the Ecole Normale Supérieure, and two years later he was already teaching Greek in that newly founded institution. Cousin's most important intellectual associations at this time were Degérando, Pierre Laromiguière, F. P. G. Maine de Biran, and Pierre-Paul Royer-Collard, who were all transitional figures between the Idéologues and the Doctrinaires and who were all seeking, in the wake of the 'pre-critical' philosophy of Descartes and Condillac, the truth about 'ideas'.

After Degérando's extraordinary survey of the history of philosophical systems, it might be thought that Cousin had little to add. In fact Cousin was never very impressed with Degérando's Idéologue effort, not even the new edition of 1823 which he reviewed – 'too artificial to be good'[17] – though in his funeral eulogy in 1842 he gave his elder colleague some credit as a pioneer. Nevertheless, Cousin took as his own point of departure (though without very specific acknowledgment) the view of the history of philosophy offered by Degérando, while expanding it by a much more deliberate and

---

[17] *Fragments de philosophie contemporaine* (Paris, 1856), 286.

conspicuous employment of an 'eclectic' method in practice as well as theory and by distancing himself from the 'materialism' of Condillac, whose approach, he thought, 'mutilated the human spirit'.

Cousin had three other acknowledged sources of inspiration. One was Maine de Biran, who for Cousin was the premier psychologist of the day because of his criticism of the physiological approach fashionable in those years. The other was Laromiguière, who lectured on philosophy at the Ecole Normale in 1811–12 and whose influence led to Cousin's conversion to a philosophical calling. 'This was the day that decided my whole life', he wrote of his first class with Laromiguière.[18] The third influence was Royer-Collard, who had founded a society of spiritualist philosophy to counter the materialist legacy of the Revolution; and Cousin, a member of this group, shared its attitudes.[19] In 1815, through the good offices of Royer-Collard, Cousin succeeded Laromiguière in the chair of philosophy in the Ecole and began denouncing

> this tradition of materialism and atheism, blind hatred of Christianity, and revolutionary violence [which] at the beginning of the Restoration weighed on people's minds and souls and prevented the establishment of liberty as well as of true philosophy.[20]

In the philosophical vacuum of Bonapartist France, Cousin, following Royer-Collard, turned to the Scottish common-sense school for guidance, though correcting this 'sensualist philosophy' with a characteristic dash of 'spiritualism', betokening cordiality both toward Christian religion and toward idealist – Kantian and Hegelian as well as Platonic – philosophy, not to mention the spirit of the new bourgeois age. Cousin devoted his study and teaching first to elementary philosophical problems: the philosophical trinity of the ideas of the True, the Beautiful, and the Good – and then, in the fashion of Degérando, to the study of philosophical 'systems'. It was at this point that Cousin encountered, or (as he preferred to think) devised, an eclectic approach as a way both of organizing the history of thought for his young students and of claiming a 'method' of attaining truth. 'In our eyes Eclecticism is the true historical method, and for us it has all the importance of the history of philosophy', Cousin declared in 1816; 'but there is something which we place above the history of philosophy, and thus above eclecticism – philosophy itself'.[21]

---

[18] Barthélemy-Saint-Hilaire, *M. Victor Cousin*, I, 36.
[19] See Royer-Collard, 'Fragments philosophiques', in Thomas Reid, *Œuvres complètes*, trans. T. Jouffroy (Paris, 1828), 299ff.
[20] *Philosophie sensualiste au dix-huitième siècle* (Paris, 1864), ii–iii.
[21] *Du Vrai*, (Paris, 1816), 35.

In his search for a new philosophical system Cousin was not long content with the 'sensualism' of the Scottish school; by 1817 he was moving on to German idealism, and by 1820 he was beginning to study Kant. In that same year Cousin collaborated in publishing a translation of Dugald Stewart's *General View of the Progress of Metaphysical, Moral, and Political Philosophy since the Revival of Letters*; and in this connection he brought to the attention of French readers the virtually unknown *Scienza nuova* of Giambattista Vico, later translated by Jules Michelet.[22] Cousin himself encouraged this publication, as also that of the work of J. G. Herder on 'the idea of the philosophy of history' by Michelet's friend Edgar Quinet.[23] That the writings of Vico and Herder represented a fundamental critique of the sort of 'spiritualism' taught by Cousin did not prevent them from being incorporated into the eclectic canon. For Cousin, Vico was significant mainly for his theory of the *corsi* and *ricorsi* of gentile civilizations, a theory which Cousin, with characteristic superficiality, likened to Polybius's notion of constitutional cycles.[24]

In the conservative climate following the assassination of the Duke of Berry, Cousin was dismissed from his teaching post (the Ecole Normale itself being closed), and he devoted himself more intensely to scholarly pursuits and travels of intellectual discovery. In 1817 he had taken his first break from teaching and made his first *deutsche Reise*, establishing intellectual contacts in Heidelberg, Göttingen, Berlin, and Weimar, including Hegel, Schelling, Jacobi, and Goethe.[25] In philosophical terms, he recalled, Germany was 'on fire' at that time, and from these foreign flames Cousin lit his own philosophical torch. This was in the heyday of what one contemporary called 'the philosophical alliance between France and Germany'.[26]

In 1824 Cousin returned to Germany with some notoriety, found himself arrested, and spent some time in a Berlin prison before being released, with the help of Hegel. He gained a considerable reputation, especially among Hegelians, and he soon began an even more extensive correspondence with German philosophers. Heinrich Heine was one of the few to cast doubt on the scholarly legend which, in Germany, represented Cousin as a leader of

---

[22] *Histoire abrégée des sciences metaphysiques, morales et politiques depuis la renaissance des lettres*, trans. J. A. Buchon (Paris, 1820), ded. to Cousin; see Michelet, *Œuvres complètes*, I (Paris, 1971), for his trans. of Vico's *La Science nouvelle* (1827).

[23] Herder, *Idées sur la philosophie de l'histoire*, trans. Quinet (Paris, 1827).

[24] *Histoire abrégée*, 369.

[25] Michel Espagne and Michael Werner (eds), *Lettres d'Allemagne: Victor Cousin et les hégéliens* (Tusson, Charente, 1990).

[26] Barchou de Penhoes, *Histoire de la philosophie allemande depuis Leibniz jusqu'à Hegel* (Paris, 1836), I, 9.

French philosophy already in the mid-1820s, and, in France, as having laid the foundations of his Kantian expertise in his Berlin prison. This was impossible, remarked Heine, since the book was in German and since Cousin did not really know German. Heine would not be the last to doubt that Cousin actually grasped the German philosophy about which he talked and wrote so much.[27]

Nevertheless, Cousin was an extremely active scholar during his forced retirement in the 1820s, preparing editions of Proclus, Abelard, and Descartes and translations of Plato and of the great history of philosophy by the Kantian, Tennemann, which became another vehicle of – and supplied much more material for – Cousin's eclectic philosophy.[28] In this work Cousin found and celebrated a long tradition of the 'history of ideas' (*histoire des idées*) going back especially to the earlier school of modern eclecticism centered at the University of Halle and to the monumental history of J. J. Brucker, whom Cousin honored as 'the father of the history of philosophy'[29] and whose scholarship he did not scruple to plunder.

In his monumental *Critical History of Philosophy* Brucker had classified virtually all philosophy from Bacon's system as 'eclectic', and his German successors in the century between him and Cousin continued this tradition. Though Cousin had claimed ignorance of this tradition, it was hardly unknown in France; for in a report on 'the progress of learning' since 1789, prepared for Napoleon in 1808 and published in 1810, Dacier had referred to 'the eclectic philosophers of Germany';[30] and Degérando's work of 1804 showed familiarity with the work of Tiedemann and Tennemann as well as Kant – not to mention the 'eclectic' school of antiquity. In the end it was Cousin who, in France at least, reaped this rich eclectic harvest, however carelessly gathered, interpreted, and distributed, and scorned by later generations.

Cousin took a deliberately derivative view of the history of philosophy, which he surveyed in a textbook that had at least a dozen editions during the century.[31] Philosophical systems were all 'products of the human spirit', he taught, including the 'philosophy before philosophers' expressed in oriental myth and poetry; but the philosophy he recognized began with the Greeks.

---

[27] In 1834 Schelling had published an appraisal of Cousin criticizing his views as naïve and essentially pre-Kantian, published in *Système de l'idéalisme transcendental*, trans. Paul Grimblot (Paris, 1842), 377ff.

[28] See above, note 1.

[29] *Course of the History of Modern Philosophy*, I, 236.

[30] Dacier, *Tableau historique de l'érudition française* (Paris, 1862), 344, remarking also that France had no history of philosophy at that time.

[31] *Histoire générale de la philosophie*, ed. Barthélemy-Saint-Hilaire (Paris, 1884⁹).

After surveying the schools established by Plato, Aristotle, and the Stoics, Cousin remarked on the ancient predecessors of his own school. 'Situated between Africa, Asia, and Europe', he wrote, 'it was indeed natural that Alexandria should want to unite the oriental and the Greek spirits; but in this union it was the oriental spirit that was dominant.'[32] Thus ancient eclecticism slid into mysticism and, under the destructive force of skepticism, initiated the 'slow agony and death of the Greek tradition', which was terminated by Justinian's closing of the Academy of Athens in 529.

'The circle of systems had thus been run,' he remarked, and the following chapters traced another turn of the wheel from Christian beginnings down to the turn toward mysticism of late scholastic philosophers like Jean Gerson. A new cycle began with 'the Philosophy of the Renaissance', which declared its independence from scholastic servitude but which was still in a disorderly state until the founding of the major modern schools of empiricism ('sensualism'), idealism, and a revived skepticism. It was Cousin's intention to appropriate the rich legacy of these modern systems by his post- and anti-sectarian view. Eclecticism, he was persuaded and tried to persuade others, 'is the muse which must preside over a truly philosophical history of philosophy and which we invoke here'.[33]

Despite his wide-ranging learning and cosmopolitan pretensions, Cousin remained within a narrowly conceived French tradition. For him the central question of philosophy was still that posed by his French forebear and founder of 'modern philosophy', Descartes. This question concerned the self – the *Cogito* – from which epistemological puzzle issued, according to Cousin, all the problems of philosophy.[34] Subjectivity – the domain of the *Ego*, the *Ich*, the *Moi* – was also a preoccupation of contemporary German philosophers, most notably Fichte; and Cousin's inquiries were also very much *à la mode* in this search for an 'eternal Moi'.[35] In the early nineteenth century, however, there was another issue tied to the self, and this was its chief social and ultimately political manifestation – namely, selfishness, or 'egoism'. In the July Monarchy there was a veritable 'cult of the ego' (*culte du Moi*) which, devoted to material success, lay at the roots of the Social Question and provoked the objections of a wide range of 'socialist' critics, most of whom had contempt for the academic and ideological role of Cousin

---

[32] Ibid., 175.
[33] Ibid., 29.
[34] *Premiers essais*, 48.
[35] See Hippolyte Castile, *Les Hommes et les mœurs en France sous le règne de Louis Philippe* (Paris, 1853), 18ff.

– the 'mythologue du Moi' – in promoting bourgeois selfhood and the material well-being of the Cartesian *Cogito*.

Philosophically and historically, the consequence of the focus on the thinking subject was an obsession with the primary creations of this subject – that is, since Plato, 'ideas'. Cousin's work was in large part focused on the analysis of ideas and especially on the 'history of ideas'. His celebrated course of 1828–29 was devoted to the 'idea of philosophy' (inaugural lecture), the 'fundamental ideas of history' (fifth lecture), and to many particular ideas (especially 'the True, the Beautiful, and the Good') in the Platonic mold.[36] By that time Cousin had already begun making his scholarly contributions to ancient philosophy, including his translation of Plato and his edition of Proclus; and these further reinforced the 'spiritualist' quality of his teachings. ('Our true doctrine, our true flag is spiritualism', he declared.[37]) In his translation of Tennemann's manual of the history of philosophy Cousin listed 'the history of ideas, principles, and other particular doctrines' which scholars had treated, including that of the true God (Christoph Meiners), atheism (Jakob Thomasius), fate (Grotius), the soul (Joseph Priestley), adiaphora (C. C. Schmid), the association of ideas (Michael Hissmann), and others whose work Cousin indiscriminately plundered and whose authority he vicariously enjoyed.

As a teacher and as an academic administrator Cousin had a remarkable success. His trajectory carried him from being a 'guru' and political martyr in the 1820s to an 'official philosopher' in the 1830s and 1840s and finally, after 1848, back to his books.[38] From the age of twenty-three he had been a charismatic lecturer, stirring and even subversive to his young auditors. Restored to his chair of philosophy in 1828, he pursued the eclectic cause of liberty, goodness, and beauty with evangelical fervor. Even his severest critics admitted that he was without peer as an orator – though such praise of his 'rhetoric' was a left-handed compliment, especially coming from philosophers.

In general Cousin affected contempt for philosophical schools, but his magisterial presence was felt by several generations of students; and he had enthusiasts and fanatics, as Simon recalled, if not true disciples. Like modern *Annaliste* historians, he was fond of the academic and implicitly authoritarian 'We': 'He said "we have"', according to Simon, 'the way the king says "We

---

36 *Cours de l'histoire de la philosophie* (Paris, 1847).

37 *The True, the Good and the Beautiful*, 9.

38 See especially Alan B. Spitzer, 'Victor Cousin and the French Generation of 1820', in *From Parnassus: Essays in Honor of Jacques Barzun*, ed. Dora B. Wiener and William R. Keylor (New York, 1976), 177–94.

wish".'[39] Cousin was especially contemptuous of the philosophical aspirations of women (even though he counted many among his devotees), it may be added; and (in good classical fashion) his ideas were derived from others committed to the life of the mind.

In his early years Cousin was considered something of a radical; but his provocations, like his ideals, were highly intellectualized. Politically, he was a 'liberal' but of the most cautious variety, and even in 1830 he was never caught up in the enthusiasm of the *Trois Glorieuses* that replaced the Bourbons with the Orleans dynasty; for him a change of cabinets would have been enough. Cousin also had to tread lightly in matters of religion, which was not only a creed but also, politically and socially, a code which it were unwise to violate. According to Jules Simon, again, 'From 1815 to 1830 one was often asked in the salons, "What do you think of God?"'[40] More than once Cousin defended himself against charges that he was a 'pantheist'. In the final analysis Cousinian eclecticism was not a philosophy of action, and eventually this failing was enough to turn away the younger generation, whose idea of the 'Good' was more activist and socialized than that of the complacent professor.

In fact Cousin's eclecticism had a religious as well as a philosophical dimension, and he made serious concessions to accommodate his secular ideas to the Catholic faith which he professed and urged on younger students and correspondents. In the 1850s he struggled with ecclesiastical authorities, including Pope Pius IX himself, to prevent his book *On the True, the Good and the Beautiful* from being placed on the Index of Prohibited Books. He submitted to questioning by Lamennais, Lacordaire, and agents of the Holy See, and defended his philosophical position and orthodoxy at length against the urging of the Pope to beware of secular learning and German philosophy in particular.[41] In the end, through the personal intervention of Pius IX, the sentence of the Congregation of the Index was suspended, and the matter was dropped, leaving Cousin in a sort of ecclesiastical limbo, though secure in his own mind about the power of eclectic philosophy to resolve, or dissolve, such problems.

Cousin's intentions were of the best. He both consciously sought useful ideas in his studies of Greek, German, Italian, and French philosophical tradition and also argued that philosophical truth was itself best served by this alliance with erudition. Unfortunately Cousin's conceptual mill, though it used everything as grist, ground exceedingly coarse, and the contradictions of his position

---

[39] *Victor Cousin*, 5. Cf. Richard Cobb, '"Nous" des *Annales*', in *A Second Identity* (London, 1969), 76–83.

[40] *Victor Cousin*, 54.

[41] Barthélemy-Saint-Hilaire, *M. Victor Cousin*, II, 6, 42, 73, and so on.

attracted disapproval from the beginning. To some critics eclecticism was little more than a confused sort of plagiarism. There was some doubt that he really grasped Hegel, whom he cited alongside Brucker without noting the philosophical contempt which the former felt for the latter's pedantry.[42] In historical judgment Cousin was sufficiently vague, his level of generality sufficiently high, that he could find not only intellectual affinities but also influence between thinkers as different as Montesquieu and Vico.[43] For him 'ideas' represented a currency of exchange acceptable in many different historical contexts throughout the Republic of Letters and across many centuries, and he was remarkably undiscriminating in his historical investigations of the history of ideas in various contexts. After 1830, in any case, he was widely regarded as (in the words of Sainte-Beuve) one of the 'prophets of the past' – not a bad sobriquet for a practicing historian of ideas.[44]

Cousin was a capable scholar; despite his idealist rhetoric, he approached the history of philosophy, or at least of particular philosophical texts, as a philologist, and in this respect he was carrying on the foundational task of the German eclectic tradition, with its emphasis on erudition. He was also an immensely popular teacher; his classroom platitudes were applauded, echoed, and diluted still further by epigones like Théodore Jouffroy, Jules Simon, and Amédée Jacques. Cousinian orthodoxy continued to be promoted, at least until the Revolution of 1848 shook up the complacent discussion of received ideas and the career lines associated with Cousinian eclecticism.[45]

The growing criticism levelled at Cousin was that there was no philosophy behind his rhetoric and learning. According to George Henry Lewes, writing in 1857, 'Cousin's celebrated Eclecticism is nothing but a misconception of Hegel's *History of Philosophy*, fenced round with several plausible arguments', while Cousin himself was but 'a brilliant rhetorician utterly destitute of originality'.[46] French critics brought more serious charges. In 1838 P.-J.-B.

---

[42] See Paolo Bechi, 'Hegel e Cousin: storia di plagi e di censure', *Verifiche*, 23 (1994), 211–35.

[43] *Course of the History of Modern Philosophy*, I, 219, 'The *new science* is the model and perhaps the source of the *spirit of the laws*.'

[44] *Les grands écrivains*, 188.

[45] See Sainte-Beuve, *Œuvres* (Paris, 1956), I, on Jouffroy and Lerminier; also Jouffroy, *Mélanges philosophiques* (Paris, 1875), 273–7 ('De l'éclecticism en morale'); and cf. Simon, *Histoire de l'école d'Alexandrie*, Jacques, *Aristote considéré comme historien de la philosophie* (Paris, 1827), and H. Roux-Ferrand, *Histoire des progrès de la civilisation en Europe depuis l'ère chrétienne jusqu'au XIX siècle* (Paris, 1847), I, 144; also Alaux, *La Philosophie de M. Cousin*.

[46] George Henry Lewes, *The Biographical History of Philosophy* (New York, 1857), II, 7.

Buchez, for example, published a philosophical treatise 'from the point of view of Catholicism and progress' charging eclecticism with being 'a Protestant philosophy invented by the Protestants' and traceable ultimately to Luther, who unleashed religious liberty and individualism upon the world.[47] Cousin had simply reduced philosophy and especially the ideas of the Good, the Beautiful, and the Just to varieties of egoism: the *bon* being what is useful to me, the *beau* what amuses me, and the *juste* what serves me. 'The foundation and point of departure of eclecticism', wrote Buchez, 'is the sovereignty of the ego.' In the opinion of the socialist Pierre Leroux, Cousin had found his *ideé fixe* from his study of Proclus and his German trips; but mainly his inspiration and support were political. The notion of a 'happy medium' was ultimately the hypocritical doctrine of the Orleanist government – 'a dose of monarchy, a dose of aristocracy, and a dose of democracy' was the prescription – whence arose this 'miserable political syncretism' hiding behind the myth of a united 'nation'. For Leroux this false and static synthesis seemed to be a rejection not only of philosophy but also of the idea of progress as conceived by socialists like himself. Seconding this critique, the former disciple of Cousin, Joseph Ferrari, launched a sarcastic assault on the 'salaried professors' who, under Cousin's leadership and the deceptive slogan of 'liberty of thought', had established an expensive monopoly over the teaching of philosophy based on the primacy of the *Moi*. Indeed, complained Ferrari in 1849, 'it is eclecticism that has forced us to become socialist'.[48]

Yet before the revolutions of 1848 and the triumph of positivist (and Positivist) 'science', eclecticism did in fact prevail in the French academic establishment and, for good or for ill, has left its impact on France and beyond.[49] At the end of the nineteenth century it was, according to Lucien Lévy-Bruhl, 'still the philosophy officially taught in France'.[50] For all its philosophical vacuity, pedagogical pretentiousness, and pernicious political associations, Cousinian

---

[47] *Essai d'un traité complet de Philosophie de point de vue du Catholicisme et du progrès* (Paris, 1838), II, 418; and cf. *Introduction à la science de l'histoire* (Paris, 1842), 435; also M. l'Abbé Roques, *M. V. Cousin et ses adversaires* (Paris, 1858).

[48] *Les Philosophes salariés* [1849] (Paris, 1983), 63.

[49] The influence can be seen in the *Dictionnaire des sciences philosophiques par une Société de professeurs de philosophie*, ed. A. Franck et al. (6 vols; Paris, 1844–52) and in the many textbooks published in the wake of Cousin's work, including those of J.-B. Bouvier (1841), the Abbé E. Barbe (1846), le duc de Caraman (1845), and Salinis and Scorbiac (1847). In general see Ulrich Johannes Schneider, 'A Bibliography of Nineteenth-Century Histories of Philosophy in German, English, and French (1810–1899)', *Storia della storiografia*, 21 (1992), 141–68.

[50] *History of Modern Philosophy in France*, trans. G. Coblence (Philadelphia, 1899), 438.

eclecticism marks a striking broadening of horizons and a deepening perspective on the history of ideas. Despite the ideological objections of critics, eclecticism did have a claim on some aspects of the western philosophical heritage; and it merits more historical appreciation than it has enjoyed.

3. History of Philosophy

Whether or not modern eclecticism was a dark, misguided, or boring chapter in the history of *philosophy* is debatable; what is undeniable is its significance for the *history* of philosophy and the history of ideas.[51] In either case it represents a vital part of the debate, continuous from the late eighteenth century down to the present, about the role of history in philosophy. Since Hegel's time this problem has been known as the 'philosophy of the history of philosophy'; and it is, in effect, an early version of Thomas Kuhn's question about 'a role for history' in scientific inquiry, although it has been directed toward philosophical tradition and the cultural past more generally.[52]

From the very beginning philosophy has laid claims to a transcendent status, first as a providential 'gift' and keeper of the flame of true wisdom, then as an expression of rigorous science. In Neoplatonism philosophy celebrated its divine origins; after Kant the pretensions of philosophy have taken a more secular form through the conceptual hegemony of 'pure reason', but the effects have been no less imperial and universalist. The prison of idealism in which the history of philosophy was also trapped was made more secure by the common assumption that the history of philosophy was essentially psychology writ large. 'In the study of systems one should follow the same order in which they developed', as another of Cousin's admirers put it. 'This order is nothing else than that in which our faculties develop: sensibility before reason, sensationalism before idealism, and so on.'[53]

The result has been a neglect of the vagaries of the human condition, the vicissitudes of historical change, and the cultural moods of a particular age.

---

[51] See Gueroult, *Histoire*, III, 737ff.

[52] See K. L. Reinhold, 'Über den Begriff der Geschichte der Philosophie', in *Beyträge zur Geschichte der Philosophie*, ed. G. G. Fülleborn (Zullichau, 1791), and Lutz Geldsetzer, *Die Philosophie der Philosophiegeschichte im 19. Jahrhundert* (Meisenheim, 1968); and cf. Richard Rorty, J. B. Schneewind, and Quentin Skinner (eds), *Philosophy in History* (Cambridge, 1984), A. J. Holland (ed.), *Philosophy: Its History and Historiography* (Dordrecht, 1985), Bernard P. Dannerhauer (ed.), *At the Nexus of Philosophy and History* (Athens, GA, 1987), and Peter H. Hare, *Doing History Historically* (Buffalo, 1988).

[53] M. C. Hippeau, *Histoire de la philosophie* (Paris, 1838²), 14.

'This is particularly true of the history of ideas, and especially the history of philosophy', Pierre Bourdieu has remarked. 'Here the ordinary effects of de-realization and intellectualization are intensified by the representation of philosophical activity as a summit conference between "great philosophers" ... ', when in reality it is a 'philosophical doxa carried along by intellectual rumour – labels of schools, truncated quotations, functioning as slogans in celebrations or polemics – by academic routine and perhaps above all by school manuals ... '.[54]

The 'philosophy of the history of philosophy' seeks to look behind the comfortable premises of academic tradition and to pose human and historical questions. Of what use is history for the projects of philosophy as they have appeared in the course of time? Is there a wisdom beyond time and outside of particular cultural contexts? Why study intellectual and cultural history? Is the record of human thinking and creating a blessing or a curse, a help or a hindrance? The fortunes of eclecticism and the more general field of the history of ideas are bound up with such questions about the value of studying the human past, and it is in the light of these issues that this inquiry will be pursued.

The rise of the history of philosophy to prominence in Cousin's time – and in no small part thanks to his efforts – can be seen in the organization of the new university which was founded by Napoleon and in which Cousin became a leading figure. From the law of 1802 the curriculum required a year of philosophy, including logic, metaphysics, ethics, and 'the history of the opinions of philosophers', a provision that was preserved in the Restoration.[55] With the Revolution of 1830 Latin was officially replaced by French for philosophy examinations and dissertations, and efforts were made to repair the neglect of the history of philosophy. In the ministry of Guizot in 1832 an official plan proposed ten questions concerning this field, beginning with methods, periodization, the succession of schools from antiquity to modern times, and finally the question which so absorbed Cousin and all the eclectics – namely, 'What advantages are there in the history of philosophy for philosophy itself?'

One of the most popular topics of discussion in the age of Cousin was the Neoplatonic 'School of Alexandria', founded by Ammonius Saccus in the second century AD and ended in 529 by decrees of Justinian. Alexandria in these years of contentious overlap between paganism and Christianity was a

---

[54] *The Field of Cultural Production*, ed. R. Johnson (New York, 1993), 32.

[55] Documents published in Cousin, *Défense de l'Université et de la philosophie* (Paris, 1844), 346ff.

play- and battle-ground of eclecticism, and its traditions were of special interest to Cousin and his contemporaries. In 1822 Jacques Matter published a history of this school, and of course Cousin featured the topic in his own lectures, as did his *protégé* and successor Jules Simon, who published his work in 1845.[56] In 1842 the Académie des Sciences Morales et Politiques, with the encouragement of Cousin, Minister of Public Education, offered a prize for the best study of this school, including its 'monuments', its fortunes down to the Renaissance, and its philosophical value and errors – a perfect summary of the agenda of eclecticism. The winner of the prize, according to the official judgment of another *protégé* of Cousin (as well as his future biographer), Barthélemy-Saint-Hilaire, was the work by Etienne Vacherot (one of four submitted).[57]

For Simon, Alexandria was the 'first eclectic school'. As he wrote in 1839, 'The avowed aim of the school of Alexandria was to construct a system in which all earlier philosophies would be founded and united.'[58] Descended spiritually from Plato and Pythagoras, the pagan members of this school fell into various errors of idealism (ideas divorced from sense), 'mysticism', and the confusion of theology and philosophy. Thus Plotinus's notion of the trinity was taken over by Christian fathers like Clement of Alexandria, who found the 'road to grace' even as he preserved Platonic ideas.[59] Vacherot, with due acknowledgment to Cousin and Jouffroy, traced Alexandrine thought on God and the soul from Plato and the earlier schools down to the major figures, Plotinus and Proclus, as well as the Gnostics, Philo and the Jewish school, and the early Fathers of the Church. In a third volume published later, he followed the posthumous story of Neoplatonism from the questionable books of hermeticism down to *la Renaissance*, including the derivative work of Trapezuntius and other Byzantine scholars, Marsilio Ficino, and Giordano Bruno.

According to these interpretations, the Alexandrine school was, despite its syncretistic flaws, the very prototype of eclectic philosophy and its historicist foundation. Philosophy was itself cumulative, but Alexandrine eclecticism was a collective work on a grand and global scale. 'Stoicism, Peripateticism, and Platonism summarized [*résumé*] earlier philosophy', Vacherot wrote;

---

[56] Matter, *Histoire de l'école d'Alexandrie comparée aux principales écoles contemporaines* (Paris, 1840²); and Simon, *Histoire de l'école d'Alexandrie*.

[57] Vacherot, *Histoire critique de l'école d'Alexandrie* (3 vols; Paris, 1846–51); J. Barthélemy-Saint-Hilaire, *De l'école d'Alexandrie, rapport à l'Académie des sciences morales et politiques* (Paris, 1844), citing the Academy's charge.

[58] *Du Commentaire de Proclus sur le Timée de Platon* (Paris, 1839), 45.

[59] Simon, *Histoire de l'école d'Alexandrie*, II, 616.

'and in exploiting this triple source the School of Alexandria collected all the elements of Greek philosophy'.[60] It tried also to absorb Christian teachings, and it was at this point – marked also by the decision of the Emperor Justinian to legislate the end of pagan influence – that it met failure. Vain efforts to mix things human and divine subverted philosophy in antiquity; would they do the same for theology in modern times?

Such at least was the suggestion of the Cousinian Jouffroy, who offered a more general explanation for this curious, generational phenomenon, 'how dogmas come to an end'.[61] Dogmas arise because they seem true; they are accepted uncritically by later generations; then they become corrupted and error-ridden, while remaining the basis for social and political control. Against this appears a new faith, which begins as negative and skeptical critique and so is subject to censorship and persecution; then comes a stage of satire and mockery, as common people watch, and suffer from the division; and a final crisis occurs before the 'revolution of ideas' which brings a 'new generation', which sees the errors of both the defenders of the old faith and the skeptics and which understands what a revolution truly is and what it is designed to accomplish in material as well as spiritual terms. 'Thus the ruin of the party of the old dogma is completed, and the new one introduced', concluded Jouffroy. 'As to the old dogma itself, it has been dead for a long time.' This was a disguised picture of the eclecticism of Jouffroy's own day, but it is also, perhaps, a parable of the end of ideology and of faith in the permanence of ideas.

4.   A Liberal Triumvirate

French eclecticism developed within the Liberal, or Doctrinaire, movement of post-Napoleonic France. Politically, it supported the restored monarchy of the Bourbons and celebrated the Charter, which guaranteed free speech, free press, and political equality as well as property and Catholicism as the official religion. Within this constitutional establishment eclecticism, as envisioned and established by Cousin, reached out beyond its national base to cosmopolitan and historical ideals – receiving inspiration and reinforcement from sources ancient as well as modern, eastern (especially Indian) as well as western, German and Italian as well as English and Scottish. As Metternich would preside over a concert of

---

[60] Vacherot, *Histoire*, II, 435.

[61] 'Comment les dogmes finissent', *Mélanges philosophiques* (Paris, 1875), one of several articles published on eclecticism in the *Globe* (1825–27); English trans. in George Ripley, *Philosophical Miscellanies* (Boston, 1838), II, 121–42.

Europe, so Cousin, with his Hegelian connections, saw a holy alliance of European philosophers and philosophies, in which ideas of the True, the Good, and the Beautiful would establish hegemony, and in which Civilization, under the leadership of intellectuals, would triumph. This was the larger context – a modern liberal version of the old 'Republic of Letters' – in which Cousin and his colleagues performed their public actions, published their scholarly opinions, and attracted their disciples.

Cousin established himself during what has been called 'the golden age of the Sorbonne' in the decade before the Revolution of 1830. The shining stars of this golden age made up, during the 1820s, a triumvirate of liberal intellectuals – forming the basis of what Régis Debray has called 'la monarchie des professeurs' – in which Cousin was not the most influential.[62] It is true that Cousin, still in his mid-twenties, held hundreds of young men of his own generation spell-bound with his celebrations of the past and the power of European and French philosophy; but Cousin's colleague Abel-François Villemain attracted even greater throngs (according to Sainte-Beuve and other contemporary witnesses)[63] with his lectures on European and French literature; and the professor of history, François Guizot, was the most celebrated of the three. Goethe spoke favorably of this trio and their influence, especially of Guizot, his favorite. 'They combine perfect knowledge of the past and the spirit of the nineteenth century', he remarked, 'and the result is wonderful.'[64]

Each of these academic intellectuals was cast in opposition to the Restoration Monarchy (Cousin and Guizot were dismissed from their teaching posts, and Cousin spent time in prison for his political views); and all three became part of the political élite of the July Monarchy, serving in the government of Louis-Philippe, especially in the department of public education, and Guizot at higher levels. As scholars and teachers, all three were fundamentally devoted, too, to the history of European and especially French *civilisation* as it emerged in the wake of the French Revolution, in the context of Liberal (or Doctrinaire) ideology, and in the company of the 'conquering bourgeoisie' of the Orleanist Monarchy. Politically, they have had a bad press, but intellectually they represent cornerstones of the emerging study of intellectual history.

---

[62] *Teachers, Writers, Celebrities: The Intellectuals of Modern France*, trans. David Macey (London, 1981), 53; and see Jacques Billard, *De l'Ecole à la Republique: Guizot et Victor Cousin* (Paris, 1998).

[63] P. F. Dubois, *Cousin, Jouffroy, Damiron: Souvenirs*, ed. Adolphe Lair (Paris, 1902), 334, and Sainte-Beuve, *Correspondance générale*, ed. Jean Bonnerot (Paris, 1935), I, 110.

[64] Johann Peter Eckermann, *Gespräche mit Goethe* (Munich, 1984), 286; *Goethe's Conversations with Eckerman* (London, 1930), 305.

In 1816 Villemain assumed the chair of the history of literature at the Sorbonne and gave a series of extraordinarily successful lectures which established him, in the eyes of his many disciples, as the founder of the modern field of literary history – and especially of 'comparative literature' (his phrase).[65] For Villemain the term 'literature' invoked not only the old encyclopedic conception that encompassed virtually everything rendered into writing – 'letters' – but also the more modern and 'Romantic' view that identified Literature (capital L) with 'good letters' (*bonae litterae*; *belles-lettres*). In either sense literature encompassed philosophy and, in a similar but even more comprehensive way, 'civilization' and its history. It included the history of society, he declared in 1828, and indeed became its single force (*la seule puissance*). French literature was of great importance, and even more so French Criticism (capital C), together with its history, especially in its critiques of the cultural heritage of the old regime underlying the Revolution, the attendant 'change of spirits', and the coming of the present 'new era' in which Villemain, his colleagues, and his students were both participants and observers. However, at present, Villemain admitted, it was the influences of England (the revolution of 1688) and of Germany (idealist philosophy) that were central to 'the development of the human spirit'.[66]

In this triumvirate Guizot was the most conspicuous figure, first, on his academic stage, celebrating the glories of middle-class culture and then, in a political capacity, recommending to a wider audience to 'enrich yourselves'. Guizot was lecturing on the eve of the Glorious Revolution of 1830, which brought him into power as the king's chief minister and leading political figure until the next wave of revolutions in 1848. As a professor as well as a statesman, Guizot spoke and wrote to defend the historical superiority of French 'civilization' and to demonstrate a consistent pattern of historical progress in all areas of national endeavor – material, intellectual, moral, and political. In the middle ages humanity accomplished this partly through 'ideas from beyond the horizon of existence', but later this Christian progress was secularized. Although Guizot recognized, at least for rhetorical effect, a providential plan behind material and moral progress, he insisted, in a formula similar to Vico's (which Michelet was then asserting through his translation of the *New Science* in 1827), that 'It is man himself who makes the world.'[67]

---

[65] See especially Hutcheson Macaulay Posnett, *Comparative Literature* (London, 1886).

[66] Ibid., 336.

[67] *Michelet, Œuvres complètes*, ed. Paul Viallaneix, I (Paris, 1971), 54.

Cousin was carrying on the same ideological campaign; but in the grand tradition of academic philosophers like Hegel (with whom Cousin was just then, in 1828, in correspondence), Cousin thought of his as the highest role, philosophy – 'the worship of ideas', as he called it – being 'the last victory of thought' after centuries of struggle,[68] and its history occupied a similar position. 'The history of civilization', Cousin declared to his (frequently applauding) students, 'is the pedestal of the history of philosophy.'[69] The history of civilization had other dimensions, including the history of arts, religion, law, wealth, and geography, Cousin added; but it was philosophy that constituted the culmination of all of these processes – and eclecticism in its French form that was the culmination of all philosophy.

The efforts of this intellectual (and political) triumvirate offer an appropriate introduction to the central theme of this book. As Guizot confronted the question of civilization in general, especially through its material and political foundations, Villemain cast his net more narrowly in order to explore the tradition of literature in a comparative way, following the lead of Degérando, but reaching out also to larger cultural patterns; and Cousin, with a similar but much more 'spiritualist' orientation, took a philosophical view of the European past and 'ideas' as the primary vehicle of the progress of civilization.

These professors represent three of the major perspectives on European intellectual history which will be taken up in the following chapters: the story of the history of ideas as, *avant la lettre*, it developed within the history of philosophy from Greek antiquity to the Renaissance; the problem of knowledge in historical, linguistic, and hermeneutical terms; the formation of the modern school of eclecticism in Germany; and the shift, in the work of certain scholars, from the 'internal' to the 'external' history of thought, from the history of philosophy to intellectual and cultural history and the history of civilization. In this complex and sometimes amorphous story the concept of 'ideas' is the protagonist, first as the primary vehicle of spiritual and intellectual change, second as an expression of cultural life, and finally as a target of historical inquiry and criticism. My purpose here is to follow these story lines in their various permutations through a wide variety of cultural contexts from the ancient beginning of the debates over 'ideas', through the dispersal of the original philosophical project into rival schools, down to the emergence of the history of ideas as a modern field, and then its decline, occultation, and transformation at the end of the old (and now beginning of the new) millennium in the form of intellectual history.

---

[68] *Course of the History of Modern Philosophy*, I, 25.
[69] Ibid., 66.

Chapter 2

Eclecticism in Retrospect

> In a word *Eclecticism* is Aristotle's idea
> of history. It was implicit in Plato; it
> was the glory of Aristotle to be the first,
> in the infancy of this science, to raise it
> to the high dignity of a principle.
> Amédée Jacques

Sixteen centuries before Victor Cousin's innovations a new movement emerged among the contending philosophical schools of the age in which Christianity and paganism overlapped. 'Not long ago', Diogenes Laertius reported in his *Lives and Opinions of Eminent Philosophers*, a work written probably in the early third century AD, 'an Eclectic school was introduced by Potamon of Alexandria, who made a selection from the tenets of all the existing sects' – including Platonists, Aristotelians, Epicureans, Stoics, and Cynics.[1] The mysterious Potamon thus broke with the conventions of discipleship imposed on ancient schools of philosophy (and carried over into rival religious doctrines) and encouraged his pupils instead to learn from a variety of masters. His approach, selective and necessarily comparative, was also in effect historical, at least as interpreted by later scholars, who took it as a prototype of the more self-conscious eclectic ideas, first German and then French, which emerged in modern times. From this perspective Potamon defined both the primary point of intersection between history and philosophy and one significant precedent, *ante litteram*, of intellectual history.[2]

---

[1] *Lives of Eminent Philosophers*, trans. R. D. Hicks (2 vols; Cambridge, MA, 1980), I, 19. And see the work by Cousin's disciple, Jules Simon, *Histoire de l'école d'Alexandrie* (Paris, 1845).

[2] See the comprehensive survey by Michael Albrecht, *Eklektik: Eine Begriffsgeschichte mit Hinweisen auf die Philosophie- und Wissenschaftsgeschichte* (Stuttgart, 1994).

1. Eclecticism and History

In this perspective, too, the problem of eclecticism and the question of history had been implicitly present at the very birth of philosophy. In the first place Greek philosophy was notorious for its exploitation of earlier cultures, which all claimed, in various ways, the possession of wisdom. Compared to the Egyptians, the Greeks were 'children', Plato suggested, and had to take wisdom from their elders.[3] Moreover, the whole project of *philosophia* in the Greek sense – the love and pursuit of wisdom rather than its unproblematic possession – was the transmission of ideas and arguments from teacher to pupil, and this 'succession' was an indelibly human and retrospectively historical phenomenon.

A striking and seminal example of this can be seen in the career and legend of Pythagoras, who, as Cicero and others agreed, was the first to designate himself 'philosopher'. Pythagoras was systematically unscrupulous in exploiting the ideas of earlier thinkers.[4] As his biographer Iamblicus put it, 'He neglected no doctrine valued in his time, no man for understanding, no rite honored in any region, no place where he expected to find some wonder.'[5] He pursued his course of study 'according to each system of thought, no particular school being preferred, but all being approved according to their merits, and ranked higher than mere human studies ... , ascending as by a sort of bridge or ladder'.[6] Thus Pythagoras drew his ideas from all the cultures accessible to him, and his legend and tradition formed a link between authentic Greek and the controversial 'barbarian' philosophy that worried Christian scholars from Clement of Alexandria down to J. J. Brucker and Victor Cousin.

Yet if Pythagoras followed a vague sort of eclectic procedure, he never actually preached what he practiced. Iamblicus, drawing on Porphyry's earlier biography, explained 'how [Pythagoras] handed down [the special practices of his philosophy] and how he exercised each new generation embarking on philosophy'.[7] Despite his own eclectic background, then, Pythagoras followed a pedagogical method which was, according to tradition, authoritarian in the extreme. To his students he was 'the god-like one', or simply 'That man'. He was the Master, the *Magister*, who passed on to his disciples all that he had learned *except* the eclectic and elective freedom of choice on which his own wisdom had been based.

---

[3] *Timaeus*, 22b.
[4] Cicero, *Tusculan Disputations*, V, 8–10; and cf. *Lives*, VIII, 8.
[5] *On the Pythagorean Life*, trans. Gillian Clark (Liverpool, 1989), 8.
[6] Iamblicus, *The Exhortation to Philosophy*, trans. T. M. Johnson (Grand Rapids, 1988), 21.
[7] *On the Pythagorean Life*, 42.

Ironically enough, it was one of Descartes's most faithful disciples, Pierre Sylvan Régis, who most disparagingly portrayed Pythagoras as a paradigm of dogmatic philosophy, recalling that the opinions of this storied philosopher were cited by his *discipuli* to resolve questions 'not by reason but by authority', according to the Pythagorean formula, *Ipse dixit*.[8] Nothing was more common, remarked an early eighteenth-century biographer of Pythagoras, than 'to insinuate into men the will and command of God through such formulas'.[9] As the founder of the Italic sect, Pythagoras passed on his magisterial habits (learned, perhaps, from the Egyptian priests he had visited) to Socrates, Plato, and Aristotle. Not until the sixteenth century, Régis concluded, was philosophy finally 'liberated' from such servitude. Eclectic critics of Descartes doubted such self-serving claims but shared the goal of achieving liberation from the magisterial authority and discipular bondage on which philosophy had always depended – so said the loyal disciple of Descartes.

With Plato, who drew extensively on Pythagorean ideas, philosophy moved from myth to history, and yet the authoritarian and charismatic tone of philosophy was preserved. Although Plato's 'divinity' was proclaimed well into the modern age, he had his human forebears. Indeed, there was a recognizable kind of proto-philosophical tradition beginning with designated wise men (not to mention poets) whose ideas he appropriated as well as criticized. In his characteristic dialogical style Plato examined and reproached Heraclitus, Parmenides, and others; and in effect his judgments often fixed the place in history for contemporaries, most notably Socrates and most invidiously the 'sophists'. In *The Sophist* Plato represented his Presocratic predecessors as 'giants and gods' – that is, materialists and idealists – battling over the nature of existence. This he did, however, in terms not of intelligible ideas but of cryptic story-telling, illustrating the Mythos-to-Logos theme which later historians of philosophy incorporated into their tradition. Like Pythagoras, Plato had a large and amorphous following, extending into various kinds of derivative Neoplatonic reworkings, and the fortune of his teaching has conventionally been associated with eclectic views throughout the history of philosophy.

A new story begins with Plato's errant pupil Aristotle, who gave form and endorsement to the Greek canon and thereby acquired the reputation as the 'father of the history of philosophy'.[10] In surveying philosophy down to

---

[8] *Discursus philosophicus in quo Historiae Philosophiae Antiquae et Recentioris recensetur* (n.p., 1705), 25.

[9] J. J. Syrbius, *Pythagoras* (Jena, 1701), 25.

[10] Emile Brehier, *L'Histoire de la philosophie* (Paris, 1951), I (1), 36; and see W. K. C. Guthrie, 'Aristotle as Historian', in *Presocratic Philosophy*, ed. D. J. Furley and Reginald E. Allen (New York, 1970), I, 239–55.

Empedocles, 'the question of arranging these thinkers in order of priority' was of secondary consideration to Aristotle, but he did not ignore it. His critical (if rudimentary) sense of history was part of his characteristic tendency not only to juxtapose his own views to the 'observed facts' but also to compare them with the 'greatest number and most authoritative' opinions of earlier thinkers, usually to refute them but also to treat 'the question of arranging these thinkers in order of priority'.[11] To attain true knowledge, he declared in the *Metaphysics*, one had to consider not the question itself but also 'the other opinions which some have held on first principles'. This eclectic procedure was also followed by Aristotle in his *Physics*, *De Anima*, and *Nicomachean Ethics*; and many of his ideas, especially the famous 'four causes', seem to have been adapted in almost serial fashion from earlier authors. With Aristotle the history of philosophy seems to emerge not only as a prerequisite for philosophizing but also, in the words of Martial Gueroult, as a 'special discipline'.[12]

It is this aspect of Aristotle that attracted modern eclectics. Brucker had already attributed an eclectic method to Aristotle as well as to Plato.[13] In 1827 Amédée Jacques, an eclectic follower of Cousin, published a book to show that Aristotle had treated his predecessors, including Plato, in an 'eclectic' and historical as well as a critical fashion (though this claim has been denied by more recent and authoritative scholars).[14] Aristotle did not treat the history of philosophy directly or scientifically, admitted Jacques, but he did benefit from a rich legacy of earlier speculation and recognized his own role, and he acknowledged that the review of his predecessors was the 'touchstone', 'the sovereign rule', to understand and to 'purify' earlier efforts to grasp the principles of nature. For

> what is denied to a single man, in his weakness and in the short duration of his life, can be accomplished by humanity as a whole, which never dies and which concentrates in itself and in its collective development, the combined forces of all individuals.

The Cousinian message was unmistakable:

> In a word *Eclecticism* ... is Aristotle's idea of history. It was implicit in Plato; it was the glory of Aristotle to be the first, in the infancy of this science, to raise it to the high dignity of a principle.

---

[11] *Metaphysics*, 984b31; and see Harold Cherniss, *Aristotle's Criticism of Plato and the Academy*, I (Baltimore, 1944).

[12] Martial Gueroult, *Histoire de l'histoire de la philosophie* (3 vols; Paris, 1984–88), I, *En Occident, de Condillac à nos jours*, 27.

[13] *Philosophia historica*, II, 189, referring to *Nicomachean Ethics*, I, 4.

[14] *Aristote considéré comme historien de la philosophie* (Paris, 1827).

With Aristotle, then – as with modern eclectics – the object of history became philosophy itself, not vulgar doxographical fascination with the 'lives and opinions' of its practitioners but rather the ideas necessary for the understanding of man and nature.

In this perspective eclecticism (and thus a potentially historical view of ideas) was built into the Greek genre of philosophy. In a fragment on 'nature' Epicurus distinguished 'between the constructive use of someone else's doctrines and the "confused mixture" of ideas derived from different sources' – in effect between eclecticism and indiscriminate and deplorable syncretism. According to one modern scholar, Middle Platonism 'fused Plato with much Stoic ethics and Aristotelian logic',[15] and Middle Stoicism was likewise informed by Platonic ideas. In late antiquity, from Antiochus to Boethius, and again in early modern times, from Pletho and Bessarion to Père Rapin and Leibniz, efforts were made to reconcile Plato and Aristotle within the mission of philosophy in general; and the influx of 'barbarian philosophy', eastern religions, and Christian doctrine reinforced such eclectic practices. The history of philosophy could not avoid following suit.

2.   The Laertian Model

The history of philosophy, as a genre and as a canon, begins with the problematic and much maligned yet indispensable work of Diogenes Laertius, the first to report on the 'eclectic' method and indeed to use the term [*eklektike*] in this way.[16] Diogenes's book is a collection of lives, opinions, documents, anecdotes, memorable sayings, and poems (including his own) based not only on oral tradition but also on a mass of previous writing – historical treatises, such as that 'On the succession of philosophers' by Sophion and Alexander Polyhistor, and comments of philosophers on their predecessors, such as Zeno, Gorgias, the Pythagoreans Alcmeon and Archytras of Tarentum, and Speucippus and Xenocrates, who were successors to Plato in the Academy.

Diogenes Laertius has often been denigrated as 'foolish' and 'uncritical'; and indeed, whether a skeptic or an eclectic, he was more concerned with

---

15 Henry Chadwick in *Cambridge History of Later Greek and Early Medieval Philosophy*, ed. A. H. Armstrong (Cambridge, 1967), 170–71; and see A. A. Long, *Hellenistic Philosophy: Stoics, Epicureans, Sceptics* (Berkeley, 1986; 2nd edn), 228.

16 *Lives*; for background and analysis see Richard Hope, *The Book of Diogenes Laertius: Its Spirit and Method* (New York, 1930), and Allen Brent, 'Diogenes Laertius and the Apostolic Succession', *Journal of Ecclesiastical History*, 44 (1993), 367–89.

bio-bibliographical data, whatever its quality, and with colorful anecdotes, whatever their provenance, than with philosophical truth – although he has also been taken as anticipating the aphoristic method made famous by Nietzsche.[17] Inadvertently, one might say, he took a 'constructionist' view of philosophy and the history of ideas. He was also the purveyor of many legends of philosophical genius and supernatural insight into the workings of nature, human as well as physical, though he had virtually nothing at all to contribute to the pursuit of wisdom itself. What his book accomplished was to suggest some of the 'external factors' at work in the philosophical enterprise, institutional as well as psychological. Not only did he attend to the formative influences of education, travel, and political involvement, but he arranged the order of thinkers according to particular doctrinal 'successions' (*diadoxai*), beginning with the Ionian (Presocratic) and Italian (Pythagorean, Eleatic, Democritean, and so on), thus providing a useful taxonomy as well as chronology. For good or for ill, his book – historically inaccurate, philosophically trivial, and scarred by the effects of time and uncritical copyists though it undeniably is – has been essential for the history of ideas in antiquity and established the framework for the story of philosophy down to modern times.

If Plato and Aristotle, together with an endless line of their commentators, stood at the head of eponymous philosophical and 'sectarian' canons, Diogenes Laertius, in his unreflective and gossip-ridden narrative, defined a larger and eclectic intellectual continuum – a canon of canons – which came to be known as the history of philosophy (*historia philosophica*) and of which Brucker and Cousin were among the beneficiaries. The anecdotal panorama of ancient *philosophia* reflected in Laertian doxography illustrated most of the enduring features of the philosophical project still being pursued professionally: the institutions of the formal academy and the doctrinal 'sect' which demanded allegiance and loyalty; the formulation of defining ideas, dogmas, theories, perhaps systems and '-isms'; continual and repeated doctrinal controversies; the specialized language and literary conventions of philosophical dispute; the recognition of charismatic leaders and masters (*scholarchs*) and a regularized succession (*diodoche*) of doctrines; the basic divisions of human knowledge (which according to Diogenes Laertius, following the Stoics, were natural philosophy, moral philosophy, and logic); and the vacillation between concern for individual psychology and larger human and superhuman values and projects – between doxography and the history of philosophy.

---

[17] Gilles Deleuze, *The Logic of Sense*, trans. Constantin V. Boundas (New York, 1990), 128.

The trajectories of the transmission of ideas in time were set by Laertian doxography. The conventions of 'philosophizing', sharing the structure of Greek *paideia* as a whole, entailed a dialogue between master and disciple, or a debate between rival masters, and the invocation, interpretation, or criticism of predecessors. This diadochic – *magister–discipulus* – relationship gave continuity and a deep structure to philosophical tradition; and disagreements and revolts, usually over commonly accepted issues, provided further coherence to the philosophical canon, which took shape in the Hellenistic period. In this dialogical and eristic canon philosophers were portrayed as heroes or villains, founders or destroyers, father-figures or 'corrupters of youth', self-absorbed solitaries or public-minded reformers. They created not only reputations and traditions but also anecdotes, legends, and posthumous debates, such as those reported by Diogenes Laertius; and out of these emerged, on the one hand, conventional doxography and history of philosophy and, on the other hand, chronicles and critiques of philosophical and theological error and heresy.[18] The parallel with theology is again striking, except that with the latter fatherhood replaced mastery as the symbolic relationship. 'For when any person has been taught from the mouth of another', explained Irenaeus, 'he is termed the son of him who instructs him, and the latter is called his father.'[19]

Philosophy also generated its characteristically élitist institutions and social patterns, including, in several incarnations, the Academy and the so-called Alexandrine 'university' as well as the medieval reincarnations of these ancient establishments.[20] After Plato and Aristotle the formal academic successions tried to preserve and to disseminate doctrine – 'dogma' it has been called ever since, as 'heresy' has designated deviation from it. Like religious movements, Greek philosophy featured charismatic teachers, inspired conversions, demanded allegiance, established doctrinal credos and canons, posed theological questions (especially about God and the soul), provoked debate and censure, and produced sects (288 of them by Varro's count) and endless '-isms' for later eclectics to accommodate and for historians to chronicle and to interpret.[21] In the classical curriculum, philosophy assumed an increasingly hegemonic position and, concerned with moral and political as well as practical

---

[18] See Hope, *Book of Diogenes Laertius*, 99.

[19] *Adversus haereticos*, 4, 41.

[20] H.-I. Marrou, *A History of Education in Antiquity*, trans. George Lamb (New York, 1956), 282.

[21] Arthur Darby Nock, *Conversion* (Oxford, 1933), 164; David Sedley, 'Philosophical Allegiancein the Greco-Roman World', in *Philosophia Togata*, ed. Miriam Griffin and Jonathan Barnes (Oxford, 1989), 97–119'; and John Clark Smith, *The Ancient Wisdom of Origen* (Lewisburg, NY, 1992), 18ff. On Varro see Augustine, *City of God*, 19.1.

goals, became a sort of surrogate religion and prototype of the development of Christian theology, although the 'master–disciple' relationship took a somewhat more transcendent form in the latter.

The great schools or 'sects' and the foundational ideas of Greek thought – especially the concept of 'idea' itself – were established in the fourth century BC (Platonism, Aristotelianism, and Pyrrhonism) and in the third century were joined by Stoic, Epicurean, and Cynic competitors for the attention and allegiance of youth. Competition for pupils and official favor raised the level stakes of philosophical debate. Philosophers who could not be fitted into this scheme were dismissed as 'sporadic'.[22] In later generations these schools not only changed internally (being designated as 'old' and 'new', 'middle', and 'late'), but also interacted and intermingled with each other, exchanging ideas, denouncing errors, and debating the roles and relevance of doctrinal ancestors. Efforts were made in particular to reconcile the doctrines of Plato and Aristotle and later to accommodate these to Stoic, Epicurean, and skeptical thought. It was in this context that eclectic notions and practices appeared most conspicuously and that the history of philosophy, which was charged with judging and discriminating between these schools, was given a seminal impulse.

As disciples followed masters, so schools followed other schools, and sects other sects. So it was, according to Brucker, with Platonism, which had emerged from the Ionic, Socratic, and Heraclitean sects, and with eclecticism, which was 'generated' by Neoplatonism.[23] Though a 'new philosophy', the *secta Eclectica*, praised by both Plato and Aristotle, followed practices that could be traced back to the 'barbarian philosophy' of Egypt. Ancient eclecticism was the product of wide and indiscriminate learning and, from the very beginning, extensive voyages of philosophical inquiry; and it thrived in the multicultural environment of Hellenism and especially Alexandrine Egypt, with the doctrinal bedlam created by the confrontation between paganism and Christianity and the scholarly traditions which were brought to bear on philosophical as well as Homeric and biblical texts.

3.　The First Eclecticism

In its most specific formulation eclecticism referred to a particular method of determining truth, which Diogenes Laertius defined with reference to

---

22 *Lives*, VIII, 50.
23 Brucker, *Historia philosophica* II, 189: 'Plato et Aristoteles eclecticam viam laudeverunt et commendaverunt ... '

Potamon's now lost *Elements of Philosophy*, setting down the criteria of truth as follows:

(1) that by which the judgment is formed, namely, the ruling principle of the soul; and
(2) the instrument used, for instance the most accurate perception. His universal principles are matter and the efficient cause, quality, and place; for that out of which and that by which a thing is made, as well as the quality with which and the place in which it is made, are principles. The end to which he refers all actions in life made perfect is all virtue, natural advantages of the body and environment being indispensable to its attainment.[24]

Such an abstract formulation hardly justifies the notion of a 'school', a stage of the Academy, or even a distinctive method, though it may suggest an open-minded attitude that contrasts with more dogmatic conceptions of conventional sectarian philosophers.

Despite its tolerant stance, ancient eclecticism has had a very bad press, especially among philosophers, and Cousin, among others, expressed serious reservations about it. Even today the word 'eclecticism' does not have a pleasant ring, suggesting as it does indecision, confusion, lack of definition, and neglect of logical consistency.[25] The classic unfavorable judgment, enshrined eventually in the nineteenth-century work of Eduard Zeller, was pronounced by J. J. Brucker: 'Upon the foundations of the Platonic philosophy, with an abundance of heterogeneous materials collected from every other sect, was erected an irregular, cumbrous and useless edifice, called the *Eclectic School*.'[26] Calling it a 'school' is characteristic of the tendency of the history of philosophy to hypostatize magisterial '-isms'; judging it so harshly is a more modern inclination, arising in part from the distaste, among Protestant as well as Enlightened philosophers, for the curious alliances between classical philosophy and religious movements of late antiquity – the mixtures between 'things divine and human'. For skeptics and rationalists such Gnostic or

---

[24] *Lives*, I, 21.

[25] Or a form of instrumentalism, such as the 'eclectic' method attributed to Galen, on which see Owsei Temkin, *Galenism: Rise and Decline of a Medical Philosophy* (Ithaca, 1970), 17.

[26] *Historia critica philosophiae* (6 vols; Augsburg, 1766), in the translation of William Enfield, *The History of Philosophy* (London, 1840), 55. See also E. Zeller, *Die Philosophie der Griechen in ihrer geschichtlichen Entwicklung* (Leipzig, 1904[4]), 547; Giovanni Reale, *Storia della filosofia antica*, III, *Sistemi dell'età ellenistica* (Milan, 1980); and Pierluigi Donini, 'The History of the Concept of Eclecticism', in J. M. Dillon and A. A. Long (eds), *The Question of 'Eclecticism'* (Berkeley, 1908), 15–33. The relevant section of Zeller's work was translated as *A History of Eclecticism in Greek Philosophy*, trans. S. S. Alleyne (London, 1883).

Neoplatonic concoctions were monstrous examples of intellectual mis-cegenation, and even for Christians they were not marriages made in heaven. As Brucker concluded about the ancient school,

> The Eclectic school, thus raised upon the foundations of superstition, enthusiasm, and imposture, proved the occasion of much confusion and mischief both to the Christian religion and to philosophy.[27]

Denis Diderot followed Brucker in the effort to reconstruct a history of ancient eclecticism, giving it his own critical spin. For Diderot eclecticism began by declaring independence not only from sectarianism but also from those more insidious enemies of enlightenment – prejudice, tradition, antiquity, universal consent, and authority.[28] Yet eclecticism also brought confusion and error. As old as the world, it began nominally with Potamon and a succession of over twenty philosophers, beginning with Potamon's disciple, Ammonius Saccus and his pupils, Plotinus, Porphyry, and Iamblicus; Longinus, who traveled extensively in the near east; Proclus, 'the maddest eclectic of all'; and the apostate Emperor Julian – Diderot does not include any Christians. Eclecticism also included women philosophers, especially (whatever her religion) the beautiful, intellectually peerless, and ill-fated Hypatia, whose death, said Diderot, marked also the end of ancient eclecticism.[29]

In scholarly retrospect Brucker and Diderot may have speculated and protested too much; for according to more recent scholars, this eclectic 'school' was a figment of historical imagination. There is little evidence of an institutional or conceptual tradition associated with this cryptic statement made by a notoriously untrustworthy author. Despite the assertion of Brucker, Degérando, Cousin, Zeller, and others, there was no real 'school' of eclecticism comparable to the Aristotelian Lyceum or Platonic Academy (though eclecticism has been associated with the Fourth or Fifth Academy). Potamon had no traceable following; and indeed it was characteristic of eclecticism that, on principle, students were free to listen to other, 'dogmatic' philosophers. Nor was there a theory of choice, which is what eclectic method would seem to require. In this strict sense it is hard to disagree with the view of a recent scholar that 'No ancient philosopher was an eclectic.'[30]

---

[27] Brucker, *Historia philosophica* I, 86.
[28] *Œuvres complètes*, VII, *Encyclopédie*, ed. J. Lough and J. Proust (Paris, 1976), 36.
[29] Brucker, *Historia philosophica* II, 351; and see Maria Dzielska, *Hypatia of Alexandria*, trans. F. Lyra (Cambridge, MA, 1995).
[30] Sedley, 'Philosophical Allegiance', 119.

Yet many historians of ideas, taking a less literalist view, have judged otherwise, finding evidence for eclectic (small e) attitudes if not Eclectic (capital E) theory. The great schools which grew up in the aftermath of the fifth-century Greek Enlightenment became increasingly fragmented and diffuse, as did their Epicurean and Stoic rivals. Mutual borrowing and awareness of tradition led these schools to practice, even if they did not preach, a general sort of eclecticism – as Cousin and his disciples were at pains to demonstrate, though with the usual Christian anxieties about possible impieties.

With Arcesilaus (died 242 BC) begins the 'Middle Academy', according to Diogenes Laertius,[31] and with him, too, begins a deliberate skeptical attitude which led to eclectic practices. Though, like Socrates, he worked in an oral tradition, Arcesilaus reportedly (via Cicero) doubted the possibility of knowledge based exclusively on the senses. 'He was the first to suspend his judgement owing to the contradictions of opposing arguments', according to Diogenes. 'He was also the first to argue both sides of a question, and the first to meddle with the system handed down by Plato.' For Diogenes, Arcesilaus was a 'chimera', with 'Plato the head of him, Pyrrho the tail, midway Diodorus'.[32] He did not hesitate to 'recommend his pupils to hear other philosophers', and sometimes he seemed to argue merely from authority, whether his own or that of others. No wonder – even if he had not been, as Diogenes remarked, 'fond of boys' – he was called 'a corrupter of youth and a shameless teacher of immorality'. This byproduct of mastership, too, represents an important precedent in the history of philosophy, at least in the public image of philosophers represented by historians.

In the Hellenistic age a growing historical perspective (or at least a range of backward-looking learning) led philosophers to draw on older traditions. In Cicero's time, for example, Antiochus of Ascalon tried to revive the Old (the original and orthodox Platonic) Academy by connecting it – through an antique sort of canon-formation, or reformation, which had eclectic overtones – with the Stoicism of his day.[33] This historical perspective also underlay the new science of 'philology'; and while the great achievement of Alexandrine scholarship might threaten to eclipse philosophy and trivial literary studies, and while historical matters might overshadow the larger question of wisdom (*sophia, sapientia*), it was essential for Laertian doxography and for the

---

[31] *Lives*, I, 405.

[32] Ibid., 409.

[33] *Academica*, I, 13; see also John Glucker, *Antiochus and the Late Academy* (Göttingen, 1978), Harold Tarant, *Scepticism or Platonism? The Philosophy of the Fourth Academy* (Cambridge, 1985), and Paul MacKendrick, *The Philosophical Books of Cicero* (New York, 1989).

history of philosophy more generally. One result, however, has been that eclecticism and the history of philosophy have generally leaned away from analysis and toward concerns for quantitative erudition and textual criticism. Such was conspicuously the legacy of Brucker and Cousin.

The freedom suggested by eclecticism and the large horizons opened up by the history of philosophy had some disturbing drawbacks. For most critics eclecticism has suggested not pure ideas but congeries of 'opinions' (*doxa*), according to Plato's invidious distinction.[34] It was characteristic not of the *polis*, on which Plato's and Aristotle's works were a sort of nostalgic, or ironic comment, but of that multicultural mélange that brought confusion as well as subtlety to the intellectual life of the Hellenistic world. The cultural contacts and shock produced by Alexander the Great's expedition of 324–323 BC created conditions for the development of eclectic practices as well as the spread of Stoicism.[35] The decline of the freedom of the city-states, the withdrawal from public life, the cosmopolitan horizons which opened on 'barbarian' cultures, eastern as well as Roman, and the crisis of values and social turmoil of Greco-Roman imperial civilization turned philosophy in upon itself and its past. The classical canon weighed heavily on masters and students, whose concerns in any case shifted from speculation to practical philosophy and ways of coping with the vicissitudes of fortune, against which reason seemed increasingly ineffective. Moral philosophy became the cynosure of philosophical attention, and not the city but the soul – not the *polis* but the *psyche* – became the center of anxieties and debates.

Modern eclectics, like the faithful Cousinian Jules Simon, tried to make a virtue of the confluence of doctrines in the Hellenistic period. Simon argued that after the exhaustion of the dogmatic schools, philosophy was saved by the infiltration of oriental ideas – mysticism, Neoplatonism, Gnosticism, and so on – down to the time of Plotinus and the efforts to reconcile East and West.[36] 'The philosophy of Plotinus', wrote Simon, 'embraced everything.'[37] The other side of this story was a conspicuous drift toward skepticism, especially 'Academic' (rather than Socratic or Pyrrhonist) skepticism; and this, too, tended to reinforce eclectic tendencies by challenging the doctrines of particular schools and reinforcing the principle of free choice.

---

[34] *Republic* 478[b]; cf. *Cratylus* 420[b]; and see Yvon Lafrance, *La Théorie platonicienne de la Doxa* (Montreal, 1981).
[35] Reale, *Storia della filosofia antica*, III, 343–5.
[36] *Histoire de l'école d'Alexandrie*, I, 101.
[37] Ibid., II, 2.

In general ancient eclecticism represented hardly more than congeries of practices and attitudes that served both to extend and to confuse philosophical speculation – extend it by suggesting that philosophical problems were common to all sects and nations, and confuse it by interpreting terms (as Brucker said) 'in a sense different from that of their original authors'. In trying to reconcile various ideas, by analogy or allegory, eclectics made it impossible, continued Brucker, 'to form an accurate notion either of the Platonic, the Peripatetic, the Stoic, the Egyptian, or the Oriental philosophy'. Yet in late antiquity and in the wake of eclectic practice philosophical tradition moved beyond sectarianism, and this remained its state throughout the period of what Brucker and other Protestant scholars, in their confessional chauvinism, called the Middle Age of philosophy or, adapting the term applied by Diogenes Laertius to non-Greeks, the 'centuries of the New Barbarians'.

Central to the history of philosophy in general and to eclecticism in particular is skepticism, especially in its radical Pyrrhonist form. The aim of skepticism was to find a way around the practice of dogmatizing by suspension of judgment.[38] According to Sextus Empiricus, this was to be accomplished through ten modes, or 'tropes', which classify the natural and human conditions of perceiving and thinking. Most relevant to the history of philosophy was the last mode, which was 'derived from customs, laws, beliefs in myths, compacts between nations and dogmatic assumptions ... '.[39] The just and the unjust, the bad and the good, the civilized and the barbarian are all relative – culturally constructed, in today's parlance – and so were the doctrines of philosophers. Philosophers have always resisted this most rigorous line of philosophical argument, but (as Hume remarked) it always returns to haunt dogmatic claims to truth.

The epistemological basis for this skepticism had been suggested by Epicurus, who pointed out the preconceptions (*prolepsis* was his term) inherent in experience and language and which were prior to and perhaps constitutive of philosophical speculation. Recognizing such prejudices was far from modern empiricism; yet the result was to reduce philosophy to a form of opinion (which – philosophically – was supposed to be its opposite).[40]

---

[38] *Outlines of Pyrrhonism*, trans. R. G. Bury (Cambridge, MA, 1976), 49–93 (1.36–163). See Myles Burnyeat (ed.), *The Skeptical Tradition* (Berkeley, 1983).

[39] *Lives*, II, 493–9.

[40] 'By preconception [*prolepsis*] they mean a sort of apprehension or a right opinion [*doxa*] or notion, or universal idea stored in the mind; that is, a recollection of an external object often presented; e.g. Such and such a thing is a man: for no sooner is the word "man" uttered than we think of his shape by an act of preconception, in which the senses take the lead ... Opinion they also call conception or assumption,

The results for the history of philosophy were profound, though 'dogmatists'
and most eclectics could not accept the relativist conclusions which cast
doubt on the possibility of philosophical truth and so perhaps of philosophy
itself.

There was, it should be recalled here, another anti-philosophical counter-
current, running parallel to and inadvertently reinforcing skepticism, which
had its roots in the sophist movement and which found expression in the
tradition of rhetoric.[41] While philosophy prized truth above all intellectual
virtues, rhetoric had a different scale of values, attaching importance also to
encyclopedic learning, moral and political goals, and human concreteness
and immediacy, for which the study of history was essential. 'Sophist' was
Plato's term for his conceptual rivals, whose myopic and mercenary teachings
he deplored; but however low their standing in the history of philosophy,
their attitudes have been of major significance for historians of philosophy
down to the time of Cousin – whose position indeed was denounced by some
critics as 'rhetorical' in the most pejorative sense.

Rhetoric was almost as old as philosophy (and indeed Socrates himself was
called a 'sophist'), and this profession, too, found a prosopographical historian
to celebrate its canon. Even earlier than Diogenes Laertius, Philostratus wrote
his equally anecdotal *Lives of the Sophists*, which traced this parallel tradition
from Protagoras down to the 'Second Sophistic' of the third century AD. 'The
men of former times applied the name "sophist," not only to orators whose
surpassing eloquence won them a brilliant reputation', wrote Philostratus,
'but also to philosophers who expounded their theories with ease and
fluency.'[42] Unlike many philosophers, however, the sophists pursued philosophy
without the skeptical attitude of Socrates and with greater attention to the
power and social uses of language. Protagoras was also, Philostratus noted,
the first to charge a fee for his lectures.

Diogenes, who had a similar sense of history (or at least of chronology and
pedagogical succession), was more concerned with doctrinal matters. For him
Protagoras, who had studied under Democritus, 'was the first to maintain

---

and declare it to be true and false; for if it is true it is subsequently confirmed or if it
is not contradicted by evidence, and false if it is not subsequently confirmed or is
contradicted by evidence.' (*Lives*, II, 563; and cf. II, 605; and cf. Sextus Empiricus,
Adversos mathematicos, 7.210–16, citing Epicurus).

[41] See especially Brian Vickers, *In Defense of Rhetoric* (Oxford, 1988), and *The
Rhetoric Canon*, ed. Brenda Deen Schildgen (Detroit, 1997).

[42] *The Lives of the Sophists*, trans. Wilmer Cave Wright (Cambridge, MA, 1921),
13, including also Eunapius, *Lives of the Philosophers and Sophists*; and see Graham
Anderson, *Philostratus: Biography and Belles Lettres in the Third Century A.D.*
(London, 1986).

that there are two sides to every question ... , and he even argued in this fashion, being the first to do so'.[43] This anti-logical argument was linked to his famous *Homo-mensura* aphorism – 'man is the measure of all things' – and implicitly and ultimately a way of politicizing and relativizing philosophy by subsuming it, along with its imperialist truth-claims, under the art of rhetoric. If this is 'sophistry' in a pejorative sense, it also allows philosophy to be monitored by skeptical criticism and, implicitly, supplemented by a rudimentary kind of historical understanding.

Less appreciated are the linguistic premises of rhetoric which must apply to philosophy, too, although the connections are often neglected or denied; namely, the force of inherited language in conceptualization, suggested by the Epicurean notion of *prolepsis*.[44] For philosophers things have 'always already' (in Heideggerian terms) been named, connections made, conventions formed, issues defined, and goals set. The recognition of the 'forestructure' not only of knowledge but also of philosophizing places philosophy in history's field of vision. In any case this old debate between rhetoricians and philosophers would be renewed in the age of modern eclectic philosophy, when the disparity between scientific and literary traditions was even greater, when the question of the relation between truth and probability was raised, and when the conceptual stakes were considerably higher.

4. Roman Appropriations

Rhetoric also offered the Romans a way to rescue practical philosophy from sectarian dispute. Virtue was not the monopoly of the *philosophi*, Quintilian declared; for only the *orator*, as master of all knowledge, had 'a genuine title to the name of philosopher'.[45] Quibbling about trivial matters of 'opinion' for centuries, philosophers had withdrawn from public affairs, and only the orators were the true wise men (*civiles sapientes*). Preoccupied with ideas and propositional logic, philosophers also undervalued the force of linguistic ambiguity and the complexity of social reality, and so became slaves to certain words.[46]

---

[43] *Lives*, II, 463. See the recent works of Edward Schiappa, *Protagoras and Logos: A Study in Greek Philosophy and Rhetoric* (Columbia, SC, 1991), and Susan C. Jarratt, *Rereading the Sophists: Classical Rhetoric Refigured* (Carbondale, IL, 1991).

[44] See Stephen Everson, 'Epicurus on Mind and Language', in *Language* (Companions to Ancient Thought, III), ed. Everson (Cambridge, 1993), 74–108.

[45] *Ars oratoria*, I, pr., 17–18 and 9; also X, i, 35.

[46] Ibid., VII, iii, 16, and ix, 1.

The Romans could not avoid being eclectics in the sense that they went to school with the Greeks, and indeed were called 'children' by the Greeks, as the Greeks had been by the Egyptians. Yet they would not play disciple to master in any slavish way.[47] In the famous words of Horace, repeated endlessly by modern eclectics, 'I am not bound over to swear as any master dictates' (*non jurare in verba magistri*).[48] Such Roman declarations of liberty were of course intensified by their inclination toward rhetoric, which (in the famous pedagogical image) emphasized the open hand of invention over the clenched fist of logic. In their imperial fashion their aim was to trace new paths of thought on the old maps drawn by the Greeks. 'I am a friend of Socrates … , a friend of Plato, a friend of Aristotle', according to the old topos; 'but above all I am a friend of truth.' This formula illustrates the ultimate basis for the eclectic attitude of the Roman epigones of the Greeks and applicants to their schools.

There was of course a strong skeptical element in this declaration of intellectual liberty from Greek mastery, as with Antiochus's pupil Cicero.[49] Whether or not an 'eclectic', Cicero displayed a Platonic as well as a skeptical face in his later works. In his dialogue, *Academica*, Cicero assigned to his friend Varro the task of defending Antiochus's famous 'turn' back to the original Academy of Plato. This was the Varro whose message to his friends was to 'go to the Greeks, so that they may draw from the fountain heads rather than seek out mere rivulets'. By contrast Cicero defended a notion of a sort of eclectic progress. 'What then?', he asked. 'Is our friend Antiochus to have more liberty to return from the new school to the old, than we are to have to move out of the old one into the new?' And he added that 'there is no question that the newest theories are more correct and free from error'.[50]

In the second book, Lucullus, speaking for Antiochus, complained that the members of the New Academy invoked the great philosophers, even Plato and Socrates, just as demagogic politicians tried to borrow glory from 'famous personages of antiquity', alleging that they all belonged to the same party. '[O]ur New Academy allows us wide liberty', Cicero remarked, 'so that it is within my right to defend any theory that presents itself to me as most probable';

---

[47] Seneca, *Ad Lucilium epistulae morales*, 33.7.

[48] *Epistulae*, 1.1.14. See Capasso, *Historiae philosophiae synopsis* (Naples, 1728), 165; also Wilhelm Schmidt-Biggemann, *Theodizee und Tatsachen: Das philosophisches Profil der deutschen Aufklärung* (Frankfurt, 1988), 203; and Paul Dibon, *La Philosophie néerlandaise au siècle d'or* (Paris, 1954).

[49] Glucker, in *The Question of 'Eclecticism'*, 34–69; and see Miriam Griffin and Jonathan Barnes, *Philosophia Togata* (Oxford, 1989).

[50] *Academica*, 1.13.

and elsewhere he declared, 'I say anything that strikes me as probable; and so I alone am free' ('free' in the sense of not being 'tied to any school').[51]

The advantage of skepticism was that one became one's own master, but in practice that often meant drawing freely on many masters and holding many opinions. This was also the view of Seneca, for as he remarked in one of his moral essays, 'I, too, have the right to form an opinion.'[52] In his letters, recalling that the Ancients should be followed not as masters but as guides (*non domini … sed duci*), he confessed: 'That is my habit; I try to extract and render useful some element from every field of thought, no matter how far removed it may be from philosophy.'[53] One of the benefits of history is that, through literary memory, it permits such dialogues with the dead. 'We can discuss with Socrates, doubt with Carneades, overcome human nature with the Stoics, or reject it with the Cynics', he wrote. Moreover, 'Since nature allows us to enter into all ages, why should we not escape from the confines of our narrow existence to share eternal meditations with these nobler spirits?'[54] Philosophizing for Seneca – invoking another famous classical motif – was not unlike the behavior of bees in gathering honey.[55]

This eclectic attitude might seem to preclude originality or even suggest unauthorized borrowing: 'What are you doing with another's property?' Epicurus asked – but Seneca's answer could justify plagiarism as well as eclecticism: 'Any truth, I maintain, is my own property' (*quod verum est, meum est*).[56] Thus the transmission of ideas was given legitimacy as a sort of common inheritance, which indeed has become a dominant metaphor in intellectual history, being revived in the eighteenth century, for example, by Bishop Warburton, who argued that 'An exclusive Property cannot be obtained in every Idea that we pursue.'[57]

Of course the legacy of inherited ideas and intellectual or rhetorical consensus may be something quite different from the 'truth', and both the study of history and eclectic method have been criticized for obscuring this distinction. On this point theologians have been even more insistent than philosophers, especially in the age of 'primitive Christianity', which was seeking, through faith, its own path to truth and so its own view of the transmission of ideas.

---

[51] *Tusculan Disputations*, 4.4.7.
[52] *Moral Essays*, II, trans. John W. Basore (London, 1951), 105–7 (*De Vita beata*, 3.2).
[53] *Epistulae*, 58.16; 80.1.
[54] *De brevitate vitae*, I, xiv.
[55] Albrecht, *Eklektik*, 52.
[56] *Epistulae*, 12.11.
[57] *An Enquiry on the nature and origin of literary property* (London, 1762), 3.

Christianity represented both a repudiation of and a confiscation of ancient thought. From its transcendent position, the message of the Gospel and the canon it accumulated cast suspicion on the hubris, the worldliness, and the materialism of Greco-Roman philosophy. 'Beware', preached Paul, 'lest any man spoil you through philosophy and vain deceit after the traditions of men.'[58] Platonism, and especially the 'reformed Platonic philosophy' (as Brucker called it), seemed congenial in some ways, but it remained a seed-bed of errors; and its assimilation was highly selective and interpretative. Aristotelianism was even harder to swallow and, despite employment of dialectical method, was not received until the twelfth century. A historical view of ancient ideas was thus possible only within a very restricted compass and underwritten by an indisputable 'truth' fixed by Holy Scriptures. As a result the history of philosophy and of thought more generally was to a large extent the history of error – or at least suspect ideas that had to be reconciled with preestablished theological doctrine. This assumption, which would be shared by modern eclectic scholars, informed all efforts, direct or indirect, to create a 'Christian philosophy' that would both draw on pagan wisdom and yet not be a contradiction in terms.

5. Between Paganism and Christianity

Eclectic practices entered into a new and even more contentious stage with the conflict of religions in the last centuries of the Empire. In the later Roman Republic, with the inroads of skepticism and eclecticism, the great schools had entered into a period of decline and confusion, further complicated by the influx of occult doctrines and oriental religions. Historians of philosophy have tried to pick their way through this labyrinth by fixing on particular thinkers and assigning them to – or analyzing their various ideas in terms of – older traditions. In general all the conventional dogmatic schools, including Platonism, Aristotelianism, and Stoicism, became hopelessly and irremediably 'eclectic' and difficult to identify in the doctrinal pandemonium of late antiquity. As Gregory of Nazianzen wrote in the fourth century, 'the philosophers have crept into the church just like the Egyptian plague'. Officially this invasion ended only with Justinian's famous edict of 529, closing offices and schools to pagans and the 'contamination' they carried.[59] In modern

---

[58] *Colossians*, 2:8, the only usage of the term in all the Scriptures.

[59] Alan Cameron, 'The Last Days of the Academy of Athens', *Proceedings of the Cambridge Philological Society*, n.s., 195 (1969), 7–29.

western retrospect the main story to be told is that of the conflict between pagan philosophy and patristic Christianity – the great rivalry referred to by Tertullian between Jerusalem and Athens, and by Jerome between Cicero and Christ – each party regarding the other as 'barbarian'; and in this turmoil eclectic practices were elaborated, systematized, and made into a model for later philosophers and historians of philosophy.

Despite the rise of Alexandrine learning, philosophy had tended to be, intellectually, a rather parochial affair. There were limits to the most flexible eclecticism and syncretism, and in general the horizons of philosophers of all sects stopped short of the alien conceptions of the non-Greek 'barbarians' – Egyptians, Assyrians, Chaldeans, Persians, Indians, and Hebrews. Doubts were occasionally expressed. Diogenes Laertius admitted at the outset of his work that 'There are some who say that the study of philosophy had its beginnings among the barbarians.' But he added immediately that 'not merely philosophy but the human race began' with the Greeks; the very word, coined by Pythagoras, could not be rendered into barbarian tongues. Such Hellenophilia has colored the history of formal philosophy down to the present century.[60] Thus Gadamer began his book on the beginning of philosophy with Plato and Aristotle as the only way of access into the Presocratics: 'Everything else', he concluded, 'is historicism without philosophy.'[61]

In general, despite marginal admissions and favorable mentions by Plato and other Greek thinkers, the contributions of these barbarians were for the most part ignored – at least until Jewish and Christian critics of Greek chauvinism tried to correct this imbalance in favor of other, no less chauvinistic, doctrinal traditions. One seminal example was Philo Judaeus, who took Moses as the main source of philosophy as well as the law, yet at the same time defended the 'encyclopedic' learning of the Greeks and drew on most of the ancient schools, including even the skeptics, according to methods that for most commentators have appeared to be 'eclectic' as well as allegorical. It is mainly on these grounds that Harry Wolfson regarded the work of Philo Judaeus – 'Church Father *honoris causa*, he has been called'[62] – as the beginning of modern European philosophy.[63]

In this search for a usable past we can see a practical and partisan kind of intellectual history *ante litteram*. Christian apologists agreed that secular

---

[60] A point curiously not followed up in Martin Bernal's *Black Athena*.
[61] *The Beginning of Philosophy*, trans. Rod Coltman (New York, 1998), 10.
[62] David T. Runia, *Philo in Early Christian Literature* (Minneapolis, 1993), 3.
[63] *Philo: Foundations of Religious Philosophy in Judaism, Christianity and Islam* (Cambridge, MA, 1948).

wisdom was older than the Greek love thereof: 'For which of your institutions have not been derived from the Barbarians?' asked Tatian of the Greeks.[64] Justin Martyr, Clement of Alexandria, and Origen all made efforts to derive Greek philosophy from Judaism. These early theologians all found anticipations of Christian doctrine in paganism; and some modern scholars, such as Theophilus Gale in the seventeenth century, imported these beliefs into the history of philosophy and came to share the 'eclectic' label. As Thomas Gale argued in the seventeenth century, the 'New Platonists'

> made it their businesse to choose what they found excellent in any other Sect: whence they were called *hairesis eklektike*, an Eclectic Sect, also *eklektikoi*, Eclectics.[65]

This line of argument (for Brucker, too) was very much in keeping with a sort of eclectic method, although it also threatened to lapse into syncretism, which most Christian scholars despised.

Of all the ancient schools, the most congenial to Christian doctrine was Platonism, which seemed to mark at least a stage in the pursuit of wisdom and perhaps even (in Eusebius's famous phrase) a 'preparation for the Gospel'.[66] 'Are we Greeks or Barbarians or intermediaries between the two?', Eusebius wondered. 'What innovations have we made?' In either case, 'Why do we use their books, which have nothing in common with us?' Like the Hebrew Scriptures,[67] the fables of the Egyptians, transmitted to and transformed by the Greeks, formed a sort of historical continuum which, Eusebius assumed, Christians should not ignore.

In efforts to understand divinity Justin Martyr tells of applying successively to a Stoic, a Peripatetic, and a Pythagorean before receiving a clue from a Platonist and – the final 'conversion' – full satisfaction in Holy Scripture.[68] In antiquity's version of the Quarrel between the Ancients and the Moderns Justin sided with the latter. 'Common sense dictates', he wrote, 'that those who are truly pious men and philosophers should honor and cherish only

---

[64] Cited by Etienne Gilson, *History of Christian Philosophy in the Middle Ages* (New York, 1955), 13. In general see the anthology of Albert Warkotsch (ed.), *Antike Philosophie im Urteil der Kirchenväter: Christlichen Glaube im Widerstreit der Philosophien* (Munich, 1973).

[65] *The Court of the Gentiles* (Oxford, 1672), part II.

[66] *Praeparatio Evangelium.*

[67] *Acts*, 7:22: 'And Moses was learned in all the wisdom of the Egyptian priests, and was mighty in words and in deeds.'

[68] Saint Justin Martyr, trans. Thomas B. Fells (New York, 1948), *The Dialogue with Trypho*, 150.

what is true, and refuse to follow the beliefs of their forefathers, if these beliefs are worthless.'[69] Yet Justin also celebrated the party of the Ancients to the extent that, in his view, the Greeks had been anticipated by an older tradition – and indeed derived their wisdom from it. Plato himself had learned from their prophets, Justin argued, even though he had feared to admit it to his fellow citizens.[70]

In the early third century Clement of Alexandria also proposed to 'run through the opinions which the philosophers ... assert confidently about the gods'.[71] Like Justin, Clement was critical of all the old schools, especially the Peripatetics and the Stoics, whom he regarded as 'atheists'. Far preferable, among the buzzing swarm of pagan philosophers, was Plato, whom he accepted as 'a fellow worker in the search' with at least some sense of the One True God of Judeo-Christian tradition. 'What is Plato but Moses talking Greek?', he asked (quoting Numenius the Pythagorean).[72] 'But we will not rest content with philosophy alone', he wrote. 'Let poetry also approach – poetry, which is occupied entirely with what is false, – to bear witness at last to truth, or rather to confess before God its deviation into legend.'[73] In his *Stromata* Clement not only surveyed the semi-legendary history of Greek speculation, beginning with Orpheus and the other ancient poets, but also celebrated the value of philosophy in this selective and purified form, which was the product of a method that was literally 'eclectic' (*eklektikon*).[74] Within this panoramic scope Clement also located the barbarians, for in his opinion they 'invented not only philosophy but practically every form of technical skill'.[75]

It should be added that such invocation of pre-Christian wisdom was not to be confused with misguided efforts to reconcile paganism and true religion; and in this sense, as Jean Le Clerc argued in the early seventeenth century,

> Clemens would not stick wholly to any Sect, lest he should take for Philosophers such as perhaps had only that manner of Philosophizing called *Eclectick*, that is to say, the Method of those [like Potamon] who chose, out of all the Opinions of the Philosophers, those which seemed most rational to them, and made a system of them for their private use.[76]

---

[69] Justin, *The First Apology*, 34.
[70] Justin, *Exhortation to the Greeks*, 406.
[71] *Exhortation to the Greeks*, trans. G. W. Butterworth (Cambridge, MA, 1982), 147.
[72] *Stromateis*, trans. John Ferguson (Washington, DC, 1991), 135 (1.22.4).
[73] *Exhortation to the Greeks*, trans. G. W. Butterworth (London, 1919), vi (163).
[74] Ibid., 49 (1.7.6).
[75] Ibid., 79 (1.16.74).
[76] *The Lives of the Primitive Fathers* (London, 1701), 16.

For this was the deplorable error of syncretism, although there was indeed a fine line (and a shared rhetoric) between the syncretistic desire for peace and the eclectic search for truth.

Following Clement's line of thought, Origen contrasted the dogmatic view of Celsus about a single 'ancient doctrine' preserved by 'wise men', with an appreciation of ideas fashioned by 'barbarians' as well as Greeks:

> How much better than Celsus is Numenius the Pythagorean, a man who showed himself in many works to be very learned and who by studying several doctrines made from many sources a synthesis of those which seemed to him to be true.[77]

In Origen's trinity of wisdom the 'wisdom of this world' was superior to the false 'wisdom of the rulers of the world', but it could never ascend to knowledge of divine things.[78] For Origen, as for Philo, the consummation of this search for truth was to be found in the Christian Logos, of which pagan precursors had only the vaguest of premonitions.

Although Christianity began as a religious movement, in many ways it came to model itself after the 'sects' of philosophy. 'What novelty is it', Tertullian asked of the *Christiani*,

> if some way of life gives its followers a name drawn from their teacher? Are not philosophers called after their founders – Platonists, Epicureans, Pythagoreans? yes, and the places they gathered, where they took their stand – Stoics, Academics?[79]

Later Christians would continue the imitation of philosophical tradition by defining its own 'dogmas', excluding 'heresies', and establishing institutional bases. Of course Tertullian reversed the priority – and in this way inverted the canon – arguing that the pagan poets and philosophers (*sophistae*) 'had drunk from the fountain of the prophets' and 'borrowed from our books'.[80] They were all bees, so to say, gathering the same honey from an essentially religious source.

---

[77] *Contra Celsum*, trans. Henry Chadwick (Cambridge, 1953), 59. And see Clark Smith, *Ancient Wisdom of Origen*.
[78] *Origen on First Principles*, trans. G. W. Butterworth (Gloucester, MA, 1973), 224 (III, 3).
[79] *Apology*, trans. T. R. Glover (Cambridge, MA, 1977), 21 (3.6).
[80] Ibid., 207 (47.2).

6. The Hunt for Wisdom

What Nicholas of Cusa called the 'hunt for wisdom' (*venatio sapientiae*) did not end with the closing of the schools in 529, although there was small and poorly lit space for philosophy. The 'dark' or 'middle' ages is a pejorative coinage of Italian humanists, beginning with Petrarch, to designate and to denigrate the time between classical antiquity and its modern recovery; and the centuries between Augustine and Petrarch, painted dark by the humanists, were blackened further by Protestant scholars.[81] Lutheran historians of philosophy in particular took over this concept in their own efforts to define the 'modern' period of their canon. This tripartite division – the philosophy of ancients (*veteres*), authors of the middle ages (*medium aevum*), and moderns (*moderni, recentiores,* or *novatores*) beginning with the 'restoration of letters' and the new eclecticism issuing from this revival – was inherited by Brucker from his predecessors, refined to admit subdivisions and non-western authors, and passed on to later historians of ideas. Embedded in six centuries of the 'literature', this threefold periodization has also been indelibly inscribed on the mentalities of western scholars (with revisions and self-magnifying efforts to add a 'postmodern' appendage).[82]

In the middle period philosophy was often idealized, or personified, especially in the form of a woman, as for Martianus Capella, pagan contemporary of Augustine, and for Boethius, who represented philosophy as a beautiful lady carrying books in one hand and a scepter in the other and recalling the 'ancient days before the time of my child, Plato', when she was already struggling against folly.[83] But Christian philosophy – or, as Brucker preferred to call it, *philosophia apud Christianos* – was informed by a new structure of authority that subordinated the quest for wisdom to what, within the Laertian framework, could only be regarded as a 'barbarian' myth, that is, the Creation story of the Jews extended and complicated by the Christian view of the Fall, which was produced by an excessive, disobedient, and impious desire for knowledge. Thus the philosophical enterprise was from the beginning placed under a curse. Adam had no doubt been the first philosopher, but with Eve's

---

[81] Lucie Varga, *Das Schlagwort vom 'Finsteren Mittelalter'* (Baden, 1932).

[82] Codified in the textbooks of Conrad Cellarius, *Historia antiqua* (1685), *Historia medii aevi* (1688), and *Historia nova* (1696); and see Wallace K. Ferguson, *The Renaissance in Historical Thought* (Boston, 1948).

[83] *Martianus Capella and the Seven Liberal Arts*, II, *The Marriage of Philology and Mercury*, trans. William Harris Stahl and Richard Johnson (New York, 1977), 32; and Boethius, *The Consolation of Philosophy*, trans. W. V. Cooper (Chicago, 1981), 4.

misstep and his own complicity original wisdom was lost, and along with it the language of paradise that expressed natural and human reality with immediate and pristine clarity. Only the desire remained, and the Babel of tongues to which the progeny of Adam and Noah had been reduced.

Even under the regimen of sin philosophy was undoubtedly a divine gift, but – like all things Greek in provenance (as the barbarian Trojans had learned) – Christians worried about what accompanied the legacy. Was philosophy the 'holy fire' stolen by Prometheus or some terrible thing out of Pandora's box, and in any case could Christian truth be caught in pagan terms? For philosophical debate was much complicated by the ambiguities in concepts crucial to both theology and philosophy, most notably the Logos, the illuminating Word which could refer to Christ or to divine reason that human thought sought to imitate, and the Neoplatonic ideas that were associated not only with human concepts but also with the doctrine of immortality. Not only was nature joined to supernature in a hierarchical structure – the Great Chain of Being where the Creation story was retold in terms of Plato's mythical Forms and what Giovanni Filoramo has called a 'bureaucracy of the invisible' appended to the animal hierarchy – but human psychology was formulated in the very same terms.[84]

Recent scholarship, drawing on manuscript sources, has shown that twelfth-century authors had a much greater appreciation of ancient philosophy than was previously thought. Under the influence of Plato's *Timaeus* (the only substantial Platonic work known before the fifteenth century) and associated galenic and hermetic texts, the natural dimensions of the human condition were given new prominence; and man was seen as a kind of universe, a 'microcosm', a conceit that opened up a world of anthropological analogies, especially when combined with the philosophical psychology deriving from Aristotle's *De Anima*.[85] In this connection the ancient debate over the nature and human condition of ideas (in the form of the 'problem of universals' taken up by Abelard and others) became the center of dispute and the foundation of science, though not accompanied by the interest shown by Plato and Aristotle in Presocratic thought.

For centuries both philosophical language and the history of philosophy have been tied to these epistemological assumptions, placing abstract reason at the top of a ladder of learning, at the end of a process of enlightenment. Such was the 'theophany' of the Syrian mystic Pseudo-Dionysius, in which the image of the Creator was to be seen not in humanity but in his natural

---

[84] *A History of Gnosticism*, trans. A. Alcock (Cambridge, MA, 1990), 30.
[85] F. E. Cranz, 'Perspectives de la Renaissance sur le "De Anima"', *Platon et Aristote à la Renaissance* (Paris, 1976), 359–76.

Creation – although unlike God, the author added (and as Vico later argued), human observers find only indirect understanding of things, which was human science.[86] God knows the language of nature, while humanity had to translate this into its own imperfect tongues to approach, but not reach, absolute truth. 'Human souls also possess reason', taught Pseudo-Dionysius, 'and with it they circle in discourse around the truth of things.'[87]

But human souls possess memory, too; and the past of philosophy was not forgotten in the middle ages. Even Isidore of Seville has been claimed as a 'historian of philosophy', though the derivative views collected in his encyclopedic *Etymologies* followed neither logical nor chronological order.[88] With the recovery of Greek science in the twelfth century, however, medieval intellectuals extended their knowledge of *auctores* and so access to the philosophical past. Not only authority but also reason and method were employed in the examination of this ancient legacy; and the chief instrument of the new science was Aristotelian dialectic, which divided the generations and cast Christian learning into centuries of discord. 'For', as Adelard of Bath told his nephew, 'I have acquired one type of learning, with reason as guide, from my teachers, while you, fettered by the appearance of authority, follow another, as a halter ... '[89]

The key to this new (or renewed) rationalism was the Aristotelian dialectic taught by the medieval *scholasticus* (the immediate source of 'scholasticism') and transmitted from the 'trivial' arts to the high sciences. As a historical construct scholasticism took shape first as an invidious humanist stereotype and then as a Protestant caricature, which represented it as producing a divorce between language and thought. To early modern historians of philosophy like Georg Horn, scholastic philosophy was a system of elementary mistakes which, introducing vain subtleties and habits of disputation into philosophy, ultimately corrupted all branches of knowledge.

A leading champion of this new science was Peter Abelard, whose colorful career and rash arguments made him a popular subject for historians of

---

[86] *De divinis nominibus* (PG, III, col. 585), ch. 7, 'De Sapientia, mente, ratione, veritate, fide': 'Hac igitur Deus res cognoscens, non scientia rerum, sed scientia suiipsius novit.' The Pseudo-Dionysian corpus was translated into Latin in the ninth century by John Scottus Eriugena.

[87] *De Divinis nominibus*, VII, 2; trans. C. Luibheid in *The Complete Works* (New York, 1987), 106.

[88] Jacques Fontaine, *Isidore de Seville et la culture classique dans l'Espagne wisigothique* (Paris, 1959), II, 707.

[89] *Quaestiones naturales*, cited in Peter Dronke (ed.), *A History of Twelfth-Century Philosophy* (Cambridge, 1988), Introduction, 11; and see Tina Stiefel, *The Intellectual Revolution in Twelfth Century Europe* (New York, 1985), 80.

philosophy like Brucker and Cousin. Abelard was the prototypical 'intellectual'.[90] Drawing crowds of students (including women) in Paris to listen to his new philosophy, he was the Cousin of the twelfth century. 'As a professor his success was prodigious', Cousin told his own large following, and it contributed much to the establishment of the University of Paris.[91] Like Adelard of Bath, Abelard contrasted reason with authority and mere 'opinion', and his *Sic et Non* – first discovered and published by Cousin in 1836 – revived many old heresies through questions raised presumably in order to refute them.[92] Along with this rationalism came a new, or renewed, sympathy with ancient authors who were allowed, by readers like Abelard (in the words of a modern scholar), 'to speak truer than they knew' – and in a way to 'prefigure' later ideas.[93] This sort of strong interpretation, or cooptation of earlier authors into a later school, and so a canon, is one of the conventions which make it possible to impose historical form on philosophy and to impute continuity to ideas.

In its more radical forms scholastic philosophy turned to Latin Averroism, in which the errors of naturalism and atheism threatened religious faith; but it was scientific curiosity rather than the siren song of infidel philosophy that encouraged scholars to read suspect texts. This was the case with Robert Grosseteste and Roger Bacon, whose purpose, wrote Richard Southern, was to alter Christian doctrine so:

> first, that it should master the philosophical and scientific resources of its enemies with a view to meeting them on their own ground; and secondly, that it should clarify its own position by discarding harmful accretions and concentrating on the central documents of its tradition.[94]

This is a fair statement of the aims of eclectic philosophy in the early modern period, which was (in the seventeenth-century formula taken up again by Martial Gueroult) to consider the history of error (*historia stultitiae*) as well as the history of wisdom (*historia sapientiae*) in the pursuit of truth.[95]

---

[90] Mariateresa Fumagalli Beonio Broccheri, 'The Intellectual', in Jacques Le Goff (ed.), *Medieval Callings*, trans. Lydia G. Cochrane (Chicago, 1987), 187.

[91] *Lectures*, II, 22, citing his fuller portrait in his *Fragments philosophiques*, II (Paris, 1840).

[92] *Sic et Non*, ed. Blanche B. Boyer and Richard McKeon (Chicago, 1976); cf. *Ouvrages inédits*, ed. Cousin (Paris, 1836).

[93] Winthrop Wetherbee, in Dronke, *History*, 38; and see D. E. Luscombe, 'Peter Abelard', ibid., 279–307.

[94] R. W. Southern, *Robert Grosseteste: The Growth of a Medieval Mind in Medieval Europe* (Oxford, 1986), 15.

[95] *Histoire de l'histoire de la philosophie*, I (1984), 83, adopting the formula of Thomasius and Brucker.

Like his namesake four centuries later, Bacon celebrated the value of experience. Seeking the sources of philosophical error, he found them in tradition; and his remedy was threefold – to prefer strong to weak authorities, reason to custom, and opinions of the wise to those of the prejudiced.[96] For its implementation his program required experience in the tradition not only of British empiricism but also philology and history, that is, the reading of many books, for 'philosophy is merely the unfolding of the divine wisdom by learning and art'. Thus the history of philosophy came into play as it did later for Francis Bacon.[97]

According to the review of the history of philosophy given in Bacon's *Opus Majus*, philosophy was 'perfect' in its scriptural form, yet not entirely absent in the works of unbelievers, pagans as well as the Arabs. There was intellectual 'gold' to be found in Egypt, as both Moses and Plato discovered; and Plato went on to learn Hebrew so that he could read *Genesis* and learn about the true God. Drawing on pagan authors as well as the Bible, Bacon sought chronological order and a general pattern in the fortunes of wisdom: perfect in the minds of Noah and his sons; corrupted in the unbelieving poets and sages who followed and were adored as gods (Zoroaster, Prometheus, Hermes Trismegistus, Apollo, and others); restored to perfection by Solomon; then corrupted through sin; finally restored again by the Greek wise men, and especially Aristotle, who 'purged away the errors of preceding philosophers' and completed philosophy 'as far as possible for that time'.[98] Not only did Bacon give a certain historical shape to the history of wisdom, or philosophy, but he also opened a prospect of future progress, following the first achievements of theology and 'supply[ing] what the ancients lacked':[99]

> Therefore Christians desiring to complete philosophy ought in their works not only to collect the statements of philosophers in regard to divine truths, but should advance far beyond to a point where the power of philosophy as a whole may be complete.[100]

The way to accomplish this was through a program of study that can only be called eclectic, such that

> Christians can unite many authorities and various reasons and very many opinions from other writers besides the books of unbelieving philosophers, provided they

---

[96] *The 'Opus Majus' of Roger Bacon*, ed. John Henry Bridges (London, 1897), I, 17; *The Opus Majus of Roger Bacon*, trans. Robert Belle Burke (New York, 1962), I, 19.
[97] See below, Chapter 3.
[98] *Opus Majus*, 63, 65.
[99] Ibid., 66 (Lat., I, 57): 'vias philosophorum infidelium complere'.
[100] Ibid., 73.

belong to philosophy, or are common to it and theology, and must be received in common by unbelievers and believers.[101]

Bacon was exceptional, though not unique, in his sense of philosophy as a process of accumulation and criticism. A thirteenth-century *Summa philosophiae* (wrongly ascribed to Grosseteste) surveyed philosophical tradition as a hierarchy of thinkers ranging from 'theosophists' (inspired authors like Moses, the prophets, and Christ), theologians (the authoritative Augustine, Jerome, and Pseudo-Dionysius to uninspired makers of modern summaries such as Peter Lombard and perhaps himself), and the pagan philosophers of antiquity, whose authority he ranked above the Moderns.[102] This author also recognized two basic methods: one was Plato's direct assault on truth and the other Aristotle's habit of arguing with his predecessors – the latter, of course, coming to prevail in the medieval *Studium*.

On the whole, as Etienne Gilson has concluded, 'The masters of the thirteenth century were making history, not writing it.'[103] Yet their writings constituted as much a critical history of commentary as an achievement of 'science', and long before humanism, Franciscan critics denounced the source of this science, Aristotle himself, as the 'worst philosopher'.[104] It is ironic that the propositionalist bias of medieval philosophizing produced, in the long run, not incontrovertible logical proofs but rather long and growing lists of *opiniones* and a method that often resorted not to truth but rather to consensus – to that rule of probable truth called the *communis opinio*. Humanists had complained about the endless accumulation of 'glosses on glosses of glosses', but in a longer run this growing deposit of opinion furnished material for historians of philosophy to report and to interpret, finally provoking still later critics, during the Enlightenment, to revolt against this pedantic 'scholasticism'.

The recovery of Plato opened a wider perspective on ancient philosophy and the possibility of reconciling Christian and pagan thought in the endless 'hunt for wisdom' (*venatio sapientiae*). In a little treatise of that title Nicholas of Cusa presented a review of the history of philosophy, pointing in particular

---

[101] Ibid., 74; Lat., I, 64: 'Propter quod philosophans Christianus potest multas auctoritates et rationes et sententias quamplurimas de scriptis aliis, quoque de libris philosophorum infidelium adunare, dummodo sint propria philosophiae, vel communia ei et theologiae, et quae communiter habent fideles et infideles reperire.'

[102] Gilson, *Christian Philosophy*, 266–72; and see Charles King McKeon, *A Study of the* Summa Philosophia *of the Pseudo-Grosseteste* (New York, 1948).

[103] *Christian Philosophy*, 427.

[104] Edward P. Mahoney, 'Aristotle as "The Worst Natural Philosopher" (*pessimus naturalis*) and "The Worst Metaphysician" (*pessimus metaphysicus*)', in *Die Philosophie im 14. und 15. Jahrhundert*, ed. Olaf Pluta (Amsterdam, n.d.).

to the Platonic concept of ideas to define this wisdom and to join pagans and Christians in the hunt.[105] Cusanus was one of a number of fifteenth-century scholars who sought intellectual and religious harmony in the confluence of several traditions. In the aftermath of the fall of Constantinople in 1453 he wrote a dialogue between men of several cultures – an Italian, a Tartar, an Englishman, a Bohemian, and others – in which he envisioned and called not for conformity but for a unitary wisdom that would bring philosophical and religious 'peace' to all humanity. After this multicultural discussion Cusanus staged a book exhibit, including the works of Varro and Eusebius, who had commented tolerantly on the diversity of religion.[106]

Cusanus's pacifist, or syncretistic, dream was pursued later by Pico, Jean Bodin, Guillaume Postel, Leibniz, and other scholars who sought not only intellectual concord but also peace in a larger human sense. But this was utopian syncretism, verging on heresy, and not the truth-seeking eclecticism which more orthodox authors hoped to extract, or to distill, from the tradition of western philosophy and scholarship. And it was the revival of the concealed or missing parts of this tradition of thought and learning, beginning especially in the fourteenth century, that – according to Brucker, Cousin, and other scholars of their conciliatory persuasion – showed the best route to the illusive goal of wisdom. It was the encyclopedic scholarship of the Renaissance, in short, that gathered and arranged the materials for the new eclecticism of the modern age.

7. The Language of Ideas

Philosophy was one thing, learning another: thinking gives access to living ideas, but reading restores the past and its dead (of whom, Novalis believed, we have a duty to think). 'In books I find the dead as if they were alive', wrote Richard de Bury in the fourteenth century; 'in Books I foresee things to come; in books warlike affairs are set forth; from books come forth the laws of peace.'[107] Disapproving of the scholastic worship of Aristotle and in general the habit of 'studying antiquity more than truth', Bury sided with the Moderns; yet he celebrated the fact that books, which 'alone are liberal and

---

[105] *De Venatione sapientiae*, in *Operun clariss. P. Nicolai Cusae Card.* (Paris, 1514), fol. CCI–CCXVIII^r.

[106] *Nicholas of Cusa's De Pace Fidei and Crobratio Alkorani*, trans. Jasper Hopkins (Minneapolis, 1970), 70.

[107] *Philobiblon*, trans. E. C. Thomas (Oxford, 1970), 13.

free', offer access to the ancient wisdom of the eastern precursors of 'the approved divinity of Plato'.[108] Anticipating modern eclectics, Bury posited an idea of progress – 'the gradual perfecting of books' – based on the accumulation of other people's learning, recalling that even Aristotle used both books and reason in his philosophy, so that he could see 'with lynx-eyed penetration ... through the sacred book of the Hebrews, the Babylonians, the Chaldeans, the Persians and the Medes, all of which learned Greece had transferred into her treasures'.[109] So it would be in the future, for 'Being dead, they cease not to teach, who write books of sacred learning.'

The reading of books is a special vocation, and brings up questions of language underlying philosophy. Students of antiquity were members of what a recent scholar has called a 'referring culture', in which most of what was important had already been said better than a 'modern' writer could hope to do.[110] But how, in the hunt for wisdom in the words of others, can one capture the intellectual quarry hiding in these words? If medieval authors lost the sense of context, continuity, and succession that had prevailed in the ancient schools, they still faced the problem of gaining 'access' to these authors, an exegetical method traceable to the Greek commentators, which dealt with questions of intention, utility, order, and genre, and asking the readerly – and rhetorical – questions of who, what, why, how, and where.[111] In this effort medieval scholars were assisted by an elaborate and flexible theory of interpretation, which recognized spiritual and figurative – moral, allegorical, anagogical – as well as literal, 'historical' constructions of texts.[112] So Hellenistic commentators had done for Homer, Philo for Judaism, and Origen for Christianity. Such a hermeneutical theory and practice formed intellectual connections and continuities essential to the reconciliation of Christian and pagan learning and to the writing of the history of philosophy.

One feature of scholasticism relevant to this problem – to questions of interpretation, transmission of ideas, and the history of thought – is the

---

[108] Ibid., 71.

[109] Ibid., 109–11.

[110] Ruth Morse, *Truth and Convention in the Middle Ages* (Cambridge, 1991), 17.

[111] Rita Copeland, *Rhetoric, Hermeneutics, and Translation in the Middle Ages* (Cambridge, 1991), 67; and see Edwin A. Quain, 'The Medieval *Accessus ad auctores*', *Traditio*, 3 (1945), 215–64.

[112] See Henri Lubac, *Exégèse médiévale* (Paris, 1959–64); Hennig Brinkmann, *Mittelalterliche Hermeneutik* (Tübingen, 1980); and *Sensus-Sensatio*, ed. M. L. Bianchi (Florence, 1996); and Kathy Eden, *Hermeneutics and the Rhetorical Tradition* (New Haven, 1997); also Wilhelm Dilthey, 'Schleiermacher's Hermeneutical System in Relation to Earlier Protestant Hermeneutics' (1860), *Hermeneutics and the Study of History*, in *Selected Works*, IV, ed. Rudolf Makkreel and Frithjof Rodi (Princeton, 1996), 33.

acceptance of Latin as the medium of exchange and in effect as a universal language forming an ideal vehicle for the description of God's Creation and man's small additions thereto. God spoke Hebrew and then Greek, but never so clearly as Latin, which indeed became the first language of the 'Republic of Letters', as the international literary community was called from the fifteenth century.

But the language of the universities was a very peculiar sort of Latin, joined as it was to the conviction that disputation was the best road to mastery of knowledge, the achievement of correct intellectual conclusions, and the transmission of these dogmas from *magister* to *discipulus*. 'Omnis scientia esset logica,' as Duns Scotus put it.[113] On such assumptions proof and persuasion relied exclusively on a kind of verbal algebra or textbook shorthand in which the terms, 'taken out of context', were arranged in simple and unqualified propositions. Memorable examples of this were the condemnation of certain theses of Aristotle in 1277, of Pico della Mirandola in 1488, of Luther in 1520, and of Ramus in 1542; but the practice can be seen also in the seventeenth-century tendency to reduce philosophy to univocal and decontextualized terms, discrete and 'stripped' propositions, and logical demonstrations. So reduced, history itself could become reasoned, conjectural, even apriori. Such reductive propositionalism was quite in keeping with the assumption of enduring and exchangeable 'ideas' conceived as existing apart from oral or written discourse and identifiable and communicable by historians as well as philosophers.

Not all scholars were captives of this view. In his *Metalogicon* John of Salisbury, student of Abelard, celebrated not only Aristotelian logic but also eloquence as the means of translating ideas into words; and in this connection he defended Aristotle, whom (he recalled) Quintilian had praised on stylistic as well as intellectual grounds. John recognized the public role of intellectuals and, ignoring the legendary teaching of Abelard, prized publication above oral accomplishments, remarking that 'He who speaks is judged merely by one or a few persons; whereas he who writes exposes himself to criticism by all, and appears before the tribunal of the whole world and every age.'[114] John also had a sense of the dynamics of intellectual change, for 'men always change the opinions of their predecessors' – nor, he added, was he himself immune from this principle.

---

[113] Gilson, *Christian Philosophy*, 462.
[114] *Metalogicon: A Twelfth-Century Defense of the Verbal and Logical Arts of the Trivium*, trans. Daniel D. McGarry (Berkeley, 1955), 117 (II, 18); and see Edouard Jeauneau, 'Jean de Salisbury et la lecture des philosophes', in *The World of John of Salisbury*, ed. Michael Wilks (Oxford, 1984), 77–108, and Janet Martin, 'John of Salisbury as Classical Scholar', ibid., 179–201.

In some ways it may be anachronistic to attribute a 'sense of history' to twelfth-century scholars, even the humanist avant-garde of the school of Chartres; but they showed a sense of wonder, sometimes cultural shock, and developed sensitive methods of reading ancient philosophers (*lectio philosophorum*) even as they adapted them to modern 'questions'. As a modern scholar concludes, 'It is largely their willingness to engage an ancient source, directly and as nearly as possible on its own terms, that distinguishes the work of Thierry, Bernard of Chartres, and William of Conches from that of their contemporaries.'[115] One result was a revival of ancient sectarian habits, imputations of continuity with ancient lines of argument, and a renewal of the grandiose 'scientific' pretensions of philosophy and imperial claims over other disciplines.

What is more, philosophers at this time again began to find a place in society, and a use for their ideas and arguments, as a result of the appearance of the new institution of learning which organized itself as a 'university'.[116] Legend had it (and still in a sense accepted by Cousin) that the University of Paris was descended from the Carolingian schools, with a 'translation of studies' accompanying the 'translation of empire' by which Charlemagne became 'Roman' emperor.[117] In fact the university emerged from the cathedral schools of Abelard's time as first an ecclesiastical and then a royal institution, becoming in the course of generations an intellectual – philosophical as well as theological – monopoly and the center of an international academic network 'prefiguring' the 'Republic of Letters' of a later age.

The medieval *Studium* was an extraordinary planting- as well as battle-ground of ideas. In the first century after their founding, the intellectual history of the universities, especially Paris and Oxford, was a reprise of the old battles between paganism and Christianity, but now in the institutional context of the faculties of arts, philosophy, and theology, with controversy further inflamed by the rivalry between the Dominican and Franciscan Orders, established in the University of Paris in the early thirteenth century. Ecclesiastical authorities examined the varieties of Aristotelianism developed from ancient texts and commentaries, and extracted from them certain errors, especially concerning ideas of the soul, of time, and of nature in their relationship to God. In 1277 an inventory of these errors – 179 philosophical and 40 theological – was published and condemned by decree of the Bishop

---

[115] Wetherbee, in Dronke, *History*, 32.

[116] Hilde de Ridder-Symoens (ed.), *A History of the University in Europe*, I, *Universities in the Middle Ages* (Cambridge, 1992).

[117] *Lectures*, II, 13, deriving 'scholastique' from the Carolingian *scolae*.

of Paris. But despite the temporary setback, the study of these doctrines and the process of 'philosophizing' flourished, as did a variety of new schools and '-isms'.[118]

Like the ancient academies, the university was a place to listen, to talk, to exchange ideas; it was a course of study, a *Studium*, an embodiment of the ancient ideal of *encyclios paedeia*, a basis for an international network of scholars in agreement about the questions to be disputed, if not answers to be reached. This new institution was, as Etienne Pasquier remarked about the University of Paris in the sixteenth century, 'built of men'.[119] It was also transformed by men, as they followed various career lines and served different masters. Medieval professors, like their ancient forebears, followed the generational pattern of master and disciple; and in the unending dialogue thereby formed, medieval 'doctors' acquired, or adapted from the Ancients, an extraordinary vocabulary to express the complex relationships created in the medieval *Studium* – the vocabulary of inquiring, erring, opining, knowing, doubting, criticizing, and transmitting the ideas and the wisdom to be found in ancient authors.[120]

The story continued in the following chapters traces intellectual efforts to understand first the philosophical inheritances and then other creations of the 'human spirit' constituting humanity in its different cultural guises. As told by doxographers and historians of philosophy, the story takes the form of an intellectual progression from wisdom to philosophy; then, beginning in the fifteenth century, from philosophy to a new sort of 'eclecticism'; and finally circling back to a broader sort of modern wisdom involving intellectual and cultural history and the human sciences more generally.

---

[118] Ferdinand van Steenberghen, *Aristotle in the West* (Louvain, 1955), and Gordon Leff, *Paris and Oxford Universities in the Thirteenth and Fourteenth Centuries* (New York, 1968).

[119] *Recherches de la France* (Paris, 1621), IX, 19; and see Stephen C. Ferruolo, *The Origin of the University: The Schools of Paris and their Critics 1100–1215* (Stanford, 1965).

[120] See Pierre Michaud-Quanten, *Études sur le vocabulaire philosophique du moyen age* (Rome, 1970).

Chapter 3

The 'Light of Philosophy Reborn'

First comes writing, then philosophizing.
Friedrich Nietzsche

Philosophy began by word of mouth but long since has become part of scribal culture, with all the conditions this implies, and the art of printing intensified these conditions. In ancient schools oral tradition prevailed; in the age of the printed book the relationship of instructor with student becomes more remote and problematic, and the intermediate role of the critic is magnified. The Renaissance restored a more direct knowledge of the ancient schools, including primary texts as well as Laertian doxography; but it was the Reformation (no less than the new science) that set philosophy on its modernizing course, Luther's 'liberty of conscience' being succeeded and conceptually fulfilled by Protestant – and eclectic – 'liberty of philosophizing' (*libertas philosophandi*) and implicitly, perhaps, freedom of thought, if not the marketplace of ideas. So at least eclectic historians of philosophy saw the conceptual implications of Lutheran reform and the purified tradition it constructed, and Catholic historians did not seriously dispute the phenomenon, only its meaning and value. This constitutes the philosophical context of the early study of intellectual history, which continued in a more subtle way the 'hunt for wisdom' that transcended particular doctrines.

1. Renaissance of Letters

In the wake of the Renaissance of learning conventionally credited to Petrarch and his followers came what one early modern historian of philosophy called the 'light of Philosophy reborn' (*renascentis ... Philosophiae lux*).[1] This first dawning was due not to self-proclaimed philosophers but to grammarians and scholars – not to the system-builders of the thirteenth century or to the 'modern way' that succeeded these, but rather to such humanist 'restorers of

---

[1] Adrian Heereboord, *Meletemata philosophica* (Nijmegen, 1664), 5.

65

philosophy' as Ficino, Pico, Valla, Poliziano, Agricola, Erasmus, and Melanchthon. In its modern incarnation philosophy was the product of what Appiano Buonafede saw as the 'great revolutions' of philosophy initiated by the 'elegant and erudite' Renaissance scholars and completed by modern and mimetic disciples of ancient masters. Following Brucker, however, Buonafede surveyed not only the restorers of ancient doctrines (*restauratori Aristotelici, Pitagorici, Platonici, Cabbalisti*, and so on) but also the founders of new ones, although these could usually be seen as building on the old and so likewise subject to historical discussion.[2]

Obviously, the old philosophies were themselves 'new' in that they were reinterpreted in Christian terms to suit modern conditions. In the Renaissance as in antiquity, philosophy and its history were dominated by the magisterial figures of Plato and Aristotle, who posthumously spawned not only new ('neo-') schools and a massive 'literature' but also a vast mythology; and the history of philosophy was shaped by the battles between the epigones of these two conceptual titans. In the later middle ages 'philosophy' referred almost exclusively to the work of Aristotle.[3] Yet no less than Plato, Aristotle was embedded in eclectic commentary, being associated with certain 'natural books' of Neoplatonic provenance, while Plato appeared mainly in philosophical legend and tradition by way of Diogenes Laertius, Cicero, and Augustine.[4] It was this tradition that led Petrarch, though he lacked any Greek, to his famous revisionist remark (itself supported by ancient testimony), that 'Plato is praised by the greater men, Aristotle by the bigger crowd.'[5]

Petrarch did not really know much philosophy, but he knew what he liked and disliked.[6] He had little knowledge of the sophists, founders of the rhetorical tradition on which he drew; and following Platonic convention, he applied the term 'sophist' pejoratively to the scholastic dialecticians of his day, whose true 'ignorance' (compared to his own ironically Socratic 'ignorance') he despised. The Platonic doctrine of ideas he knew by way of Cicero and Macrobius, and he regarded it as a product of ancient and 'poetic' theology, following Aristotle's

[2] *Della restaurazione di ogni filosofia ne' secoli XVI, XVII e XVIII* (Venice, 1785).

[3] Charles Schmitt, *Aristotle and the Renaissance* (Cambridge, MA, 1983).

[4] Raymond Klibansky, *The Continuity of the Platonic Tradition during the Middle Ages* (London, 1939).

[5] 'On his Own Ignorance and That of Many Others', trans. Hans Nachod, in *Renaissance Philosophy of Man*, ed. Ernst Cassirer et al. (Chicago, 1948), 111. 'The judgment that Plato was the greater authority *in divinis*, Aristotle *in naturalibus* goes back to antiquity', notes James Hankins, *Plato in the Italian Renaissance* (Leiden, 1990), I, 5.

[6] Charles Trinkaus, *The Poet as Philosopher: Petrarch and the Formation of Renaissance Consciousness* (New Haven, 1979).

famous statement that the poets were the first theologians. But philosophy transcended its doctrinal purveyors, and so Petrarch became an unashamed eclectic, 'for I do not love sects but the truth', he wrote. 'Therefore I am at one time a Peripatetic, and at another a Stoic and sometimes an Academic.'[7]

Petrarch's views were carried on by Coluccio Salutati, Leonardo Bruni, and other disciples. Salutati recalled one of the central episodes, or myths, of the philosophical canon, namely the 'Socratic revolution', celebrated by Cicero and many others. This, the first of many intellectual 'turns' in modern times, shifted emphasis from the wonders of physical nature to the realities of social life and the pressures of moral choice. It was a turn that Petrarch had taken, most famously in his ascent of Mount Ventoux, when he shifted his attention from mountain scenery to reflection and self-knowledge.[8]

Bruni, who stood at the center of the modern turn from natural to moral philosophy, was the first humanist translator of Aristotle's (and a few of Plato's) works, at least those in 'practical philosophy'. Like his predecessors, Bruni honored the connections between philosophy and poetry, which (he recalled) both Plato and Aristotle had studied. He admitted the disputes between the ancient sects over moral philosophy but played them down as differences of style and terminological preference. In his life of Aristotle he indulged in a good bit of doxographical detail, culled mainly from Diogenes Laertius.[9] In general Bruni believed that humanity owed less to Plato than to Aristotle, who had arranged all the disciplines into a single, teachable system, who held opinions more in keeping with 'normal usages and ways of life', and who displayed great eloquence, though unappreciated by his later expounders, who were quite ignorant of classical literature. As George Holmes has remarked, 'Bruni did not regard philosophy as a live study to which original contributions might be made.'[10]

The modern history of philosophy is inextricable from the ancient rivalry between Platonic and Aristotelian philosophy.[11] The choices in general were between the contemplative and the active, and between spiritualism and naturalism – between ideas and the senses, as some might say. The old debate

---

[7] *Rerum familiarum libri I–VIII*, trans. Aldo S. Bernardo (Albany, 1975), VI, 2.

[8] 'Ascent of Mount Ventoux', trans. Hans Hachod, in *Renaissance Philosophy of Man*, ed. Cassirer et al., 56.

[9] *The Humanism of Leonardo Bruni*, trans. G. Griffiths, J. Hankins, and D. Thompson (Binghamton, 1987); and see Ronald G. Witt, *'In the Footsteps of the Ancients': The Origins of Humanism from Lovato to Bruni* (Leiden, 2000).

[10] *The Florentine Enlightenment 1400–1450* (New York, 1969), 112.

[11] For example, Bernardino Donato, *De Platonicae atque Aristotelicae Philosophiae differentia* (Paris, 1541).

was revived in the fifteenth century through renewed contacts with the Eastern Empire during efforts to end the schism between the Greek and Roman Churches before the Turkish conquest of Constantinople. During the Council of Florence discussions were carried on by doctrinal adversaries – Roman and Greek Christians as well as Aristotelians and Platonists – with new perspectives and choices of canons opening up; and these debates continued after the fall of Byzantium in 1453. Two years later John Argyropoulos, lecturing on Greek literature in Florence, appeared to his students to have 'stepped into Florence from antiquity itself'.[12]

The Byzantine contribution, according to a recent scholar, was to represent the work of Plato, his antecedents, and his successors, as 'a unified philosophical tradition'. Plato's greatest champion was George Gemistos Pletho, who composed an invidious analysis of *Differences between Plato and Aristotle*. Formerly Plato had been more highly esteemed, Pletho argued, but was recently eclipsed by Aristotle, through the noxious influence of the Arabic commentators (also scorned by Petrarch). Pletho rehearsed what would be standard arguments for the inferiority of Aristotle – that he had brought logical inconsistencies, a deterministic theory of causation, a materialistic notion of the soul, and a degrading idea of virtue. Moreover, Aristotle had denied the theory of ideas (derived, Pletho thought, from Pythagoras), and so, at least implicitly, a creating God.

Pletho's polemic against Aristotle and idealization of Plato provoked a long controversy central to the modern history of philosophy. The first major response was George Trapezuntius's *Comparison of Plato and Aristotle*. A defector from Platonism to Aristotelianism and a champion of orthodoxy, Trapezuntius concluded that 'depraved Platonic hedonism corrupted the empire and in the end brought it to ruin'; and to it he attributed as well 'all the heresies that beset the early church'. His target was the distinguished exile Cardinal Bessarion, who wrote his own treatise 'against the calumniators of Plato' in the conciliatory spirit of contemporary efforts to reconcile the Churches. Drawing on the eclectic heritage of Platonism (that is, Neoplatonism), Bessarion gathered a wealth of testimonies about the congeniality of Platonic doctrine to Christian faith – for Plato recognized God in a spiritual sense even if he called him 'Jove'.[13]

In this debate over the father-figures of philosophy, religion furnished the controlling subtext, especially in the cases of Plato's alleged ideas of free will,

---

[12] Arthur Field, *The Origins of the Platonic Academy of Florence* (Princeton, 1988), 109.
[13] *Bessarion in calumniatorem Platonis libri IV*, ed. and trans. L. Moliter (Paderborn, 1927), 233: 'non verbis sed re ipsa constat'.

immortality, and the spiritualist doctrine of ideas. All these seemed to contrast with the materialism and determinism of Aristotle, at least in scholastic form, while the spiritualism of Plato seemed more easily, if often figuratively, reconcilable with Christian faith. For these reasons, too, Plato had come again to eclipse Aristotle. 'For all the ancients', wrote one Renaissance scholar, 'all the men of the middle ages [*medie tempestatis homines*], all the most learned men of our age, all Greeks, barbarians and Christians, revere, honor and preach Plato as though he were an oracle.'[14]

The consummation of Plato's revival appears in the heroic labor of Marsilio Ficino in translating the whole work of Plato – and, what is more, of interpreting it as a unified corpus. Ficino had great respect for the restorative powers of history, for 'what is itself mortal, through history attains immortality; what is absent becomes present, what is ancient becomes new ... ' This reconstruction is just what he hoped to perform for Plato. However, there was a serious ambivalence in the idea of making something ancient into something new, for Ficino's Plato was embedded in a vast tradition of Neoplatonic and hermetic commentary and merged into Ficino's own syncretistic theology.

This was the 'divine' Plato who had attained a status hardly less immortal than that of his ideas and who, in Florence, became the spiritual father of a community devoted to philosophy in the ancient style. If the 'Platonic Academy' associated with Ficino was largely a creation of the imagination of later historians,[15] it nonetheless symbolized a sort of philosophical circle familiar to any reader of Diogenes Laertius. This cooperative ideal, celebrated as an alternative to and a refuge from the hostile intellectual terrain of scholasticism, became a basis for ideas of intellectual continuity and synthesis which sought to reconcile the squabbling sects of philosophical tradition.

Yet what Buonafede and other later historians of philosophy celebrated was not merely the revival of the ancient sects or their eponymous heroes, but rather 'the restoration of philosophy in general'. While drawing on ancient sources and often professing allegiance to particular ancient schools, philosophy was given new life by the innovators (*novatores, reformatores, recentiores*) and adjusted to modern contexts.[16] Whatever form it took, philosophy was trying to attain – or to regain – the status of a 'science', with all the privileges, honors, and rewards pertaining thereto.

---

14 Giovanni Andrea de' Bussi, cited by Hankins, *Plato in the Italian Renaissance*, I, 209.

15 James Hankins, 'The Myth of the Platonic Academy of Florence', *Renaissance Quarterly*, 44 (1991), 429–75.

16 See Franco Venturi, *Italy and the Enlightenment*, trans. Susan Corsi (New York, 1972), 59.

In a sense philosophy was reasserting in a secular way an earlier claim that, in the words of Ficino, 'philosophers as a class are divine'.[17] One influential expression of this was Jacopo Sadoleto's dialogue *In Praise of Philosophy* (1543), which defended this 'divine science' in a Christian perspective.[18] Sadoleto established the connection to pagan views through Augustine's famous invocation of Cicero's (lost) *Hortensius*, which had turned – 'converted' – him to philosophy. Answering traditional rhetorical objections, Sadoleto insisted on the transcendent unity not only of truth but also, despite endless disagreement on particular issues, of philosophy itself. For him reason was 'another god' in the body, philosophy the most exalted creation of this divinity, and the history of philosophy in effect a celebration of both of these more-than-human phenomena.

In these arguments Sadoleto was followed by the young French Platonist Louis Le Caron, for whom true philosophy was not only 'divine' but also 'sovereign'.[19] Although opposed to 'opinion', it had the highest practical utility to humanity. In particular he identified the doctrine of Plato with the 'true philosophy' of law; and in this juridical form he hoped to naturalize philosophy and conscript it into the service of the French monarchy. In short, Le Caron was a sort of 'civic Platonist' (though his term was 'courtier', anticipating the 'court philosophy' of the next century) who wanted to reconcile philosophy and rhetoric, the contemplative and the active life, private truth and public utility; and it was in such terms that he viewed the history of philosophy. As Sadoleto had argued, moreover, philosophy was a purely Greek invention not to be confused with the 'bastard philosophy' of the barbarians who speculated and mythologized before Pythagoras.

In their efforts to raise their discipline to the top of the hierarchy of learning, modern philosophers were faced with an ancient problem. Let us grant that philosophy is a science; the object of science is truth; and truth, in contrast to opinion, is one – *una est veritas*, according to the ancient proverb which had been passed from pagan to Christian writers. The problem was how this unitary, Platonic truth could be determined in the crush of learning

---

[17] Michael J. B. Allen, *Icastes: Marcilio Ficino's Interpretation of Plato's Sophist* (Berkeley, 1989), 220: 'philosophorum genus esse divinum'.

[18] *De Laudibus philosophiae libri duo* (Lyon, 1543), and a modern translation by P. Charpenue, *L'Attaque et la défense de la Philosophie* (Paris, 1864); and see Richard M. Douglas, *Jacopo Sadoleto 1477–1547: Humanist and Reformer* (Cambridge, MA, 1959), 78–81.

[19] *Les Dialogues*, ed. John A. Buhlmann and Donald Gilman (Geneva, 1986), and see also D. R. Kelley, 'Louis Le Caron Philosophe', *Renaissance Essays in Honor of Paul Oskar Kristeller* (New York, 1976).

produced in an age of proliferating schools, printed books, religious and political disputes, and a riot of ideas drawn from many different times and places. Truth was supposed to be the 'daughter of time'; but so, to judge from the excavations of Renaissance scholarship, was error. How could modern philosophy even begin to establish its identity in the midst of so many problematic rival doctrines that had been retrieved from antiquity and inherited from the middle ages?

This is to rephrase the old problem underlying the famous Quarrel between the Ancients and the Moderns, and its resolution depended on historical and linguistic as well as philosophical judgment.[20] Could the Moderns think as deeply and as widely as the Ancients had done, and was it possible to express their thoughts in their own vulgar languages? It was in response to these questions that serious inquiry, conceptual as well as doxographical, into the history of philosophy was begun, though the first efforts of formulation seem, from a contemporary standpoint, to owe more to imagination and occult tradition than to memory or reason. In any case they represented an extraordinary effort of scholarship aimed at the recovery of the literary remains of over two millennia of magisterial philosophizing.

2. Republic of Letters

Philosophy and its history were pursued over an ever-expanding network of teachers and authors, students and readers, in which criticism was promoted and institutionalized. The legacy of western learning was the common property of scholars belonging to that international community, which since the fifteenth century has been called the 'Republic of Letters'.[21] Like the congregation of the faithful and communion of saints and the modern 'public sphere', this scholarly community transcended time and nationality, although unlike sainthood, erudition was a matter of purely human effort and achievement. What held this 'republic' together was not virtue but learning, including a

---

[20] Classic account in Henri Rigault, *Histoire de la Querelle des Anciens et des Modernes* (Paris, 1859).

[21] Barbaro, in *Two Renaissance Book Hunters*, trans. Phyllis Walter and Gordon Goodhart (New York, 1991). See Paul Dibon, *La Philosophie néerlandaise au siècle d'or* (Paris, 1954), I, 154; *Commercium Litterarium: La Communication dans la république des lettres 1600–1700*, ed. Hans Bots and Françoise Waquet (Amsterdam, 1994); Maria Fattori (ed.), *Il Vocabulario della République des lettres* (Florence, 1997); and Anne Goldgar, *Impolite Learning: Conflict and Community in the Republic of Letters, 1680–1750* (New Haven, 1995).

common language (a more or less classical Latin, with its treasury of topics and tropes), a common, if highly disputed, view of the Christian past, and a devotion to the literary tradition essential for communication and meaningful disputes between both contemporaries and between 'Ancients and Moderns'.

As the contemporary scholar Noel d'Argonne observed, with a nice mixture of historical sense and idealism,

> The Republic of Letters is of very ancient origin ... and existed before the Flood. Never has a republic been so great, so populous, so free, and so glorious. It embraces the whole world and is composed of people of all nations, social conditions, ages, and sexes, neither women nor even children being excluded. All languages, ancient as well as modern, are spoken. Arts are joined to letters, and the mechanical arts also have their place in it. But its religion is not uniform, and its manners, as in all republics, are a mixture of good and bad, both piety and libertinage being found.

This Republic was coterminous with Christendom, he continued, but differed from it in political as well as ecclesiastical terms:

> The politics of this State consists more in words, in maxims and reflections, than in actions and in accomplishments. People take their strength from eloquence and reasoning. Their trade is entirely spiritual and their wealth meager. Glory and immortality are sought above all things ...

In contrast to the medieval ideal of religious and political unity, the Republic of Letters was deeply divided in confessional and professional ways:

> Sects are numerous, and every day new forms appear. The whole State is divided among philosophers, medical doctors, jurists, historians, mathematicians, orators, grammarians, and poets; and each has its own laws.

Most divisive of all, for d'Argonne, was the art of criticism, which recognized no superior in things literary or philosophical and which set itself up as the final arbiter of meaning:

> Justice is administered by the Critics, often with more severity than judgment ... They cut, slice up, or add as they please, and no author can escape once he falls into their hands.[22]

Though based at first on the network of late medieval European universities and then on scholarly correspondence, the Republic of Letters came to include private scholars and any authors who found access to, or gained recognition

---

[22] [Noel d'Argonne], *Mélanges d'histoire et de littérature* (Paris, 1740, 4th edn), II, 166–7; and see Paul Dibon, *Régards* (Paris, 1990), 154.

through, the channels of communication provided by the printing press. Old-fashioned bibliomania was magnified and commercialized by printed books, and the office, and business, of judging books was given systematic and bibliographical foundation.[23] What put the Republic of Letters on the map, beyond scholarly correspondence and *itinera*, was the extraordinary increase of printed books and periodicals in the seventeenth and eighteenth centuries.[24] Literature produced its own disciplines – *Literaturwissenschaft, Buchwissenschaft, Bibliothekwissenschaft*, and so on – and the old classical topos lamenting the proliferation of books and 'the literature' of particular disciplines acquired new dimensions that made traditional polyhistorical learning truly beyond human capabilities.[25] So the works of all ages, translations as well as editions, appeared, making man literally (in the phrase of Daniel Heinsius) 'contemporaneous with the universe'.

Along with this spectacular increase in information and opinion came a parallel growth of official scrutiny, management, and censorship; and this pressure gave new encouragement and meaning to the old traditions of private and public – esoteric and exoteric – knowledge. Historians of philosophy, too, had to tread carefully between the mundane truths to which the historical art pretended and the revealed truths guarded by religious authority.

Of the contributors to the history of philosophy in particular there were German, French, English, Italian, and Dutch authors, though almost all wrote in Latin. Most were university professors, including teachers of theology, philosophy, law, history, and literature (classical languages); but all were *érudits*, virtuosi of encyclopedic learning, and joined in a common enterprise, which was to study philosophical tradition and especially to accommodate ancient and modern ideas. Though signalled normally by mastery of ancient languages, membership was eventually extended to vernacular writers as the community was itself vernacularized – 'Deutsche Republik der Gelehrten', 'Republyk der Geleerden', 'République des lettres', 'República literaria', and 'Republic of Letters'.[26]

---

23 Adrien Baillet, *Jugements des savans sur les principaux ouvrages des auteurs* (Amsterdam, 1725).

24 See the data in Siegelunde Othmer, *Berlin und die Verbreitung des Naturrechts in Europa* (Berlin, 1970).

25 See Baillet, *Jugements des savans*, xi, on 'la multitude des livres qui augmentent tous les jours d'une manière prodigieuse' and the consequent 'nécessité de choix'.

26 Herbert Jaumann, 'Ratio clausa: Die Trennung von Erkenntnis und Kommunikation in gelehrten Abhandlungen zur *Respublica literaria* um 1700 in der europäische Kontext', in *Respublica Literaria*, ed. S. Neumeister and C. Wiedemann (Wiesbaden, 1987), II, 409–29, and Gunter E. Grimm, *Literatur und Gelehrtentum in Deutschland* (Tübingen, 1983).

Socially, this Republic formed an estate within European society, with a claim (long associated with the sciences of law and medicine) to noble status and pretensions to a distinctive sort of academic 'liberty' going beyond the privileges of the conventional three estates. Yet while bound together by common interests, values, and means of communication, this community nevertheless displayed fundamental divisions – religious, national, disciplinary, doctrinal, and generational – and there were perhaps as many motives and interpretations as there were authors. Not only particular schools – all the old 'sects' and some new ones – but also universities, religious orders, courts, national enthusiasms, generational differences, and confessional allegiances provided inspiration for particular projects. These made up the 'external history' of philosophy which had always been at least implicitly part of the doxographical agenda.

The scholarly projects and missions of the Republic of Letters were carried out in a tumultuous context, defined in the first instance by the religious and political divisions of Counter-Reformation Europe, which for philosophers was most apparent in the large and provocative schism between Catholic establishments such as the University of Paris ('mother of science' and seed-bed of academic controversies and legends) and the new Protestant foundations, such as the University of Halle, which became the center of the new eclectic philosophy. What further deepened divisions between orthodoxy and criticism was the rise of the new science, which not only drew on mainstream philosophy but also employed practical experience and cooperative research in a new intellectual community that rivaled and in some ways eclipsed the international network formed by medieval universities and even the humanist Republic of Letters.

For the history of philosophy the Protestant universities of Germany were of particular significance for Aristotelianism, which was given new life in the sixteenth and seventeenth centuries. What Lutheran professors found in Aristotelianism – a reformed and de-scholasticized Aristotelianism to be sure – was a way of consolidating their doctrine and organizing it in a pedagogically effective way to ensure possession of the hearts and minds of generations to come.[27] This Protestant Aristotelianism, promoted first by Melanchthon in his

---

[27] See Peter Petersen, *Geschichte der aristotelischen Philosophie in protestantischen Deutschland* (Leipzig, 1921); Max Wundt, *Die deutsche Schulmetaphysik des 17. Jahrhunderts* (Tübingen, 1939); Ulrich Gottfried Leinsle, *Das Ding und die Methode: Methodische Konstitution und Gegenstand der frühen protestantischen Metaphysik* (Augsburg, 1985); Ernest Lewalter, *Spanisch–Jesuitische und Deutsch–Lutherische Metaphysik des 17. Jahrhunderts: Ein Beitrag zur Geschichte der iberisch–deutschen Kulturbeziehungen und zur Vorgeschichte des deutschen Idealismus* (Hamburg, 1935);

reform of Lutheran education, was to prevail in German higher education for almost two centuries both in philosophy and in theology and to figure prominently in the early stages of modern eclecticism. Continuing attempts to compare, to contrast, or to reconcile Aristotelianism with other ancient and modern schools, especially Cartesianism, gave further impetus to the historical study of philosophy and to the new 'eclectic method' established by seventeenth-century scholars, philosophers, theologians, jurists, and medical doctors.

In the Republic of Letters the stress was normally on the 'public' aspect of intellectual exchange and propagation of ideas, but the intimidation of authority and institutions of censorship encouraged another dimension of discourse, which was 'clandestine literature'. In recent years scholars have uncovered a vast amount of anti-Christian literature, in which skepticism, libertinism, free thought, naturalism, 'atheism', Judaism, and Spinozism, commingled in a counter-culture based on the circulation of published and manuscript materials – most spectacularly the quasi-legendary treatise on the 'Three Imposters' (Moses, Jesus, and Mohammed).[28] This is a whole world of subversion which is still in the process of being mapped. All this figures in the more distant 'backgrounds of intellectual and cultural history' being considered here.

3. Literary History

In the modern age philosophy, and especially the history of philosophy, was a matter not just of words but (even within the classroom) of written words, and one condition of philosophizing which was shared by scholastic and humanist scholars was a sort of bibliomania that was already well established before the invention of printing. Books, declared Johann Trithemius – speaking of manuscript books – enrich the Church, preserve faith, destroy heresy, promote morality, and offer many other forms of instruction.[29] For Trithemius the printed book represented an unwelcome but fortunately (he believed) passing

---

Josef Bohetec, *Die cartesianische Scholastik in der Philosophie und reformierten Dogmatik des 17. Jahrhunderts* (Leipzig, 1912); and Denis Des Chene, *Physiologia: Natural Philosophy in Late Aristotelian and Cartesian Thought* (Ithaca, 1996).

[28] See *Heterodoxy, Spinozism, and Free Thought in Early-Eighteenth-Century Europe: Studies in the* Traité des trois imposteurs, ed. Silvia Berti, Françoise Charles-Daubert, and Richard H. Popkin (The Hague, 1996), and Antony McKenna, 'Spinoza in Clandestine Manuscripts: A Bibliographical Survey of Recent Research', in *Disguised and Overt Spinozism around 1700*, ed. Wiep Van Bunge and Wim Klever (Leiden, 1996).

[29] *In Praise of Scribes. De Laude scriptorum*, ed. Klaus Arnold, trans. Roland Behrendt (Lawrence, KA, 1974), 35.

fashion, and he urged that the monk should keep writing according to monastic tradition in order to 'ensure lasting remembrance for himself and for his text'. Communication and continuity of thought over time depended on the artificial memory and superhuman force of *scriptura* – and notwithstanding Trithemius's doubts about paper, the book in printed form was as enduring as, and more effectively broadcast than, the parchment and calligraphy of the scribes.

'Primum scribere', said Nietzsche, 'deinde philosophari.'[30] For early modern scholars philosophy was not only a set of intellectual practices but also an accumulation of centuries of texts; and by the seventeenth century a critical perspective had been opened upon this intellectual tradition so essential for the history of philosophy, yet so unstable. The common view was summed up by Francis Bacon: 'Even the Works of Knowledge, tho' the most excellent among human Things, have their Periods: for after Kingdoms and Commonwealths have flourished for a Time, Disturbances, Seditions and Wars often arise.' Then come 'barbarous Times', when 'the river Helicon dips underground', followed by a 'Course of Changes', when 'Learning rises again, and shows its Head, though seldom in the same Place, but in some other Nation.'[31] First 'renovation' and then 'translation of studies', passing from Italy to the nations north of the Alps; and Bacon hoped that England would be the current beneficiary.

The study of history was a key both to this scientific community and to the continuing projects of philosophy.[32] The Renaissance 'art of history', like its classical model, referred to actions accomplished, things done (*res gestae*); but from at least the sixteenth century it also reached out for words recorded, things written (*res literariae*), and especially works printed; and the upshot was a new discipline of literary history (*historia literaria*; *historia literaturae*). This inversion of the old topos subordinating words to things (*res non verba*) was linked directly to what was called the 'renaissance of letters' (and in the nineteenth century abbreviated, abstractly, to simply the 'Renaissance'). Letters, literature, meant not capital-L Literature (which was rather 'good letters', *bonae litterae*, *belles lettres*), but anything set down in writing, or printing – that making of books which, even in antiquity, seemed to have no end and which in modern times was becoming overwhelming.[33]

---

[30] *The Gay Science*, trans. Walter Kaufmann (New York, 1974), 54.

[31] 'Orpheus', in *The Mythology of Concealed Knowledge of the Ancients* (*De Sapientia veterum*), trans. Peter Shaw. See Charles Whitney, *Francis Bacon and Modernity* (New Haven, 1986), and especially Paolo Rossi, *Francis Bacon: From Magic to Science*, trans. Sacha Rabinovitch (Chicago, 1968).

[32] See especially Arno Seifert, *Cognitio Historica* (Berlin, 1976).

[33] Thomas Cooper, *Thesaurus linguae Romanae et Brittanicae* (London, 1565): '*Literatura*: Grammar: learning, writing: cunning.' In general see Adrian Marino, *The*

Down to the eighteenth century, 'literature' covered the whole range of arts and sciences in the ancient, medieval, and modern encyclopedia of learning. Such was the usage of Francesco Filelfo, contrasting *Litteratura* to *Latinitas* in his letter to Lorenzo de' Medici;[34] Guillaume Budé in his *De Studio literarum* (1532); Konrad Gesner in his pioneering bibliography, *Bibliotheca universalis* (1548), both a critical classification of books by discipline and a cornerstone of modern library science;[35] Christophe Milieu in his *De Scribendis universitatis rerum historia* (1551), providing 'narratives' (*narrationes*) of the history of literature and wisdom (*sapientia*) as well as civil science (*prudentia*) and nature; and Louis Le Roy, in his *De la Vicissitude ou variété des choses en l'univers* (1575), which compared modern and ancient 'literature' in all intellectual fields.[36] For G. J. Vossius, a historian of philosophy as well as a philologist, 'literary history' (*historia literaria sive scholastica*) treated 'the lives and writings of learned men and the invention and progress of the arts'. 'What Vossius called "literary history"', writes a recent scholar, 'was really what would now be called cultural history.'[37]

Although Bacon's motto was 'things not words', nevertheless he recognized the value of the 'history of literature' and even Laertian doxography, as a supplementary and vicarious form of experience. As he wrote in the *Advancement of Learning*:

> Let there be added the sects and most celebrated controversies that have occupied the learned: the calumnies by which they suffered; the praises and honors with which they were decorated. Let there be noted the principal authors, the most famous books, the successors, the academies, the societies, the colleges, the orders.[38]

The history of literature was ancillary to Bacon's proper method, but it was quite in keeping with his ideals of empirical and cooperative research through the analogous history of nature.

Biography of 'the Idea of Literature' from Antiquity to the Baroque, trans. Virgil Stanciu and Charles M. Carlton (Albany, 1996).

[34] Cited in Angelo Mazzocco, *Linguistic Theories in Dante and the Humanists* (Leiden, 1993), 66.

[35] Luigi Balsamo, *Bibliography: History of a Tradition*, trans. William A. Pettas (Berkeley, 1990), 33ff.

[36] 'Writing Cultural History in Early Modern France: Christoph Milieu and his Project', *Renaissance Quarterly*, 52 (1999), 342–65.

[37] Nicholas Wickenden, *G. J. Vossius and the Humanist Concept of History* (Assen, 1993), 73; see also C. S. M. Rademaker, *Life and Works of Gerardus Joannes Vossius (1577–1649)* (Assen, 1981), 55.

[38] *De Dignitate scientiarum*, in *Works*, ed. Spedding et al. (Boston, 1816), II, 199–200.

In any case philosophy rested inescapably on a literary base and was tied to a literary tradition, and modern philosophers were urged to master the bibliographical 'literature' of their discipline, of which Guillaume Morel's was perhaps the earliest.[39] Chronological listings of authors are important antecedents of the history of philosophy, being concerned, as Johann Fries wrote, with the circumstances of philosophers, including the period in which they lived, whether before or after Christ, the dating of their works, and where they stood in the diadochic 'succession' of doctrine – beginning, for him, with legendary founders like Orpheus, Mercury (Hermes) Trismegistus, and a number of proto-'Homers' before 'Homerus poeta'.[40] Important contributions to this genre include Vossius's history and classification of philosophical sects (1658) and Johann Jonsius's bibliographical collection (1659), listing all known historians of philosophy since antiquity.[41] For Jonsius the history of philosophy could treat either particular disciplines or philosophers and their intellectual genealogies, in either case beginning with Homer. As another Protestant scholar put it, philosophy was connected to the other intellectual disciplines as by Homer's 'golden chain' linking earth with the heavens.[42]

For the encyclopedist Johann Alsted, too, the key was chronology, 'the light and eye of history', as he called it, as he arranged the 'succession of philosophers' (like that of apostles, heretics, and jurists) according to both genealogy and chronology in a sort of temporalized version of his more famous encyclopedic works.[43] In this *Thesaurus of Chronology* Alsted also

---

[39] *Tabula compendiosa de origine, successione, aetate, et doctrina veterum philosophorum* (Basel, 1580 [1547]).

[40] *Bibliotheca philosophorum classicorum authorum chronologica* (Zurich, 1592), preface, distinguishing *veteres*, *neoterici*, and *recentes authores* (drawing on the work of Guillaume Morel), and see Michael Jasenas, *A History of the Bibliography of Philosophy* (Hildesheim, 1973).

[41] Jonsius, *De Scriptoribus historiae philosophiae libri I* [1659] (Jena, 1716); and see B. G. Struve, *Introductio in notitiam rei literariae et usum bibliothecarum* (Jena, 1710); J. F. Reimann, *Versuch einer Einleitung in die historiam literariam antediluvianum* (Halle, 1709); C. A. Heumann, *Conspectus Reipublicae literariae sive via ad historiam literariam iuventuti studiosae* (Hanover, 1718); Gottlieb Stolle, *Anleitung zur Historie der Gelahrheit* (Jena, 1727) and *Introductio in historiam litterariam* (Jena, 1728); Nicholas Gundling, *Historie der Gelahrheit* (Frankfurt, 1734); and Gabriel Naudé, *Advice on Establishing a Library* [1627] (Berkeley, 1950). For an older view of the 'emergence of literary history' see George Saintsbury, *A History of Criticism and Literary Taste* (New York, 1902), 545.

[42] Christian Breithaupt, *Aurea Jovis catena coelo demissa: Nexus historiae philosophiae cum superioribus disciplinis ad audiendas in historiam philosophicam praelectiones* (Helmstadt, 1718); and see Pierre Lévêque, *Aurea Catena Homeri* (Paris, 1959).

[43] *Thesaurus chronologiae* (Herborn, 1650, 4th edn), 290.

included the eclectic school (*secta electiva*), which he saw being continued by Pico, Ramus, and others in the modern age.[44]

In the seventeenth century, then, philosophy still, for many authors, occupied a central place in the old classification of learning; and its freedom was restricted by association with conventional doctrines, ancient preconceptions, and 'prejudices'. Philosophy might be 'systematic', as illustrated by Bartholomew Keckermann's dozen or so works published with this designation; but the 'system' in question was not a logical structure, dialectic being only one minor part of the system. Rather, it took the form of an encyclopedia or a universal library, and it was accountable to all the other arts and sciences as well as to logic and to reason.[45]

Alsted, for example, defined philosophy as the 'knowledge of everything intelligible' (*philosophia est omnis scibilis cognitio*), including 'opinion' and 'probable' knowledge.[46] He founded 'restored philosophy' on preconceptions (*praecognita*) which included an analysis of the disciplines making up philosophy – their 'principles', their 'nature' and 'difference', how they are taught and given encyclopedic form.[47] Daniel Morhof defined wisdom (*sapientia*) as a kind of library of polymathic knowledge and the product of 'literary history', and he distinguished between the Laertian 'history of philosophy in general' and the history of particular schools, both ancient (beginning with Pythagoras) and modern (the *novatores*, including the 'nature philosophers' as well as Cartesians).[48] Gottlieb Stolle, in one of the standard

---

[44] Ibid., 477.

[45] Helmut Zedelmaier, *Bibliotheca Universalis und Bibliotheca Selecta* (Cologne, 1992); W. Schmidt-Biggemann, *Topica Universalis* (Hamburg, 1983); Leroy E. Loemker, *Struggle for Synthesis: The Seventeenth-Century Background of Leibniz's Synthesis of Order and Freedom* (Cambridge, MA, 1972); Joseph S. Freedman, *European academic philosophy in the late sixteenth and seventeenth centuries: the life and philosophy of Clemens Timpler (1563/4–1624)* (Zurich, 1988); and Richard Yeo, *Encyclopedic Visions: Scientific Dictionaries and Enlightenment Culture* (Cambridge, 2001).

[46] Johann Heinrich Alsted, *Philosophia digne restituta libros quatuor* (Herborn, 1615), 10; also his *Scientiarum omnium Encyclopedia* (Lyon, 1649), *Panacea Philosophica* (Herborn, 1610), and *Theatrum scholasticum* (Herborn, 1620); and see Howard Hotson, *Johann Heinrich Alsted: Between Renaissance, Reformation, and Universal Reform* (Oxford, 2000).

[47] Cf. Aristotle, *Posterior Analytics*, 1.1.

[48] *Polyhistor* (Lübeck, 1708), I, 9; and II, 1, on the history of philosophy. See *Mapping the World of Learning: The Polyhistor of Daniel Georg Morhof*, ed. Françoise Waquet (Herzog August Bibliothek, Wolfenbüttel, 2000), especially the articles by Paul Nelles, Ann Blair, Constance Blackwell, Anthony Grafton, and Martin Mulsow; also Waquet, 'The *Polyhistor* of Daniel Georg Morhof, lieu de mémoire de la République des Lettres', *Les lieux de mémoire et la fabrique de l'œuvre*, ed. Volker Kapp, *Biblio*, 17 (1993), 47–60.

handbooks of literary history, placed the history of philosophy within the history of learning in general (*Historie der Gelahrheit*), following and depending on the liberal arts (*die freyen Künste*); and he distributed it further into particular branches, including logic, psychology (*Pneumatik, Geisteslehre*), moral philosophy, and natural law.[49]

Such was the condition of philosophizing and the impediments to philosophers in the early modern period before the assaults of skeptics, champions of pure reason, and counter-encyclopedic literary critics recently discussed by Nicholas Kenny.[50] As Montaigne famously complained, 'There is more ado to interpret interpretations than to interpret things, and more books upon books than upon any other subject; we do nothing but intergloss one another.'[51] By the early eighteenth century this was true not only of philosophy but also of its history. In his (pre-Bruckerian) *Critical History of Philosophy* of 1737, A. F. Boureau-Deslandes remarked that, 'An infinity of authors, some distinguished by intelligence [*talens de l'esprit*] and others by great erudition, have written the history of philosophy.'[52] In the light of this warning, who could doubt the historicity and culturality of philosophy? Who could doubt that, from one standpoint, it was a form of literature, subject to the same limitations and fortunes, and so to the same sort of scholarly criticism? This is a situation which many philosophers have sought to deny, or to evade, for two centuries and more, but historians have embraced it for their own purposes.

4.   Literary Criticism

Down to the time of Kant, then, philosophy was in effect subsumed under the rubric of 'literature' and 'literary history' and so subjected to the rules and standards of literary – and in that connection historical – judgment and criticism. From such a standpoint the light of philosophy had to shine through the written, or printed, page, and to this extent, long before Jacques Derrida's

---

[49] Gottlieb Stolle, *Anleitung zur Historie der Gelahrheit* (Jena, 1718); and cf. C. A. Heumann, *Conspectus Reipublicae literariae* (Hanover, 1718), 8th edn 1791.

[50] *The Palace of Secrets: Béroalde de Verville and Renaissance Conceptions of Knowledge* (Oxford, 1991).

[51] *Les Essais*, III, 13 ('De l'expérience').

[52] *Histoire critique de la philosophie, où l'on traite de son origine, de ses progrès, et des diverses Revolutions qui leur sont arivées jusqu'à notre tems* (Amsterdam, 1737), xv. See Rolf Geissler, *Boureau-Deslandes: Ein Materialist der Frühaufklärung* (Berlin, 1967), and 'Boureau Deslandes, historien de la philosophie', *L'Histoire au XVIIIe siècle* (Aix, 1980), 135–52.

grammatology, philosophy became entangled in the world of narration (*narratio*), writing (*scriptura*; *écriture*), and print (*typographia*); and this has been a fundamental condition of the modern history of philosophy. As a form of literature philosophy was obviously subject to literary examination and criticism, and the history of philosophy depends most fundamentally on the reception and interpretation of this literature. As Bacon wrote, 'As the principal part of the tradition of knowledge concerneth chiefly writing of books, so the relative part thereof concerneth reading of books.'[53] This brings up the fundamental problem of reading methods and practices – the field of hermeneutics and its literary offshoot, the study of reception (*Rezeptionsgeschichte*) – which form the principal pedagogical and psychological grounds of intellectual tradition in its *longue durée*.

How have philosophical texts been read? Early medieval practices of meditative reading, which were intended to reinforce monastic piety, were succeeded by a more complex kind of reading that was 'historical' in the sense of a more or less literal-minded absorbing of information or doctrine and by the 'scholastic' method, that set a premium on logical analysis, propositional reduction, and disputation of 'questions'. Another mode of interpretation that had ancient roots and was preserved and extended by medieval scholars was 'allegorical', construing difficult or cryptic texts through analogical, figurative, or symbolic correlates, dependent to a large degree on the reader's imagination. These customary approaches may all be contrasted with humanist rhetorical efforts of 'imitative' reading, which were part of an effort to acquire the conventions, standards, and style of ancient writing. They may also be contrasted with modern 'critical' reading, which seeks to learn the original, authorial meaning of texts and perhaps to know more about them than the author himself had known (*Besserverstehen*), and with 'aesthetic' interpretation, which subjected texts to larger literary, artistic, or historical standards.[54]

The humanist reading of texts, including philosophical texts, was founded on the art of grammar, promoted to the science of philology, which produced that modern discipline called the art of criticism (*ars critica*): capital-C 'Criticism' (as Jean Jehasse has represented it) joining its similarly capitalized associates, Literature and Philosophy.[55] This approach had little to do with criticism

---

[53] *Advancement of Learning*, 130.

[54] See Hankins, *Plato in the Italian Renaissance*, I, 18–25; also Ernst Behler, 'What it Means to Understand an Author Better than He Understood Himself: Idealist Philosophy and Romantic Hermeneutics', in *Literary Theory and Criticism*, ed. Joseph P. Strelka (Bern, 1985), I, 69–92.

[55] Jehasse, *La Renaissance de la critique: l'essor de l'humanisme érudit de 1560 à 1614* (Saint-Etienne, 1976), and Reinhard Koselleck, 'The Process of Criticism', in

deriving from appeal to standards of truth based on reason or religion – philosophy or theology.[56] Rather it emphasized textual accuracy, fidelity to authorial intention, and so submission to a specifically literary sort of authority. It concentrated on 'sources rather than streams', in the topos repeated by Marsilio Ficino (*fontes potius quam rivulos*);[57] and it carried interpretations which were not logical but rather philological and which included emendations both literal and conjectural. Thus criticism set itself apart from the standards of all the so-called 'sciences', including philosophy and theology, and accepted the authority of received and canonized texts and, in this connection, what humanist scholars had celebrated as the 'authority of antiquity'.

In this way ancient philosophy encountered the new science of philology, likewise ancient in origin and Greek in provenance. For Budé *philologia* was the key to the restoration of ancient wisdom; and so philosophy, like law and theology, became one of the humanities (*studia humanitatis*). 'Once an ornament', Budé wrote, 'philology is now the means of restoration.' In his *De Studio literarum*, referring to Plato, he remarked,

> It is surely a great accomplishment to judge the great geniuses of antiquity according to the representations of them which have been left to us and which one or two generations have, on the basis of sadly corrupt monuments, restored to a condition almost as splendid as the original.[58]

A second Flood, a second wave of 'barbarism' – that is, the middle ages – had inundated letters, but the efforts of textual critics and the 'miracle' of printing had restored them to life.

Drawing on the devices of grammar and rhetoric, humanist scholars focused their attention not simply on some sort of doctrinal truth but on the human meaning of texts, which was not limited to logical or propositional characterization. As Erasmus urged, it was necessary to attend 'not only to what is said, but also by whom it is said, with what words it is said, in what time, on what occasion, what precedes and what follows'.[59] This approach to texts was applied to the history of philosophy as well as to literature in

---

Critique and Crisis (Cambridge, MA, 1988), 103; also *Handwörterbuch der Philosophie*, 'Kritik'.

[56] See the *Encyclopédie* entry 'Critique', distinguishing between 'restitution de la Littérature ancienne' and judgment of 'productions humaines'.

[57] *The Letters of Marsilio Ficino*, trans. Language Department, School of Economic Science, I (London, 1975), 152.

[58] *L'Etude des lettres*, trans. M. M. de la Garandarie (Paris, 1988), 50.

[59] *Ratio Studiorum*, cited by Marjorie O'Rourke Boyle, *Erasmus on Language and Method of Theology* (Toronto, 1977), 92.

general. For Vossius criticism was in fact a part of philosophy; for the office of the textual critic was to gain true understanding of the ancient mind.[60] Thus it was not original conceptualizing but historical interpretation and scholarly judgment (rhetorical *judicium* in a special sense) that was essential for a grasp of philosophy in particular as well as 'literature' in general.[61] Such critical scholarship demanded recourse to the whole circle of classical learning.

The relations between philology and philosophy in the early modern period were complex, uncertain, and often strained. Some scholars were inclined to think that philology, because of its emphasis on memory, was positively an obstacle to productive thinking. The Ancients used their own mother tongue while we waste much time on old languages, argued Le Roy (a vernacularizer who happened also to be Regius Professor of Greek in the Collège Royal) – 'Which is the cause that we have not at this day [1575] such eminent persons in *Philosophie*, as Pythagoras, Thales, Plato, Aristotle, and Theophrastus ... '[62] Their noses buried in old books, scholars forgot not only the marvels of Creation but also that pursuit of self-knowledge which had been the motto of philosophy since the Seven Sages. What Jonathan Swift called the 'malignant deity' of Criticism seemed to usurp the place of the Muses and indeed philosophy itself.[63]

Some enthusiasts of literary learning had a very different way of looking at the opposition between it and philosophy – placing faith in the letter and casting doubt on the role of reason in the interpretation of texts. In his *Court of the Gentiles* (1672) Theophilus Gale tried to prove the 'vanity of pagan philosophy' and the priority of Holy Scriptures entirely on the basis of textual erudition. 'Now the mater of this Discourse', he wrote, 'is not *Logic* but *Philologic*, touching the spring-head and Derivation of human Arts and Sciences.'[64] At the other extreme were champions of mathematics and

---

[60] *De Philosophia et philosophorum sectis libri II* (The Hague, 1658), 171, 'etiam Critice partus est Philosophiae'; 172: 'finis Criticis est veram cognoscere veterem mentem'.

[61] See Baillet, *Jugements des savans*, II, 65 (on *philosophes*), and the comments of Rémy Saisselin, *The Literary Enterprise in Eighteenth-Century France* (Detroit, 1979), 19ff.

[62] *Of the interchangeable course, or variety of things in the whole world*, trans. Robert Ashley (London, 1594), fol. 125ᵛ.

[63] *The Battle of the Books*, in *The Prose Works*, ed. Temple Scott (London, 1907), 75.

[64] *The Court of the Gentiles or, a discourse touching the traduction of human literature both Philologie and Philosophie from the Scriptures and Jewish Church: as also the Vanity of Pagan Philosophie, and Subservience of Reformed Philosophie to Theologie* (Oxford, 1672), 7.

metalanguage for whom erudition was a record of error and misconception. Standing between these extremes was Giambattista Vico, whose extraordinary life work was an attempt to join philology and philosophy in a 'new science' of humanity that accommodated and indeed embodied the entire tradition of western learning.

For scholars who maintained their allegiance to humanist learning, it was a fundamental condition of modern philosophy that it required not merely logical argument but also historical and rhetorical judgment (*judicium*). As Vossius wrote, 'Judgment I call that on the basis of which the historian, after the narration of the facts, forms his opinion.' So the history of philosophy was, according to the eclectic J. F. Buddeus, fundamentally 'hermeneutic'. 'Why hermeneutic?', he asked:

> While many truths have been discovered by learned men, it is not necessary to express them by the investigation and study of their works, but it is enough if we extract them from these writings and monuments; but this cannot be done unless we rightly understand these writings, whence we say 'hermeneutic'.[65]

The question of interpretation was germane to modern philosophy in more than one sense, and it was not necessary to wait for the desperate insights of Nietzsche to appreciate the problems presented by language. For the communication of ideas often depends not only on verbal agreement between discussants – speakers and listeners, authors and readers – but also on translation from one language to another (the most basic meaning of 'interpretation'), which has profound and often distorting effects.[66] As Heidegger explained the disparity, '*Roman thought takes over the Greek without a corresponding equally authentic experience of what they say, without the Greek text. The rootlessness begins with this translation.*'[67] Since Cicero at least, the rendering of classical into barbarian tongues has made possible cross-cultural transmission and modernization, but it has also changed original meaning and magisterial intention. This is another reason why philosophy and its history often needed to resort to the devices of literary criticism.

---

[65] J. F. Buddeus, *Elementa philosophiae instrumentalis seu institutionum philosophiae eclecticae* (Halle, 1714), 180. And cf. J. C. Dannhauer, *Idea Boni Interpretis* (Strasbourg, 1630), 12: 'fines hermeneuticae esse verum orationis sensus exponere atque falso vindiciae'.

[66] Rita Copeland, *Rhetoric, Hermeneutics, and Translation in the Middle Ages* (Cambridge, 1991), and more generally Andrew Benjamin, *Translation and the Nature of Philosophy* (London, 1989), and, on 'vulgarization' and 'discipleship', Robert Denoon Cumming, *Phenomenology and Deconstruction* (Chicago, 1991), I, 66.

[67] Heidegger, 'The Origin of the Work of Art', *Poetry, Language, Thought*, trans. Albert Hofstadter (New York, 1971), 23.

5. Succession of Doctrine

'Knowledge of history means choice of ancestors,' wrote Lord Acton,[68] and this was especially true for the history of ideas, which for him was central to the modern study of history. From the sixteenth century the choice of philosophical canons was vastly expanded beyond the Platonic and Aristotelian monopolies, as many other schools and counter-schools joined the array of doctrines and systems revealed by Renaissance scholarship. The most notable of these were new ('neo') versions of ancient schools – Stoics, Epicureans, and skeptics (as well as neo-scholasticism, both Catholic and Protestant) – but to these were added an endless variety of modern sects which would fill the pages of the histories of philosophy then being assembled. And this is not to mention the skeptical and anti-philosophical ideas likewise derived from antiquity but taking their place in that eclectic and problematic complex which historians define as Modernity.

How were scholars to cope with this modern Babel of words and Pandemonium of ideas? In the search for a way out of the labyrinth of doctrine created by the revival of learning, one strategy was recourse to syncretism (the term itself perhaps coined by Georg Horn in his pioneering history of philosophy published in 1655) – that is, efforts of 'conciliation' between rival sects aimed at a *pax philosophiae* and what Rudolphus Goclenius, in his *Conciliator Philosophicus* of 1609, called 'God's truth' (*veritas Dei*).[69] The intellectual prototype was the ancient program of religious syncretism, associated with Neoplatonism, hermeticism, and the mystery religions, and so suspect in the eyes of religious and political authorities.

In modern times the pioneer in the effort to bring harmony to contending philosophical and religious traditions was Pico della Mirandola, the 'Prince of Concord' in more than one sense. Invoking the Horatian formula of intellectual independence, Pico laid out his agenda in this way, beginning with the Horatian code-phrase of intellectual liberty (and of eclecticism) signaling the eclectic: 'Pledged to no one's words, I have decided to let myself roam through all the masters of philosophy, to look at every scrap of opinion

---

[68] *Essays in Religion, Politics, and Morality*, ed. J. Rufus Fears (Indianapolis, 1989), 620, 643, citing the Acton MSS.

[69] *Conciliator Philosophicus* (Kassel, 1609), 1; cf. Petro de Abano, *Conciliator differentiarum philosophorum et medicorum* (Venice, 1520); Mutius Pansa, *De Osculo seu consensu ethnicae et Christianae Philosophiae, Tractatus* (Marburg, 1605); René Rapin, *La Comparaison de Platon et d'Aristote, avec les sentimens des Peres sur leur Doctrine, et quelques reflexions Chrestiennes* (Paris, 1671); G. Mazzoni, *In universam Platonis, et Aristotelis Philosophiam Praeludia, sive de Comparatione Platonis et Aristotelis* (Venice, 1697); and so on.

and to know all the schools.'[70] For the ecclesiastical authorities of his day Pico roamed altogether too widely – proposing, in his heaven-storming 900 theses, to bring 'concord' not only to Plato and Aristotle but also to a riotous mélange of scholastic, Jewish, Arabic, and hermetic philosophy.

In the Renaissance some of these synthetic efforts took a historical form – syncretism, as it were, historicized. This was the case with Ficino, who also traced philosophy back into a mythical past and a *prisca sapientia*, in which the Egyptian priest Hermes Trismegistus, regarded as a contemporary of Moses, founded a tradition featuring Orpheus, Philolaus, Aglaophemus, Pythagoras, and Plato. 'In this way', Ficino wrote, 'from a wondrous line of six theologians emerged a single system of ancient theology, harmonious in every way, which traced its origins to Mercurius and reached absolute perfection in the divine Plato.'[71] So it was, too, with Pico, whose reading in hermetic texts led to his famous observation – repeated later by Lipsius and others – that 'All wisdom comes from the east.'[72]

This line was followed by many later Neoplatonists, including Francesco Patrizi, whose 'new philosophy', as a recent scholar has written, 'reaffirmed the historiography proposed by Ficino'.[73] Another example was Symphorien Champier, whose somewhat discordant 'symphony' of Platonic and Aristotelian doctrines was likewise given a sort of historical ordering. 'Champier's view of intellectual history as an unbroken line', D. P. Walker has written, 'which includes the middle ages, was shared by Lefèvre and La Boderie; and it is of course the view of Pico and Ficino, but with the difference that in the Italians the strong patriotic motive is lacking.'[74] In his survey Appiano Buonafede later gave prominent place to the restoration of syncretism through the 'way of concord'.[75]

---

[70] 'Oration on the Dignity of Man', in *Renaissance Philosophy of Man*, ed. Cassirer et al., 138.

[71] *The Letters of Marsilio Ficino*, I, 50. And see Ingrid Merkel and Alan G. Debus (eds), *Hermeticism and the Renaissance: Intellectual History and the Occult in Early Modern Europe* (Washington, DC, 1988), especially Brian Copenhaver, 'Hermes Trismegistus, Proclus, and the Question of a Philosophy of Magic in the Renaissance' (79–110).

[72] William G. Craven, *Giovanni Pico della Mirandola, Symbol of his Age: Modes of Interpretation of a Renaissance Philosopher* (Geneva, 1981); and see et al. (eds), *Storia delle storie generali della filosofia*; Giovanni Santinello et al. (eds), *Storia delle storie generali della filosofia* (4 vols, Padua, 1981–1988); Eng. trans. of vol. I, *Models of the History of Philosophy*, ed. C.W.T. Blackwell (Dordrecht, 1993), 127.

[73] Brian Copenhaver and Charles B. Schmitt, *Renaissance Philosophy* (Oxford, 1992), 190.

[74] Walker, *The Ancient Theology* (Ithaca, 1972), 78; and see Brian Copenhaver, *Symphorien Champier and the Reception of the Occultist Tradition in Renaissance France* (The Hague, 1977).

[75] *Della restaurazione*, I, 125.

The perspective displayed in these Neoplatonic and hermetic interpretations suggested that history had roots in mythology. The rise of philosophy was associated in particular with the myth of Prometheus, who had brought the 'divine light' (*divinum lumen*) down from heaven and with it 'the gift of all the sciences'. Budé, who followed the line of Ficino, elaborated on this theme. 'What does the myth of Prometheus signify', he asked, 'except that philosophy is the inventor of the arts?'[76] Prometheus was indeed the creator of man (*hominum inventrix*), but '"to make man" means to give him perfection in his class, so that he achieves the knowledge of things divine and human'. Thus, Budé wrote,

> I believe that Prometheus signifies the intellect of the man of philosophy who, in order to gain ability in physiology, astronomy, or other parts of philosophy, raises himself by reason alone to the level of things divine, or tries to do so.

For Budé the secular philosophy of Prometheus was a symbol of intellectual bondage which, after his deliverance at the hands of Hercules, was succeeded by a higher form of thought, liberated from pagan error, called 'philotheory'. In his *De Transitu Hellenismi ad Christianismum* (1535) Budé, writing in the context of confessional strife, recapitulated the painful ancient passage from paganism to Christianity, from *philologia* to *philotheoria*.

The Vatican librarian Agostino Steuco published a work in 1540 on 'perennial philosophy', which followed Pico's line of thought in a more systematic fashion. Steuco's purpose was fundamentally diadochic: to trace the 'succession of doctrine from the beginning of the world' (*successio doctrinae ab exordio mundi*) through its three principal stages. In this magisterial and mystical procession of wisdom Steuco identified three modes and three periods, beginning with the perfect wisdom vouchsafed Father Adam and Mother Eve; second the degenerate knowledge after the Fall; and third, philosophy, for which the desire, if not the reality, had been preserved.[77] The task of modern philosophers (*recentiores Philosophi*) was to recover this original wisdom (*prisca sapientia*, which was also *prisca philosophia*) that excessive desire for knowledge had lost.

---

[76] *De Philologia* (Basel, 1532), 170: 'disciplinarum inventrix'.

[77] *Perenni Philosophia Libri X* (Venice, 1591), on which see Mariano Crociata, *Umanesimo e teologia in Agostino Steuco: Neoplatonismo e teologia cella creazione nel 'De Perennis philosophia'* (Rome, 1987); H. J. de Vleeschauwer, *Perennis Quaedam Philosophia* (Praetoria, 1968); and Charles B. Schmitt, 'Perennial Philosophy: From Agostino to Leibniz', *Journal of the History of Ideas*, 27 (1966), 505–32. The same phrase (*successio doctrinae*) was used contemporaneously by Melanchthon in tracing the course of 'true religion'; and he, too, had conciliatory tendencies uncharacteristic of Lutheran doctrine.

Fantastic genealogy, imaginative canon-formation, or historical reconstruction, this retrospective vision of pre-philosophy vision exerted a powerful influence on the first historians of philosophy. A similar perspective is apparent in the derivative summary of Polydor Vergil, which invoked the argument of Eusebius's *Preparatio Evangelium* that philosophy had begun with the Jews and then passed to the ancient Greeks, whose major contribution was to lay the foundations for moral philosophy – Socrates (in the famous words of Cicero) bringing wisdom down from the heavens into the households of men.

Juan Luis Vives, writing in 1518, also provided a sketch of the 'origins of philosophy'. For him the story of philosophy was one of progressive enlightenment – 'little by little learning was carried forward' – and out of myth came the ordered discipline (*mathesis, disciplina*) of philosophy. The trajectory had begun in Egypt, from which Theut – or more likely Abraham – introduced both letters (the alphabet) and the learning they contained to the Greeks; and it passed on to the Pythagoreans and Plato and thence to the various sects, including the succession of 'old', 'middle', and 'new' academies and 'less distinguished' schools. In the spirit of Alexandrine scholarship Vives emphasized the importance to philosophy of that circle of learning the ancients called 'encyclopedia'. He was sure that the transmission of doctrine depended on such critical learning and that the obscurity of ancient writings, including those of Aristotle, arose largely 'from our laziness and neglect'. Yet Vives also paid deference to 'mother theology', and he was well aware (especially from his labors as editor of Augustine) that ancient ideas had to be restored in a Christian context.

A still broader view of the history of thought was taken by Louis Le Roy, disciple and first biographer of Budé as well as Professor of Greek at the Collège Royal and translator of Plato and Aristotle. Le Roy's *Vicissitude or Variety of Things in the Universe* (1575) celebrated both the positive and the negative aspects of mutability and change, both acquiring and forgetting knowledge, both lighting and extinguishing what he called the 'torch' of learning, and the 'revolutions' in studies and in political organization. Praising the 'new inventions' of the latest 'heroic age' beginning in the fifteenth century, especially the art of printing, Le Roy defended the Moderns against the Ancients and criticized the spirit of 'imitation' which modern philology had encouraged and even the superfluity of books, especially those in classical languages, which he found so time-consuming and narrowing. Reason resided also in modern vernacular languages, and like the Ancients the Moderns had ultimately to follow their own lines of thought. 'The road', Le Roy concluded, 'is open.'[78]

---

[78] *La Vicissitude ou varieté des choses en l'univers* (Paris, 1575), fol. 255^r, 'Le chemin est ouvert.'

Francis Bacon took up and refined the argument of Le Roy, embellishing it especially with biblical wisdom, issuing warnings against the extremes of antiquity and novelty, and recommending the advice of Isaiah, 'Stand ye in the old ways, and see which is the good way, and walk therein.'[79] Bacon paid special attention to the places, the books, and the persons of learning – including institutions, libraries, and rewards which sustain this trinity of 'the progression of knowledge'. Nor should the arts and sciences be studied merely en route to the professions, Bacon argued, but rather cultivated for their own sake and for the fruit which the tree of knowledge will finally bear. Whence Bacon proceeded to his exposition of the organic structure of philosophy, the method on which it rested, the ways in which errors could be eliminated, and his suggestions about its future advancement. For him, too, the road was open, beckoning historians and philosophers alike.

There was another succession of doctrine linking modernity and antiquity and reinforcing this sense of openness and independence. The early modern period saw the emergence not only of a number of rivals to Neoplatonic and Neo-Aristotelian philosophy but also of that ancient source of doctrinal ferment, the philosophy of doubt, including first the academic skepticism of Cicero and then the Pyrrhonism transmitted by Sextus Empiricus.[80] In certain respects skepticism was a reaction to the syncretism displayed by Neoplatonists and champions of 'concord' like Pico; and it represented still another approach to the reading of texts – still another theory of hermeneutics. 'It occurs to me, however', wrote Pico's nephew, Gianfrancesco Pico, who was an early reader of Sextus Empiricus, 'that it is more proper and more useful to render the teachings of the philosophers uncertain than to reconcile them as my uncle wished to do.'[81] This position served to provide a more accurate and discriminating understanding of ancient authors. It was the approach, too, of encyclopedic scholars like Pierre Bayle, who strove for a more 'critical' understanding of philosophical tradition, including doxography as well as doctrine.[82]

---

[79] *Advancement of Learning*, 58, citing *Jeremiah*, 6:16, 'Thus saith the Lord, Stand ye in the ways, and see, and ask for the old paths, and walk therein, and ye shall find rest for your souls. But they said, We will not walk therein.'

[80] See Richard H. Popkin, *The History of Scepticism from Erasmus to Descartes* (New York, 1979), and Charles B. Schmitt, 'The Development of the Historiography of Skepticism: From the Renaissance to Brucker', *Skepticism from the Renaissance to the Enlightenment*, ed. R. Popkin and C. B. Schmitt (Wiesbaden, 1987).

[81] Cited by Charles Schmitt, *Gianfrancesco Pico della Mirandola (1469–1533) and his Critique of Aristotle* (The Hague, 1967), 48.

[82] See Pierre Rétat, *La Dictionnaire de Bayle et la lutte philosophique au XVIIIe siècle* (Lyon, 1971), and Elizabeth Labrousse, *Bayle*, trans. D. Potts (Oxford, 1983).

Skepticism had its positive value, especially in protecting Christian doctrine from pagan error; but it could also serve to encourage a dreaded threat which always lurked in the shadow of skepticism, namely 'atheism', whether construed narrowly as doubt about the existence of God or more broadly as rejection of beliefs regarded as essential to orthodoxy.[83] The existence of a creating God was the alpha and omega of philosophical study, representing either a 'preamble to faith' or a key proposition to be proved in a rational theology. Without this preconception or indisputable proof skepticism would indeed reign on every level of human thought, life, and hope. This question was always on the minds of early modern philosophers – formed at least a subtext of their discourse – even when they were discussing such apparently neutral questions as the nature of matter, the processes of change, and scientific method.

Skepticism had a corrosive effect not only on the theological forestructure of knowledge but also on philosophical tradition, rejecting not only the doctrine of ideas but also, in its extreme form, the very possibility of philosophy – 'Does philosophy exist?' (not the old scholastic question, *quid sit philosophia?*, but a new scholastic question, *an philosophia existat?*), asked one seventeenth-century author.[84] Nor (as history suggests and David Hume famously insisted) have such doubts ever disappeared from the philosophical conversation.[85]

Of course a skeptical attitude was also essential for historical understanding, since this sort of knowledge could not (as Christian Thomasius and others insisted) be more than probable. According to René Rapin, himself a champion of the Ancients, 'it is no small progress in Philosophy to have learnt how much obscurity and uncertainty is mingled with our exactest knowledge, and to be satisfied to be ignorant of that which cannot be known'.[86] But this was different from the Pyrrhonism that was radically destructive of knowledge; and it was precisely to evade such categorical doubt (as well as to find an

---

[83] François Berriot, *Athéismes et athéistes au XVIe siècle en France* (Lille, 1976); Alan Charles Kors, *Atheism in France, 1650–1729*, I, *The Orthodox Sources of Belief* (Princeton, 1990); Michael Hunter and David Wootton (eds), *Atheism from the Reformation to the Enlightenment* (Oxford, 1992). See Adam Tribbechow, *Historia naturalismi* (Jena, 1700).

[84] [J. B. DuHamel], *Philosophia vetus et nova ad usum scholae accommodata* (Paris, 1684), 42.

[85] *A Treatise of Human Nature*, I, iv, 3.

[86] René Rapin, *Reflexions on Ancient and Modern Philosophy*, trans. A. L. (London, 1678), 82, cited by Beverley Southgate, '"Torn between Two Obligations": The Compromise of Thomas White', in *The Rise of Modern Philosophy: The Tension between the New and Traditional Philosophies from Machiavelli to Leibniz*, ed. Tom Sorell (Oxford, 1993), 124.

alternative to the still prevailing Aristotelian philosophy) that modern writers turned to other ancient schools – Justus Lipsius to Stoicism, for example, and Pierre Gassendi to Epicureanism.[87] Both of these scholars approached their subjects as philologists and historians, but both sought also to make the opinions of their ancient author 'new' by finding in it answers to modern questions and reconciling it with modern assumptions and values. In this effort they contributed significantly to the history of philosophy, if in a markedly apologetic and utilitarian fashion. In any case, like Descartes, they refused to remain in the conceptual limbo of skepticism and sought a way out, whether old, new, or an eclectic combination of the two.

Yet in most ways the modern study of the history of philosophy continued to adhere to the classical Laertian model, which offered a major challenge to philological therapy as well as historical criticism. Diogenes Laertius's *Lives and Opinions of Eminent Philosophers* found a new life among the Moderns. The book was published first in Latin translation in 1472 and in its Greek original in 1533. Corrupt and full of errors as the work was, it put Christian biography to shame. 'I say it sadly', wrote Melchior Cano, 'that the lives of the philosophers have been written with more care by Laertius than the lives of the saints have been written by the Christians.'[88] The work was the target of a long series of reconstructive translations and commentaries, culminating in Gilles Menage's 'observations and emendations'.[89] Together with an accumulation of auxiliary texts and fragments culled from classical and Christian sources and a long tradition of literal exegesis, *Lives* became a major vehicle of the new field of 'philosophical history' (*historia philosophica*) and – if only because of its flaws – one reason for the philological turn which this new field had taken from the beginning.[90]

---

[87] See Howard Jones, *The Epicurean Tradition* (London, 1989); Margaret J. Osler (ed.), *Atoms, Pneuma, and Tranquillity: Epicurean and Stoic Themes in European Thought* (Cambridge, 1991), and 'Ancients, Moderns, and the History of Philosophy: Gassendi's Epicurean Project', in Sorell (ed.), *Rise of Modern Philosophy*, 129–43; Lynn Sumida Joy, *Gassendi the Atomist: Advocate of History in an Age of Science* (Cambridge, 1987), and Jason Saunders, *Justus Lipsius: The Philosophy of Renaissance Stoicism* (New York, 1955); also Magnen, *Democritus Reviviscens* (Leiden, 1648).

[88] Cited by Richard Hope, *The Book of Diogenes Laertius: Its Spirit and Method* (New York, 1930), 2.

[89] *In Diogenem Laertium Aegidii Menagii observationes et emendationes* (Amsterdam, 1692). Menage supplemented Diogenes Laertius with a *Historia mulierum philosophorum* (Lyon, 1690).

[90] Among the early Laertian surveys (before 1600) are those by J. B. Buonosegni (1458), Hermann Busch (1507), J. Walleis (1511), J. Reusch (1518), J. Flaminius (1524), G. Morel (1547), J. Riolan (1565), R. Boivin (1566), A. Pisarius (1567), D. Chytraeus, J. Grunius (1587), J. Frisius (1592), J. Crispius (1594).

6. Philosophy Reformed

If the history of philosophy was a byproduct of the 'renaissance of letters', no less significant – certainly for Brucker and the Lutheran tradition on which he drew – was that other face of the 'new learning', the 'reformation of religion'. Though concerned with different words, the history of theology sang many of the same tunes as the history of philosophy, especially those which celebrated a spiritual, foundational, and perhaps original truth and which identified, criticized, and sometimes suppressed error – 'heresy' and 'sect' being synonymous terms. Indeed, it is hardly too much to say that the history of philosophy was a secular surrogate of the history of theology.

The parallels are striking. The history of theology recognized the history of error as well as truth: just as martyrologists like Crespin and Foxe traced the fortunes and heroes of 'true religion', so Heinrich Bullinger followed the career of popish falsehood in his *Origins of Errors*. Historians of philosophy followed suit, denouncing the errors of the scholastic interpreters of Aristotle and praising the insights of reformers of thought and language from Valla to Ramus, so that anti-scholasticism became virtually identified with the (new) 'modern' philosophy.[91] Even Descartes, according to the argument of Johann Clauberg, took a kind of historical approach as distinguished from the disputatious method of scholasticism.[92]

For early modern scholars like Brucker, modern philosophy began with the extension of humanist attitudes into the domain of professional philosophy, and this meant above all the rejection of scholasticism. This proto-evangelical argument began with the criticism of Valla and other humanists and was continued in a more positive spirit by later 'castigators of barbarism' such as Agricola, Erasmus, Vives, Melanchthon, Lefèvre d'Etaples, Ramus, and Nizolio. Whether by the 'new logic' or the 'new rhetoric', these scholars proposed to join the humanist arts of language to hard philosophical reasoning in opposition to the barbaric 'pseudo-philosophers' of the medieval universities.

Of these scholars Mario Nizolio was one who, according to his modern editor, saw 'himself and his work in the perspective of the history of

---

[91] F. X. Gmeiner, *Literaturgeschichte des Ursprungs und Fortganges der Philosophie* (Graz, 1788), 488, 'Anti-Scholastiker oder Novatores'.

[92] *Opera omnia philosophica* (Amsterdam, 1691), 1230: 'Cartesiana Philosophia describitur et editor tanquam historia, qua res ipsae cum omnibus suis circumstantiis comprehendentur ... Scholastica Philosophica non ita historice propagatur, sed continuis disputatoribus et litibus, consistitque maximam partem in controversiis et *logomachias*.'

philosophy'.[93] He saw this history largely as a story of derivative commentary from antiquity and decline, especially from the time of Porphyry and especially of Boethius; and while he displayed some respect for Aquinas, it was only as a 'one-eyed man among the blind'.[94] Classical authors and Moderns like Pico, Vives, and Valla were to be recommended but read selectively and critically. Nizolio was a particular admirer of Cicero and, on the basis of this precedent, wanted to dissociate philosophy from medieval dialectic and metaphysics and to enhance and correct it through the graces and clarity of rhetoric. This was the lesson that Leibniz learned from Valla, Vives, and Nizolio, whose *True Principles* he edited and commented on.

Lutherans followed humanists in promoting the black legend of scholastic philosophy, and indeed interpreting it as a kind of second 'barbarism'. According to the sixteenth-century chronicle of Cario, which in Melanchthon's editorial hands became a quasi-official Lutheran history, 'The Scholastics invented a new doctrine designed to attract and entice men into error and superstition.'[95] This view became a cliché in the work of later Lutheran historians of philosophy, such as Adam Tribbechow and Friedrich Gentzken, for whom 'Scholastic philosophy was extremely barbaric, obscure, confused, and tangled', and filled with 'litigious and perplexing subtleties'.[96] Worst of all, it mixed together things divine and human – philosophy and theology – to the detriment of both. As Protestants denied the existence of modern miracles, so they were determined to keep the projects of philosophy on their proper secular foundations.[97]

This disrepute did not, however, apply to Aristotle himself or to the notion of a logical system of philosophy. After the spiritual euphoria of the initial 'liberation' from corrupt Romanist tradition, Luther's disciples fell back into more mundane intellectual habits, beginning with the old sectarian division into doctrinal factions, the moderates following Philip Melanchthon and the ultras – 'gnesiolutherans' – Flacius Illyricus. They also turned back to the sort

---

[93] *De Veris Principium et vera ratione philosophandi contra pseudophilosophos*, ed. Q. Breen (Rome, 1956), lxv; also Breen, 'Marius Nizolius: Ciceronian Lexicographer and Philosopher', *Archiv für Reformationsgeschichte*, 46 (1955), 69–87.

[94] *De Veris Principium*, lxvi.

[95] Cario, *Chronique et histoire universelle* [trans. S. Goulart] ([Lyon], 1579), I, 779. In general see James H. Overfield, *Humanism and Scholasticism in Late Medieval Germany* (Princeton, 1984).

[96] Gentzken, *Historia philosophiae* (Hamburg, 1724), 147, and Tribbechow, *De Doctoribus scholasticis* (Jena, 1717).

[97] See D. P. Walker, 'The Cessation of Miracles', in Merkel and Debus (eds), *Hermeticism and the Renaissance*, 111–24.

of philosophical and pedagogical system associated with Aristotelian logic, though they pursued this quest within an encyclopedic rather than scholastic context, thus tying philosophy to the other disciplines.

Both Melanchthon and Flacius also had considerable respect for the study of history in a doctrinal as well as a human sense, but they diverged somewhat about the correct approach. Flacius's aim was to celebrate the proto-Lutheran 'witnesses to truth' (*testes veritatis*), while Melanchthon turned back to patristic tradition (*testimonia patrum*) as a way – an eclectic way – not only of defining Lutheran doctrine but also of making a sort of Erasmian peace between rival Churches and confessions.[98] Both had a conception of a spiritual tradition of 'true religion', set apart from ecclesiastical institutions and going back to the 'primitive Church'; both sought a kind of spiritual continuity which gave Lutheranism a respectable – that is, an ancient – pedigree; and both suggested a religious model for the eclectic history of secular philosophy (*Weltweisheit*, as it was called and taught in German universities by Thomasius and others), which likewise had to attend to the history of errors as well as truth.

The analogy is especially apparent in the work of Leibniz and Thomasius's pietist contemporary Gottfried Arnold, who carried on the spiritualist view of doctrinal history taken by Lutherans of all colors – not only the moderate Melanchthon but also the ultra Flacius; *Catalogue of the Witnesses of Truth* represented an honor roll, a doctrinal hagiography, a 'Whiggish' history of proto-Lutherans (*Vorläufer*) throughout history. Gottfried Arnold featured these same 'witnesses of the truth' (*Zeugen der Wahrheit*) in his controversial *Nonpartisan History of Heretics and the Church* (1698–1700), and he celebrated the same 'rebirth' of doctrine (*Wiedergeburt*; *conversio*) as did historians of philosophy such as Georg Horn, Thomas Stanley, and Abraham Grau.[99] Like these scholars, Arnold wanted to separate truth from error in the doctrinal past – including the so-called 'heresies' so often misconstrued by Catholic authorities – and to represent the history of religion, at least in human terms, as a process of enlightenment. What further reinforced this tradition was the comparisons made between Protestant and philosophical 'martyrs' – who both (as the Greek word indicated) were 'witnesses' to a transcendent truth.

Out of Lutheran theology, too, especially in the work of Flacius Illyricus, came a theory of interpretation – *ars hermeneutica*, Leibniz called it – which

---

[98] See especially Peter Fraenkel, *Testimonia Patrum: The Function of the Patristic Argument in the Theology of Philip Melanchthon* (Geneva, 1961).

[99] *Unpartheyische Kirchen- und Ketzer-Historien* (Schaffhausen, 1740), and see Peter C. Erb, *Pietists, Protestants, and Mystics: The Use of Late Medieval Texts in the Work of Gottfried Arnold (1666–1714)* (Metuchen, 1989).

reinforced this spiritualist notion of intellectual progress through reform and purification.[100] This theory of how to read biblical texts, standing at the beginning of a tradition leading from Flacius through Chladenius and Schleiermacher to Gadamer and Jauss, formed the basis of modern philosophical hermeneutics, which also tries to join history with more transcendent goals.

In early modern Germany the study of philosophy was carried on in a continuing context of religious controversy, especially through the conflicts between hard-line Lutheran orthodoxy, in which a new brand of Aristotelian doctrine became established in the universities reformed by Melanchthon, and a new spiritualism which inspired the pietist movement of the seventeenth century.[101] Pietism emphasized individual belief and action over formal theology and ritual and envisaged a spiritual community on the basis of such ideals. In this sense pietism was quite in keeping with an eclectic approach to philosophy, which likewise sought a higher truth above the formal doctrines, sects, and systems of philosophy; and it strongly informed many early efforts to write broad, ecumenical, and non-partisan histories of philosophy.

What the Aristotelianism of the Protestant (no less than the 'second Scholasticism' of the Catholic) universities favored was a revival of metaphysics as 'first philosophy', which humanists had so eloquently deplored. Metaphysics represented the 'triumph of philosophy' – the title of a book by one of its enthusiasts – and with this triumph came the tendency to identify logic with psychology, to identify reality with the ideas inferred from that reality, and so to separate reason from the contingent and expressive medium of language.[102] With metaphysics, too, came an impetus toward system and prideful individual constructions – 'my book', 'my system', 'my doctrine', and so on – that also undermined the notion of wisdom as a collective inheritance and, indirectly, the value of history as a partner in the philosophical quest.[103] Philosophers,

---

100 'Anweisung, wie man die Heilige Schrift lesen soll ... ', in *Seminar: Philosophische Hermeneutik*, ed. Hans-Georg Gadamer and Gottfried Boehm (Frankfurt, 1976), 43–52.

101 See Klaus Deppermann, *Der hallesche Pietismus und der preussische Staat unter Friedrich III* (Göttingen, 1961).

102 N. Taurellus, *Philosophiae Triumphus* (Arnheim, 1617).

103 Argonne, *Mélanges d'histoire*, 215, citing Pascal ('toujours un *chez moi* à la bouche'). And see Max Wundt, *Die deutsche Schulmetaphysik des 17. Jahrhunderts* (Tübingen, 1939), 56; *Die deutsche Schulphilosophie im Zeitalter der Aufklärung* (Tübingen, 1945); Siegfried Wollgast, *Philosophie in Deutschland zwischen Reformation und Aufklärung* (Berlin, 1988); Leinsle, *Das Ding und die Methode*; and Hans M. Wolff, *Die Weltschauung der deutschen Aufklärung in geschichtlicher Entwicklung* (Bern, 1949).

no less than humanists, were entangled in the web of language, and drew, consciously or not, on the intellectual heritage of their culture; and it was one of the main purposes of historians of philosophy to throw light on this process.

7.   Philosophical History

Like philosophy, history was regarded as a form of wisdom – 'philosophy teaching by example', according to the ancient topos. 'History describes what science is, and philosophy for what purpose it exists,' declared Jonsius.[104] Then he added a distinction which later became a commonplace in nineteenth- and twentieth-century historicism: 'History considers singulars, and philosophy considers universals.' It was partly to resolve this modern version of the old problem of universals that scholars turned to the history of philosophy as a record or legacy of opinions aimed at the discovering and formulating of truth. The history of philosophy treated not the universals of speculative wisdom but the singulars of the search, therefore – the post-Laertian study of the 'lives and opinions' of philosophers.

In the sixteenth century the history of philosophy, *ante litteram*, was carried on – if often implicitly or inadvertently – in a variety of conflicting modes. Though difficult to define clearly and to separate cleanly, there are at least four approaches that deserve mention. First was the old tradition of Laertian doxography reinforced by the rival genres *de viris illustribus* and *vitae sanctorum*; second, the 'succession' of Christian doctrine, constituting a prototype of the history of secular ideas and disciplines; third, the ('dogmatic') effort to find in one of the ancient systems a basis for modern scientific 'method'; and fourth, the historical and skeptical critique of these systems which might clear the way for a 'new philosophy'. This crucial question, arising from the philosophical aspect of the larger Quarrel between the Ancients and Moderns, was fought by philosophers as different as Zabarella, Campanella, Bacon, and Descartes, and defined the fundamental terms for interpreting the modern history of philosophy: 'Whether it is useful for Christian philosophy to construct a new philosophy after that of the pagans', as Campanella put it, 'and if so, on what grounds.'[105]

---

[104] Jonsius, *De Scriptoribus*, 1.

[105] M.-P. Lerner, 'Campanella, juge d'Aristote', *Platon et Aristote à la Renaissance* (Paris, 1976), 335–58; and see John M. Headley, *Campanella and the Transformation of the World* (Princeton, 1997), 147.

A 'new philosophy': from the sixteenth century 'novelty' was in the air, whether as a goal or as a threat.[106] Yet despite the invasion of curious and occult ideas and the pursuit of strange gods, the history of philosophy proceeded for the most part in familiar channels. Under the intimidating tutelage of theology, the story of philosophy commonly began not with the evidence of secular history but with the final stages of *Genesis*. This was the perspective of the two seventeenth-century founders of the history of philosophy – who at the same time were culminating figures in the earlier doxographical tradition. Both Thomas Stanley and Georg Horn, whose books both appeared in 1655, began their surveys not *ab urbe* but *ab orbe condita*, and from this standpoint the first philosopher – as well as the first speaker – was Adam.[107] Before the Fall humanity had possessed 'perfect wisdom' (*vera sapientia*), created as it was in the image of God's own Creation. True, this *prisca philosophia* had been lost; but it remained an epistemological ideal for modern philosophers, especially those who retained a proper sense of sacred history and 'barbarian philosophy' beyond the narrow confines of Laertian doxography. Such a perspective was vital for the new 'reformed philosophy' which many Protestant scholars sought.

Georg Horn's *Historia philosophica* offered a summary of the Lutheran view of 'the origin, succession, sects, and lives of the philosophers from the beginning of the world down to our own time'. Arising from naturalistic wonder (*admiratio*), philosophy culminated in Christian truth. Making an inviolate distinction between 'ancient' and 'modern' philosophy – though separated by a 'middle' period – Horn surveyed the divine, barbaric, and poetic origins of philosophy expressed in the 'wisdom of the ancients' (*sapientia veterum*) and traced the genealogy of proto-philosophy from Adam to its first and second restorers (*instauratores*), Noah and Christ, through proliferating sects, ancient and modern, and the 'nine centuries of barbarism' which Horn lamented, before the third restoration, beginning with the revival of ancient letters and the liberation theology of Luther.

After the work of Stanley, who followed Diogenes Laertius closely, English historians of philosophy, especially in association with the Cambridge

---

[106] Lynn Thorndike, 'Newness and Craving for Novelty in 17th-Century Science and Medicine', *Journal of the History of Ideas*, 12 (1951), 584–98.

[107] Georg Horn, *Historia philosophica libri septem* (Leiden, 1655), and Thomas Stanley, *The History of Philosophy* (London, 1655), 60; also Theophilus Gale, *Philosophia generalis* (London, 1676), 8; Thomas Burnet, *Archeologia Philosophiae seu doctrina antiqua de rerum originibus* (London, 1692); Christian Dreier, *Sapientia seu philosophia prima* (Regiomon., 1644), 'Disputationes in Primam Philosophiam, Prima de origine et progressu philosophiae' (Königsberg, 1643), and Nicolaus Gundling, *Historiae Philosophiae moralis* (Halle, 1706), which begins 'ab ovo'.

Platonists, continued his efforts in a more interpretative way, following what Thomas Burnet called the 'peregrinations of wisdom' and attempting to trace what Theophilus Gale called the 'sacred pedigree' of this wisdom back to Moses.[108] Gale tried pagan philosophy in his Protestant 'court' and condemned its practitioners as not philosophers (*philosophoi*) but only 'philodoxers' (*philodoxoi*).[109] The 'reformed philosophy' which he sought rejected both the 'ipse dixit' and the errors of Greek tradition, including Aristotle and his scholastic followers. The sources of such errors, according to Gale, were ignorance, curiosity, pride, 'carnal confidence', 'litigation about words', 'opiniatrie and dogmatizing', idolatry, mythology, and other deplorable intellectual faults.[110]

Gale was followed in this criticism by Ralph Cudworth, who attacked all forms of 'fatalism', especially that associated with 'Atomical-Atheism', which he traced back to the Presocratics and indeed to a time before the Trojan War. The human root of this deterministic error was 'a Dull and Earthy Disbelief of the Existence of Things beyond the Reach of Sense'.[111] What Cudworth wanted above all was to vindicate the world of the spirit, which meant human free will, reason, and the Christian God, whose existence was, he repeated, demonstrable from the 'Idea' of God which ancient pagans as well as modern 'atheists' possessed. 'Cudworth ... ', John Passmore remarked, 'looked upon philosophy as an arena of conflict';[112] and the history of philosophy involved the critical review of doctrines judged according to standards of theology and a Christian 'reason' appropriate to this theology.

Defenders of empirical philosophy and sensationalism, beginning with Bacon, seemed to be a world away from Cudworth and other Cambridge Platonists philosophically; but they, too, sought the sources of error and ways to avoid it. Bacon had identified three idols which corrupted understanding; and similarly Joseph Glanvill attacked dogmatizing, opinions divorced from experience, and 'the prejudice of custom and education'.[113] He singled out in particular 'the Schoolmen and Peripatetick Dogmatists' for their neglect of

---

[108] Burnet, *Archeologia Philosophiae*, 89, and Gale, *Court of the Gentiles*, 8; and see Ernst Cassirer, *The Platonic Renaissance in England*, trans. J. P. Pettegrove (Edinburgh, 1953), and Gerald R. Cragg, *The Cambridge Platonists* (New York, 1968).

[109] *Court of the Gentiles*, 89.

[110] *Court of the Gentiles*, 25.

[111] *The True Intellectual System of the Universe* (London, 1678), 176.

[112] *Ralph Cudworth: An Interpretation* (Bristol, 1990), 13.

[113] *Scepsis scientifica*, ed. John Owen (London, 1885), 106; 2nd edn of *The Vanity of Dogmatizing* (London, 1661).

sense-experience and their 'Pedantick Adoration' and 'Reverence to Antiquity and Authority', making their doctrines 'inept for New discoveries; and therefore of no accommodation to the *use* of *life*'.[114]

More radical yet was Anthony Collins, who defended 'Free-Thinking' in a sense that went far beyond the 'liberty of philosophizing' called for by Lutheran historians of philosophy. According to Collins, the freedom to judge arguments according to evidence and testimony was both a right and a duty; and moreover it constituted an honorable tradition going back to Socrates, 'the divinest Man that ever appear'd in the Heathen World', who had actually (according to the judgment of the Fathers) become a 'true Christian'.[115] Collins went on to propose a canon of such free-thinkers, including Plato, Aristotle, Epicurus, Varro, Cicero, Seneca, Solomon, Josephus, Origen, and in modern times Bacon, Hobbes, and Tillotson.[116] Only the fear of boring his readers, Collins added, prevented him from discussing other participants in this honored tradition, such as Erasmus, Sarpi, Scaliger, Descartes, Gassendi, Locke, and others, who were also part of the hunt for wisdom and the long search for 'true meaning'.

Aristotle himself had not hesitated to break with authority, fleeing from Athens (Collins quoting Origen here) so that the Athenians 'might not be guilty of a Double crime against Philosophy' – referring to 'the Wickedness they committed against Socrates'.[117] Yet Aristotle had spawned the most slavish followers and a different sort of tradition, including those who, as Johann Hermann von Elswich put it, 'would rather err with Aristotle than be right with another author'.[118] Against such were ranged the enemies of scholastic 'barbarism', beginning with humanists like Petrarch, Valla, Erasmus, and Vives, and including skeptics like Glanvill and historians of philosophy like Adam Tribbechow, who identified scholasticism with popish heresy.[119] Between these extremes were scholars like Adrian Heereboord, Jean-Baptiste Du Hamel, and even Leibniz, who thought that the 'old' Aristotelian philosophy could accommodate the 'new' ideas of Descartes and other Moderns

---

114 *The Vanity of Dogmatizing* (London, 1661), 136.

115 *A Discourse of Free-Thinking, Occasion'd by The Rise and Growth of a Sect Called Free-Thinkers* (London, 1713), 123.

116 Collins's brief survey of the history of philosophy as free thought was rejected by Richard Bentley, *Remarks upon a late discourse* ... (London, 1737).

117 Ibid., 129; cf. Origen, *Contra Celsum*, trans. Henry Chadwick (Cambridge, 1953), 60.

118 *De varia Aristotelis in scholis protestantium fortuna schediasma* (Wittenberg, 1720).

119 *De Doctoribus scholasticis* (Jena, 1719).

– thus preserving the continuity of philosophical tradition.[120] A less partisan position was taken by François de Launoy, who told the story of Aristotle in the University of Paris as a 'historian' not a 'disputant', including attacks on Aristotle from the thirteenth century and defenses, not only by Catholics, but also by Protestants like Melanchthon.[121]

But doctrinal enthusiasm or anxiety was what fueled most essays in the history of philosophy, and subjects of most concern were particular ideas, schools, or '-isms' which threatened the doctrinal *status quo* defined by religious authority. 'Atheism', 'naturalism', and 'Spinozism' were among the targets of orthodox criticism that gave impetus to historical research as well as theological polemic. Preserving scholastic habits, the history of philosophy was adversarial to an extreme. For every doctrine, moreover, there was an equal and opposite anti-doctrine, even if it had to be invented – as in the case of 'atheism'.[122] So there were factors of intellectual as well as doxographical continuity in the history of philosophy, although philosophy 'itself' was by consensus above these human conditions of philosophizing.

What was the relationship between philosophy and its history? The first differed from the latter in the same way that memory differed from reason, and the consequence was that a very different sort of ordering was required. This was the point made by J. S. Bailly in his history of one central branch of natural philosophy. 'A science is a sum of truths', he wrote about modern astronomy. 'To link [*enchaîner*] them, to present them in their order from the simplest to the most complex is the object of elementary exposition; but the chain of these truths is not the order of their discovery'.[123] This insight was also present in the great enterprise of the French *Encyclopédie*, which likewise added a historical dimension to the 'chain' of sciences envisioned by D'Alembert in his 'preliminary discourse'; and it received definitive expression in Comte's distinction between a 'historical' and a 'dogmatic' or systematic approach.[124]

On the threshold of the Enlightenment the history of philosophy emerged between two poles, one being the attitude of Galileo and Descartes, relegating it to the history of error and untrustworthy 'opinion'. Descartes was disillusioned with philosophy because 'it has been cultivated for many centuries

[120] Heereboord, *Meletemata philosophica*, 378; and see Santinello, *Storia*, I, 216, and so on.
[121] *De varia Aristotelis in Academia Parisiensi fortuna* (Paris, 1653).
[122] Kors, *Atheism in France, 1650–1729*, I.
[123] *Histoire de l'astronomie ancienne*, in *Sur l'Histoire des sciences*, ed. M. Fichaut and M. Péchaux (Paris, 1969), 143.
[124] *Cours de philosophie positive*, ed. Ch. Le Verrier (Paris, n.d.), I, 145.

by the best minds ... and that nevertheless no single thing is to be found in it which is not the subject of dispute'; and so it was with the other human sciences.[125] His solution was in effect to separate reason from memory. His first 'rule for the direction of the mind' warned against 'certain special investigations' and the distractions they offered to the advance of 'universal wisdom'. The third rule was to attend 'not to what others have thought, nor to what we ourselves conjecture, but to what we can clearly and perspicuously behold and with certainty deduce'.[126] The model of Cartesian wisdom, at least in its vulgar form, is the solitary mathematician working with the simplest analytical concepts, unencumbered by past learning, and enchanted by the vision of an enlightened future purged of prejudice and error.

Contrast this with the view of Descartes's nemesis, Pierre-Daniel Huet, who (like Descartes) prefixed an autobiographical declaration (1692) to his profession of philosophical faith:

> From my school reading so ardent a love and esteem of ancient philosophy had pervaded my inmost, that from that period classical literature seemed to me the handmaid of this science. By this passion I was led to obtain a knowledge of the sects of those ancient high-priests of philosophy which are treated of in Diogenes Laertius ... , [which], compared with the observations of others gave me an intimate acquaintance with the history of philosophy.[127]

For Huet philosophical understanding was inseparable from this 'boundless' science founded by Diogenes Laertius, whose work (he confessed) he took as his 'companion' in all his travels.

Here indeed is an opposition that suggests a meeting of 'two cultures', one devoted to ideals of certainty and logical closure, the other to accommodation and encyclopedic coverage. The new science, especially in its Cartesian and Newtonian forms, seemed to fulfill the agenda of the first; but the more conventional view of philosophy seemed to many critics little more than an accumulation of doctrine and what was scorned as 'pedantry'. As Pope lamented,

> Philosophy, that lean'd on Heav'n before,
> Shrinks to her Second cause and is no more.[128]

---

[125] Discourse on Method, part I.

[126] Règles utiles et claires pour la direction de l'esprit en la recherche de la verité (The Hague, 1977).

[127] Huet, Memoirs of the Life of Pierre Daniel Huet, trans. John Aikin (London, 1810), II, 203.

[128] Dunciad, I, 643–4, the 'second cause' being, presumably, the material cause, or simple substance of philosophical literature.

In the eighteenth century the history of philosophy was pursued along many doctrinal and confessional lines. Accounts ranged from minor orations, such as those of Christian Dreier (1643) and Ephraim Gerhard (1711), to major textbooks, such as those of Friederich Gentzken (1724), J. B. Capasso (1728), A. F. Boureau-Deslandes (1737), and Samuel Formey (1760), and one history of women philosophers, that of Gilles Menage (1690). Syncretism and credulous inquiries into the occult traditions of pre-Hellenic philosophy continued, too, though critical learning had cast doubt on such metahistorical speculation. On such grounds the history of philosophy claimed status as a legitimate science. History offered a perspective from which philosophy itself seemed less than divine, for as one of the champions of the Ancients, René Rapin, remarked, 'We have seen these philosophies being born, and we shall see them die.'[129] This, too, was one of the premises accepted, lessons taught, or prejudices acquired, by modern eclecticism.

The conceptual role of history in philosophy came under fire in the late eighteenth century, especially as a result of the debate over what was called the 'philosophy of the history of philosophy' (*Philosophie der Philosophiege-schichte*). In this *Methodenstreit* several questions were posed.[130] Was the history of philosophy actually a part of philosophy, Kant himself asked? Were philosophy and its history separate disciplines, Christian Weiss asked in 1799? – or identical sciences, as C. Hippeau proposed in 1837? These problems have never been resolved, and indeed they are still being debated in much the same terms today.

For many philosophers in the age of the Kantian 'revolution', history seemed increasingly futile. In an early Latin essay on the history of philosophy Kant's friend Christian Garve described his early enthusiasm for the subject and then its sad aftermath. 'But how can I describe how much my hope was disappointed?' he asked. 'Out of that great and splendid apparatus nothing has issued except the lives of philosophers and the listing of dry opinions.'[131] There were also religious overtones to the suspicion of *Philosophiegeschichte*, which to many Lutheran thinkers recalled old prejudices against 'human

---

[129] *La Comparaison de Platon et d'Aristote*, 242.

[130] Lutz Geldsetzer, *Die Philosophie der Philosophiegeschichte im 19. Jahrhundert* (Meisenheim, 1968), 22, 'Ob die Geschichte der Philosophie selbst ein Teil der Philosophie sein könne'; 43, 'Geschichte darf nicht Philosophie und Philosophie darf nicht Geschichte werden'; and 122, 'Nous sommes de ceux qui regardent la philosophie et l'histoire de la philosophie comme deux sciences identiques.'

[131] *De Ratione scribendi historiam philosophiae* (Leipzig, 1768); cf. G. G. Fülleborn (ed.), *Beiträge zur Geschichte der Philosophie* (Züllichau, 1791), XI, 88; and see below, Chapter 9.

traditions'. As Hamann put it, 'There is an idol in the temple of learning which bears the inscription, "The History of Philosophy".'[132]

In this controversy, then, the ideals of pure reason (as well as unfettered piety) and philosophy as a purely rational 'science' were set in opposition to the history of philosophy represented as a creation of 'pedantry' that never rose above the level of doxography. As the Kantian J. C. A. Grohmann believed – a prediction that has been heard more than once over the next two centuries – 'The history of philosophy is the end of all philosophizing.'[133] ('The history of philosophy', remarked Michelet more radically, 'kills philosophy.'[134]) Barren as it may have been, however, it was present at the birth – and seminal for the cultivation – of the modern study of intellectual history, as post-Enlightenment scholarship would demonstrate.

---

[132] *Socratic Memorabilia*, trans. James O'Flaherty (Baltimore, 1967), 145.
[133] Geldsetzer, *Philosophiegeschichte*, 30.
[134] *Cours au Collège de France*, ed. Paul Viallaneix (Paris, 1995), II, 205.

Chapter 4

The Way of Ideas
and the Ways of Words

> In one of its principal aspects the
> New Science is a history of ideas.
> Giambattista Vico

By the eighteenth century the history of ideas had taken both its shape and its name, at least within philosophical tradition, but from this time on the practice of intellectual and cultural history diverges from the old philosophical canon into other disciplinary paths, and chronology does not suffice to pursue the subject. Intellectual and cultural history has been tied to philosophy, and so, at least indirectly, to religion; and the later (Christian) Neoplatonic and Neo-Aristotelian canons have tended to preserve this spiritualist orientation. But from the beginning – from the time of the sophists and the Alexandrine philologists – alternative traditions appeared that shifted attention from thought to culture, from philosophy and religion to their human conditions, texts, and contexts – marking what I have called the 'descent of ideas'.[1] These linguistic and cultural turns and returns have given substance and direction to the practices and theories of intellectual history from the late middle ages to the present. At the center of these rivalries has been the age-old dispute about the relationship between ideas and language – and by implication their history.

1. The Old Way

Both philosophers and intellectual historians take 'ideas' as their common currency, but they look at the question in wholly different ways. For philosophers, whatever their choice of definitions, ideas are in some sense

---

[1] See D. R. Kelley, 'The Old Cultural History', *History and the Human Sciences*, 9 (1996), 101–26; also *Faces of History: Historical Inquiry from Herodotus to Herder* (New Haven, 1999) and *Ventures in History: Historical Inquiry from Herder to Huizinga* (New Haven, forthcoming).

mental phenomena that are adequately represented and communicated in the philosopher's oral or written discourse and argument. For historians, however, ideas are in the first place social and cultural constructions, and the product of a complex process of inference, judgment, and criticism on the part of the scholar. The history of ideas has long been situated in the midst of this semantic confusion, and it is important to move carefully between the conflicting demands of historical accuracy and philosophical clarity.

How did the pioneering historians of philosophy, especially after the summary and foundational work of Brucker on the *History of the Philosophical Doctrine of Ideas* (1723), conceive of their enterprise? What was the subject of their investigations and representations? On the most elementary level – the Laertian level – it was the 'lives and opinions of the great philosophers', if not an even more unreflective survey of the pertinent 'literature'; but from the seventeenth century, as Leibniz suggested in the famous letter to his mentor Jakob Thomasius, a larger goal was emerging, which was the career of a newly hypostatized – or idealized – 'philosophy'.[2] This quest presumed more continuous and enduring vehicles than individual participants in the projects of philosophical inquiry or even than particular schools of thought; and these more permanent protagonists were found above all in the 'ideas' to which philosophers were committed, out of which certain systems were constructed, and in terms of which at least approximations to truth were vouchsafed to a fallen humanity.

The evolution of the concept of *idea* from its Platonic source to its Cousinian employment as a vehicle for the history of philosophy is complex and even conjectural, but it is an essential part of the story of intellectual history. Its first appearance, so cryptic as to be almost mythical, has been assigned to Parmenides, to the extent that he distinguished between the way of truth and the way of opinion, associating the former with unchanging Being and the latter with fluctuating illusion. The vision of a perennial truth has haunted philosophy and its historiography of philosophy ever since Plato's formulation.

Early in his life, according to Plato, Socrates was enlightened by Parmenides and Zeno about the nature of ideas. Plato was certain that there were ideas of ideals such as the just, the beautiful, and the good; but about the elements, or human beings, he was doubtful. To this question Socrates responded, 'I have often been very much troubled, Parmenides, to decide whether there are ideas

2 *Philosophical Papers and Letters*, trans. Leroy E. Loemker (Dordrecht, 1969), 93 (20/30 April 1669): 'You will give us the history of philosophy, not of philosophers.' This letter was published as the preface to Leibniz's edition of Nizolio's *De Veris principis et vera ratione philosophandi* (Frankfurt, 1680).

of such things or not.'[3] The reason for this, Parmenides remarked in a dramatic prophecy, was that Socrates was still young; 'Philosophy has not yet taken hold upon you', he added, so that 'you still consider other people's opinions, on account of your youth'. With age and mastery Socrates would come to reject such popular 'opinions'. In later dialogues the Platonic theory of ideas is worked out more fully and became, Werner Jaeger wrote, '*the problem of philosophy*' in Plato's Academy.[4] As Plato put it in *The Republic*, 'We suppose an idea to exist when we give a name to many separate things'; but this did not imply that ideas were mere onomastic inventions. On the contrary, ideas formed an eternal and unchanging world of higher, paradigmatic reality, governed by the idea of the good, populated by other generalized ideals, and accessible only by means of thought, that is, Socratic *diaeresis* and recollection. According to Rudolf Eucken, the doctrine of ideas 'is a revolution and a revaluation of the most radical description; the intellectual history of man knows none greater'.[5]

The theory of ideas marked the first point of divergence between Plato and his greatest disciple, Aristotle, as well as a central theme in the history of philosophy over the centuries.[6] The basic issue between Platonists and Aristotelians was whether ideas required a material, or natural, base and whether, consequently, they were independent of language. In the first book of his *Metaphysics* Aristotle described the history of Greek philosophy as a search for first principles in which, with Plato, the focus shifted from the nature of things to their universal forms, or Ideas, which were the cause of all things and a higher sort of reality. But Aristotle had a different notion of cause and of reality. He was not persuaded by Plato's idealist arguments, since for him ideas contribute nothing either to sensible things or to the understanding of them; and he replaced Plato's theory with his own system of fourfold causality, representing natural reality as a process of generation and corruption, lowering Platonic ideas to the level of mere opinion (*doxa*) and sending the philosopher back into the Platonic cave. It was an Aristotelian

---

[3] *Parmenides*, 130b. See Henri-Dominique Saffrey, 'Origine, usage et signification du mot "IDEA" jusqu'à Platon', in M. Fattori and M. L. Bianchi (eds), *Idea*, VI Colloquio internazionale (Rome, 1990), and Peter Brommer, *EIDOS et IDEA: Etude sémantique et chronologique des oeuvres de Platon* (Assen, 1940), 1–11.

[4] Jaeger, *Aristotle: Fundamentals of the History of his Development*, trans. Richard Robinson (Oxford, 1934), 195; cf. John M. Rist, *The Method of Aristotle* (Toronto, 1989), 38.

[5] *The Problem of Human Life*, trans. Williston S. Hough (New York, 1912), 19–20.

[6] Gail Fine, *On Ideas: Aristotle's Criticism of Plato's Theory of Forms* (Oxford, 1993).

principle, though not found in Aristotle, that 'there was nothing in the intellect that had not been previously in the senses' – *nihil in intellectu quod non fuerit prius in sensu* was the scholastic formula, Aristotelian in spirit if not in letter – and it had an extraordinary fortune in modern philosophy down to the time of Leibniz, Brucker, and Cousin.[7]

Other students of Plato continued to teach his theory of ideas. Attempts were made by eclectic-minded philosophers like Antiochus to rescue Platonic ideas by joining them to Stoic principles, especially 'seminal reason', according to which ideas emerged from the 'seeds' of knowledge.[8] Cicero, in his rhetorical fashion, also seemed to accept the theory, while noting Aristotle's criticism, and he rendered the Greek term *idea* coined by Plato into Latin as 'species' or 'form'.[9] Seneca regarded Plato's 'ideas' a fifth cause to append to the Aristotelian set of four causes.[10] Some Christian authors, such as Tertullian, rejected 'ideas' as 'imaginary forms' invented by unenlightened pagans; but others, including Philo, Augustine, and Boethius, welcomed them into theology by regarding them as attributes of God in his role as the creating Word.[11] For Clement of Alexandria an idea is a 'thought of God'.[12] According to Philo, the Logos was the idea of ideas, the very center of the world of ideas (*ho ek ton ideon kosmos*) and basis of its unity. Dionysius the Areopagite spoke of 'principles, which the Greeks call "ideas", that is, species, eternal forms, and unchangeable reasons of things, through and in which the visible world is formed and ruled'.[13] Ideas, declared Augustine, are 'the fixed and unchanging reason of things which are themselves not formed and persist therefore eternally and always in the same way, being contained in the divine intellect'.[14]

In the flurry of opinions stirred up by the cross-winds of Hellenistic and early Christian doctrines, the poles of the debate continued to be the Aristotelian rejection of ideas as imaginary and the theological defense of

---

[7] P. Cranefield, 'On the Origin of the Phrase *Nihil est in intellectu quod non prius fuerit in sensu*', *Journal of the History of Medicine*, 25 (1970), 77–80; and see Thomas M. Lennon, *The Battle of the Gods and the Giants: The Legacies of Descartes and Gassendi 1655–1715* (Princeton, 1993), 334ff.

[8] See Maryanne Horowitz, *Seeds of Virtue and Knowledge* (Princeton, 1997).

[9] *Academica*, 1.8; *De Natura deorum*, 1.12.

[10] Norma E. Emerton, *The Scientific Reinterpretation of Form* (Ithaca, 1984).

[11] See the references in *Historisches Wörterbuch der Philosophie*, ed. J. Ritter et al. (Basel, 1976), and *Wörterbuch der philosophischen Begriffe*, ed. Rudolf Eisler (Berlin, 1927), IV, 682–99; and the articles on patristic and medieval usage in Fattori and Bianchi, *Idea*, 13–87.

[12] *Stromateis*, 5.3.16.

[13] *De Divisione naturae*, 2.2.

[14] *De vera religione*, cited by M. C. D'Arcy, in *A Monument to Saint Augustine*, ed. D'Arcy et al. (New York, 1930), 167–8.

ideas as divine creations – as figments of human imagination or thoughts in the mind of God.[15] In medieval philosophy the problem turned on the reality of universals. Many authors invoked the Platonic ideas with approval and even mystical enthusiasm – Bernard of Chartres, for instance, made them 'coeternal' with God and the primary vehicles of Creation. On this interpretation Aristotle was wrong: ideas existed but only in the mind of God, and only through these 'divine essences' could humanity attain, however imperfectly, a vision of philosophy. There was then such a thing as purely intellectual reality. 'Indeed', Duns Scotus wrote,

> this is demonstrated by Plato, who first introduced the term 'idea'; for he asserted that beyond the sensible world there is an intelligible world in the divine mind; and he called this ... the idea of the sensible world ... [which however] is nothing but the external world as it exists objectively in being known in the divine mind.[16]

Scholastic philosophers found a homology, if not an identity, between these divine creations and those produced by human effort; and in this way they invested man with powers of creation similar to those of God himself, thus introducing an epistemology later defined as the 'maker's knowledge', according to which one could know only what one had created.[17] For Thomas Aquinas, 'The word "idea" signifies a certain form thought of by an agent in the likeness of which he intends to produce an external work.'

In their own way critics who followed the 'modern way', such as William of Ockham, while rejecting the reality of universals as defended by the 'ancient way' of scholastics such as Duns Scotus, seemed to accept at least a theological sort of realism. 'Ideas are intellectually and objectively in God', Ockham wrote; 'indeed they are the creatures themselves'.[18] But on the level of human psychology Ockham took what was in effect an internalized view of ideas, that is, of their natural 'reality' as signs, as creations of the human mind (*termini concepti*) and accommodated to its greatest intellectual creation, the science of logic – which was represented by Leibniz as well as by scholastic tradition as a sort of 'divine psychology'.

---

[15] *Cambridge History of Later Greek and Early Medieval Philosophy*, ed. A. H. Armstrong (Cambridge, 1967), 55, suggesting Seneca as the first to express this view.

[16] Cited by Stephen Nadler, *Arnauld and the Cartesian Philosophy of Ideas* (Princeton, 1989), 149.

[17] Antonio Perez-Ramos, *Francis Bacon's Idea of Science and the Maker's Knowledge Tradition* (Oxford, 1988).

[18] Cited by Frederick Copleston, *A History of Philosophy*, III (1) (Westminster, MD, 1953), 67; and see Marilyn McCord Adams, *William Ockham* (New York, 1987), I, 1054.

According to the medieval consensus in general, ideas were both products of the human mind and preexisting realities in the mind of God – primary, principle, or intelligible species, exemplars, or archetypes, as they were variously called. According to Etienne Gilson, 'After Augustine this notion of the divine Word, conceived as full of the Ideas after whose pattern God has created the world, will become the common property of practically all the Christian theologians'[19] – and, we might add, of philosophers and historians of ideas.

2. The Doctrine of Ideas

The question of ideas became central to Renaissance philosophy and its history, especially in connection with the many comparisons and contrasts between Plato and Aristotle which were begun in antiquity (for example, by Plutarch), revived in the Byzantine East, and imported into the West in the fifteenth century. In his famous assault on Aristotle, Pletho rejected the thesis of a sensuous origin of ideas, and he gave them their usual Neoplatonic place of honor in the mind of God. Aristotle was wrong too, he thought, in assigning the doctrine of ideas to Plato, since Pythagoras had held similar views long before.[20] Ideas were part of the 'perennial philosophy'. Discussions of the doctrine of ideas were continued by Platonizing humanists like Ficino and Pico.[21] They were followed by other scholars, such as Bernardino Donato and Jean Riolan, who began placing the issue in a wider and more eclectic intellectual context. 'What is an idea?', asked Donato. 'Nothing else than the eternal and perfect understanding of God.'[22] Riolan was concerned above all to reconcile Platonic exemplars with Aristotelian forms. Following Ficino and others into what he called the 'labyrinth of philosophy', Riolan – inspired more by curiosity and scholarly appetite, perhaps, than by logical clarity – ventured from the exposition of philosophy and celebration of its dignity into questions of its origins and historical dimensions.[23]

---

[19] Etienne Gilson, *History of Christian Philosophy in the Middle Ages* (New York, 1955), 71–2.

[20] C. M. Woodhouse, *Gemistos Plethon, The Last of the Hellenes* (Oxford, 1986), 205.

[21] See Michael J. B. Allen, *The Platonism of Marsilio Ficino* (Berkeley, 1984).

[22] Donato, *De Platonicae atque Aristotelicae Philosophiae differentia* (Paris, 1541), fol. 10ᵛ, 'ipsius Dei intelligentia aeterna atque perfecta'.

[23] *Disputatio de origine Philosophiae* (Paris, 1565), 3; and *Exertatio ad Ideas Platonici* (Paris, 1568).

With many Renaissance philosophers, as Ernst Cassirer and Paul O. Kristeller have shown, the problem of knowledge becomes the principal context for the debate over ideas. Platonists took the view that human understanding was essentially not discourse but reason – not *oratio* but *ratio*. This was challenged by philologists like Valla and Nizolio, who insisted on the primacy of literal over spiritual meaning; but such literary critique of philosophy was not fully appreciated in, or fully received into, mainstream philosophy. Neo-Aristotelians, too, contributed to the discussion of ideas. The old question of the 'immortality of the soul', the cause of so much anxiety among commentators on Aristotle's *De Anima*, turned in part on the mechanical problem of how ideas arose from mere sense-impressions – how, in other words, universals were derived from particulars in a psychological and epistemological sense. On this subject there was an unending flood of opinions, but the terms for the debate were set by the Latin versions of Aristotle, beginning with the thirteenth-century rendering by William of Moerbeke, which provided the basic vocabulary of philosophical psychology, including *anima, intellectus, sensitivum, sensibile, intellectivum, phantasia, phantasma,* and *species*. In the sixteenth century Pietro Pomponazzi defended a naturalistic approach to ideas. In his treatise *On the Immortality of the Soul* he reviewed the opinions held by 'judicious men', including not only Plato and Aristotle but also Alexander of Aphrodisias, Averroes, and Thomas Aquinas, and then reasoned his way in scholastic fashion to his own solution, that, philosophically if not theologically, the soul was dependent on the body and material images for purposes of forming ideas. For his pains Pomponazzi was often condemned by later critics and historians as one of those 'naturalists' or 'atheists' who operated outside the framework of orthodox theology. This itself became one of the themes, or myths, of intellectual history in its search for conceptual ancestors.

In the sixteenth century the term 'idea' designated a truly 'eclectic' notion in every sense of the word – a form or archetype, an ideal, a mental image, something conceived or imagined in the mind, an object of thought, and so on. Here is the definition of what Leibniz called this 'splendid honorific' given in Thomas Cooper's Latin dictionary of 1565:

> Idea: the figure conceived in Imagination, as it were, a substance perpetuall, being as paterne of all other sorte or kinds, as of one seale proceedeth many printes, so of one Idea of man proceede many thousands of men.

By the seventeenth century, then, the term and concept *idea* had an extraordinarily rich and contentious history, having been a staple of Christian theology, metaphysics, psychology, logic, and other branches of philosophy, and having entered and enhanced literary and common language, including the vernaculars. Even champions of the new science – though claiming to be of the 'party of nature' rather than of the spirit – paid homage to the doctrine of ideas.[24] As Bacon wrote, in a famous play on words,

> There is a great difference between the idols of the human mind and the ideas of the divine [*divinae mentis Ideae*]. That is to say, between certain empty dogmas, and the true signatures and marks set upon the works of creation as they are found in nature.[25]

In the mathematical philosophy of Galileo and Kepler, ancient ideas were assimilated to the natural laws of God's Creation and associated – as they had been in antiquity – with the rationality and regularity of geometry and mathematics. The Neoplatonic conviction was that God himself was a mathematician and that it might indeed be possible to read the divine mind, in which these mathematical ideas reposed, and so recapitulate Creation in a new science. But the problem still remained of how to join this transcendent view of ideas to the sensual foundations of ordinary human knowledge – of how to reconcile common-sense positivism with a higher mathematical, or lower empirical, realism.

3.   The New Way

The post-Renaissance obsession with 'method' (and, for some, the culmination of method in a 'system' of ideas) led to foundational questions concerning not only the 'nature of things' but also, and still more fundamentally, the knowledge of the nature of things. As Cassirer argued at the beginning of the last century, epistemology represented the central theme of modern philosophy – deriving not only from Descartes and his reformulation of Platonic 'ideas' as *cogitationes* but also from humanist views of human nature and those of Neoplatonists like Nicholas of Cusa – not to speak (as Cassirer in fact did not speak) of scholastic commentators on Aristotle's *De anima*. Underlying the Cartesian *Cogito*, in short, was a vast legacy of speculation about the human mind (*anima, mens, intellectus*, and so on) and its ideational creations. The 'quest for certainty' and the nature of ideas were inextricable from

---

[24] See Michael Albrecht, 'Thomasius – kein Eklektiker?', in Werner Schneiders (ed.), *Christian Thomasius 1655–1728* (Hamburg, 1989), 78.

[25] In *Valerius Terminus* as well as *Advancement of Learning* and *Novum Organum*; see Perez Zagorin, *Francis Bacon* (Princeton, 1998), 66.

questions of method; and when historical perspective, or a sense of tradition, was added to this project, one result was the formation of an eclectic view of philosophy, and one of the byproducts was the history of ideas.

This is some of the background to the endless debates among modern philosophers over what John Locke famously defined as 'the original, certainty, and extent of human knowledge'.[26] This intellectual heritage weighed heavily on the advocates of the new science even when, like Descartes, they affected to reject it. Descartes himself, notoriously, brought many of the premises of scholastic philosophy back into his structure of thought.[27] Locke remarked about his 'new way of ideas' that 'if it be new, is but a history of an old thing'.[28] If the language was new, the music was much the same; the substance of their arguments embodied the concerns of the new science, but the forms retained the premises of the old, especially in relation to theology.[29] Speculation was caught between the Scylla of spiritualism and the Charybdis of materialism,[30] and a consensus was never reached about the precise link between general ideas and particular sense-impressions. 'It's rather sad to have so many ideas', remarked Voltaire, 'and not to know the nature of ideas precisely.'[31]

---

[26] *Essay*, I, 1. See John Yolton, *John Locke and the Way of Ideas* (Oxford, 1956), and Michael Ayers, *Locke* (2 vols; London, 1991), I, *Epistemology*.

[27] Etienne Gilson, *Index Scholastico-cartésien* (Paris, 1913); and see Stephen Menn, *Descartes and Augustine* (Cambridge, 1998).

[28] See E. J. Ashworth, 'Do Words Signify Ideas or Things? The Scholastic Sources of Locke's Theory of Language', *Journal of the History of Philosophy*, 19 (1981), 299–326. In general see the articles in Fattori and Bianchi, *Idea*, on the use of the term in Descartes, Locke, Leibniz, Malebranche, Berkeley, Wolff, Kant, Schelling, Hegel, and others.

[29] According to Jean Nicot, *Trésor de la langue française tant ancienne que moderne* (Paris, 1606), '*Ideas* are imaginations that people construct in their thoughts: *Ideae, idearum*. These are also the images of things that are impressed on our soul. Platonists say that there are some eternal models and portraits of all things in God, which they call ideas.' Also Rudolph Goclenius, *Lexicon Philosophorum* (Frankfurt, 1613), 196. 'What idea is: 1. Idea is the architectural rationale [*ratio architectatrix*] in the mind of the maker, that is, the reason according to which the fabrication is carried out. It is therefore a relative Being, that is, the essence of the idea is said to consist in its relation to something else, or to be referred to something else, that is, to be the exemplar of something else or its archetype. Thus both the first idea and the first exemplar are called *archetypon* exemplar.' On this see Roger Ariew and Marjorie Grene, 'Ideas, in and before Descartes', *Journal of the History of Ideas*, 56 (1995), 87–106.

[30] So that the term might also be employed in a pejorative sense, as with Thomas Burnet, *The Sacred Theory of the Earth* [1688] (Cambridge, 1965), 71. 'That the Explication we have given of an Universal Deluge is not an IDEA only, but an account of what really came to pass in the Earth … '

[31] *Philosophical Dictionary*, trans. Peter Gay (New York, 1962), 309.

In any case the seventeenth century began, in the wake of the *Cogito*, what Ian Hacking has called 'the heyday of ideas'.[32] Descartes is usually given credit for conferring new meaning on the old term 'idea' and making it the primary locus of modern philosophical discussions of the problem of knowledge. Like his scholastic forebears, he admitted an ambiguity, distinguishing between ideas as creations of the mind and as representations of reality – and yet from the outset he was careful to separate his idea of 'idea' from theological associations and to tie it directly to language.[33] As he later explained, 'I used the term "idea" because it was the standard philosophical term used to refer to the forms of perception belonging to the divine mind, even though we recognize that God does not possess any corporeal imagination', he wrote, adding, 'besides, there was not any more appropriate term at my disposal'. In this way – Descartes playing Humpty Dumpty, making words mean only what he wanted them to mean – the old Platonic form was in effect psychologized. As Descartes added, 'I cannot possibly satisfy those who prefer to attribute a different sense to my words than the one I intended.'

But attaching different senses to words was precisely what kept philosophical debate – and indeed the history of philosophy itself – going. The new 'way of ideas' was never free of old intellectual habits, especially those arising from a theological forestructure presupposing a role for God. The arch-reconciler Leibniz saw no contradiction between the old and the new ways:

> As to the old controversy whether we see all things in God (an old opinion which, properly understood, is not entirely to be rejected) or whether we have some ideas of our own, it must be understood that even if you understood things in God, it would still be necessary to have our own ideas also ... as affections or modifications of our mind corresponding to the very object we perceive in God.

---

[32] Ian Hacking, *Why Does Language Matter to Philosophy?* (Cambridge, 1975), part I.

[33] 'Idea. I understand the term to mean the form of any given thought, immediate perception of which makes me aware of the thought. Hence, whenever I express something in words, and understand what I am saying, this very fact makes it certain that there is within me an idea of what is signified by the words in question' (*The Philosophical Writings of Descartes*, trans. John Cottingham, Robert Stoothoff, and Dugald Murdoch (2 vols; Cambridge, 1984), II, 113). See also Nicholas Jolly, *The Light of the Soul: Theories of Ideas in Leibniz, Malebranche, and Descartes* (Oxford, 1990); Robert McRae, '"Idea" as a Philosophical Term in the 19th Century', *Journal of the History of Ideas*, 26 (1965), 175–84; Emily and Fred S. Michael, 'Corporeal Ideas in Seventeenth-Century Psychology', ibid., 50 (1989), 31–48; and especially Roger Ariew and Marjorie Grene, 'Ideas, in and before Descartes', showing how Descartes drew on and conflated contemporary literary usages.

Either way, whether divine archetypes or psychological creations, ideas were a mark of immortality that set humanity apart from the rest of Creation. Whether following Malebranche's traditional, Augustinian view of ideas as divine archetypes, or Arnauld's psychologistic, Cartesian doctrine, ideas were placed above the vagaries of opinion and the forces of history. In effect 'ideas' were taken off the agenda of criticism, out of the world of discourse and textual analysis, and beyond the reach of history. Like the world of 'spirit' of which they were a part, they were not subject to the mutability of the sublunar world.[34]

This was in keeping with the premises both of Neoplatonic idealism and of Cartesian clarity, but it was also an invitation to another kind of skeptical criticism. It seems almost an act of dogmatic desperation to claim, as did Arnauld in his fourth 'rule of reasoning' in the 'Port-Royal Logic', that it was an error 'to ask for definitions of terms that are clear in themselves', most notably as the words 'think' and 'exist' in the formula, 'I think, therefore I exist.'[35] For Cartesians, in other words, ideas seemed to be above analysis and beyond debate. But of course this assumption was as vain as it was desperate, for awkward questions about the nature of human thought and forms of its expression continued to be posed.[36]

The persistence of disagreement was itself an encouragement to a historical approach to philosophy, and this was further reinforced by the philosophical phase of the contemporary Quarrel between the Ancients and Moderns. Some scholars resisted the notion of a radical break with the past in these issues, particularly in the case with the doctrine of ideas. The insight 'I think, therefore I am', for example, was also to be found in Plautus. Concerning the alleged Cartesian breakthrough, some could find a suggestion for the *Cogito* in Aristotelian philosophy, while Arnauld pointed to a source in Augustine.[37] An even more fundamental parallel with the egocentric Cartesian *Cogito*, it was also suggested, was the Jehovan 'I am that I am.'

---

[34] *Spiritus: IVe Colloquio internazionale del lessico intelletuale Europea*, ed. M. Fattori and M. Bianchi (Rome, 1984), and Rudolph Hildebrand, *Geist* (Halle, 1926); and see Elmar J. Kremer, *The Great Arnauld and Some of His Philosophical Correspondents* (Toronto, 1994).

[35] Antoine Arnauld and Pierre Nicole, *La Logique ou l'art de penser*, ed. P. Clair and F. Girbal (Paris, 1981), 39; *Logic or the Art of Thinking*, trans. Jill Vance Buoker (Cambridge, 1996), 25.

[36] Richard A. Watson, *The Breakdown of Cartesian Metaphysics* (Atlantic Highlands, NJ, 1987).

[37] Joseph Bohatec, *Die cartesianische Scholastik in der Philosophie und reformierten Dogmatik des 17. Jahrhunderts* (Leipzig, 1912), 108, citing a thesis of G. P. Roetenbeck; and Arnauld, *On True and False Ideas*, trans. Stephen Gaukroger (Manchester, 1990), 52. See Augustine, *De Trinitate*, 15.12.21.

Admittedly, this line of argument was unpopular, as René Rapin remarked, 'in a time when only novelty was desired and when everyone claimed to be a philosopher in his own way'.[38] Yet there were conservative authors who sided with the Ancients. One conspicuous example of the attitude of *déjà-vu* and *nihil novum sub sole* was Louis Dutens, who, extending the 'heumatological' efforts of Polydore Vergil's *Inventors of Things*, repeated both these claims and reached further back – to the Chaldean oracles – for the origin of Platonic ideas. He applied such speculative *Quellenforschung* to other self-proclaimed innovators, including Locke, who had adopted his empirical approach from Aristotle. Infected with the 'precursor virus' (as it has been called), he went on to make more fundamental claims about the unoriginality of Descartes in a polemical book of 1766, 'in which is demonstrated how our most celebrated philosophers have taken their learning from the works of the Ancients'.[39]

So the problem of knowledge, especially in the form of 'ideas', absorbed many distinguished minds but has produced no consensus. Were ideas objects of human apprehension, acts of the human mind, or merely 'dispositions'? Sense-perceptions, mental images, or concepts? There were defenders of all these positions, as well as eclectic combinations of these and other arguments. All sought truth and strained to avoid 'prejudice'; yet all were in fact bound to some preconceptions, whether physical theory or theological conviction. The problem was the circularity of arguing, through words, about reason. The rule of the *Port-Royal Grammar*, repeated by Destutt de Tracy in the early nineteenth century, was that 'in order to understand the fundamentals of grammar it is necessary to understand what happens in our mind'.[40] But in human terms it was exactly the opposite.

The one thing on which virtually all discussants seemed to agree was the basically neutral character of ideas and, in the words of Ian Hacking, 'the priority of mental discourse to public speech'. Moreover, ideas – 'clear and distinct' ideas anyway – were born without any significant social, political, cultural, or gender attributes. Divine souls could see ideas 'through time', Ficino had argued, and so apparently could philosophical geniuses like

---

[38] *La Comparaison de Platon et d'Aristote, avec les sentimens des Peres sur leur Doctrine, et quelques reflexions Chrestiennes* (Paris, 1671), 3.

[39] *Origine des découvertes attribuées aux Modernes, Où l'on demonstre que nos plus célèbres Philosophes ont puis de leurs connoissances dans les Ouvrages des Anciens, et que plusieurs vérités importants sur la Religion ont été connues des Sages du Paganisme* (Paris, 1812; 4th edn), 52. See Georges Canguilhem in *A Vital Rationalist*, ed. F. Delaporte and trans. A. Goldhammer (New York, 1994), 50–51.

[40] *Elémens d'Idéologie* (Paris, 1817; 2nd edn), II, 17.

Descartes.[41] Thus ideas were colorless, ageless, classless, raceless, genderless: 'the mind has no sex', in the famous feminist aphorism of the Cartesian Poulain de la Barre,[42] or any accidental and subjective qualities that might interfere with logical analysis. 'I will now close my eyes', Descartes wrote in his pursuit of self-knowledge, 'I will stop my ears, I will turn away my senses from their objects.'[43] Like Euclidean geometry, it would seem, ideas were proof against the inconstancy of the human condition and the vicissitudes of historical change. Yet Neo-Aristotelian empiricism did not surrender in the face of such rationalist attacks, and Leibniz was not alone in believing that Aristotelian ideas could be reconciled with the new philosophy. 'There is nothing in the intellect that was not previously in the senses', Leibniz quoted, and adding, famously – 'except perhaps the intellect itself.'[44]

4. Ideas and History

By Locke's time, in any case, 'ideas' were already the subject not only of attempts to reconcile Platonic idealism and Aristotelianism, or to extricate conceptualizing altogether from such sectarian traditions, but also of historical reflection – that is, following the 'fortune' of particular ideas. Although multiform, these ideas did seem to have a conceptual stability over time which appeared to be independent of human fallibility. For Thomas Stanley they constituted fundamental principles comparable to matter and God himself, and he summarized his view in this way: '*Idea*, as to God, is the *Notion* of God, as to us, the primary *Intelligible*, as to matter, a *manner*, as to this sensible World, an *Exemplar*, as to it self, *Essence*.'

With Descartes and his disciples and critics, this *fortuna* entered a new, more secular and more 'mechanical' phase, which was also received into the philosophical canon. At the same time the celebrated 'doctrine of ideas' was projected, in spirit if not letter, into 'barbarian philosophy' and traced through its various Christian and humanist contexts. That Platonic ideas were consonant with 'true, orthodox, and Christian philosophy' had been argued by Justin, Clement, and other Church Fathers; with their Neo-Pythagorean,

---

[41] Michael J. B. Allen, *Marsilio Ficino and the Phaedran Charioteer* (Berkeley, 1981), 154.

[42] Siep Stuurman, 'Social Cartesianism: François Poulain de la Barre and the Origins of the Enlightenment', *Journal of the History of Ideas*, 58 (1997), 617–40.

[43] *Meditations*, III.

[44] *New Essays on Human Understanding*, trans. P. Remnant and J. Bennett (Cambridge, 1981), I, ii, 20, 'nisi intellectus ipse'.

mathematical base they also joined with modern rational philosophy modeled on geometry. This was the view taken by Brucker, whose *History of the Philosophical Doctrine of Ideas* of 1723 (a work preparatory to his *Critical History of Philosophy*, published later) provided a history of the idea of 'ideas' from Plato down to his own 'eclectic' age.[45]

After inquiring into the possibility of Presocratic origins, Brucker examined the many differences of opinion about the Platonic doctrine of ideas; but against the authority of Aristotle he preferred to believe that these divergent views could be reconciled in a modern context. Here Brucker invoked the assurance of Justin and Clement that 'Plato's theory of ideas is [in accord with] orthodox Christian philosophy' and a variety of medieval and modern interpretations, including such scholars as Vives and Erasmus. What rendered the ancient theory of ideas useful to the Moderns was the emergence of the 'rational philosophy' of philosophers such as Leibniz, Descartes, Arnauld, Malebranche, Locke, and Christian Thomasius, the 'restorer of purer philosophy'. The origin of ideas was indeed a 'vexed question', Brucker admitted, especially in their connections with sense-impressions; but for the *history* of philosophy 'ideas' located the problem of knowledge; Brucker believed that from a comprehensive and erudite history of this tangled problem truth would, in time, emerge; for such was the premise of the new 'eclectic' method.[46]

In these various ways 'ideas' became the common currency of the history of thought. The crucial step was taken by Vico, who denominated his 'new science', in one of its principal aspects, as 'the history of ideas' (*la storia delle idee*, the phrase adapted from Brucker's *Historia philosophica doctrina de ideis*). Vico's point of departure was one of his first axioms, that 'Doctrines must take their beginning from that of the matters of which they treat.' Applying this axiom to philosophy itself, Vico found Brucker's book to be fundamentally mistaken in tracing the question of ideas and their origins only from its Platonic source and failing to realize that the doctrine in question was not just philosophical but belonged to a more general and more profound category of conceptualizing, that of 'wisdom', which Brucker would divorce from true philosophy.

Vico, finding 'this history of human ideas ... strikingly confirmed by the history of philosophy itself',[47] told a different story. Philosophy began with

---

[45] Brucker, *Historia philosophica doctrina de ideis* (Augsburg, 1723); and see Constance Blackwell, 'Epicurus and Boyle, Le Clerc and Locke: "Ideas" and their Redefinition in Jacob Brucker's *Historia philosophica doctrinae de ideis*, 1723', in Maria Fattoria (ed.), *Il Vocabulario della République des lettres* (Florence, 1997), 77–92.

[46] J.A. Goldfriedrich, *Die historische Ideenlehre in Deutschland* (Berlin, 1982).

[47] *Scienza nuova*, para. 499.

the contemplation of the heavens (*admiratio*) and theology; and theology, the 'queen of the sciences', he argued, 'took its start not when the philosophers began to reflect [*riflettere*] on human ideas' (as, he adds, in the 'erudite and scholarly little book' recently published by Brucker), 'but rather when the first men began to think humanly' (*umanamente pensare*). In other words the history of ideas begins not with Plato but with myth and poetry. It was on this poetic wisdom that Plato had drawn in the formulation of his theory of ideas and that Vico would base his 'history of ideas'.

Yet Vico's historicization of ideas was not much noted in his own day nor followed up by historians of philosophy. Nature seemed to guarantee the universal and enduring quality of ideas. As Turgot wrote, 'The same senses, the same organs, and the spectacle of the same universe, have everywhere given man the same ideas, just as the same needs and inclinations have everywhere taught them the same arts.'[48] The classical theory of ideas persisted into the nineteenth century in the form of 'Ideology' – a materialist and anti-metaphysical conception descended from Locke and Condillac and given its new name by Destutt de Tracy.[49] This 'science of ideas' was based on the Lockean thesis that all knowledge was derived from the senses. Talk of innate ideas amounted to spiritualist superstition and 'metaphysics'. Not 'I think, therefore I am,' was Destutt de Tracy's motto, but rather 'I sense, therefore I exist.' Yet in the end Ideology preserved a simplistic, scientistic, psychologistic, and even 'zoological' conception in which not only religion but also history was denied a significant role.

French eclecticism was not much more cordial to the implications of Vico's approach. Though an admirer of Vico, opposed to Ideology, and devoted to 'the history of ideas', Cousin retained a similarly unhistorical view, essentially that of Plato, for whom 'There is no science of the transitory'[50] – though Cousin indeed traced this unhistorical view historically, in order to establish the canon of eclectic 'spiritualism' and to reinforce the 'fixed, immutable principles' which Restoration France sorely needed. For Cousin, ideas, 'thought in its natural form', were 'the proper object of philosophy', and modern philosophy in particular 'bears the date of 1637' – when the *Discourse on Method* appeared. Cousin was neither a base empiricist, a naïve nominalist,

---

[48] *Turgot on Progress, Sociology and Economics*, ed. Ronald L. Meek (Cambridge, 1973), 42.
[49] See Brian William Head, *Ideology and Social Science: Destutt de Tracy and French Liberalism* (Dordrecht, 1985), and R. Emmett Kennedy, *Philosophe in the Age of Revolution: Destutt de Tracy and the Origins of 'Ideology'* (Philadelphia, 1978).
[50] *The True, the Beautiful, and the Good*, 39.

nor an 'absurd realist'. 'No, ideas are not things or beings', he told his students; 'they are not simply words and not beings; they are conceptions of human reason' – following Thomas Reid's view that ideas were not things but rather operations of the mind.[51] As such ideas had their own 'intellectual laws' existing beneath the ordinary laws of nature. Consciousness was a given, a 'fundamental fact'; and so was the ego (*le Moi, das Ich*), along with its identity, integrity, and creative powers; and the history of ideas should be pursued in these psychological (and perhaps phenomenological) terms.

Nevertheless, the 'history of ideas' became, in name and in effect, a major concern of post-Revolutionary intellectuals, especially eclectic scholars like Cousin and his *protégés*. If for Cousin ideas were a large presence in history, for his younger eclectic colleague Jouffroy they were a mighty force. 'Logic is the queen of revolutions', Jouffroy wrote; 'a revolution is only the development of an idea, and the development of an idea is nothing other than logic.'[52] Another historian of ideas of that period was Eugène Lerminier, Professor of Comparative Law at the Collège de France, who believed that 'from one century to another ideas prolong their relevance; and the more powerful and accepted they are in one particular period, the slower they will be to die and give way to others which they have produced'.[53] In particular Lerminier seized upon what he called 'the history of one of the essential ideas of humanity', namely the influence of the social ideas of the Enlightenment on legal reform and on the improvement and 'sociability' of Restoration France.

Still another eclectic historian of ideas was Jules Barni, Cousin's former secretary, a liberal, a pacifist, and later a republican politician. For Barni, too, the eighteenth century was 'the age of ideas', especially the moral and political ideas which were in the process of transforming the world; and in his lectures at the Academy of Geneva (1861) he outlined the historical approach to this subject. On the lowest level was narrative history, which rendered an account of events; next was philosophical history, which went on to offer causal explanation; and finally, the history of ideas – 'philosophical history *par excellence*', but being at once more general and more concrete than the academic history of philosophy as Cousin practiced it, by placing itself in the service of humanity,

---

[51] Cousin, *Cours de l'histoire de la philosophie* (Paris, 1843), 90; and cf. Keith Lehrer, *Thomas Reid* (London, 1989), 84.

[52] *Globe* (17 November 1827), cited in Douglas Johnson, *Guizot: Aspects of French History 1787–1874* (London, 1963), 365.

[53] *De l'Influence de la philosophie du XVIIIe siècle sur la législation et la sociabilité du XIXe siècle* (Paris, 1833), 291; and cf. *Philosophie du droit* (Paris, 1831). See also Bonnie G. Smith, 'The Rise and Fall of Eugène Lerminier', *French Historical Studies*, 12 (1982), 377–400.

which (he was sure) was continually marching toward peace and liberty. For Barni the history of ideas was the story of true enlightenment realized.

For historians and philosophical critics – in contrast to idealist speculators – the question revolved around *other people's* ideas. 'Sometimes, in popular language a man's ideas signify his opinions', wrote Thomas Reid. 'The ideas of Aristotle, or of Epicurus, signify the opinions of these philosophers' – especially in France, he added, noting also that 'Bruckerus, a learned German, wrote a whole book giving the history of ideas' in this mundane sense.[54] In his work on the human intellect Reid offered his own history of ideas. For philosophers, as distinguished from 'the vulgar', this term refers to something in a mind that thinks; but Reid admitted that, 'in explaining the opinions of others', he occasionally would use the word in this way, that is, as 'a mere fiction of philosophers'. This occasional usage was absolutely normal for historians, whereas philosophers are methodologically incapable of 'historicizing' their own ideas.

Perhaps the root of this difference was, again, a residue of religious belief, that is, notions of consciousness and the soul. 'The very existence of ideas constitutes the soul', George Berkeley wrote – and the soul can hardly usefully be admitted as grounds for understanding history.[55] Debates about ideas could only be over words, and Horne Tooke pointed out that Locke's *Essay concerning Human Understanding* was really not about 'the *composition of ideas*' but rather 'the contrivances of Language' – the names of ideas – a subject which Locke had originally wanted to avoid.[56] Reversing Locke's complaint, Tooke remarked that 'the perfections of language, not properly understood, have been one of the chief causes of the imperfections of our philosophy'.

Scottish philosophy also contributed to the historicization of ideas, as scholars like William Robertson, Adam Ferguson, and Dugald Stewart investigated the material dimensions of intellectual development. What they produced was an idea of Progress, given precise form in the 'four-stage' thesis of historical development – hunting, pasturage, agriculture, and commerce.[57] Before the century's end this thesis, supported by Turgot, Smith, Meiners, and others, became a cliché of 'conjectural history', as Stewart called it. In his survey of intellectual history from the 'revival of letters' down to his own day, Stewart adapted the image of the 'torch of science' being passed from the

---

[54] *Essays on the Intellectual Powers of Man* (Cambridge, 1969 [1813–15]), 15–16.

[55] See *Principles of Human Knowledge*, para. cxxxixff.

[56] John Horne Tooke, *Diversions of Purley* (London, 1860), 19.

[57] *Turgot on Progress, Sociology, and Economics*, trans. Meek; and see Ronald L. Meek, *Social Science and the Noble Savage* (Cambridge, 1976), and *Smith, Marx, and After* (London, 1977).

'great *lights of the world*' across the generations, like the Olympic flame.[58] Stewart also opposed the growing disciplinary specializations, arguing that the division between history, philosophy, and poetry is no longer adequate for the purposes either of science or for anyone aspiring to be what Stewart called 'the historian of Human Mind'.[59]

The tradition of Scottish philosophy continued for almost two centuries, and the man who has been called 'the last original thinker of the Scottish school' of philosophy, the Victorian scholar Robert Flint, marked the intersection with intellectual history, and indeed at one point he defined himself as a 'historian of ideas'.[60] In his *History of the Philosophy of History* (1874, expanded in 1894) Flint proposed 'to trace the course of human thought in its endeavors to explain human history, that is, to give an account of the rise and progress of reflection and speculation on the development of humanity'.[61] Flint was one of the first enthusiasts for the writings of Vico in the Anglophone world, and not surprisingly he gave special note to the eclectic philosophy of Cousin, which professed to be 'the outcome of all the philosophies of the past'. With Flint, as with Cousin, we rejoin the mainstream of the history of ideas.

5. The Mirror of Understanding

Ideas, Borges wrote, 'are not, like marble, everlasting'.[62] Ideas take shape in language, change shape in communication, and undergo deeper transformations

---

[58] The simile was borrowed from Plato, *Laws*, book VI, and Lucretius, *De rerum natura*, II, 75: 'Et quasi cursores vitaï [sic] lampada tradunt' (*Dissertation*, I, 32, n. 1).

[59] 'Dissertation First: Exhibiting a general view of the Progress of Metaphysical, Ethical, and Political Philosophy since the Revival of Letters in Europe', in *Works*, ed. William Hamilton (Edinburgh, 1854), I, 14–18. The French translation by J. A. Buchon, with additional reflections by Cousin, is *Histoire abrégé des sciences metaphysiques, morales et politiques depuis la Ren. des lettres* (Paris, 1820), 28; the comments on Vico (369) provided the impulse for the Vichian revival in France culminating in Michelet's translation of the *New Science* (1827). That Stewart's views were commonplace is suggested by Roger L. Emerson, 'Science and Morality in the Scottish Enlightenment', in M.A. Stewart (ed.), *Studies in the Philosophy of the Scottish Enlightenment* (Oxford, 1990), 27, citing a course in Aberdeen on 'the Nature, Progress and Origins of Philosophy' in 1743–44.

[60] Preface to Bernhard Pünjer, *History of the Christian Philosophy of Religion from the Reformation to Kant*, trans. W. Hastie (Edinburgh, 1887), ix; and see George Elder Davie, *The Democratic Intellect: Scotland and her Universities in the Nineteenth Century* (Edinburgh, 1961), 272.

[61] *History of the Philosophy of History* (New York, 1894), 1.

[62] 'las ideas/ no son eternas como el mármol': Borges, 'Daybreak' (Amanecer).

with the passage of time. However fundamental they may be, Goethe's Mephistopheles (if not Goethe himself) reminds us, they depend on language for expression, communication, and indeed meaning:

In general stay with words,
So to find the right door
To the temple of certainty.[63]

Humanity sometimes needs the devil to remind it of this inescapable and ultimate condition of its condition and its projects. Historians, including historians of philosophy, are less troubled by this warning, since they do not normally expect admission into the temple of certainty and must be satisfied with the way-stations of probability.

Clarity and distinctness notwithstanding, there remained, between ideas and understanding, thought and its communication, the problematic medium of language. 'Language', declared J. B. Merian, 'is the greatest problem of the human spirit.'[64] About this cultural creation in which their work was done philosophers were in two minds. Was it a window or a veil? Potentially, it was (in Leibniz's words) 'the bright mirror of understanding',[65] but in fact it never escaped the curse of Babel. This tension between the linguistic ideal and the reality, natural or social, at hand has informed philosophy and its history almost from the beginning. The Stoics were aware of ambiguity (*amphibolia*) and took account of context and different linguistic communities;[66] and philosophers still struggle with the disparity between their intellectual goals and the 'prison house of language' which lodges and at the same time restricts their understanding.

Within the philosophical tradition language has figured as a human reality that is yet a mystery, linking uncontrolled sense-impressions with higher processes of thought and will, but whether by nature or convention was endlessly debated. 'This is the order of nature', wrote the polyhistor Johann

---

[63] Johann Peter Eckermann, *Gespräche mit Goethe* (Munich, 1984), 260; *Goethe's Conversations with Eckermann* (London, 1930), 283, Goethe quoting (inaccurately) from *Faust*, I, 1990ff. The student (speaking perhaps for Goethe himself) answers the advice of Mephistopheles by protesting, 'Yet in the word must some idea be.'

[64] *Analyse de la dissertation sur l'origine du langage qui a remporté le prix en 1771*, in *Königliche Akademie der Wissenschaften, Memoires* (Berlin, 1783), 347.

[65] Hans Aarsleff, *From Locke to Saussure* (Minneapolis, 1982), 85; G. A. Padley, *Grammatical Theory in Western Europe 1500–1700: The Latin tradition* (Cambridge, 1976), 269, 325, language as the 'mirror of thought' or 'mirror of things'. See also Nancy Struever (ed.), *Language and the History of Thought* (Rochester, 1995).

[66] Catherine Atherton, *The Stoics on Ambiguity* (Cambridge, 1993), 173.

Alsted: 'thing, mind, language': mind conceives the thing, and words expresses the conception.[67] Such was the tripartite nature of truth (*triplex est veritas*), a chain depending on the proper correlation of ideas and 'the things themselves'. The triangular relationship of things, words, and ideas generated endless and polyglot debates among scholars and philosophers. For humanist grammarians, words, that is, nouns, were taken normally to be signs of things (although they might also be things themselves, as were Egyptian hieroglyphs). In the seventeenth-century 'way of ideas', there was a shift from simple nomenclature to subjective meaning, as words were regarded as the names of perceptions or conceptions of the mind and therefore as communication became more problematic.

The ground for the intellectualization of language had been prepared by the assimilation of language to logic attempted by the old tradition of speculative grammar, which formed a province within the larger territory of scholastic philosophy. From the sixteenth century it was also pursued by a new breed of rational grammarians, such as Thomas Linacre, J. C. Scaliger, and Petrus Ramus, who in various ways tried to impose logical structure and set down the 'rules' of the Latin language, whence it was extended to vernaculars and even the exotic tongues of the New World.[68] Such linguistic formalism prepared the way for more radical efforts toward general grammar and universal language, whose premise was what has been called an 'isomorphism of linguistic structure and the structure of *thought*'.[69]

Such projects of linguistic reform and construction of universal languages all posited a mental discourse stemming from common sense and common ideas.[70] Thomas Campanella devised a 'philosophical grammar', which he regarded as a science because it linked words directly with the 'nature of things'. If everyone agreed on the same language as they do on particular ideas, John Wilkins argued in his own efforts 'toward a Real Characteristic', then 'we should be freed from that Curse in the Confusion of tongues, with the unhappy consequences of it'. The greatest benefit would be the formulation

---

[67] *Philosophia digne restituta* (Herborn, 1612), 107.

[68] W. Keith Percival, 'Grammar and the Rise of the Vernaculars', in Thomas A. Sebeck (ed.), *History of Linguistics* (The Hague, 1975), 231–75; and E. J. Ashworth, *Language and Logic in the Post-Medieval Period* (Dordrecht, 1974).

[69] G. A. Padley, *Grammatical Theory of Western Europe 1500–1700, Trends in Vernacular Grammar*, I (Cambridge, 1985), 296.

[70] James Knowleson, *Universal Language Schemes in England and France 1600–1800* (Toronto, 1975), M. M. Slaughter, *Universal Languages and Scientific Taxonomy in the Seventeenth Century* (Cambridge, 1982), Robert Markley, *Fallen Languages: Crisis of Representation in Newtonian England 1660–1740* (Ithaca, 1993), and Jean-Pierre Séris, *Langages et machines à l'âge classique* (Paris, 1995).

of a truly 'philosophical language' in which the curse of Babel would be removed, misunderstandings would be avoided, and a larger consensus, perhaps even world peace, could be achieved.

For many philosophers the problems posed by language were conjectural, a shadow cast across the 'way of ideas' which could be dissipated by the careful definition of terms and by the light of reason. Ordinary language was mainly something to be overcome, or perfected, and all it needed to achieve this was the cleansing power of reason. Most radical was the position of Descartes, for whom language was something to be eluded by devices of reason – as Ian Hacking says of him, 'proof was a device for getting rid of words' – and mathematics was presumably an improvement on language. This was the belief even of Leibniz, despite his interests in linguistics and history; and it led him, by analogy with mathematics, to his 'universal characteristic', which would replace the cumbersome old 'encyclopedia' of traditional learning with a rational dictionary containing 'characteristic numbers for all ideas'.[71] In such a state of grace and perfection language was fit for philosophy, but in its ordinary and public condition it is good only for 'opinion'.

The 'way of ideas', in its new as well as its old form, seemed to beg the question of language, assuming as it did that ideas were a stable currency, and that language, correctly employed, was at least potentially a trustworthy medium for intellectual exchange. According to Aristotle,

> As writing, so also is speech not the same for all races of men. But the mental affections themselves, of which these words are primarily signs, are the same for the whole of mankind, as are the objects of which those affections are representations, images, copies.[72]

Augustine took a similar view: 'For the thought that is formed by the thing that we know, is the word which we speak in the heart: which word is neither Greek nor Latin, nor of any tongue.'[73] And as Pico later wrote, 'An Arab and an Egyptian will say the same thing; they may not say it in Latin, but they will nonetheless be correct in saying it.'[74]

---

[71] 'Preface to a Universal Characteristic (1678–79)', in *Philosophical Essays*, ed. Roger Ariew and Daniel Garber (Indianapolis, 1989), 1–5; and see Paolo Rossi, 'The Twisted Roots of Leibniz' Characteristic', *The Leibniz Renaissance* (Florence, 1989), 271–89.

[72] *Peri Hermenias*, 16a.

[73] *De Trinitate*, xv.10.19. And see Marcia Colish, *The Mirror of Language: A Study in the Medieval Theory of Knowledge* (New Haven, 1968).

[74] 'Letter to Ermolao' (106).

The issue of words versus ideas is reflected in a famous debate carried on between Pico and Ermolao Barbaro.[75] Though Pico's work was informed by humanist values in many ways, he preserved scholastic method in his project of harmonizing many philosophies in terms of discrete propositions – 900 of them – drawn from these disparate sources. Pico's sympathetic view of scholasticism was challenged by Ermolao Barbaro, who rejected the 'barbarous and stupid method of philosophizing' of scholastics. In contrast, Barbaro elevated *oratio* above *ratio* – language and eloquence above thinking and argument. Behind the virtuoso rhetoric of both parties, this exchange is a useful illustration of the central issue of the practice of philosophizing and the transmission of ideas over time: on the one hand Pico's belief in a spiritual truth beyond particular cultural and linguistic traditions, and on the other hand Barbaro's underlying premise that attention should be given above all to the language of earlier authors as preserved in the sources, and that eloquence, mastery of language, is essential to modern philosophizing. A generation later Barbaro's position was restated in a more forthright and less jocular way by Philip Melanchthon, who was concerned less with the stupidity of scholastic philosophy than with the errors which it brought to religion and the arts.[76] For Melanchthon rhetoric was not 'adventitious adornment' but rather 'the faculty for proper and clear explication of mental sense and thought'. Not disputation but linguistic custom provided the basis of society, the means of instruction, and the road to the reform of philosophy, the arts, and religion.

Empirical philosophers – the 'party of nature' as opposed to the 'party of spirit' – had little patience with either side of this dispute, preferring the third member of the trinity, 'things', to distracting considerations of mediating thought and language. Bacon took as his motto the old rhetorical topos, 'things not words' (*res non verba*) – 'for words are but the images of matter' – and placed it in the service of natural philosophy. He denounced common language as an 'idol of the marketplace' and a major source of error. 'Words', Bacon wrote, 'are but the current tokens or marks of Popular Notions of things' and, wrongly chosen, 'do shoot back upon the understanding of the wisest'.[77]

With Hobbes and Locke 'ideas' are linked more directly with words. 'The generall use of Speech is to transfer our Mentall Discourse, into Verball',

---

[75] See Quirinus Breen, 'Giovanni Pico della Mirandola on the Conflict of Philosophy and Rhetoric', *Journal of the History of Ideas*, 13 (1952), 384–426.
[76] Ibid.
[77] *Of the Advancement of Learning*, 114.

wrote Hobbes, 'or the Trayne of our Thoughts, into a Trayne of Words.'[78] The problem was that speech was notoriously prone to a variety of abuses. Nature itself cannot err, Hobbes remarked; error arises only from the process of naming and the misuses of speech, especially in matters of generality. Nor can ideas by themselves be false, argued Locke, since 'words, in their primary or immediate signification, stand for nothing but *the ideas in the mind of him that uses them*',[79] so establishing, as Michael Ayers notes, 'the logical priority of ideas and mental predication over words and verbal predication'. Locke believed it was possible to think without recourse to the convention of names. Consciousness 'itself' was thus a peaceful realm of spirit, and it was only the Babel factor that divided humanity into warring nations, schools, and sects.[80]

The significant point is that, in the pursuit of truth and the attempt to escape error, prejudice, and mere opinion – in what has been called the 'flight from ambiguity' – philosophers were constructing, or rather imagining, a realm of pure reason and eternal ideas existing apart from social contexts of human expression, exchange, and the search, as distinguished from the grasp, of truth.[81] In the spiritualist realm of ideas – as in the state of nature – there was neither ancient nor modern, master nor slave, lord nor peasant, male nor female. Not only does the mind 'have no sex', but it has no social status, political allegiance, economic base, cultural context, or linguistic confinement. All of these conditions of thinking were relegated safely to folly or to willful error, to prejudices and the imagination or to the modern interplay between 'the passions and the interests'.

6. The Linguistic Turn

The extreme rationalism of some seventeenth-century philosophers went very much against the views – and the prejudices – of Latin grammarians and rhetoricians in the tradition of Valla, Poliziano, Barbaro, Budé, and Erasmus,

---

[78] *Leviathan*, ch. 4.

[79] *An Essay concerning Human Understanding*, III, ii, 2.

[80] Arno Borst, *Der Turmbau von Babel* (3 vols; Stuttgart, 1960); Don Cameron Allen, *The Legend of Noah: Renaissance Rationalism in Art, Science and Letters* (Urbana, 1949); Marie-Luce Demonet, *Les Voix du signe: Nature et origine du langage à la Renaissance (1480–1580)* (Paris, 1992), and James J. Bono, *The Word of God and the Languages of Man: Interpreting Nature in Early Modern Science and Medicine* (Madison, 1995).

[81] See the general discussion of Donald N. Levine, *The Flight from Ambiguity: Essays in Social and Cultural Theory* (Chicago, 1985).

who understood language in terms of custom, usage, style, and the copiousness (*copia*) provided by classical literature. In contrast to philosophical grammar of medieval speculation the new science of philology in the Renaissance was descriptive, in this sense 'historical' – 'history' was the first division of grammar, as 'method' was the second – and generally suspicious of efforts to classify and to categorize language, recalling scholastic methods and heralding the new 'universal languages' of the seventeenth century. Such metalinguistic ideals remained in the future; and modern philosophers continued to face this Babel factor which had distorted, if not broken, the bright mirror of understanding. In the sublunar world of intellectual debate the medium of exchange was not ideas but words, and so the foundational question in the philosophical search for truth – some would say the *Philosophia Prima* – is the role of language. Before the final vision of Truth, in other words, philosophers must spend their conceptual lives in the purgatory of Opinion, if not in the inferno of Error, where meaning must be sought, judgments made, and communications attempted.

Universal reason and exchangeable ideas depended above all on propositional logic, and this was a minefield of controversy. Anthony Collins defined reason as 'that faculty of mind whereby it perceives the Truth, Falsehood, Probability or Improbability of Propositions', but added immediately that propositions and the ideas they treated invariably depended on words, which depended in turn on convention, individual usage, and ultimately 'human testimony', so that 'The words must stand for those Ideas which the use of Language has appropriated them to or for what the Author or Relator says he understands by them ... '[82] History, journeys of discovery, scientific experiment, all the 'human Sciences' (Collins's term), and even religion depend on such human testimony; and the association of ideas underlying linguistic communication is an 'internal', private matter, tied to authorial intention and inaccessible to universal reason, which requires 'external evidence' as the 'criterion of truth'.[83]

There were other dangers in confusing language and thought, for, unlike mental operations, languages had tenses and other conventions which were relative, contingent, and changing. This was especially evident in the age-old problem of translation (*interpretatio*), whether to translate word for word

---

[82] *An Essay Concerning the Use of Reason in Propositions, the Evidence whereof depends upon Human Testimony* (London, 1710), 8.

[83] Ibid., 34: 'Do we not meet with Men every day that use Words for Ideas peculiar to themselves, and that may for ought we know perceive a Relation between those Ideas?'

(*verbum a verbo*) or sense for sense (*sensum de sensu*), and if the latter, how to determine such metalinguistic meaning.[84] Translation drew extensively on rhetorical theory and practice in order to achieve not merely the letter of a text but also its spirit, which for the Bible might mean the Holy Spirit, but which for ordinary works meant only the mind and the 'intention' of the author in his particular situation. Renaissance humanists accepted this as a matter of practice, and some raised it to a theoretical level. 'For ideas are only intelligible to us by means of the words which describe them', wrote Erasmus; 'wherefore defective knowledge of language reflects upon our apprehension of the truths expressed.'[85] Louis Le Roy was prepared to celebrate the powers of reason, 'But reason is of little use', he added, 'if one cannot express in speech what has been conceived in the understanding.'[86]

It was language, then, which had prevented philosophy from apprehending truth directly and which had condemned it to that lower dimension which Plato had called opinion. Before the seventeenth century not only language but particular languages had mattered to philosophers in the most concrete ways. Greek and Latin were the media of philosophical discourse, but in the Renaissance the vernaculars also joined in this chorus. One purpose of Joachim Du Bellay in his *Defense and Illustration of the French Language* (1549) was to argue that 'the French language is not incapable of [doing] philosophy' – and indeed offered the only possibility of emulating the Ancients. Italian, French, English, and (belatedly) German all contributed to international debates, and later scholars celebrated the revolutionary step of teaching philosophy in the vernacular – as Le Roy did in the sixteenth and Thomasius in the seventeenth century (for which he was derided as a 'barbarian'). In Kant's time Latin terminology, derived from the Greek and imitated by the vernaculars, continued to form the medium of exchange among the contending sects of early modern Europe. Even Arnauld, who did not think language significant in distinguishing 'true and false ideas', found Descartes's Latin arguments clearer than his French. In the eighteenth century Du Bellay's prophetic argument had been transformed into an assumption, as the Academy of Berlin formulated as its prize topic for 1777 the question – or *petitio principii* – 'Who has made the French language universal?'[87] By then there

---

[84] Rita Copeland, *Rhetoric, Hermeneutics, and Translation in the Middle Ages* (Cambridge, 1991), discussing Jerome, and Erica Rummel, *Erasmus as Translator* (Toronto, 1984).

[85] *Concerning the Aim and Method of Education*, trans. W. H. Woodward (Cambridge, 1904), 162.

[86] *Vicissitude des choses*, fol. 32ᵛ.

[87] Adolf Harnack, *Geschichte der königlich preussische Akademie der Wissenschaften*

were new challengers for primacy in philosophical discourse, including English and German, to which innovating teachers like Thomasius and Wolff turned to express their conceptualizations – and which, especially in the form of Kant's 'critical philosophy', was undermining French intellectual hegemony by Cousin's time. In this way new generations of the Moderns continued their battles with the Ancients.

The variability of language was a problem that skeptics had long acknowledged. The 'causes' of linguistic mutability were discussed by both philologists and philosophers, but only the latter lamented the fact. Drawing on humanist critiques of Aristotelianism, Francisco Sánches posed this question: 'In the realm of Latin are there not a great many words that are obsolete, while others are invented afresh every day?' The same applied to other languages, so that 'no wholly regular and uncorrupted language remains to us today', that is, none still in touch with the 'nature of things'.[88] 'Therefore', he concluded, 'there lies in words no power to explain the nature of things [*rerum natura*], except that which they derive from the arbitrary decision of him who applies them … ' Was not philosophy subject even more fundamentally to the same limitations? 'For the very reason that no man is identical to any other man', Diderot warned, 'we never understand precisely, we are never precisely understood; our speech always goes beyond or falls short of the sensation itself.'[89] Believing in 'the irreducible individuality of psychic experience', he regarded language not as a transcendent logic but rather as a 'second nature' created by the human desire to know, express, and communicate.[90] For history and the human sciences it was not the primary but this secondary nature that needed to be understood; and in this connection Thomas Reid, pointing out, moreover, the basically analogical character of language, which had to derive its most fundamental terminology from common and material experience, invoked the pseudo-Aristotelian adage, 'nothing in the intellect, which was not first in the senses'.[91]

In short, language was a product of history and transcended the community of speakers at any given time. Not only particular human beings, as Heidegger

---

zu Berlin (Berlin, 1900), I, 421: 'Qu'est-ce qui a fait de la langue française la langue universelle de l'Europe?'

[88] *That Nothing is Known (Quod nihil scitur)*, trans. Douglas F. S. Thompson (Cambridge, 1988), 219.

[89] *Œuvres complètes*, ed. J. Assézat and M. Tourneaux (20 vols; Paris, 1875–77), II, 180–81.

[90] Herbert Josephs, *Diderot's Dialogue of Language and Gesture: Le Neveu de Rameau* ([Columbus, OH], 1969), 19, 27.

[91] *Essays on the Intellectual Powers of Man*, 103.

put it, but also 'language speaks'.[92] 'Where word breaks off, no thing may be.'[93] And (for the historian) no thought either.

7. The History of Language

Like philosophy, language had a history; and by the seventeenth century this history, too, had been extensively cultivated. The story of human speech followed the biblical narrative, with its estimate of 'seventy-two' human tongues, but the legend of Babel did not function in the emergent fields of comparative grammar and philology. Instead emphasis was placed on the natural process of linguistic change and diversity. This had been the subject of various treatises on languages, including those of Konrad Gesner and Claude Duret.[94] The treatise of Olaus Borrichius (1704), dedicated to the eclectic theologian Buddeus, pointed to factors of climate and geography (which so directly affect the senses), the influence of sounds (such words as *barbara* or *clangere* being obvious examples of such natural imitation), artificial changes brought by teaching, and such social phenomena as the migrations of peoples.[95]

In the eighteenth century discussions of language and its relations to thought and to society were pursued by philologists and philosophers alike, and a consensus was not to be expected, given the speculative level of the debates and the religious, ideological, and methodological differences of the disputants. Among the scholars who published significant statements on these issues were Condillac (1746), Maupertuis (1748), Rousseau (1754), Adam Smith (1761), Samuel Formey (1762), J. D. Michaelis (1766), J. D. Süssmilch (1766), J. G. Sulzer (1767), J. G. Herder (1771), Lord Monboddo (1773), and J. G. Adelung (1781).[96] Public interest in these problems culminated in the two prize questions posed by the Academy of Sciences of Berlin in 1757

---

[92] *Poetry, Language, Thought*, trans. Albert Hofstadter (New York, 1971), 198, 210, and so on, and *On the Way to Language*, trans. Peter D. Hertz (New York, 1971), 124.

[93] *On the Way to Language*, 63.

[94] *Mithridates Gesneri. De differentiis linguarum tum veterum tum quae hodie apud diversis nationes in toto orbe terrarum in usu sunt* (Zurich, 1555), and Duret, *Le Thresor de l'histoire des langues de cest univers* (Paris, 1615); and see especially Demonet, *Les Voix du signe*, Daniel Droixhe, *La Linguistique et l'appel de l'histoire* (Geneva, 1978), and Borst, *Turmbau von Babel*.

[95] *De Causis diversitatis linguarum dissertatio* (Jena, 1704).

[96] Hans Aarsleff, 'The Tradition of Condillac: The Problem of the Origin of Language in the Eighteenth Century and the Debate in the Berlin Academy before Herder', 'An Outline of Language-Origins Theory since the Renaissance', *From Locke to Saussure* (Minneapolis, 1982), 146–209, 278–92.

and 1769. The first topic was 'What is the reciprocal influence of the opinions of a people on its language and of its language on its opinions?' and the second was 'Would men left with only their natural faculties be capable of inventing language?' – and if so, how?[97] The idea of 'influence', publicized here and shifted from its astrologico-medical usage to a socialized form, became an invaluable short-hand for undefinable connections between phenomena and human agency.[98]

About the origins of language theories abounded; whether attributing the breakthrough to gestures, animal cries, divine grace, or human ingenuity, scholars still rehearsed the old story of Psammeticus (told first by Herodotus), which had a child held incommunicado uttering its first words in Hebrew; and indeed many of the crucial arguments in the linguistic speculation of the Enlightenment, taking off from conventional notions of a state of nature, remained on a comparable level of hypothesis and naïveté.[99] Goethe was only one of those who thought the debate fruitless: if man had a divine origin, then so did language, he remarked after reading Herder's essay, and the same for a natural origin.[100] But of course there was a philosophical as well as a historical problem at stake, and this was the relationship between the way of ideas and the ways of language.

In Condillac's pioneering explorations of the origins of language, philosophy was assisted by history.[101] For Condillac, as Hans Aarsleff wrote, 'The progress of the mind becomes a question of the progress of language.'[102] While in his philosophical works Condillac treated language in terms of logic, common-sense speculation, and notions of a state of nature, in his historical works he took up questions of social causes and 'influences'. 'Languages were precise methods as long as men spoke only of things related to their primary needs', he wrote; but thereafter men 'went on to create needs out of pure curiosity, needs of opinion, finally useless needs, each more frivolous than the other'.[103]

---

[97] Harnack, *Geschichte*, I, 409, 414.

[98] See Robert S. Leventhal, *The Disciplines of Interpretation: Lessing, Herder, Schlegel and Hermeneutics in Germany 1750–1800* (Berlin, 1994), 224.

[99] Antoni Sulek, 'The Experiment of Psammeticus', *Journal of the History of Ideas*, 50 (1989), 645–51, treating later imitators.

[100] *From my Life: Poetry and Truth*, trans. Robert R. Heitner (New York, 1987), I, 301.

[101] Jean Sgard (ed.), *Condillac et les problèmes du langage* (Geneva, 1982), and Pierre Juliard, *Philosophies of Language in Eighteenth-Century France* (The Hague, 1970); also Ronald Grimsley, *Sur l'Origine du langage* (Paris, 1971), including texts by Maupertuis, Turgot, and Maine de Biran.

[102] *From Locke to Saussure* (Minneapolis, 1982), 109.

[103] *Treatise on Sensations*, III, ii, 3.

In recorded history languages had lost pretensions to such precision, for 'Commerce brought together people who exchanged, as it were, their opinions, their prejudices, as well as the products of their lands and their industry.'

In contrast to Condillac, Johann David Michaelis approached these questions as a philologist rather than a philosopher or conjectural historian, and so he emphasized the changing nature of language. 'Every word was a neologism once,' Erasmus had observed, and Michaelis attended to the invention of new words. 'Language is a democracy where use or custom is decided by the majority', he argued, following a classical notion going back at least to the Roman grammarian Varro; and 'it is from the opinions of the people and the point of view in which objects appear to them, that language receives its form' – though to be sure, philosophers, not only the scholastics but also modern eclectics like Christian Wolff, tried to alter conventional terms and to introduce new ones. In general, Michaelis concluded, 'the right of creating [new words] ... belongs only to classic authors, the fair sex, and the people, who are the supreme legislators'.[104] Far from being merely neutral and unequivocal signs, wrote Michaelis, words often tended to produce love, hatred, or other judgments; and he illustrated his point through Latin, Hebrew, Arabic, and German usage. Unlike many philosophical commentators on linguistics such as Condillac, Michaelis preferred looking at the derivation of terms to speculating about human nature. 'It cannot be imagined how much good is contained in etymology', he rhapsodized:

> It is a treasure of sense, knowledge, and wisdom: it includes truths which most philosophers do not see into, and will one day immortalize the philosopher who shall discover them, without [knowing] that, from time immemorial, they have been in every body's mouth.[105]

As J. G. Sulzer wrote in 1767, 'The etymological history of languages would indisputably be the best history of the progress of the human mind.'[106]

The modern virtuoso of etymology was Giambattista Vico, whose views about language were unknown to the French and German discussants of the question of language. Vico had made the most fundamental of all 'linguistic turns', in the sense that his 'new science' was based directly on philology, which in turn depended on a theory and practice of etymology that would

---

[104] *A Dissertation on the Influence of Opinions on Language and of Language on Opinions*, Eng. trans. (London, 1769), 2–3.

[105] Ibid., 12.

[106] Hermann J. Cloeren, *Language and Thought: German Approaches to Analytical Philosophy in the 18th and 19th Centuries* (Berlin, 1988), 14.

permit scholars to read their way back, through literary and historical study of texts, to the most primitive 'ideas' formed by humanity in its formative, 'barbaric' stages. In his own way Vico, too, sought a metalanguage, a 'philosophical grammar' – but for him this was an instrument of historical inquiry that would reveal the origins not only of language, which was as it were the baby-talk of the human race, but also of human society and culture, which represented as it were language writ large.[107]

Language owed more to imagination and social instinct than to reason. 'Poetry', as J. G. Hamann put it, 'was the mother tongue of the human race.'[108] Language was the place where reason and sociability met, where opinions flourished but truth remained only an ideal, where historical change could be sensed but perfect communication seldom be achieved. Even for Locke language was 'the great instrument and common tie of society',[109] and as such language, that is, languages as they had evolved in the postdiluvian world of man's making, offered a paradigm not for the philosopher but for the historian of ideas and culture.

This was a project, too, of Herder, who likewise approached the origin of language as a philologist and historian. Language was not an 'invention', and he regarded thought experiments using children (Condillac had imagined two children in the desert) as useless, a 'puerile' effort to apply clear and distinct ideas to a question not 'philosophical' in this abstract sense. Language is not a result of contract, as Rousseau also seemed to believe – so that the tendency in the naming of an animal was first to say, and so to think, 'baa', rather than 'sheep'.[110] Nor was there any age when humanity did not have a language of some sort. For Herder language originated in an instinctive process of imitating sounds, which thereby generated a succession of natural signs and in consequence a kind of 'interior language'. Herder was suspicious of foreign importations of every sort, beginning with philosophical Latin: 'that a Latin spirit has invaded the core of *the learned disciplines* is, I think, self-evident. Peruse the textbooks of most philosophies and a learned language, into which the concepts are woven, will be found.'[111] He criticized Kant's neglect of ordinary language at the expense of abstract philosophical jargon and rejected the vision of a linguistic utopia founded on such an unequivocal

---

[107] *Scienza nuova*, para. 433, 448 *et passim*.

[108] *Aesthetica in nuce*, in *German Aesthetic and Literary Criticism*, ed. H. B. Nisbet (Cambridge, 1985), 141.

[109] *Essay*, III, 1.

[110] *Selected Early Works 1764–1767*, trans. Ernest Menze (University Park, PA, 1991), 105 ('On the Stages in the Life of a Language').

[111] Ibid., 195.

medium of exchange. 'The Universal language advocated by Leibniz', he concluded, 'is not attainable.'[112]

Yet if Herder's vision did not aspire to a 'universal characteristic', it did offer a larger agenda than the Berlin Academy. Having reflected in a comparative way on languages, he extended the inquiry by asking significantly more refined questions:

> To what extent does the natural way of thought of the Germans also have an impact upon their language? And the language upon their literature, beginning with its basic elements, its pronunciation, and meter? How much can be explained on the basis of their environment and their language organs? On the basis of historical evidence, to what extent can the richness and poverty of their language be said to have grown out of their way of thought and life? To what extent is the etymology of its words determinable by viewpoints held in common with other nations, or peculiar to itself? To what extent do the rules of language run parallel to the laws governing their thought? And how can the particularities of the language be explained out of thought patterns? In matters essential, what revolutions did the German language have to experience? And how far has it come to date for the poet, the prose writer, and the philosopher?[113]

Thus did Herder propose to connect problems of language with the old enterprise of philosophy; for, as he insisted, 'It is through language that we learn to think *precisely*.'[114]

8.   Metacriticism and Hermeneutics

It was from this point of view that Herder undertook his criticism – that is, his 'metacriticism' – of Kant's so-called critical philosophy. The subject of Kant's work was not 'pure reason', Herder protested, but only 'human reason', and this reason cannot be separated from other faculties.[115] For Herder the main question was not 'What is Enlightenment?', but rather 'What is humanity?' – and language and history, rather than logic, metaphysics, epistemology, or theology, were the keys to it. In general, Herder argued, 'The human mind thinks with words' (*die menschliche Seele denkt mit Worten*), citing in this connection Leibniz's formula that 'language is the mirror of

---

[112] *Selected Early Works*, 159 ('Conclusion: On the Ideal Language').

[113] Ibid., 102 ('On Recent German Literature: First Collection of Fragments' [supplement to 'Briefe über die neueste Literatur'; in *Deutsche Bibliothek*]).

[114] Ibid., 102.

[115] *Verstand und Erfahrung Vernunft und Sprache, Metakritik*, in *Sämtliche Werke* (Stuttgart, 1853), XXXVII; and see Ulrich Geier, *Herder's Sprachphilosophie und Erkenntniskritik* (Stuttgart, 1981).

understanding'; for reason was a process of experience in specific (not absolute) time and space, which was to say in language and in history.

The descent of ideas into the medium of language can also be seen in the art of interpretation, *ars hermeneutica*, as Leibniz and others called it, which was an offspring of the Renaissance *ars critica* and which achieved disciplinary status in the eighteenth century. Hermeneutics had been confined to questions of textual exegesis, especially in classical, biblical, and legal scholarship.[116] Its antecedents included J. C. Dannhauer's *Idea of a Good Critic* of 1630, a large body of work on legal 'extension',[117] and an even larger literature on biblical criticism, most notably that of the ultra-Lutheran Flacius Illyricus, who sought spiritual truth through an interpretation of scripture – Luther's *sola scriptura* – rather than natural truth through logical disputation, which Flacius rejected as an evil of scholasticism.[118] Hermeneutics was a method that was applied to literature and to such 'dogmatic' disciplines as jurisprudence and theology, but it had little relevance to philosophy. 'Very little knowledge of this discipline can be found in philosophy,' wrote Johann Martin Chladenius, pioneer of the art of hermeneutics.[119] This was in 1742; a half-century later Kant made the point more strongly in his *Conflict of Faculties*, arguing that law and theology were dependent on textual authority, while philosophy (and perhaps medicine) was 'free' from such dogmatic restrictions – and even from the rules of grammatical or historical criticism and subject only to those of reason.[120]

What concerned Chladenius, however, was not rational or logical but rather human understanding. 'It is one thing to understand a proposition in itself', he wrote, 'and another to understand it as being presented and asserted by someone.'[121] In the latter case one must consider not only the 'prevailing conditions' but also the undeniable fact that 'Different people perceive that

---

[116] See Hans-Georg Gadamer and Gottfried Boehm (eds), *Seminar: Philosophische Hermeneutik* (Frankfurt, 1976); H.-E. Hasso Jaeger, 'Studien zur Frügeschichte der Hermeneutik', *Archiv für Begriffsgeschichte*, 13 (1974), 35–84; Guido Canziani and Yves Charles Zarka (eds), *L'Interpretazione nei secoli XVI e XVII* (Milan, 1993); Jean Grondin, *Introduction to Philosophical Hermeneutics*, trans. Joel Weinsheimer (New Haven, 1994); and Leventhal, *The Disciplines of Interpretation*.

[117] Ian Maclean, *Interpretation and Meaning in the Renaissance: The Case of Law* (Cambridge, 1992).

[118] *De Ratione cognoscendi sacras literas* (1567).

[119] 'On the Concept of Interpretation', in *The Hermeneutics Reader*, ed. Kurt Mueller-Vollmer (London, 1985), 60; and Gadamer and Boehm, *Seminar: Philosophische Hermeneutik*.

[120] *Der Streit der Fakultäten*, with trans. by Mary J. Gregor (Lincoln, NE, 1979), 35ff.

[121] Mueller-Vollmer, *Hermeneutics Reader*, 56.

which happens in the world differently', a principle which Chladenius generalized as 'point of view' (*Sehe-Punkt*).[122] For him interpretation demanded above all 'judgment' (*Urteil*) on the part of the reader and involved not only differences in point of view but also disagreements between various interpreters that had to be reconciled. As Goethe wrote,

> We see the world in one way from a plain, another way from the heights of a promontory, another from the glacier fields of the primary mountains ... , but we cannot say that we see more truly from any one than from another.[123]

From this circumstance – the limitations of human horizons and point of view – no human being, not even a philosopher, was exempt. In particular it was the predicament of the historian, who could never avoid interpretation – that is, asking such unphilosophical questions as: who, where, when, why, and under what conditions?

Hermeneutics flourished in the Romantic period and took a more general form. While requiring a knowledge of 'language and archeology', hermeneutics placed this erudition in the service of a higher 'spiritual' quest for the spirit of a cultural Other (not unlike the *Volksgeist*)[124] which could be carried on only by a 'philosophically trained philologist'. According to Friedrich Ast, the scholar's task was to inquire into the context of the composition of, say, the odes of Pindar: when did he live, what was his mentality, how did it develop, and under what conditions? Yet for Ast, formulator of the famous 'hermeneutical circle', these inquiries were directed at understanding the 'spirit' of this author, his work, and his time; for these were the ultimate loci not only of the 'ideas' of an author but also of historical meaning and truth. Hermeneutics was thus the more reflective successor of the discipline of philology, which Ernst Renan defined as 'the exact science of things of the spirit'.[125]

It was the theologian Friedrich Schleiermacher, following the work of Ast, who raised the hermeneutical art to the level of general understanding. The purpose of hermeneutics, following Homeric and biblical criticism, was to seek the truth not of nature but of human writing, which is to say the intention of an author. For this one must have a knowledge of language and

---

[122] Christoph Friedrich, *Sprache und Geschichte: Untersuchungen zur Hermeneutik von Johann Martin Chladenius* (Meisenheim, 1978).

[123] *Gespräche*, 390; *Conversations*, 383.

[124] Richard Palmer, *Hermeneutics* (Evanston, IL, 1969), 77; and Gayle L. Ormiston and Alan D. Schrift (eds), *The Hermeneutic Tradition from Ast to Ricœur* (Albany, 1990).

[125] *L'Avenir de la science*, in *Œuvres complètes*, ed. Henriette Psichari (Paris, 1949), III, 844.

of people and must inquire into the history and vocabulary – Schleiermacher called it the 'linguistic sphere' – of an age. The question was what light informed exegesis could throw either on the author or on the language, since texts were a product of the complex interplay between human will or genius and the cultural force of inherited language.[126] For Schleiermacher there was only one method of interpreting (not four, as medieval exegetes had posited); and though he admitted that there could be meanings of a text beyond the primary historical signification, he rejected allegorical or cabalistic interpretations. In any case, except for scriptures, all texts were time-bound; and in this connection Schleiermacher distinguished between objective-historical and subjective-historical interpretation, the first relating texts to language, requiring erudition beyond artificial lexicographical aids, and the second to the author, which required psychological empathy. Together these synthesizing efforts made possible historical reconstruction (*Nachkonstruieren*).

Looking to time future as well as time past, Schleiermacher recognized what he called objective-prophetic and subjective-prophetic interpretation. These had to do with the 'influence' of a text in the history of the language and its place in the development of the author. Because the interpreter had command of many texts over a larger span of time, Schleiermacher suggested, it was possible 'to understand the text as first as well as and then even better than its author'.[127] Ironically, it was Kant (and later Friedrich Schlegel) who first made this claim to what Dilthey called *Besserverstehen*, based on the possibility of unconscious or inadvertent expressions on the part of an author not in full command of his thoughts. Kant's argument was made, however, in connection with his discussion of the disparity between Platonic ideas and their imperfect human counterparts, while Schleiermacher was concerned more specifically with questions of cultural and historical context.[128] Not that Schleiermacher believed that perfect reconstruction was possible; for in this respect, too, history was inferior to philosophy. 'Not only do we never

---

[126] 'Schleiermacher's Hermeneutical System in Relation to Earlier Protestant Hermeneutics' (1860), *Hermeneutics and the Study of History*, in *Selected Works*, IV, ed. Rudolf Makkreel and Frithjof Rodi (Princeton, 1996), 33ff.

[127] Mueller-Vollmer, *Hermeneutics Reader*, 83; also Hans-Georg Gadamer, *Truth and Method*, trans. Garrett Barden and John Cumming (New York, 1982), 170, and Ernst Behler, 'What it Means to Understand an Author Better than He Understood Himself: Idealistic Philosophy and Romantic Hermeneutics', in *Literary Theory and Criticism: Festschrift Presented to René Wellek in Honor of his Eightieth Birthday*, ed. Joseph P. Strelker (Bern, 1985), I, 69–92.

[128] *Critique of Pure Reason*, 'Transcendental Dialectic', I, i, 'Of Ideas in General': 'by comparing the thoughts which an author has delivered upon a subject, to understand him better than he understood himself'.

understand an individual view exhaustively', he explained, 'but what we do understand is always subject to correction.' As Goethe wondered,

Why is one living mind never directly present to another?
When the soul speaks, alas,
It is no longer the soul that speaks.[129]

Johann Gustav Droysen connected hermeneutics specifically with intellectual history by making the 'interpretation of ideas' the last mode – completing pragmatic interpretation (from records), interpretation of conditions (especially space and time), and psychological interpretation (human will) through study of the cultural context or 'ethical forces' of an age.[130] Thus the scholar became a creator: just as the historian was not a mere reporter of facts, so the critic was not a mere commentator: both were devoted to the problematic and creative task of reconstructing meaning. '"Interpretation"', Nietzsche pronounced: 'the introduction of meaning – not explanation.'[131]

Thus the post-Cartesian *Cogito* came to embrace the existence not only of itself but also, through empathetic understanding, of the cultural Other – reversing in a sense the exaltation of the Romantic Ego by seeking the 'I' in the 'Thou'.[132] This was the sort of hermeneutical understanding that underlay the secularized 'sciences of the spirit' (*Geisteswissenschaften*) which Dilthey, a successor both to Kant and to Schleiermacher, tried to establish. As he wrote of the foundational art of hermeneutics,

The historical consciousness constructed on this basis has enabled modern man to hold the entire past of humanity present within himself: across the limits of his own time he peers into vanished cultures [*vergangenen Kulturen*], appropriating their energies and taking pleasure in their charms, with a consequent increase in his own pleasure.[133]

This is also a good characterization of the spiritualist tradition of intellectual and cultural history as it appeared in these same years.

---

[129] Cited by Ernst Cassirer, *The Logic of the Humanities*, trans. Clarence Smith Howe (New Haven, 1960), 112.

[130] *Grundriss der Historik* (Leipzig, 1875), 21; Mueller-Vollmer, *Hermeneutics Reader*, 131.

[131] *Der Wille zur Macht*, ed. Peter Gast (Stuttgart, 1964), 414; *The Will to Power*, trans. Walter Kaufmann and R. J. Hollingdale (New York, 1967), 327.

[132] Dilthey, *Gesammelte Schriften*, VII (Leipzig, 1927), 191 ('Entwürfe zur Kritik der historischen Vernunft'): 'Das Verstehen ist ein Wiederfinden des Ich im Du.'

[133] 'Die Entstehung der Hermeneutik', in *Gesammelte Schriften*, V (Leipzig, 1924), 317; 'The Rise of Hermeneutics', trans. Frederic Jameson and Rudolf A. Makkreel, in Makkreel and Rodi (eds), *Hermeneutics and the Study of History*, 235.

The mission of science has always been to understand the 'great book of nature' – a topos that runs through the history of European literature, along with parallel conceits of the 'book of experience', the 'book of reason', and the 'book of memory' – from Conrad of Megenberg in the fourteenth century to Goethe in the nineteenth. Natural philosophers sought to decipher the language of this book and decided, after Galileo, that this language must be mathematics; and some believed (and indeed still believe) that humanity may also be expressed in some such abstract tongue. Culture, too, may be regarded as a book, though not the clearly written volume that Galileo opened with his new sciences.[134] Rather, the 'darkness of earliest history', as the 'forgotten Romantic' J. A. Kanne put it, could be detected only 'in the Sibylline pages with which the book of human life begins'.[135] This is Herder's 'great book in which we read the sense of an unknown agent', a sense not 'outside of or "behind" the word, but rather *in the word itself*'.[136] This is the 'great dark book of [world] history' invoked by Gadamer in connection with the ideas of Dilthey, 'the collected work of the human spirit [*des menschlichen Geistes*], written in the languages of the past, the text of which we have to understand'.[137] This was the mission of intellectual and cultural history, a form of scholarly inquiry which joined forces with hermeneutics in the reading of the great book of culture – following the 'descent of ideas' into a context accessible to intellectual and cultural historians.

---

[134] Ernst Robert Curtius, *European Literature and the Latin Middle Ages*, trans. Willard R. Trask (Princeton, 1953), 317ff; also Jesse M. Gellrich, *The Idea of the Book in the Middle Ages: Language Theory, Mythology, and Fiction* (Ithaca, 1985), and Mary Carruthers, *The Book of Memory: A Study of Memory in Medieval Culture* (Cambridge, 1990).

[135] *Pantheum der aeltesten Naturphilosophie* (Tübingen, 1811), 1. See Erich Neumann, *Johann Arnold Kanne ein vergessener Romantik* (Berlin, [1928]).

[136] Cited by Leventhal, *The Disciplines of Interpretation*, 200.

[137] *Truth and Method*, 156.

Chapter 5

The New Eclecticism

> No other method of philosophizing is more
> reasonable than the Eclectic Method.
>
> J. G. Heineccius

The success of the modern eclectic school of philosophy, declared J. G. H. Feder in 1767, 'was so great that many could not regard anyone as a true philosopher who did not belong to it'.[1] Modern eclecticism was something very different from its ancient namesake, although that name was often taken in vain. For one thing the new eclecticism was developed within a Christian framework, and for another it shunned the irrational and impious 'syncretism' that gave ancient eclecticism such an unfortunate reputation. Modern eclectic philosophy proclaimed not only its freedom from authoritarian and dogmatic thinking but also the superior value of history as the royal road to enlightened piety and learned reason.[2] Both history and philosophy were forms of wisdom (*sapientia*) and so eclecticism was doubly endowed – and bound as well to the study of the history of ideas in its several German, French, and Italian phases.

---

[1] *Grundriss der philosophischen Wissenschaften nebst der nöthigen Geschichte* (Coburg, 1769, 2nd edn), 43.

[2] See the comprehensive study by Michael Albrecht, *Eklektik: Eine Begriffsgeschichte mit Hinweisen auf die Philosophie- und Wissenschaftsgeschichte* (Stuttgart, 1994), with full bibliography, but also the review by Ulrich Johannes Schneider in the *Journal of the History of Ideas*, 59 (1998), 173–82; also Schneider, 'Das Eklektizismus-Problem in der Philosophiegeschicht', in *Johann Jacob Brucker (1696–1770): Philosoph und Historiker der europäischen Aufklärung*, ed. Wilhelm Schmidt-Biggemann and Theo Stamm (Berlin, 1998), 135–58, and Constance Blackwell, 'The Case of Honoré Fabri and the Historiography of Sixteenth Century Jesuit Aristotelianism in Protestant History of Philosophy: Sturm, Morhof, and Brucker', *Nouvelles de la Republique des Lettres* II (1995), 49–77, and D. R. Kelley, 'Eclecticism and the History of Ideas', *Journal of the History of Ideas*, 62 (2001).

1. The Fourth Way

In the sixteenth century there had been essentially three recognized modes of 'philosophizing', hence of envisioning the history of philosophy.[3] First was the dogmatic or sectarian way, requiring adherence to the authority of a single schoolmaster – 'magisterism' – whether ancient, medieval, or modern. The second was some form of syncretism, which attempted to reconcile a number of such authorities on the basis of reason, intuition, or some sort of figurative interpretation. The third was skepticism, which cast doubt on all philosophical opinions, while at the same time drawing on the authority of ancient skeptics such as the Cicero of the *Academica*, the newly available Sextus Empiricus, or the second-hand accounts of Diogenes Laertius.[4]

There was a fourth possibility, however, and this was the 'eclectic' approach to wisdom, which (though overshadowed by modern science and discredited in retrospect) came into prominence in the seventeenth century. In its modern form eclecticism appeared at the confluence of several intellectual movements: the revival of learning, including ancient and patristic philosophy; evangelical religious reform, based on a tradition of spiritual truth that had to be extricated from human error; the 'liberty of philosophizing' (*libertas philosophandi*), a secular extension of the Protestant rejection of dogma; and finally, and intertwined with all of the others, the adoption of critical history as a necessary foundation for understanding. The strength of eclecticism was that it tried to accommodate this entire agenda; its weakness was its less-than-critical faith that these goals were in keeping with reason, the new science, and Christian religion. In any case it was in the scholarly arena occupied by eclecticism that the history of thought and culture was most actively pursued in the early modern period.

The inspiration for this newest of 'new ways' came once again from Diogenes Laertius's *Lives and Opinions*, in which the mysterious Potamon had been briefly described.[5] Early modern scholars repeated and embroidered upon this cryptic passage, usually in the light of Suidas's statement that Potamon lived in the time of Augustus, at least until this error was rejected.[6] Scholars

---

[3] In general see *Cambridge History of Renaissance Philosophy*, ed. C. B. Schmitt, Q. Skinner, E. Kessler, and J. Kraye (Cambridge, 1988), and Brian P. Copenhaver and Charles B. Schmitt, *Renaissance Philosophy* (Oxford, 1992).

[4] See Charles B. Schmitt, *Cicero Scepticus: A Study of the Influence of the* Academica *in the Renaissance* (The Hague, 1972).

[5] See above, Chapter 2.

[6] H. G. Gloecknerus, *De Potamonis Alexandrini Philosophica Eclectica* (Leipzig, [1745]).

also attempted to link Potamon with Plotinus on the basis of an allusion in Porphyry's life of Plotinus. Ficino was found to be wrong in inferring that Potamon had been a pupil of Plotinus, since it was to the latter and not to Potamon (as an eighteenth-century scholar pointed out) that the remark was applied about making one single school out of many.[7] In any case Potamon figured in most surveys of the history of philosophy from the seventeenth century and was often credited with being not merely the founder of a sect but also the creator of an original method (*methodus, modus, ratio,* or *genus philosophandi*).

For some historians, such as Boureau-Deslandes, the open-minded Potamon became a sort of pre-Enlightenment hero. Others of a more rationalist bent, like Diderot in his article on 'Eclecticism' in the *Encyclopédie*, refused him admission into this canon.[8] More severe critics regarded Potamon as just another sectarian, an obscure one at that, and his putative school as no less authoritarian than the others. Refusing to follow a master was a nice idea, wrote Guillaume Maleville,

> But this neat plan was wholly speculative and disappeared almost as soon as it was formed. The pupils of the Eclectic school followed the preferences of their professors just as did those in the Stoic, Epicurean, Peripatetic, and other schools.[9]

If the *locus classicus* of eclecticism was the famous passage in Diogenes Laertius, the *locus modernus* was the *Manductio ad stoicam philosophiam* of Justus Lipsius, which appeared in 1604. In that highly influential work Lipsius rhetorically addressed the eclecticism of Potamon in these terms:

> You finally appeared, O excellent philosophy, and started on the road leading to truth. You arrived and became known too late; you should have come first.[10]

---

[7] *Acta Philosophorum*, II, 332: 'ex multa secta unam faciebat'; and see below at note 76.

[8] Boureau-Deslandes, *Histoire critique de la philosophie* (Amsterdam, 1737), III, 83, and Diderot, 'Eclectisme', in *Œuvres complètes*, ed. Jean Varloot (Paris, 1975), VII, 36–111 (also the article on 'Thomasius, Philosophie de'); Jacques Proust, *Diderot et l'Encyclopédie* (Paris, 1982), ch. 7; also Nelly Schargo, *History in the Encyclopédie* (New York, 1947).

[9] [Maleville], *Histoire critique de l'éclectisme, ou des nouveaux platoniciens* ([Paris], 1766), I, 4; and see Gregorio Piaia, 'Jacob Bruckers Wirkungsgeschichte in Frankreich und Italien', in *Johann Jacob Brucker (1696–1770)*, ed. Schmidt-Biggemann and Stamm, 218–37.

[10] *Manductionis ad Stoicam philosophiam libri tres* (Paris, 1604), fol. 13ᵛ; and see Constance Blackwell (ed. English edn), *Models of the History of Philosophy* (Dordrecht, 1993), 124ff.

Lipsius meant that the method of critical choosing or election should have guided philosophers all along and helped them to avoid dogmatic errors and sectarian disputes. Since this was obviously the case, it remained for historians, according to the 'elective' or 'eclectic' argument, to review philosophical tradition from this critical standpoint.

Following Lipsius, Johann Alsted included the eclectic school in his view of the history of philosophy and went on to declare that the followers of Pico and Ramus enrolled in that school.[11] In this way the opposition between ancient and modern sects could be either joined in an ancient–modern synthesis (*philosophia novantiqua*) or else historicized according to the lights of Renaissance scholarship. From the second quarter of the seventeenth century the term and concept of eclectic philosophy gained currency, as did also the associated idea of the 'liberty of philosophizing', that is, the freedom to choose between philosophical schools.[12] By the end of the century eclecticism, despite disagreements about its nature, had become an essential justification for the history of philosophy and for its claims to be a distinctive 'science'.

The primary task of seventeenth- and eighteenth-century scholars in many disciplines was to organize and to prioritize the learning inherited over two millennia and then to analyze specific problems. This is clear not only from the treatises of major scholars but also from the thousands of dissertations presided over by professors, especially in German universities. These theses, which remain to be explored in any systematic way, defended the methods and the promise of eclectic method. They were also concerned with a wide range of questions and keywords – including *atheismus, historia* (also *historia literaria* and *historia philosophica*), *idea, intellectus, novitates, opinio, praejudicium, ratio, sapientia, scientia,* and *veritas* – which richly illustrate the dissemination of ideas and 'prejudices' of early Enlightenment learning.[13] Eclectic tendencies can be seen in the effort to treat questions in terms both of 'philosophy' and of 'history', including philological discussion of terms, thus joining past erudition of the past with present issues.

To prize bookish eclecticism was not, however, to overlook the premium placed by some philosophers on 'experience' and 'novelty', which were

---

[11] *Thesaurus Chronologiae* (Herborn, 1650 [1624]), 477: 'sectam electivam eligerunt'; see Albrecht, *Eklektik*, 160, and in general Howard Hotson, *Johann Heinrich Alsted: Between Renaissance, Reformation, and Universal Reform* (Oxford, 2000).

[12] For example, Johannes Reinboth (1628), Johann Conrad Dannhauer (1634), Johannes Phocylides (1651), and others discussed in Albrecht, *Eklektik*.

[13] For example, J. C. Sturm (1679), J. Esperus (1695), and A. A. Dysing (1698), and F. Gotter (1730); and in general Hauspeter Marti, *Philosophische Dissertationen deutscher Universitäten* (Munich, 1982).

associated with the lowly 'mechanical arts'. These practical disciplines were excluded in large part from the encyclopedia, although arts such as painting, sculpture, architecture, and (the performing of) music were applying for admission to membership in the society of disciplines graced by intellectual 'method'. But 'experience' meant not merely the accumulation of sense-impressions and knowledge based on practice or history in a Baconian sense; it also referred to the vicarious experience to be found in books (the 'experience of tradition', Gadamer has called it[14]), as even Bacon acknowledged in passing; and 'novelty' implied not merely the serendipitous and the unprecedented, that is, the original creations of the *Novatores*, but also appreciation of the old in contrast to which it claimed innovation. This is where not only eclecticism but also the 'history of literature' (*historia literaria*) came in – and where modernizing philosophers lodged their protest against history.

The accumulation of miscellaneous lists, organized bibliographies, biographical collections, and historiographical accounts of the philosophical tradition, as taught in the universities and in the public domain created by print culture, was essential to the project of eclectic philosophy.[15] Modern eclecticism appeared in the wake of the revival of this 'literature' but only after the principle of authority had been challenged and the 'prejudice of antiquity' overcome – the party of the 'Moderns' achieving parity with that of the 'Ancients', or rather a truce being called between these two old combatants.

Freedom from intellectual servitude or myopia was a founding principle of eclecticism, as expressed in the aforementioned slogan, the 'liberty of philosophizing'.[16] This was a view associated with the anti-authoritarian attitudes of Renaissance humanists like Valla, Pico, and Erasmus, who rejected the notion of 'Magister dixit' in favor of the old Horatian motto, 'I am not bound over to swear as any master dictates', according to the endlessly repeated maxim of Horace.[17] For Erasmus the Pythagorean 'Ipse dixit', which migrated from oracular discourse into common speech, was altogether too

---

[14] *Truth and Method*, trans. Garrett Barden and John Cumming (New York, 1982), 321ff.

[15] See above, Chapter 3, note 25.

[16] Albrecht, *Eklektik*, 235.

[17] *Epistulae*, 1.1.14, 'non jurare in verba magistri'. See Capasso, *Historiae philosophiae synopsis* (Naples, 1728), 165; also Wilhelm Schmidt-Biggemann, *Theodizee und Tatsachen: Das philosophisches Profil der deutschen Aufklärung* (Frankfurt, 1988), 203; Paul Dibon, *La Philosophie néerlandaise au siècle d'or* (Paris, 1954); Robert B. Sutton, 'The Phrase Libertas Philosophandi', *Journal of the History of Ideas*, 14 (1953), 310–16; and Albrecht, *Eklektik*, 112ff.

close to the biblical 'Thus saith the Lord.'[18] In his campaign to reform Aristotelian dialectic Peter Ramus also pursued this quest for 'philosophical liberty', claiming membership in the *secta veritatis* – 'the sect not of Aristotle, of Plato, or of any man, but only of truth'.[19]

In this sense eclecticism was not a mere accumulation of knowledge or even a reconciliation of doctrines but rather, according to its own lights, a method of separating truth from opinion and falsehood, science from superstition, and so a process of intellectual enlightenment and human progress. Intellectual tradition was thus seen as a sort of Dantean Comedy of Ideas, founded on the premise of free will, with Criticism leading Erudition from the depths of Error through many levels of Opinion and Prejudice to the highest reaches of Wisdom, that is, the final 'critical' Philosophy.[20] Along the way the student, or reader, would be introduced to the major figures of pagan and Christian thought, who are judged and given appropriate places in the account, with the most blessed and celebrated philosophers appearing before the culminating vision – although this vision, unlike the final scene of Dante's *Commedia*, was situated in the future and given rational rather than mystical form.

This in any case was the attitude toward authority taken over by followers of Luther, associated with his resistance to ecclesiastical authority, joined to encyclopedic erudition, assimilated to the aims of eclectic philosophy, and reinforced by the familiar classical tags from Horace, Cicero, and Seneca and by the standard biblical text (1 Thessalonians 5: 21): 'Prove all things; hold fast that which is good.'[21] It was the story passed down by modern scholars and summarized in canonical form in J. B. Brucker's *Critical History of Philosophy*. Intellectual history is by no means adequately described by this narrative; but it has evolved within the conceptual and chronological framework associated with the doxographical tradition leading from Diogenes Laertius to modern historians of philosophy like Horn and given legitimacy by eclectic and encyclopedic interpretations.

---

[18] *Adages*, trans. R. A. B. Mynors, II, v, 82, in *Collected Works*, XXXIII (Toronto, 1991), 279.

[19] *Animadversiones Aristotelicae* (Paris, 1543), 30ʳ.

[20] Werner Schneiders, *Aufklärung und Vorurteilskritik: Studien zur Geschichte der Vorurteilstheorie* (Stuttgart, 1983).

[21] *Omnia autem probate: quod bonum est tenete*; the Vulgate has *quod donum est* ('what is given') instead of *quod bonum est*. See Albrecht, *Eklektik*, 57ff., *passim*.

2. The Eclectic Turn

In the seventeenth century 'eclecticism' became a word to conjure with, though its meaning was seldom clear. In 1631 G. J. Vossius described how, as a young student, he had served successive philosophical apprenticeships under the Aristotelians, Platonists, Stoics, and Epicureans; and he concluded, 'Clearly, I have become an eclectic.'[22] In the last years of his life Vossius continued to defend the value of ancient eclecticism (*secta electiva ... sive electrix*), which had acknowledged the weakness of human understanding, as a permanent condition of philosophizing, and urged that it pointed the way to wisdom. On the potential of eclecticism in an age of confessional strife and destruction he speculated in these terms:

> How would it be in the future if we should be not [followers of] Ionic philosophers, or Italians, Eleatics, Platonists, or Peripatetics, not Stoics, Epicureans, Skeptics, or any other such sects, but all of these?[23]

This was one cornerstone of the new eclectic school, which seldom omitted to look back to its ancient antecedents.[24] Twenty years later Thomas Gale, whose project was 'to make an universal Inquisition into all Opinions', associated the new 'reformed philosophy' with the ancient 'Eclectic sect', which included 'those most distinguished men Potamon, Plutarch, Ammonius Saccus, and Plotinus, and others of this "golden succession" (*Aurea successionis*) that joined pagan wisdom and Christian truth'.[25]

Modern eclecticism took its point of departure from the liberation of scholars from dependency on one sectarian view. Yet it also bound them in a sense to tradition, since one of its premises was the belief that truth was the

---

[22] 'Nempe eclecticus factus sum', cited by C. S. M. Rademaker, *Life and Works of Gerardus Joannes Vossius (1577–1649)* (Assen, 1981), 30.

[23] *De Philosophia et philosophorum secta* (The Hague, 1658), 117; and see Rademaker, *Life and Works*.

[24] See Albrecht, *Eklektik*; Wilhelm Schmidt-Biggemann, *Topica Universalis: Eine Modellgeschichte humanistischer und barocker Wissenschaft* (Hamburg, 1983); Helmut Holzhey, 'Philosophie als Eklektik', *Studia Leibnitiana*, 15 (1983), 19–29; Werner Schneiders, 'Vernünftiger Zweifel und wahre Eklektik: Zur Entstehung des modernen Kritikbegriffes', *Studia Leibnitiana*, 17 (1985), 142–61; Horst Dreitzel, 'Zur Entwicklung und Eigenart "Eklektischen Philosophie"', *Zeitschrift für historische Forschung*, 18 (1991), 281–343; and Timothy Hochstrasser, *The Natural Law Tradition and the Historiography of Moral Philosophy in the Enlightenment* (dissertation, Cambridge University, 1990).

[25] *Philosophia generalis, in duas partes determinata. Una de Ortu et progressu philosophiae ejusque Traductione e Sacris Fontibus* (London, 1676), 9.

product not of individual but of collective effort. According to Francis Bacon (who was admitted posthumously into the eclectic canon), 'The perfection of the sciences is to be looked for not from the swiftness and ability of one inquirer; but from a succession.'[26] This assumption owed something not only to the Baconian program of cooperative research but also to the skeptical view of individual genius. As Francisco Sánches had asked,

> But, after all those great men, what fresh contribution can *you* possibly make? Was Truth waiting for *you* to come upon the scene?[27]

This intellectual humility also entailed examining philosophical error, so that wisdom could be distinguished from falsity – *sapientia* from *stultitia*; *Weisheit* from *Narrheit* – as historians of theology had long done and as historians of philosophy (and historians of the history of philosophy) would continue to do.[28] For all these reasons history was given a privileged position in the study of philosophy, in accordance with the axiom that there could be no valid philosophy without the history thereof. Thus the aim of eclecticism was to join the old, unreflective, doxographical tradition with the scientific search for truth in order to give philosophical legitimacy to the history of philosophy – and, conversely, historical legitimacy to the practice of philosophy.

In this quest not only for certainty and truth but also for historical knowledge of error, neither philology nor doxography was any longer adequate; and scholars looked for conceptual depth and scientific validity as well as scholarly precision in philosophy. The foremost among these was Leibniz, who was an *érudit* as well as an advocate of the new science. Leibniz seemed to find this combination in the work of his own mentor, Jakob Thomasius, who taught dialectic and rhetoric at the University of Leipzig and whose essay on the history of philosophy appeared in 1665.[29] Thomasius's work marked a departure from doxographical convention. 'Most of the others are skilled

---

[26] *De Sapientia veterum*, 'Prometheus', in *Works*, II, 654. In general see Steven Shapin, *A Social History of Truth: Civility and Science in Seventeenth-Century England* (Chicago, 1994).

[27] *That Nothing is Known*, ed. and trans. E. Limbrick and D. Thomson (Cambridge, 1988), 169.

[28] See Martial Gueroult, *Histoire de l'histoire de la philosophie*, I (Paris, 1984), 87, and *Zwischen Narretei und Weisheit*, ed. Gerald Hartung and Wolf Peter Klein (Hildesheim, 1997), from Plotinus to William Hamilton.

[29] *Schediasma Historicum* (Leipzig, 1665); also *Dissertationes ad Stoicae philosophiae et caeteram Philosophicam Historiam facientes argumenti varii* (Leipzig, 1682); and see Giovanni Santinello et al. (eds), *Storia delle storie generali della filosofia*, I, Dalle origini rinascimentali alla 'historia philosofica' (Brescia, 1981), I, 409.

rather in antiquity than in science and have given us lives rather than doctrines', Leibniz wrote in his famous letter to Thomasius in 1669.[30] 'You will give us the history of philosophy, not of philosophers.' What Thomasius would do, too, was to teach the younger generation 'that it is wrong to give our moderns credit either for everything or for nothing'; for such had been the inclination of Bodin, Nizolius, Galileo, Bacon, Hobbes, Descartes, and other egoistical, dogmatic, or innovationist thinkers, 'among whom', added Leibniz, 'the mantle of philosophy is being torn apart'.

The elder Thomasius identified philosophy with the whole 'circle of learning' preserved in the encyclopedic tradition;[31] but he did not embrace this learning uncritically. Like Arnold and other historians of religion, he looked at both sides of the doctrinal coin – the 'history of error' as well as 'history of wisdom' – and indeed he was praised by Leibniz for correcting misconceptions of philosophical tradition.[32] In accord both with Lutheran doctrine and with his own discriminating sense of history, Thomasius insisted on separating philosophy from the higher truths of Christianity; for him the main source of error was the failure to preserve this distinction. This had been the trouble with Gnosticism and the ideas associated with the false Hermes Trismegistus ('Pseudo-Mercurius'), with medieval scholastics and mystics, and with the specious 'conciliatory' interpretations of Steuco, Postel, Lipsius, and Gassendi. This lesson was not lost on Leibniz, who later remarked, 'We cannot judge Plato's teachings by Plotinus or Marsilio Ficino, for they have perverted his fundamental doctrine in their scurryings after the miraculous and the mystical.'[33]

In his pioneering interpretations of western philosophy Thomasius described the chief schools in terms of their concepts of God and nature but rejected attempts to Christianize these ancient doctrines and looked with suspicion on the idea of the 'liberty of philosophizing' associated with such innovators as

---

[30] Preface (20/30 April 1669) to Nizolio, *De Veris principis et vera ratione philosophandi contra pseudophilosophos libri IV* (Frankfurt, 1680), fol. 2ᵛ ('non philosophorum, sed philosophiae historia'); also in *Philosophical Papers and Letters*, trans. Leroy E. Loemker (Dordrecht, 1969), 93. For Leibniz's and Thomasius's exchanges on the history of philosophy see *Leibniz–Thomasius: Correspondence 1663–1672*, ed. and trans. Richard Bodéüs (Paris, 1993).

[31] *Schediasma*, 3: 'Philosophia vocabulum, quo totum alias artium nostrarum circulum designamus ... '

[32] Martin Pott, 'Christian Thomasius und Gottfried Arnold', in *Gottfried Arnold (1666–1714)*, ed. Dietrich Blaufuss and Friedrich Niewöhner (Wiesbaden, 1995), 247–65.

[33] Letter to Remond (10 January 1714), cited in Ernst Cassirer, *The Platonic Renaissance in England*, trans. James P. Pettegrove (Austin, 1953), 154.

Grotius, Bacon, Descartes, and Hobbes. His own preference was for the true and 'reformed' Aristotle; and in good Lutheran fashion he was most critical of the perverted Aristotelianism of the scholastics. Aristotle's 'being as being' (*ens quatenus ens*), for example, referred not, pantheistically, to the divine Creator, as later scholars argued, but to his Creation; for 'God is not being but above being.'[34] Syncretism was not history, argued Thomasius: 'Nothing more viciously corrupts our history of philosophy than efforts to conciliate Plato, Aristotle, Stoic, and other pagans with Christian faith.'[35] For Thomasius such corrupting modernizers (*novantiqui*, or *novatiores*, as he called them) were worse than skeptics and libertines.

Over the next two generations the teaching of the elder Thomasius was extraordinarily influential, not only through the work of Leibniz but also through his son, Christian Thomasius, who published some of his father's works in *Historia Sapientiae et Stultitiae* (1693), and the editions of his works appearing in the *Acta Eruditorum*. It is ironic that these two pupils both continued the efforts to 'reconcile' ancient and modern philosophy – although by 'modern' they meant the 'reformed philosophy' of Lutheran tradition.

What the elder Thomasius had accomplished was a negative task of historical, or conceptual, emendation; and it was the following generation, still employing historical methods, that proposed to shift from preoccupation with error to a quest for truth. In retrospect scholars saw in this shift the makings of a new school, which by the end of the seventeenth century assumed the name of 'eclectic'. Among other adherents of this school, or at least conspicuous employers of the term – *verbum* if not *res* – were J. C. Sturm, J. F. Buddeus, C. A. Heumann, Nicolas Gundling, J. G. Heineccius, Ephraim Gerhard, Arnold Wesenfeld, Giambattista Capasso, Brucker, and their students in many dissertations written in the late seventeenth and early eighteenth centuries.[36]

Just as there were eclectics *ante litteram*, so there were eclectics *sine titulo*. Parallel lines of argument were pursued by Jean-Baptiste Du Hamel, member of the Oratory, professor at the Collège Royal, and author of *De Consensu*

---

[34] *Schediasma*, 11: *Deum non esse ens sed super ens.*

[35] *Dissertationes ad Stoicae philosophiae et caeteram Philosophicam Historiam facientes argumenti varii*, 22.

[36] On all these see the comprehensive work of Santinello, *Storia*, I (with updated bibliography), and more recently, Ulrich Schneider, 'Eclecticism and the History of Philosophy', in *History and the Disciplines: The Reclassification of Knowledge in Early Modern Europe*, ed. D. R. Kelley (Rochester, 1997), 83–102, and Martin Mulsow, 'Gundling and Buddeus: Competing Models of the History of Philosophy', in ibid., 103–26.

veteris et novae philosophiae (1663); Adrian Heereboord, who viewed the history of philosophy from the standpoint of a 'Cartesian scholastic' in his *Meletemata philosophica* (1664); and Abraham de Grau, Dutch teacher of philosophy and author of a *Historia philosophica* (1674). Heereboord defended the 'liberty of philosophizing' and emphasized the variety and variability of philosophy;[37] Grau, celebrating the relighting of the torch of philosophy, argued that Descartes's method of doubt was in no way superior to that of Aristotle and was indeed part of scholastic tradition;[38] and Du Hamel tried to reconcile not only Plato and Aristotle but also Epicurus, Descartes, and others.[39] For Du Hamel philosophy was a family affair devoted not to quarrels but to its proper object, the human mind (*mens humana*) and its creations, including especially the Platonic 'ideas'.

As in the case of the ideas and influence of Potamon, there has been a debate among modern scholars about the definition of and the doctrinal reality behind the term 'eclectic'. Indeed it was one of the features of the terminology of eclecticism that it was widely praised or denounced with little concern for precision.[40] It is difficult, historically and philosophically, to distinguish eclecticism as a method (beyond simple declarations of independence from philosophical authority) from old-fashioned syncretism; and indeed it is only in retrospect (and by employing retrospective logic) that we can discriminate between arguments for 'concord' and historical synthesis. Leibniz himself, at this point, was studying the history of philosophy to reinforce his own conciliatory views, first following Ciceronian Mario Nizolio, who had sought 'the true method of philosophizing [directed] against the pseudo-philosophers', and employing the same sort of optimistic syncretism underlying the Protestant Aristotelianism established by the efforts of the 'Preceptor of Germany', Melanchthon, and other reformers of German religion and education (which also informed Leibniz's hope for religious pacification). 'In fact', Leibniz went on in his letter to Thomasius (published as a preface to

---

[37] *Selectarum ex philosophia disputationum* (Leiden, 1650), 750; cf. *Meletemata philosophica* (Nijmegen, 1664); and see Santinello, *Storia*, I, 211.

[38] *Specimen philosophiae veteris* (Franeker, 1673), 'praefatio'; and see Blackwell, *Models*, I, 259.

[39] *Philosophia vetus et nova ad usum scholae* (Paris, 1684), 48; and see Santinello, *Storia*, II, 22.

[40] Albrecht, *Eklektik*, 18ff., makes a distinction between eclectic philosophers defined by a principle of methodological selection (*Auswahl-Eklektiker*) and those defined by doctrinal independence (*Selbständigkeit-Eklektiker*); but this nice distinction, more theoretical or rhetorical than practical, was not honored in the early modern period, when eclectics were steering between the extremes of dogmatism and skepticism in the dangerous waters of religious controversy.

his edition of Nizolio's work), 'I venture to add that the whole of Aristotle's eight books can be accepted without injury to the reformed philosophy' (*philosophia reformata*).[41]

Although Thomasius disagreed with this flexible (and unhistorical) position, it was quite in keeping with Protestant Aristotelianism – Melanchthon if not Luther himself – that had flourished in German universities since the Reformation. Leibniz made his own 'choice of canons' from the history of philosophy and, in his criticism of Locke, stationed himself in the Platonic line because of his belief in innate ideas, while Locke was assigned to Aristotelian tradition for his materialist position on this crucial issue.[42] So historical perspective and conciliatory attitudes collaborated to accommodate these two rivals to ancient tradition (in opposition to the innovationist rhetoric of modern philosophy) – and indeed medieval tradition, too; for as Charles Schmitt remarked, 'Protestant Aristotelians were influenced by Catholic ones, but not vice versa.'[43]

In this connection an important parallel to the history of philosophy should be noted; and that is the history of law, which also claimed to be a form of wisdom (*rerum divinarum humanarumque notitia*) and which had long followed its own 'eclectic' road, sifting through authorities in the search for truth – or at least defensible and 'common' (that is, by majority) opinion. The 'new' or 'reformed' jurisprudence, like its philosophical counterpart, centering first in France and then in the Netherlands and Germany, based its method not only on ancient civil law and later commentators but also on the other parts of the encyclopedia, including philology, rhetoric, history, and philosophy; and like philosophy and theology, it encountered ideas of 'naturalism', especially in the form of modern natural law (*jus naturale*).

Among the historians of philosophy, the younger Thomasius, Leibniz, and J. G. Heineccius were also jurists who wrote, also eclectically, on jurisprudence; and both Thomasius and Heineccius published editions of the work of François Baudouin, who in 1561 (under the influence of Melanchthon) first promoted an alliance between the art of history and the science of law as well as reconciliation between Huguenots and Catholics.[44] By many of its practitioners 'civil science' was regarded as a form of wisdom, which was defined by jurists and philosophers alike as the 'knowledge of things divine and human' – and

---

[41] Preface, 77.

[42] See Nicholas Jolly, *Leibniz and Locke: A Study of the New Essays on Human Understanding* (Oxford, 1984), 6.

[43] *Aristotle and the Renaissance* (Cambridge, MA, 1983), 28.

[44] D. R. Kelley, *Foundations of Modern Historical Scholarship* (New York, 1970), ch. 3.

which, for historians of law, subsumed, since it was prior to, 'philosophy'.[45] These attitudes were reflected, for example, in Christian Thomasius's *History of Natural Law* (1619), which presented a survey, parallel to the history of philosophy and likewise based on natural reason, from barbaric times down to the seventeenth century.

The common historical interpretation of eclecticism can be inferred from the Leipzig dissertation of Roman Teller of 1674, which treated the name and the tradition of what was taken to be an ancient sect comparable to Aristotelianism or Platonism.[46] Drawing on the work of Lipsius, Heinsius (edition of Horace, 1610), Horn, and Vossius, and invoking the tell-tale topoi of doctrinal liberty (*nullius jurare*, and so on), Teller recognized the foundational achievement of Potamon, while admitting into this school Cicero, Horace, Clement of Alexandria, Origen, and others. Thus the genealogy of modern eclecticism was established, and its academic legitimacy affirmed. In the end eclecticism did not come to prevail even in Germany; but it supplied an alternative to the old and new schools. Moreover, it remained an issue for another century and more, and down to the time of Cousin it continued to maintain the role of history in philosophy.

3. Christian Thomasius

By the last quarter of the seventeenth century the eclectic method – or at least the vocabulary and rhetoric of 'eclecticism' in its modern sense – was evident in the study not only of philosophy but also of law and theology. The first major work to display the label was that of J. C. Sturm, professor of natural philosophy at Altdorf, whose thesis, *De Philosophia sectaria et electiva*, was published in 1697.[47] Rejecting sectarian 'prejudice' as well as the 'serpent of atheism', Sturm proposed to apply the eclectic method praised by Vossius to physical science. Unlike Vossius, however, Sturm distinguished modern eclecticism from the uncritical practices of Potamon and other ancients, Christian as well as pagan, and associated it rather with the advice of Bacon, who warned against a premature formulation of 'method'. It was most likely through Sturm that Christian Thomasius turned to this new eclectic method

---

[45] D. R. Kelley, 'Vera Philosophia: The Philosophical Significance of Renaissance Jurisprudence', *Journal of the History of Philosophy*, 14 (1976), 267–79.

[46] *Disputationem de Philosophia Eclectica* (Leipzig, 1674), on which see Albrecht, *Eklektik*, 302ff.

[47] J. C. Sturm, *Philosophia sectaria et electiva* (Nürnberg, 1697).

and, because of his more prominent position, gained a reputation as a founding figure of modern eclecticism – 'der erste Eklectische Philosophus in Deutschland', he was called by J. G. Walch.[48]

Christian Thomasius, according to Diderot (following Brucker), has a place 'among the reformers of philosophy and the founders of a revived eclecticism'.[49] Drawing not only on the teachings of his father and Leibniz, but also on the methods of the legal tradition and on his Lutheran upbringing, Thomasius – 'the Gottfried Arnold of philosophy' – had brought his ideas to the new University of Halle, which he helped to establish in 1694.[50] In the judgment of Brucker he was the one who 'introduced eclectic freedom into the German schools'. He was, if not head of the eclectic school (*eclectica philosophia*; *Wahl-Philosophie*), then at least the major representative of an eclectic method which sought a middle way between Aristotelianism and Cartesianism and proposed to liberate secular thought without discarding the riches of philosophical tradition.[51] For these reasons he is still widely recognized as a founder of the Enlightenment – although his was the conservative *Aufklärung* of pious German scholars, not the radical, free-thinking, and allegedly pagan *Lumières* of the French *philosophes*.[52]

---

[48] *Philophisches Lexicon* (Leipzig, 1740), 163; and on the vocabulary of eclectic philosophy, German as well as Latin, see Dagmar von Wille (ed.), *Lessico filosofico della Frühaufklärung: Christian Thomasius, Christian Wolff, Johann Georg Walch* (Rome, 1991).

[49] *Œuvres complètes*, XIV (Paris, 1972), 892: 'éclectisme renouvelé'.

[50] Pott, 'Christian Thomasius und Gottfried Arnold'; and see Klaus Deppermann, *Der hallesche Pietismus und der preussische Staat unter Friedrich III* (Göttingen, 1961); Carl Hinrichs, *Preussentum und Pietismus* (Göttingen, 1971); Wilhelm Schrader, *Geschichte der Friedrichs-Universität zu Halle* (Berlin, 1894); Notker Hammerstein, *Jus und Historie: Ein Beitrag zur Geschichte des historischen Denkens in deutschen Universitäten im späten 17. und in 18. Jahrhundert* (Göttingen, 1972); F. Ernest Stoeffler, *German Pietism during the Eighteenth Century* (Leiden, 1973), *August Hermann Francke: Das humanistische Erbe des grossen Erziehers* (Halle, 1965); and T. J. Hochstrasser, *Natural Law Theories in the Enlightenment* (Cambridge, 2000).

[51] Thomasius's first reference to eclecticism appears in a letter to Pufendorf in 1678; see K. Varrentrapp, 'Briefe von Pufendorf', *Historisches Zeitschrift*, 70 (1893), 31.

[52] See Werner Schneiders (ed.), *Christian Thomasius 1655–1728* (Hamburg, 1989), including Hans-Jürgen Engfer, 'Christian Thomasius. Erste Proklamation und erste Krise der Aufklärung in Deutschland', 21–36; Helmut Holzhey, 'Initiiert Thomasius einen neuen Philosophentypus?', 37–51; Michael Albrecht, 'Thomasius – kein Eklektiker?', 73–94; Luigi Cataldi Madonna, 'Wissenschafts- und Wahrscheinlichkeitsauffassung bei Thomasius', 115–36; Martin Pott, 'Thomasius' philosophischer Glaube', 223–47; and Frank Grunert, 'Bibliographie der Thomasius-Literatur 1945–1988', 335–55; also Schneiders, *Naturrecht und Liebesethik: Zur Geschichte des*

Religion was the key to Thomasius's view of the history of thought. Like his father and Leibniz, he worked within a Lutheran framework; and to this was added the impulse of pietism, centered in the University of Halle, the first Lutheran university in the territories of Frederick III, Elector of Brandenburg and later king of (or 'in') Prussia.[53] Thomasius was himself an early defender of A. H. Francke and P. J. Spener, pietist leaders who had fled from the intolerance of Leipzig. The 'Halle movement' in Germany, which acquired the support of King Frederick William I of Prussia, was centered on a religious sort of wisdom (*christliche Klugheit*); but eclectic philosophy, which likewise sought to reconstruct a spiritual tradition leading away from dogma and toward the truth, was given impetus along with pietism and borrowed some of its moral credit.

Thomasius was deeply affected by this movement, and after 1693 he turned away from the naturalistic attitudes he derived from Sturm to the more spiritualist convictions of pietism, especially that of his colleague Buddeus, professor of theology. Thomasius was no less opposed to skepticism than to dogmatism (to pagan error than to Catholic doctrine), and the philosophical 'liberty' he recommended was the counterpart to the religious 'liberty' of his confessional tradition. As Heumann wrote in his *Acta Philosoporum*, 'What Luther did in the reformation of theology, Herr Thomasius did in the reformation of philosophy.'[54]

Yet unlike Luther, Thomasius did not take his stand on conscience; nor did he believe that human truth could be attained by a single clear-thinking individual – even geniuses like Galileo, Descartes, or Luther himself. Rather, and more like Luther's disciple Melanchthon, Thomasius emphasized a long-standing doctrinal and 'spiritual' tradition rooted in patristic and even pagan antiquity. For Thomasius, as for Vossius, philosophy was a collective enterprise not reducible to the teaching of one author or separable from learned tradition

---

praktischen Philosophie in Hinblick auf Christian Thomasius (Hildesheim, 1971), and 'Vernunft und Freiheit: Christian Thomasius als Aufklärer', *Studia Leibnitiana*, 11 (1979), 3–21; Max Fleishmann (ed.), *Christian Thomasius: Leben und Lebenswerk* (Halle, 1931); Rolf Liebeswirth, *Christian Thomasius: Sein wissenschaftliches Lebenswerk* (Weimar, 1955); Henrich Rüping, *Die Naturrechtslehre des Christian Thomasius und ihre Forbildung in der Thomasius-Schule* (Bonn, 1968); Hammerstein, *Jus und Historie*; Max Wundt, *Die deutsche Schulphilosophie im Zeitalter der Aufklärung* (Tübingen, 1945); and F. M. Barnard, 'The "Practical Philosophy" of Christian Thomasius', *Journal of the History of Ideas*, 32 (1971), 221–46.

[53] See Wolfgang Martens, 'Hallesches Pietismus und Gelehrsamkeit oder vom allzu grossen Misstrauen in die Wissenschaften', in *Respublica Literaria*, ed. S. Neumeister and C. Wiedemann (Wiesbaden, 1987), II, 496–523.

[54] *Acta Philosophorum*, I, 567. See below.

and a succession of teachers. 'I call eclectic philosophy', he wrote in his *Introductio ad philosophiam aulicam* (*Einleitung zur Hoff-Philosophie*) in 1688, 'not what depends on the teaching of an individual or on the acceptance of the words of a master, but whatever can be known from the teaching and writing of any person on the basis not of authority but of convincing arguments.'[55]

For this reason philosophy and logic (*Vernunftslehre*) were inseparable from the historical dimension in which they were situated – though not from the parallel history of theology to which Thomasius's friend was devoted. For him the key was the alliance between history and philosophy. 'History and philosophy are the two eyes of wisdom', he argued. 'If one is missing, then one has only half vision' (*einäugy*).[56] The results of this alliance were to give both philosophical legitimacy to history and historical legitimacy to the practice of philosophy. As Thomasius wrote,

> Philosophy is the history of the origin and progress of human wisdom and error considered apart from divine revelation. This philosophical history is in a certain way more comprehensive than ecclesiastical history, since it shows that the origin of errors in natural philosophy and civil prudence is a necessary part of ecclesiastical history ... [57]

Thus the history of practical knowledge (*Gelahrheit*) formed the substructure of wisdom (*Weisheit*, or *Weltweisheit*) and was essential to overcome that nemesis of reason – 'prejudice' (analogous to 'dogma' rather than 'heresy') – whether scholastic, Cartesian, Hobbesian, or any other sectarian doctrine, all of which Thomasius shunned.[58]

Did Thomasius represent a 'new type' of philosopher? Some of his admirers think so, partly because (beginning in 1687) he shifted from Latin to the German language and partly because of his emphasis on practical rather than theoretical philosophy (connected in part with his teaching of jurisprudence)

---

[55] *Introductio ad philosophiam aulicam* (Leipzig, 1688), translated as *Einleitung zur Hoff-Philosophie* (Berlin, 1712), following the lead of Armand de Gerard, *La Philosophie des gens de court* (Paris, 1680). See Wundt, *Aufklärung*, 19; Hammerstein, *Jus und Historie*, 53, and Paola Zambelli, *La formazione filosofica di Antonio Genovesi* (Naples, 1972), 386.

[56] *Cautelae circa Praecognita jurisprudentiae in usum auditorii Thomasiani* (Halle, 1710), 84, cited by Schmidt-Biggemann, *Topica Universalis*, 283.

[57] Thomasius, *Introductio*, and see *Einleitung zur Vernunft-Lehre* (Halle, 1691; repr. Hildesheim, 1968).

[58] 'De Praejudiciis oder von den Vorurteilung', in F. Bruggemann (ed.), *Aus der Frühzeit der deutschen Aufklärung* (Leipzig, 1938), 30; and see Schneiders, *Aufklärung und Vorurteilskritik*, and von Wille, *Lessico filosofico della Frühaufklärung*, 138–40.

and public service rather than private speculation. Thomasius's father had distinguished between the philosopher and the political man (*philosophus* and *politicus*),[59] and the son represented his own approach as that of a courtier or public person – *philosophiam aulica* or *Hoff-Philosophie* are his terms. Although he revered the tradition of learning, he had, like many eclectics, contempt for 'pedantry' (*Pedantismus*; *Pedanterey*) and the indulgences of the mere *savant*, the *littérateur, literatus*, the closeted scholar without experience of the world.[60]

Thomasius was joined by others in pursuing this eclectic line of argument, among them Arnold Wesenfeld in his essays on 'sectarian and eclectic philosophy' (1694).[61] Referring to the views of Keckermann and Bacon that not only states but also disciplines went through stages, Wesenfeld wrote, 'Not only cities, empires, nations, and families but also philosophical concepts [*res philosophia*] have their fortunes' – an allusion to the famous aphorism that 'books have their fortunes'.[62] This, too, was a premise of eclecticism. With the usual bows to canonical figures like Potamon and Lipsius (as well as Vossius, Heereboord, and Sturm) Wesenfeld likewise asserted the 'liberty of philosophizing' which would lead to doctrinal peace (*pax philosophiae*) and an end to the threats posed by skepticism, naturalism, Manichaeism, Spinozism, probabilism, atheism, and other subversive counterparts of ancient heresies. Wesenfeld contrasted the 'rationality' of the eclectic method with the 'prejudices' of Descartes, but on the whole he was more favorable to Bacon's view of the 'advancement of learning'. For Wesenfeld, eclecticism drew on both the observation of nature and the writings of others (*natura et scripta eruditorum*), and it depended on the support (as Johann Sturm had also noted) of a 'society of scholars' (*societas litterarum*) in Germany, Italy, France, England, the Netherlands, and elsewhere. 'Eclecticism', as a later scholar observed, 'is the only sect, or non-sect, that can survive in an academy.'[63]

---

[59] *Schediasma*, 2.

[60] Emilio Bonfatti, 'Vir Aulicus, Vir Eruditus', in *Respublica Litteraria*, ed. Neumeister and Wiedemann, I, 175–91, and Leonard Forster, '"Charlatanerie eruditorum" zwischen Barok und Aufklärung in Deutschland', ibid., I, 203–20.

[61] Arnold Wesenfeld, *Dissertationes philosophicae quatuor materiae selectioris de philosophia sectaria et electiva* (Frankfurt, 1694); and see Albrecht, *Eklektik*, 387ff., and Ulrich Schneider, 'Über den philosophischen Eklektizismus', *Nach der Postmoderne*, ed. Andreas Steffens (Düsseldorf, 1992).

[62] Ibid., 23: 'Habent enin non tantum urbes, imperia, gentes, familiae, sed et res philosophicae sua fata et incrementa, decrementa ... '

[63] Christian Bartholmèss, *Histoire philosophique de l'Académie de Prusse depuis Leibniz jusqu'à Schelling* (Paris, 1850), II, 63.

Thus, eclecticism projected philosophy across the Republic of Letters both backward and forward in time, joining Ancients, Moderns, and Posterity (including post-Moderns) in a continuous and worldwide intellectual pilgrimage toward enlightenment. Another strength of eclecticism was that it served utility as well as truth by accommodating ideas to the spirit of particular times and places (*ad genus seculi et locorum*). As an anonymous author put it in a work on *The Lives of the Ancient Philosophers* (1702) based on Stanley's work,

> This method, as I take it, is preferable to that of culling one General Systeme of philosophy out of all their writings, and to quoting them by scraps scattered here and there.[64]

Perhaps the most comprehensive treatment of the subject was that of Thomasius's younger colleague at Halle, J. F. Buddeus, Professor of Moral Philosophy (another sub-specialty of philosophy, overlapping in some ways with the law, that claimed autonomy). Buddeus's *Elements of Instrumental Philosophy* (1714 [1697]) surveyed philosophical history from its poetical origins down to the 'new body of philosophy'. Like Leibniz and Thomasius, Buddeus emphasized the work of the humanist reformers of dialectic (including Valla, Agricola, Vives, Melanchthon, and Nizolius) in rescuing philosophy from the 'Scholastic yoke' and in forming a philosophical method based on a critical reading of earlier writers.[65] For Buddeus, eclectic 'methodology' was inseparable from questions of language and the interpretation of texts; and it was for this reason that he presented it as a form of 'hermeneutics'.[66]

This line of argument formed another connection with Lutheran theology: 'The Protestant pastor', remarked Nietzsche, 'is the grandfather of German philosophy.'[67] One specific link was the theory of interpretation (*ars hermeneutica*, as Dannhauer, Leibniz, and others had termed it),[68] which had been inaugurated by the Lutheran theologian Flacius Illyricus as a way of

---

[64] *The Lives of the Ancient Philosophers* (1702), preface.
[65] J. F. Buddeus, *Elementa philosophiae instrumentalis* [1697] (Halle, 1714), 'philosophandi ratio verum ex aliorum scripta'; also *Compendium historiae philosophicae* (Halle, 1731), and *Historia juris civilis* (Halle, 1704); and see Serenella Masi, 'Eclettismo e storia della filosofia nel Johann Franz Budde', *Filosofia e storia della filosofia* (Turin, 1977), 163–212, and Santinello, *Storia*, II, 373.
[66] *Elementa*, 177.
[67] *Twilight of the Idols*, trans. R. J. Holingdale (New York, 1968), 121.
[68] Dannhauer, *Idea Boni Interpretis et malitiosi calumniatoris* (Strasbourg, 1630), 4; and see D. R. Kelley, 'Civil Science in the Renaissance: The Problem of Interpretation', in *The Languages of Political Theory in Early Modern Europe*, ed. A. Pagden (Cambridge, 1987), 57–78.

discerning the spirit of truth behind the letter of scripture.[69] In a methodological climate dominated by logic and mathematical proof, the process of interpretation was all but discredited among philosophers; but it was at least marginally preserved for purposes of historical and probable knowledge which was the concern of Buddeus's 'methodology'.[70]

Another champion of eclecticism was J. G. Heineccius, who was a polyhistor and professor of law at Halle and who surveyed in these terms the history both of law and of philosophy. Heineccius gave further shape to eclecticism by prescribing five methodological rules (*leges*), counterparts to Descartes's skeptical (though in their own way dogmatic) rules of reasoning. First, propositions should all be demonstrated and given proper order and then distinctions made; second, irrelevancies should be avoided (confusing law with moral philosophy, for example, as Cicero had done, or with theology, as the scholastics had done); third, in the spirit of Arnoldian nonpartisanship, contemporary controversies should not be introduced (for example, Protestants versus Catholics); fourth, discussions should be brief and concise (especially in teaching); and fifth, the actual words of authors should not be used, unless particularly eloquent or weighty.[71]

In this way 'true philosophy' could be distilled from philosophical or legal tradition, and natural law could receive the warrant of history as well as reason. Ancient and modern philosophy undoubtedly contained many errors as well as truths, he admitted; for such was the unavoidable human condition of philosophizing. For just this reason, Heineccius concluded, there were five further points to be kept in mind. No one should be satisfied with his own reason and knowledge, or build on this weak foundation; nor should one despise the ideas of others or refuse to suspect one's own. Above all, he concluded,

> one should not seek truth by oneself, nor accept or reject everything written by ancients and moderns. Therefore, no other method of philosophizing is more reasonable than the Eclectic Method.[72]

This was eclecticism at the height of its power.

---

[69] *Historia Sapientiae et Stultitiae collecta a Christian Thomasius* (Halle, 1693), 45.

[70] See *Analecta historiae philosophicae* (Halle, 1724).

[71] J. G. Heineccius, *Praelectiones in Hugonis Grotii de iure belli et pacis libros III*, in *Opera omnia* (Geneva, 1771), IX, 26, 34: 'nisi quod ponderis vel elegantiae insit'. See Santinello, *Storia*, II, 504; but there is no significant modern study of this very important scholar.

[72] *Elementa philosophiae rationalis et moralis* (Berlin, 1756[8]), 272: 'Folglich kein anderer Methodos philosophandi raisonable sey, als: METHODOS ECLECTICA.'

Of course eclecticism had its critics, too, even in the Lutheran camp, especially because of suspicious connections with syncretism. The historian J. L. Mosheim denounced the methods of the eclectic or Potamonic thinkers (*Eclectici aut Potamonici*). These misguided souls – 'whom mediocrity of genius, or an indolent turn of mind indisposed to investigating truth by the exertion of their own talents and powers' – refused to swear allegiance to a single school (alluding to the Horatian formula) and collected their ideas out of all the philosophers; and, what was worse, their errors, as Brucker also complained, had been passed on to Christians like Origen.[73] Mosheim opposed the efforts of the Jesuit scholar J. F. Baltus to defend the Fathers of the Church from this criticism, and he denounced eclecticism for its former association with the pagan errors embedded in Neoplatonism (*Platonici iuniores*), Gnosticism, hermeticism, and other errors with which it had been infected. But if Mosheim despised philosophical eclecticism, he nevertheless followed its agenda in his ecclesiastical history, which reviewed such errors and sorted them out from true philosophy and true theology.

4. Acts of the Philosophers

By this time 'methodology' (*methodologia*) was a popular topic of discussion among historians of philosophy. According to Ephraim Gerhard, writing in 1711, both history and philosophy were forms of wisdom (*divinarum humanarumque notitia*, according to the old formula); moreover, in combination they constituted a legitimate 'science', with its own method. This science remained part of 'literary history', Gerhard admitted, but its focus was very different.[74] It was not interested in trivial anecdotes about Pythagoras's father, Plato's mother, Aristotle's son, the physical condition or temperaments of philosophers. Its concern was only with their ideas and the fortune of their work over time – why Epicurus was popular among the Romans, for example, or why Plato was pleasing to the Christian Fathers.[75] For Gerhard as for Leibniz, philosophical history was not external but internal; it treated 'not philosophers but philosophy'.

---

[73] *De Turbato per recentiores platonicos ecclesia commentatio* (n.p., 1732), 8: 'Transitus Philosophiae Eclecticae ad Christianos'. Cf. *Institutions of Ecclesiastical History Ancient and Modern*, trans. Archibald Maclaine (New York, 1867), I, 20, 58; II, 180; also Brucker, III, 442.7.

[74] *Introductio praeliminaris in historia philosophica* (Jena, 1711), 2.

[75] Ibid., 8.

A clear sign of the autonomy of the history of philosophy (beyond the fact that it had been taught in universities for at least two generations) was the founding of the *Acta Philosophorum* by C. A. Heumann, the first serial publication devoted to the new discipline, the history of philosophy.[76] This journal, published in Halle from 1715 to 1721 and modelled on the *Acta Eruditorum* (if not the *Acta Apostolorum*), featured not only monographs but also reviews of recent 'literature' in the field (including the works of Thomasius, Buddeus, and Gerhard).[77] The basic question of modern philosophy, as one might infer from the bibliographical and critical concerns of these two pioneering scholarly journals, was how to cope with the crushing weight of accumulated learning deposited by tradition and piled up, often uncritically, by Renaissance scholarship.

In his extensive introduction Heumann, invoking Lipsius's praise of ancient eclecticism, declared of its modern counterpart that it was 'the best method of philosophy and, furthermore, that no one deserved the name "philosopher" who was not an Eclectic'. In this connection Heumann gave full credit to Jakob Thomasius and his *Herrsohn* Christian and celebrated the vital connection with the German Protestant tradition, yet at the same time arguing that *philosophia eclectica* was a wholly 'free' and universal method, without which there could be no philosophy. The religious connection is illustrated by the frontispiece, which represents symbolically contrasting historical visions – one of the ideal eclectic marriage (*Concord*) between theology (wife) and philosophy (husband) and the other of a lecturer on an elevated platform addressing a group of well-dressed men, with the comment, 'I see the academic robe and books, but I do not see the philosopher.' This is one example of a rich iconography of the history of philosophy produced in the eighteenth century.[78]

In successive fascicles of the *Acta* Heumann offered a comprehensive, up-to-date survey of the history of philosophy – word, concept, and discipline – from its origin (*Ursprung*) through all stages of succession and growth (*Wachsthum*), which was becoming (before overtly evolutionist conceptions) a common metaphor for intellectual progress.[79] In the course of this survey Heumann

---

[76] See Günter Mühlpfordt, 'Ein kryptoradikaler Thomasianer: C. A. Heumann, Der Thomasius von Göttingen', in *Christian Thomasius*, ed. Schneiders, 305–34; and Santinello, *Storia*, II, 437.

[77] *Acta Philosophorum, Gründl. Nachrichten aus der Historia Philosophica*, ed. C. A. Heumann (Halle, 1715–21).

[78] On the iconography of the history of philosophy see Werner Schneiders, *Hoffnung und Vernunft: Aufklärungsphilosophie in Deutschland* (Hamburg, 1990).

[79] *Acta Philosophorum*, I, 1–63; II, 1–381; II, 567–682, 'Einleitung zur Historia Philosophica'.

published an extensive dissertation on the scholarly theme and ancient topos, the trustworthiness of history, which he compared to Thomasius's analogous discussion of legal credibility (*fides juridica*).[80] As Heumann wrote,

> There are two methods of writing history; for it can be represented either in terms of disciplines, such as the history of logic and metaphysics, or of geography and chronology, to show how philosophy has been treated, according to each discipline, in different places, from the beginning of the world down to our own time.[81]

In history, of course, 'All that glitters is not gold'; and he quoted Pierre Bayle's remark, that 'The compiling of errors is a very important part of history' – for, citing a proverbial wisdom seldom recalled by philosophers, 'to err is human'. In this spirit Heumann rejected not only the proto-philosophy of 'barbarians', especially the false hermetic corpus, but also the errors of skeptics and dogmatists, especially Catholic scholars, who in his view possessed 'neither trustworthiness nor truth'.

Heumann naturally aimed at truth, but he recognized a difference between 'logical' and 'historical' demonstrations, between the truth guaranteed by reason and that offered by probability and authority. Here he confronted the problematic character of tradition, the doxographical accounts of philosophy, which kept alive the human side of philosophy and which, like religious tradition, had its heroes and 'martyrs' – not only victims of oppression but 'witnesses' (the meaning of the Greek term) to the truth. Yet tradition had also produced such modern fables as the notorious 'Pope Joan' as well as the lies that philosophers, lovers of truth as they supposedly were, regularly told about each other and that were repeated by doxographers like Diogenes Laertius. What historical truth required, as Flacius had argued two centuries earlier, was authentic testimony; and yet it was essential to recall the old rule that one testimony was useless (*ein Zeuge, kein Zeuge; testis unus, testis nullus*). Whence the need for modern critical scholarship, represented by the *Acta*, to cleanse the 'Augean stables' of human tradition and to solve such puzzles as the dating of Pythagoras and Potamon, the successions of masters and disciples in the philosophical canon, and the origins of such mottoes as 'Know thyself.'

---

[80] *Acta Philosophorum*, I, 381–462, 'De fide historica, oder von der Glaubwürdigkeit in dieser Historie', citing also Johann Eisenhart, *De Fide historica* (2nd edn; Helmstadt, 1702). See F. G. Bierling, *Commentatio de pyrrhonismo historico* (Leipzig, 1724); Arno Seifert, *Cognitio Historica: Die Geschichte als Namensgeberin der frühneuzeitlichen Empirie* (Berlin, 1976), 152; and Markus Völkel, '*Pyrrhonismus historicus*' und '*fides historica*': Die Entwicklung der deutschen Methodologie unter dem Gesichtspunkt der historischen Skepsis (Frankfurt, 1987), 128ff.

[81] *Acta Philosophorum*, I, 462.

In one vital respect, however, Heumann differed from Gerhard and Leibniz, and this was in his willingness to consider extra-philosophical factors. Philosophical self-understanding required not merely inward-looking speculation but also inquiry into the human conditions of philosophizing, since, as Heumann aphorized, 'Philosophers are made, not born' (*Philosophi fiunt, non nascuntur*). This reversal of the condition of the poet (*nascitur non fit*) suggests another major theme of the *Acta*, which is the philosopher's character or 'genius'.[82] Aside from 'heroic' figures like Luther, Heumann recognized geniuses of the first and second magnitude, ranked according to powers of judgment and criticism, freedom from prejudice, and temperamental balance – between doubt and enthusiasm, such as Cardano, who believed everything he read. (This is a nice anticipation of the views about 'tough-' and 'tender-mindedness' of William James, for whom 'The History of philosophy is to great extent that of a certain clash of temperaments.'[83]) Following Augustine, Heumann also went on to wonder if bastards had a special talent and whether women or *castrati* were capable of philosophy.[84]

Beyond psychological factors, Heumann inquired into the influence of 'external' factors such as environment, climate, the stars, and historical periods: was there a *genius locorum* or a *genius seculi*? This was an insight summed up more concisely in Glanvill's famous phrase, 'climates of opinion'.[85] 'All ages have their genius,' William Barclay wrote, and this was a condition also for historians to consider. All nations claimed cultural precedence, but such pretensions, even those of Germans, were exaggerated. Nevertheless, historians had to take factors of race and nationality into account, and to study the special quality of philosophizing in all the modern nations. None of these were questions which contemporary philosophers (with a few exceptions) asked, but they were much on the minds of historians, especially those of a humanist and eclectic persuasion.

The history of philosophy became a major and indeed a subsidized object of study in eighteenth-century Germany. In particular it was one of the four subjects encouraged by the Prussian Academy of Sciences first headed by

---

[82] *Acta Philosophorum*, I, 567–656, 'Von dem Ingenio Philosophico'. Cf. William Ringler, '*Posta nascitur non fit*: On the History of an Aphorism', *Journal of the History of Ideas*, 2 (1941), 497–504. The formulas *Criticus non fit, sed nascitur*, attributed to David Ruhnken, and *interpres not fit, sed nascitur*, are reported by Phillip August Boeck, 'Theory of Hermeneutics', in *The Hermeneutics Reader*, ed. Kurt Mueller-Vollmer (London, 1985), 139.

[83] *Pragmatism, A New Name for Some Old Ways of Thinking* (New York, 1907), 6.

[84] *Confessions*, 9.14.

[85] *Vanity of Dogmatizing* (London, 1661), 227.

Leibniz (the others being metaphysics, moral philosophy, and natural law). The publications of the 'French colony' sponsored by Frederick the Great – this 'false Julien in his false Athens', as Chateaubriand later lamented – contributed to the larger effort to form a national school to compete with those of England and France.[86] It was hospitable to eclectic philosophy as well as to the history of philosophy and featured the work of scholars involved in both enterprises, including those of the official eclectic historian of philosophy, J. J. Brucker.[87]

5. Brucker and his Book

The culmination and fruition of the first phase of modern eclecticism (and the modern field called *historia philosophica*) was Brucker's *Critical History of Philosophy*, published in four volumes from 1741 to 1743. In this monumental work, building on the labor of Heumann and other earlier scholars, Brucker defended the new discipline of philosophical history and the associated eclectic method. He offered a compendious survey of philosophy from 'barbaric' (pre-philosophical) origins down to his own enlightened day, in effect fixing the first version of the canon of academic philosophy down to the derivative handbooks of Tennemann, Cousin, Windelband, and Ueberweg (which, in its last edition, is still authoritative). He also set the terms for the debate over two fundamental questions defined in the context of his book – namely, the 'philosophy of the history of philosophy' (*Philosophie der Philosophiegeschichte*) and, though less clearly defined, the history of ideas.

In his preliminary statement of method Brucker summed up the eclectic view of the history of philosophy. While based on an exhaustive survey of opinions conveyed in the 'literature' of his subject, his enterprise was, no less than the philosophical work of Locke, a treatise on understanding:

> A history of philosophy, is a history of doctrines, and of men. As a history of doctrines, it lays open the origin of opinions, the changes which they have undergone, the distinct character of different systems, and the leading points in which they agree or disagree: it is therefore, in fact, a history of the human understanding (*historia intellectus humani*).[88]

[86] See Bartholmèss, *Histoire philosophique de l'Académie de Prusse*, I, 405; II, 63.

[87] Ibid., II, 123; and see *Johann Jacob Brucker (1696–1770)*, ed. Schmidt-Biggemann and Stamm (with comprehensive bibliography), especially the contributions by Schmidt-Biggemann, Longo, Blackwell, and Jehl; and Gregorio Piaia, 'Brucker versus Rorty? On the "Models" of the Historiography of Philosophy', *British Journal for the History of Philosophy*, 9 (2001), 69–81.

[88] Brucker, *Historia philosophica*, I, 19 (Enfield, I, 26); and in general see Santinello, *Storia*, II, 527ff.

The difference between the 'plain historical method' of Locke and Brucker's commitment to historical truth (*fides historica* was the topos) was that Brucker attended not only to internal mental phenomena but also to external factors:

> We have carefully remarked those personal circumstances respecting any author, which might serve to throw light on his opinions; such, for example, as his country, his family, his education, his natural temper, his habits of life, his patrons, friends, or enemies.[89]

Moreover, Brucker was concerned with questions of anachronism which were of little or no interest to philosophers:

> We have been particularly careful, not to ascribe modern ideas and opinions to the ancients, nor to torture their expressions into a meaning which probably never entered into their thoughts, in order to accommodate them to a modern hypothesis or system.[90]

Yet Brucker was convinced of the philosophical value of his project, which offered not only a 'register' of scientific progress but also, anticipating the famous argument of Thomas Kuhn, proof of 'the role of history in scientific discovery'.

Central to Brucker's task were questions of chronology and periodization. In the first volume of his work a diagram was reproduced from the *Acta Philosophorum* listing in organized fashion all the traditions and divisions of philosophy – western and eastern; pre-, post-, and non-Christian; dogmatic, sectarian, skeptical, and eclectic; natural, moral, and poetic. Here is displayed not only the rise and proliferation of philosophies but also the convergence between taxonomy and the chronology adopted by Brucker, following the first of the methods recognized by Heumann. Generally speaking, Brucker found 'little progress either in learning or in philosophy from the twelfth to the fourteenth century'. Following the Lutheran line of Horn, he recognized three periods of scholastic philosophy (and was followed in this by Cousin).[91] The first of these extended from Abelard to the mid-thirteenth century, in which dialectic came to prevail and in which monastic schools were replaced by public institutions and simple *magistri* by titled *doctores*.[92] The second

---

[89] Brucker, *Historia philosophica*, I, 15 (Enfield, I, 27).

[90] Brucker, *Historia philosophica*, I, 28 (Enfield, I, 19): 'nec ad nostrorum temporum habitum et sapientiae inter nos cultae ideam philosophia vetus exigenda est'.

[91] Brucker, *Historia philosophica*, III, 717ff (Enfield, 945); Cousin, *Course of the History of Modern Philosophy* (New York, 1960), II, 17–42.

[92] See Gabriel Lebras, 'Velut splendor firmamenti: Le docteur dans le droit de l'église médiévale', *Mélanges Etienne Gilson* (Paris, 1959), 372–88.

went down to 1330 and featured the great systems, and ended with William Durandus, honored as *Doctor Modernus*. Brucker's scorn is suggested by his resorting to trivial Laertian concerns, such as citing the punning and apocryphal gravestone of Durand:

> Here lies dure Durandus under this durable stone;
> Whether saved or not is neither of note nor known.[93]

The third period, representing further decline and proliferation of useless debates, followed *durus Durandus* and ended only with the Lutheran reform in Protestant universities, which put an end to such scholastic 'modernity' – at least until Melanchthon restored it in 'reformed' guise.

The culmination of Brucker's story came with the rise of the modern eclectic method grounded in the revival of learning and the reformation of true religion. 'From these laudable attempts', he wrote, 'a species of philosophy has arisen, more pure and excellent than those of any former period, which we shall distinguish by the name of the Modern Eclectic Philosophy.'[94] Unlike the so-called eclectics of antiquity,

> The true Eclectic philosopher, renouncing every prejudice in favor of celebrated names or ancient sects, makes reason his sole guide, and diligently investigates the nature and properties of the objects which come under observation, that he may ... deduce clear principles, and arrive at certain knowledge. He deems nothing so disgraceful in philosophy ... as implicitly to acknowledge the words of a master –

citing here once again the famous Horatian formula, 'I am not bound over to swear as any master dictates.'

Why had it taken so long for this method to be discovered? The Renaissance of learning was an essential foundation; but earlier scholars had unfortunately prized erudition above philosophy, while Catholic authors had a blind respect for tradition, and even Melanchthon was too attached to old sectarian habits. Brucker's predecessors were too credulous in their acceptance of legends and anecdotes embedded in the doxographical tradition or in the fabrications of later scholars, including the fantasies about 'barbarian philosophy' and the 'divine Plato'.[95] Ancient eclecticism was too confused and uncritical for the Moderns, and medieval philosophy was worse. Even Renaissance scholarship was in many ways infected with the spirit of the three false paths to wisdom – sectarianism, syncretism, and skepticism.

---

[93] Brucker, *Historia philosophica*, III, 846; cited also by Etienne Gilson, *History of Christian Philosophy in the Middle Ages* (New York, 1955), 474.

[94] Brucker, *Historia philosophica*, IV (2), 3–4 (Enfield, II, 468–9).

[95] E. N. Tigerstedt, *The Decline and Fall of the Neoplatonic Interpretation of Plato* (Helsinki, 1974).

With the Renaissance came the revival of the ancient schools, but also, and more important, powers of judgment and criticism, which made it possible to rise above sectarianism. Looking for signs of intellectual liberation, Brucker chose Francis Bacon as the first philosopher successfully to adopt the eclectic mode. He had been preceded by two other pioneers, but Bruno was too obscure and Cardano too foolish to qualify as founding geniuses of eclecticism. According to Brucker, 'Lord Bacon ... did more to detect the source of former errors and prejudices, and to discover and establish the true method of philosophizing, than the whole body of philosophers which many preceding ages had produced'; and invoking one modern myth to reinforce another, Brucker called him 'the Columbus of the philosophical world'.

For Brucker virtually all reasonable philosophy since Bacon was 'eclectic'. Of course particular traditions have preserved some identity, commanded some loyalty, and formed their own canons, but none of them has been preserved in pure form; and in any case Brucker was not inclined to make fine distinctions that might divert his triumphalist narrative. Even Descartes, though the founder of a 'sect', was admitted by him into the ranks of the eclectics, because of his independence of authority. Brucker also departed from doxographical tradition in recognizing the accomplishments of modern eclectics, including Spinoza, Locke, Grotius, and the practitioners of the new science of nature, in improving particular branches of philosophy.

In various ways Brucker was a transitional figure between eclecticism and Enlightenment, especially in his combination of learning and reverence for the powers of the human intellect. It was the union of history with reason, too, which gave Brucker the plot for the great story that he told, or retold, a plot that not only established a philosophically correct canon but also revealed a higher pattern than traditional doxography had found. This pattern was secular progress, or rather multiple progresses, which continued, despite setbacks of barbarism, ignorance, and credulity, the rise and progress not only of philosophy in particular but also of the human mind (*intellectus humanus*) in general. Such has been the more or less unexamined premise of the history of philosophy, which recapitulates the master metaphor of Plato, the philosopher emerging from the cave into the bright world of ideas – from the dark past of myth and opinion into a future of reason and progress, moral as well as scientific. As a disciple of Brucker wrote in the last years of the century, the history of philosophy offered 'not only an exposition of philosophical meanings ... but a representation of the development of the human spirit'.[96]

---

[96] Fülleborn, *Beiträge zur Geschichte der Philosophie*, I (Jena, 1796²), 41.

The history of philosophy continued under the shadow of Brucker during the eighteenth century, with at least one hundred separate publications in the genre.[97] Many of these books were popular surveys or textbooks, and few had much to add to the accumulation of scholarship assembled in Brucker's 'critical' history. The main purpose of this genre was initially to promote the imperial status of philosophy; yet there were also subversive influences at work, which, diverging from concentration on concepts and systems of thought, led to the study of a fuller expression of the human spirit, that is, of culture, and of the history of ideas.

---

[97] See Santinello, *Storia, passim.*

Chapter 6

The History of Literature

> The history of literature is the
> *ideal history of humanity* itself.
> Johann Scherr

In the nineteenth century 'literature', despite upstart aesthetic pretensions, still retained some of its former encyclopedic range. The tendency to identify literature with the tradition of general learning rather than with just the artful and imaginative work of genius persisted well into this period.[1] Yet like 'Art' and 'Science', 'Literature' had also gained a privileged status and capitalized form, becoming, for many Romantic authors, not only the highest of the arts but also, in effect, the queen of human sciences; and it was in this modernized and inflated form that literature, and in its company modern literary criticism and theory, became – as it still is – both subject and vehicle of intellectual and cultural history. As Lord Acton noted to himself, 'Literary history becoming history of thought, Ste.-Beuve to Faguet. The idea more interesting than the biography ... '[2]

1. New Literary History

The modern history of literature, as distinguished from old-fashioned *historia literaria*, received a significant impulse from the circle of German Romantics, especially Schiller, Schelling, the Schlegels, Novalis, and Hölderlin, who came into prominence in the period beginning when the French Terror provoked a turn from revolutionary enthusiasm to political and religious conservatism.[3] As Schlegel declared in 1812,

---

[1] As suggested by a comment of a certain 'C. Francis 1855' in the Harvard Library copy of La Harpe's *De l'Etat des lettres en Europe* (1797), judging Morhof's *Polyhistor* (1708) as 'the most extensive, & perhaps the best, history of Literature extant'.

[2] Herbert Butterfield, 'Acton: His Training and Intellectual System', *Studies in Diplomatic History and Historical Geography in Honour of G. P. Gooch* (London, 1961), 195.

[3] In a vast literature see Ernst Behler, *German Romantic Literary Theory* (Cambridge,

This term [*Literatur*] includes all that circle of arts and sciences which have life and man himself for their object, independently of outward act or material agency, working only through the instrumentality of language, without any corporeal matter as a basis.[4]

As Leibniz wanted a history of Philosophy, not of philosophers, so Schlegel wanted a history of Literature, not a mere sequence of authors;[5] and literature contained 'nearly the whole of man's intellectual life'. This was the basis of what René Wellek called the 'new historicism' informing nineteenth-century conceptions of literature and criticism.[6]

This historicism was intensified by Romantic infatuation with poetry as the best expression of the world of spirit. As Schiller wrote of the poet, 'His sphere is always the realm of ideas.'[7] These were the ideas not of Descartes, however, but rather of Hamann, Herder, Vico, and the Renaissance celebrators of a poetic wisdom prior if not superior to reason. Romanticism resurrected the figure of the *poeta-theologus*, inspired by divine madness – someone like Hölderlin, perhaps – who had special access to this wisdom. 'The genuine poet', wrote Novalis, 'is always a priest.'[8] Here appears the metaphorical shift traced by M. H. Abrams from the mirror to the lamp, highlighted by an illuminist view of ideas in which the poet is a maker not only of literature but also culture.[9] 'Where philosophy stops', Schlegel aphorized, inverting the Enlightenment view, 'poetry has to begin.'[10]

1993); Theodore Ziolkowski, *German Romanticism and its Institutions* (Princeton, 1990); and Georges Gusdorf, *Les Sciences humaines et la pensée occidentale*, VII, *Naissance de la conscience romantique au siècle des lumières* (Paris, 1978).

[4] *Lectures on the History of Literature, Ancient and Modern* (1815) [trans. J. G. Lockhart] (London, 1876), 6.

[5] Ernst Behler, 'Problems of Origins in Modern Literary Theory', in *Theoretical Issues in Literary History*, ed. David Perkins (Cambridge, MA, 1991), 12, and *German Romantic Literary Theory*; also Andrew Bowie, *From Romanticism to Critical Theory: The Philosophy of German Literary Theory* (London, 1997).

[6] *A History of Modern Criticism 1750–1950*, III, *The Age of Transition* (Cambridge, 1965), 16. See Bernd Witte, 'La Naissance de l'histoire littéraire dans l'esprit de la révolution: Discours esthétique chez Schlegel, Hegel, Gervinis et Rosenkranz', in *Philologiques I: Contribution à l'histoire des disciplines littéraires en France et en Allemagne au XIXe siècle*, ed. Michel Espagne and Michael Werner (Paris, 1990), 69–87.

[7] 'On Naive and Sentimental Poetry', trans. Julius A. Elias, in *German Aesthetic and Literary Criticism*, ed. H. B. Nisbet (Cambridge, 1985), 205.

[8] Cited in Rene Wellek, *A History of Modern Criticism* (8 vols; Cambridge [I–IV], 1955–65; New Haven [V–VIII], 1986–92), II, 83.

[9] M. H. Abrams, *The Mirror and the Lamp: Romantic Theory and the Critical Tradition* (New York, 1953).

[10] *Lectures*, 64, 98; and see Bowie, *From Romanticism to Critical Theory*, 53ff.

For Jakob Grimm, to say that not philosophy but 'poetry is what comes pure out of the mind into the word' was to recognize the fundamental position of myth.[11] In the nineteenth century these ideas of poetic inspiration were reinforced by the 'new mythology' associated especially with Schelling, which proclaimed the mythopoeic power of the people.[12] Myth was an area where history and aesthetics intersected; it was both an expression of national spirit and the proper subject of art. 'The kernel, the center of poetry', wrote Schlegel, 'is to be found in mythology and the mysteries of antiquity.'[13] Scholars seeking origins were also attracted to mythology: as Friedrich Creuzer found it the key to classical antiquity, so the Grimms found it for Germanic prehistory, and – more subversively – David Friedrich Strauss for the New Testament, which hitherto had been largely exempt from such methods. For Strauss the life of Christ was a perfect case of the rise of myth out of oral tradition, and a perfect target for the new 'mythical mode of interpretation'.[14]

The poet was a spokesman for tradition as well as a prophet: his song, like Homer's, was an expression of the collective experience of the People, and so were the writings of more civilized – and less 'naïve' – writers of modern times. 'The real individual is the race, the tribe', wrote J. J. Ampère; 'the poet is the voice of this collective individual and nothing more.'[15] As it was the task of scholars like the Grimms to retrieve the most fundamental forms of folk-tales and poetry, so it was the task of criticism to accommodate them to modern aesthetic judgment – and of literary history to chronicle and to celebrate them. As Johann Scherr put it, 'The history of literature is the *ideal history of humanity* itself.'[16]

If Romantic historicism exalted individual genius – and, in Cousin's famous phrase, 'art for art's sake' – it also recognized physical, social, and cultural contexts.[17] In his own contribution to cultural history the Old Testament

---

[11] Cited by Wellek, *History*, II, 284; and see Christa Kamenetsky, *The Brothers Grimm and their Critics: Folktales and the Quest for Meaning* (Athens, OH, 1992).

[12] See Manfred Frank, *Der kommende Gott: Vorlesungen über die Neue Mythologie* (Frankfurt, 1982), 73ff.

[13] *Philosophical Fragments*, trans. Peter Firchow (Minneapolis, 1991), 101.

[14] Strauss, *The Life of Jesus Critically Examined*, trans. George Eliot (London, 1892, 2nd edn), 52; and see Richard S. Cromwell, *David Friedrich Strauss and his Place in Modern Thought* (Fair Lawn, NJ, 1974); also D. R. Kelley, 'Mythistory in the Age of Ranke', in *Leopold von Ranke and the Shaping of the Historical Profession*, ed. G. Iggers and J. Powell (Syracuse, 1989), 3–20, 181–5.

[15] *Discours sur l'histoire de la poésie* (1830), cited by Wellek, *History*, III, 9.

[16] *Allgemeine Geschichte der Literatur* (Stuttgart, 1875⁵), 3: 'die Geschichte der Literatur ist die *ideale Geschichte der Menschheit* selbst'.

[17] Albert Cassagne, *La Théorie de l'art pour l'art en France chez les derniers romantiques et les premiers réalistes* (Paris, 1906), 38.

scholar J. G. Eichhorn joined the 'new world of literature' with the new 'critical–historical spirit of the modern age'.[18] He defined the 'history of literature' as

> the story of the origins and major changes in all parts of learning [described] according to the physical, political, and moral conditions of people, such as climate, national character, means of subsistence, social needs, associations, and examples of morals and language, religious and political organization, etc.[19]

From this standpoint literature is understood as an aspect of civilization, according to the famous aphorism attributed to the Comte de Bonald, 'Literature is an expression of society.'[20]

This formula, popularized by Friedrich Schlegel, Madame de Staël, and others, implied that, society itself having undergone such profound changes in the previous century, literature was also historically transformed. 'Each age has its particular physiognomy, its distinctive character, its own genius,' wrote Pierre-Simon Ballanche in 1818;[21] and historical studies were inhibited accordingly. 'Our literature of the age of Louis XIV has ceased to be the expression of society', he added; 'it is therefore already becoming for us a kind of ancient literature or archeology.' Rules of taste and criticism have changed, so that 'old ideas have become unintelligible'.[22]

In France the most influential advocate of Romantic historicism in literature was Cousin's colleague Villemain, whose lectures of 1828 argued that literature included the history of society. In particular the literature of the previous century was the product of three major influences – religion, antiquity, and the monarchy of Louis XIV – and in turn French literature was itself the source of world-wide influence.[23] But in the present age, he admitted, it was the influences of England (the revolution of 1688) and of Germany (idealist philosophy) that were central to 'the development of the human spirit'.[24]

---

[18] *Allgemeine Geschichte der Cultur und Litteratur der neueren Europa* (Göttingen, 1796), xv, xliii.

[19] *Literaturgeschichte* (Göttingen, 1812, 2nd edn), 1, 5.

[20] *Législation primitif* (Paris, 1829), II, 223; and see David Klinck, *The French Counterrevolutionary Theorist Louis de Bonald (1754–1840)* (New York, 1996).

[21] *Essai sur les institutions sociales*, in *Œuvres* (Paris, 1830), II, 20; and see Albert Joseph George, *Pierre-Simon Ballanche: Precursor of Romanticism* (Syracuse, 1945); and Charles Rearick, *Beyond the Enlightenment: Historians and Folklore in Nineteenth Century France* (Bloomington, 1974), 42–61.21.22.

[22] Ibid., 100.

[23] *Cours de littérature française* (Paris, 1840), I, 2.

[24] Ibid., 336.

Claude Fauriel, polyglot friend of Schlegel and Franz Bopp, devoted most of his life to the history of literature. His book on popular songs in modern Greece showed his concerns for popular culture, as did his later work on the troubadours. He was more concerned with the historical than the aesthetic aspects of literature, which he regarded as following certain physical laws:

> Climate, soil, social conditions, religious belief, commercial relations, the results of wars and conquests, and a thousand other circumstances endlessly modify the common basis, the original nature of literatures, communicating to each a local physiognomy, an individual character, its own beauties and defects, and a place in the scale of art.[25]

For Fauriel the succession of different ages was better reflected in literature and its external history than in politics. Thus literary history reached the status of an autonomous discipline (as it would later be for Gustav Lanson), sharing the general inclination to 'historicism' and rivaling the Rankean 'scientific history' of the later nineteenth century.[26]

2.   A Literary Triumvirate

The most impressive product of the intersection between literary and historical studies came in the work of another French triumvirate – three remarkably successful men of letters, who were dominating figures in capital-L Literature and who also qualify, retrospectively, as pioneering intellectual historians: Charles-Augustin Sainte-Beuve, Ernest Renan, and Hippolyte Taine.

To portray Sainte-Beuve in these terms is to document the famous charge made by Marcel Proust's *Contre Sainte-Beuve* in 1908, denouncing not only the critic but also the attitude toward authors which he represented and perhaps even, as Taine thought, initiated. Sainte-Beuve, Proust wrote, 'sees literature under the category of time', following a method which 'consists in not separating the man from his work'.[27] Flaubert registered a similar complaint that, with Taine, 'The masterpiece no longer has any significance except as a historical document.'[28] This was just what historians of philosophy had been

---

[25] J. B. Galley, *Claude Fauriel* (Paris, 1909), 330; and see Rearick, *Beyond the Enlightenment*, 62–76.

[26] Fernand Baldensperger, *La Critique et l'histoire littéraires en France* (Paris, 1944), 44.

[27] *Contre Sainte-Beuve* (Paris, 1954), 127; and in general see Harry Levin, *The Gates of Horn: A Study of Five French Realists* (Oxford, 1963).

[28] Cited by Wellek, *History*, IV, 11–12, Hyman, 15.

doing to the authors whom they studied in particular, extra-philosophical, chronological, geographical, cultural and historical terms.

So in this secular, journalistic, and historicizing age the old status of priesthood was denied to philosophers as well as to literary artists. What Sainte-Beuve did in his relentless and enormously popular *Lundis*, which so profoundly shaped European literary opinion, was to shift attention from the creative artist to 'another self' (*un autre moi*) expressed in letters and gossip against the background of salon culture; moreover, he did this more often with authors of inferior talent than with recognized masters. Homer, Virgil, and most Ancients escaped this sort of journalistic attention; only the Moderns suffered such demeaning scrutiny – and had occasion to complain of the treatment.

Sainte-Beuve was not only the arch-critic of the nineteenth century; he was also a pioneering intellectual historian who ranged over the whole of modern literary history from the sixteenth century to his day – from his reviews to a history of Port-Royal, based on his lectures given at Lausanne in 1837–38.[29] He recognized the significance of 'literary tradition', but even in this massive work his genre of preference was biography, the literary portrait. *Port-Royal* was remarkable in its efforts to re-create the original milieu and religious mentality, so alien to the spirit of the modern age, of the latter-day saints and scholars of the great Cistercian abbey in the age of Louis XIV.

Sainte-Beuve was uncommonly sensitive to the difficulty of entering into the mentality of a remote age like that of Descartes, Arnauld, and Malebranche:

> When one is of the nineteenth century, possessing common sense and a spirit given to positive methods and understanding, the first condition of entering retrospectively, as one must, into these metaphysical debates is not to be afraid of certain exorbitant conventions or excessive hypotheses which are accepted by all contestants: these are, so to say, the rules of the game without which there would be no game.[30]

Viewed historically, however, Port-Royal was a sort of kindergarten of modernity, continuing the '*modern* movement' begun in the sixteenth century, with the founding of the Collège Royale, 'in opposition to the University', and with an Ordinance of 1539 requiring the use of French in public acts.[31] Port-Royal carried on this secularizing impulse, supporting 'with all its strength' the originality of that age, which was 'to have absolutely ceased to speak Latin in a French manner'.

---

[29] See Paul Nelles, 'Sainte-Beuve between Renaissance and Enlightenment', *Journal of the History of Ideas*, 61 (2000), 473–92.
[30] *Port-Royale* (Paris, 1954), III, 320.30.22.
[31] Ibid., II, 464.

In general Sainte-Beuve devoted himself to exploring the psychology and external influences of literary creation; and he was sensitive to periodization and generational changes, starting with the 'new era' of Romanticism and the 'social and political revolution' of 1830, in which he began his own writing. Proust hated 'the method of Sainte-Beuve' because it implied reduction of art – or rather, the artist, the Romantic *Moi* – to external conditions;[32] but of course this is just what had led Sainte-Beuve to intellectual and cultural history, taking the same turn as eighteenth-century historians of philosophy. And he applied the same method to contemporaries such as Cousin, Guizot, Villemain, Michelet, Taine, Renan, and others who shared his interests in literary and cultural history.

For Sainte-Beuve's younger admirer Ernest Renan, writing in 1848 under the inspiration of the 'oriental renaissance' (and with Cousin's encouragement), the whole drift of scholarship was toward literary history and philology, which – extending the old thesis of Renaissance humanism – he called 'the *exact science* of things of the spirit'.[33] For Renan the sixteenth century gave new foundations to all the arts and sciences even though it also saw endless wars, literary and scientific as well as religious and political; it was 'the creative century par excellence'.[34] But in his day the genius of the French was toward rhetoric and literature, not 'positive science', the area of German dominance. Any student of the philologists Boeckh, Bopp, or Ritter was superior to any who had been thrilled by the lectures and 'brilliant generalities' of Cousin, Guizot, or Villemain; and Renan longed for a new 'renaissance' of higher education in France according to the Prussian model.[35]

Like Kant's, Renan's was an age of criticism – but in a sense closer to Renaissance than to idealist goals – and he argued that 'the union of philology and philosophy, of erudition and thought, should become the basis of intellectual work in our age'.[36] Indebted to Cousin, Renan wrote in his thesis on Averroism that 'the interest of the history of philosophy rests less in extracting scholarly information than in the tableau of the successive evolutions of the human spirit'.[37] He joined not only scientific and historical

---

[32] *Contre Sainte-Beuve*, 121ff.

[33] *L'Avenir de la science*, in *Œuvres complètes*, ed. Henriette Psichari (10 vols; Paris, 1947–61), III, 847.

[34] Ibid., I, 210.

[35] *La Réforme intellectuelle et morale* (1871), in ibid., I, 329ff; also ibid., 85.

[36] Ibid., I, 847, 829.

[37] Ibid., III, 15 ('histoire philosophique'). According to Richard M. Chadbourne, *Ernest Renan* (New York, 1941), 41, 'To this once-famous thinker [Cousin], Renan probably owes much of his terminology and ideas concerning synthesis.'

methods but also natural and human history in a cosmic vision making chemistry 'the oldest history' and biology and racial difference a prelude to universal history.

In this process Renan saw seven stages: atomic (mechanical); molecular chemistry; solar and planetary development; biological evolution; 'preconscious humanity', made accessible through the successes of philology and comparative mythology; and finally the 'historical period', which began six thousand years ago in Egypt but which had gained 'full consciousness of the entire planet and all of humanity' only three or four hundred years earlier. The story of the French nation occupied only a few years in this gigantic evolution.[38] To the understanding of this secularized view of Creation, in any case, the key was history:

> The science of languages is the history of languages; the science of literature and philosophy is the history of literature and philosophy; the science of the human spirit is the history of the human spirit, not merely analysis of the mechanics of the soul

– alluding to Averroist commentary on Aristotle's *De Anima*.[39] Modern criticism has overcome this bias by substituting the category of becoming (history) for being (philosophy).

Sainte-Beuve, without accepting Renan's method, applauded his younger friend's enterprise, which was the study of

> what he called the conscience of the human race – a sort of higher and changing mirror in which are reflected and concentrated the principal beams or features of the past, which in every age a considerable number of thinkers take to themselves and then pass on to those who follow.[40]

This perpetual 'Noah's Ark' symbolizes the project which modern philology and history have launched for the benefit of modern science and future generations.

The third member of this French triumvirate was Hippolyte Taine, who acknowledged Sainte-Beuve as a predecessor and Renan as a comrade in arms. 'No one has done [criticism] better than Sainte-Beuve', wrote Taine: 'in this respect we are all his pupils.'[41] Sainte-Beuve was also remarkable, 'for his time', for discovering the scientific method claimed by Taine himself.[42] Like

---

[38] *Œuvres*, I, 643–4.

[39] Ibid., III, 16.

[40] *Les grands ecrivains français*, ed. Maurice Allem, *XIX siècle, Philosophes et essayistes*, III (Paris, 1930), 155.

[41] Ibid., I, 10.

[42] *Contre Sainte-Beuve*, 124, referring to Taine's preface to his *L'Intelligence*. In

his colleagues, Taine revered the science of history, 'the great effort and the great work of this century'; he deplored the rhetorical habits of French thought, especially as embodied in Cousin's vague spiritualism. Every generation tries to bury its fathers, and this was the story of the shift from Enlightenment to Romanticism. 'Raised in faith, the fathers doubted', Taine wrote; 'raised in doubt, the sons wished to believe; but like the fathers, the sons clung to metaphysics'; and Taine, again in the company of Renan, preached a doctrine of 'positive' science.[43]

The difference was that, like Buckle, Taine leaned to the model of physical science rather than philology and took more seriously the disciplines of chemistry and biology. Rabelais's *Pantagruel*, for example, should be studied in just the way one would analyze a digestive process or do an autopsy, posing questions about the connections of ideas and images in his philosophy, the character of his humor and temperament, the sources of his vocabulary and verbal inventions, 'the conformity of his book with the manners of his time', and other features of this 'magic lantern' of a work.[44] In general, argued Taine, it was necessary to bring *nature* into moral philosophy and history in order to understand the 'causes' of human behavior.

These were the premises that Taine brought to his history of English literature. The famous contextualist trinity – *race, moment, milieu* – formed the framework of Taine's interpretations and the setting for the scientistic hyperbole of his rhetoric.[45] The inherited dispositions of national character, the pressures of the natural environment, and the periods of cultural growth encompass the external 'causes' of historical change and suggest historical laws analogous to those of natural science. So Taine seemed to embody the fallacy of determinism, or (Chateaubriand judged) the heresy of 'fatalism', which Sainte-Beuve, Michelet, and others rejected as an error imported from Germany.[46] As Sainte-Beuve wrote in his critique of Taine,

---

general see François Leger, *Monsieur Taine* (Paris, 1993); Regina Pozzi, *Hippolyte Taine: Scienze umane e politica nell'Ottocento* (Venice, 1993); and Paul Lacombe, *La Psychologie des individus et des sociétés chez Taine, historien des littératures* (Paris, 1906).

[43] Ibid., 296.

[44] Ibid., 338.

[45] *History of English Literature*, trans. H. Van Laun (New York, 1883), I, 17; and see Wellek, *History*, IV, 27ff.

[46] Chateaubriand, *Génie du christianisme*, ed. Maurice Regard (Paris, 1978), 468, and *Etudes historiques*, preface; Sainte-Beuve, *Œuvres*, I, 144; Michelet, *Histoire de France*, preface; see D. R. Kelley, *Historians and the Law in Postrevolutionary France* (Princeton, 1984), 35.

One can indeed show all the relations they have with the time in which they are born and live ... , but one cannot tell in advance that [the age] will give birth to a particular kind of individual or talent. Why Pascal rather than La Fontaine?[47]

Yet what most concerned Taine in the last analysis was not external factors but rather the inner, 'invisible man' and what he called 'facts of the highest kind' – modes of feeling and thought only literary efforts could reveal.[48] What revealed the human soul behind documents was the 'revival of imagination' associated with Lessing, Chateaubriand, Scott, Thierry, and Michelet.[49] Like Sainte-Beuve, who showed the human spirit behind the monastic squabbles of Port-Royal, Taine wanted to range more widely by setting psychological analysis in a larger historical tableau – a 'system [of] human sentiments and ideas' – and here he located traditional notions of literary succession, including original work of literary 'initiators' and the follow-ups by 'imitators'.

Yet Taine's extravagant scientism alienated his senior colleagues – eclectics, Voltaireans, Gallicans, and Catholics alike – Sainte-Beuve reported. Cousin and Villemain objected to the materialism and fatalism of his work and the offenses to what Cousin called 'the public conscience'. Those whom Taine called the 'clerics' of the Académie (Sainte-Beuve abstaining from the discussion) denied the Bourdin prize to his work entirely on these grounds.[50] Like Buckle, Taine pushed the analogies of natural science too far into the sphere of moral philosophy to suit an age already troubled by more humane sorts of doubt.

While Taine and Renan were themselves devoted to the history of civilization, they also became enthusiasts for scientific positivism, which led in another direction – back to the spirit of system, as illustrated by Comte, Renouvier, and later Durkheim.[51] In this connection the history of thought tended not only to be naturalized – framed in evolutionist terms – but also to be absorbed into a scientific sociology, just as it would be in the work of Durkheim and Weber. For the traditions of intellectual and cultural history this marked – as a century earlier with academic philosophy it had marked – a parting of the ways.

Other divisions appeared in the common front of historians of literature, philosophy, and science because of the academic specialization of the later

---

[47] *Grands ecrivains*, III, 213.
[48] *History of English Literature*, I, 1.
[49] Ibid., I, 6.
[50] Leger, *Monsieur Taine*, 313–16, and Sainte-Beuve, *Grands ecrivains*, 281.
[51] See Steven Lukes, *Emile Durkheim: His Life and Works* (New York, 1972), 67.

nineteenth century, including a vast expansion of books on literary history.[52] In contrast to Taine and others of an earlier generation, Gustav Lanson specifically denied that his enormously influential handbook had anything to do with the 'history of civilization' or the 'history of ideas'.[53] Literature was a matter of pleasure, and literary talent and genius took privilege over cultural environment. As Literature was an autonomous tradition of art, so literary history was a special science; and more cultural considerations were left to scholars in other disciplines. History was a 'science', too; but it was only marginally concerned, as far as the academy and the state were concerned, with intellectual and cultural matters. At the turn of the twentieth century, however, this situation would change, especially because of another 'linguistic turn' which would bring history back into play.

3. Between Literature and Language

Since the eighteenth century language has been a key to intellectual and cultural history, and the advances of linguistic science (*Sprachwissenschaft*) in the nineteenth century reinforced this position. Following Herder but from a larger perspective, Humboldt regarded language as 'a work of the spirit' and linked it to 'the growth of man's mental power'.[54] Geniuses like Dante and Luther, virtuosi of linguistic expression, stood on the shoulders not of giants but of many generations of speakers, singers, and writers. The further historians follow the chain of culture into the past, the less they are impressed with great men and the more they must take into account collective achievements, which make it 'evident how small, in fact, is the *power of the individual* compared to the might of language'.[55]

The Romantic and idealist view of language exemplified by Humboldt, which subordinated words to human ideas and intentions, was opposed by the more rigorous conceptions of comparative philologists and later by 'neo-grammarians', who sought laws of phonetic change quite independent of

---

[52] Fritz Ringer, *Fields of Knowledge: French Academic Culture in Comparative Perspective, 1890–1920* (Cambridge, 1992), and see Alain Vaillant, 'L'Ecrivain, le critique et la pédagogue (1840–1909): Elément de bibliométrie littéraire', in *Philologiques I*, ed. Espagne and Werner, 311–32.

[53] *Histoire de la littérature française* (Paris, 1896⁴), xii; and see *Essais de méthode, de critique et d'histoire littéraire* (Paris, 1965).

[54] *On Language: The Diversity of Human Language-Structure and its Influence on the Mental Development of Mankind*, trans. Peter Heath (Cambridge, 1988), 21.

[55] Ibid., 64, 63.

human will or creativity – modern counterparts of the old dispute over free will and determinism. Over several generations debates were carried on between such advocates of a 'hard' linguistic science and those favoring a historical approach, such as Herman Paul, whose *Principles of Linguistic Science* (1880) depended not on logic or history but on psychology as a way of understanding linguistic change.[56] This was the line of the so-called 'neo-linguists', such as Karl Vossler, who, inspired by his exchanges with Benedetto Croce, summed up the discussion in his *Positivism and Idealism in Linguistic Science* (1904).[57]

In the narrow sense intended by French linguists such as Ferdinand de Saussure, wrote Vossler, what exists is not human language but only individual speech. In a diachronic and historical perspective, however, language shows its 'super-social' presence as a 'vast soliloquy of the human mind which unfolds itself in untold millions of persons and characters'.[58] As a 'human custom' and vehicle of culture, language, which for us has neither beginning nor end, has power over human beings, and so words have a sort of magical and metahistorical quality, carrying echoes of bygone – and potential for future – discourse. Tensions in thought cannot be resolved by speculation or argument; and so the problematic relations between subject and object of inquiry – 'psychology of scientific *Weltanschauungen*' – '[are] no longer a matter for philosophy but one for philology and the literary sciences'.[59] Language can be a historical agent, defining language communities or nations, signaling historical change, and becoming the center of 'language wars'.[60]

Another scholar who joined historical semantics with intellectual history was the Viennese immigrant Leo Spitzer, who agreed with Vossler's basic purpose, though he thought it a bit 'premature'. Since literature 'is nothing but its language as this is written down by its elite speakers', asked Spitzer, 'can we perhaps not hope to grasp the spirit of a nation in the language of its outstanding works of literature?'[61] But Spitzer preferred to work within the confines of particular texts, and at first was content to seek the 'spirit' of a single author through the methods of exegesis and stylistics – following the

---

[56] And see Paul, *Principles of the History of Language*, trans. H. A. Strong (London, 1988).

[57] *Carteggio Croce-Vossler 1899–1949* (Bari, 1951), 46.

[58] *The Spirit of Language in Civilization*, trans. O. Geser (London, 1932), 13.

[59] Ibid., 213–14.

[60] Ibid., 137.

[61] *Representative Essays*, ed. A. Forcione et al. (Stanford, 1988), 13. See Geoffrey Green, *Literary Criticism and the Structures of History: Erich Auerbach and Leo Spitzer* (Lincoln, NE, 1982); and James V. Catano, *Language, History, Style: Leo Spitzer and the Critical Tradition* (Urbana, 1988).

famous motto of Buffon, 'Style is the man,' but with an admixture of Freudianism. In his essay on Diderot, for example, he proposed 'to penetrate into the biological nature of the writer's nature by a study of his style'.[62]

Spitzer was highly critical of the conventional 'history of ideas' divorced from texts, and he took Arthur Lovejoy to task for his alleged idealism and neglect of historical context.[63] There was no such thing as an 'unemotional idea', Spitzer scolded; 'nor may the living idea be considered apart from the movement, from the individual'; and it must not be extracted from its 'climate'. Lovejoy responded by denying the use of notions of *Geist* or climate, except to obscure the intelligibility of ideas. In fact Spitzer himself, though no admirer of philosophy, preserved a certain spiritualism, based on the hermeneutical principle, that is, the 'philological circle', a device analogous to the 'hermeneutical circle' of Schleiermacher. This exegetical technique sought the 'inward form' of a text – regarded unproblematically as an author's intentional creation – by inference from myriad word details and a vast legacy of literary erudition, all combined of course with a proper sense of style.[64]

Philologist though he was, Spitzer aspired to combine the history of words with the history of ideas – *Geistesgeschichte* was his term for this approach[65] – which is to say a set of meanings located by a family of words that could be pursued in the literary contexts of western languages. A favorite strategy was the controversial study of etymology, which for him was a pursuit of meaning in time and so 'a piece of linguistic history' and sometimes a 'miracle'.[66] There were many 'idea-histories', he wrote, but none which coupled linguistic theory with the history of ideas. This dual interest was shown most conspicuously in his studies of the terms 'milieu', 'ambiance', and 'Stimmung', and ideas associated with this cluster – especially Pythagorean 'world harmony'. This was one idea, or semantic construct, illustrating what Spitzer called 'the concrete linguistic–historical continuity from ancient Greece and Rome via the Christian Middle Ages to our modern secularized civilization'.[67] *Stimmung*

---

[62] *Linguistics and Literary History* (Princeton, 1948), 168 ('The Style of Diderot').

[63] Spitzer, 'Geistesgeschichte vs. History of Ideas as Applied to Hitlerism', and Lovejoy, 'Reply to Prof. Spitzer', *Journal of the History of Ideas*, 5 (1944), 191–203 and 204–19, repr. in *The History of Ideas: Canon and Variations*, ed. D. R. Kelley (Rochester, 1990).

[64] *Representative Essays*, 25, and 425–48 ('Development of a Method').

[65] *Essays in Historical Semantics* (New York, 1948), 6.

[66] *Representative Essays*, 9. In this neo-Isidorean spirit he traced 'quandary' back through an uninterrupted chain to 'conundrum', 'quandary' and 'quibble' to the French 'carriwichet', but neither Skeat nor Partridge agrees with these proposals.

[67] *Classical and Christian Ideas of World Harmony: Prolegomenon to an Interpretation of the Word 'Stimmung'* (Baltimore, 1963), 2.

(French *milieu*) had semantic associations with a variety of ideas, including concert, concord, and temperament; but in its German career it had both internal and external significations (analogous to Goethe's critique of the false and deadening objectivism of Newtonian optics); that is, it included not only objective and external conditions but also subjective and internal states – not only the appearance of a landscape, for instance, but also the state of mind produced in the observer.[68]

Spitzer's history of the idea of World Harmony, like Lovejoy's study of the Great Chain of Being, began with ancient Greek conceptions of order and a higher reality beyond sense-perception. For Spitzer the point of departure was the Pythagorean 'holy *tetrakus*', the idea of a fourfold harmony in the world: musical, psychological, social, and natural, reflected in the writings of Plato, Ptolemy, Cicero, Kepler, Kircher, and Leibniz.[69] In contrast to Lovejoy, however, Spitzer tried to follow not a formal philosophical idea but rather a family of terms (Greek, Latin, and vernacular) illustrated by the usage of authors, ancient and modern, joined in a field of 'discourse' defined by Spitzer's interdisciplinary erudition, linguistic conjectures, and tacitly assumed philological authority, expressed in asides critical of the scholarship of others. Here his 'philological circle' seemed to move between keywords and world-views, without the mediation of conceptual continuity.

Spitzer extended his linguistic horizons to include not only literature but also popular culture, applying in virtuoso fashion his method of *explication du texte* to American advertising.[70] He situated the 'Sunkist' orange juice label in the broadest semantic, stylistic, and iconographic field, associating the neologism with solar imagery, the fruit in Paradise, the modern 'vitamin myth', the 'poetic' resonances of the Shakespearean 'kist', and other devices borrowed from western culture for the benefit of modern capitalist needs and utopian rhetoric. In this essay, at least, Spitzer moved beyond even Vossler's search for 'spiritual' connections between words, ideas, and culture.

Spitzer's colleague Erich Auerbach likewise followed a linguistic road into the field of intellectual history and studied both the changing fortune of keywords and the changing contexts of languages over longer periods of time. For him, as for Vossler and Spitzer, the paradigm of semantic history was the decline and revival of classical Latin, divided by a long period of vulgar Latin in which the form of language, and so of thought, was transmuted.

---

[68] Ibid., 140.
[69] Ibid., 8.
[70] 'American Advertising Explained as Popular Art', *Representative Essays*, 327–56.

'Change of words means change of culture,' Spitzer wrote.[71] This was the premise, too, that led Auerbach to his interpretation of the classical and Christian fortunes of the term *figura*, which changed its meaning from representation, type, or form to secondary and symbolic representation, 'antitype', of such forms. In this sense *figura* was opposed to *historia*, since it suggested the 'figuration' of a literal reality, a copy of an original model – a version of the problem of the representation of reality taken up in Auerbach's *Mimesis*, where, Auerbach wrote, 'Our purpose was to show how on the basis of its semantic development a word may grow into a historical situation and give rise to structures that will be effective for many centuries.'[72]

Another question that preoccupied Auerbach was the rise, in a long perspective, of the literate 'public' for which literary authors wrote and the 'spirit or culture' created by classical Latin which it made possible.[73] He found the roots of this conception in the 'publication' of ancient works referred to by Pliny and the invocation of a readership by classical authors. This literary culture virtually disappeared between 600 and 1100, until the 'almost miraculous' revival of Latin in the eleventh century and the subsequent emergence of vernacular literature, especially Dante, who resumed the classical style of addressing a readership (and a posterity). However, it was after the joining of 'La cour et la ville' in the seventeenth century – and under conditions of what Vico called the 'world of nations' – that nobility and bourgeoisie came together to form the modern, and especially a reading, 'public'. Modern discussions of the 'public sphere' have generally ignored this earlier background.

Acknowledging the influence of Vossler, Spitzer, and Curtius in particular, Auerbach nevertheless insisted that 'My purpose is always to write history.'[74] Central to Auerbach's idea of cultural change was what, referring to the foundational work of Vico, he called 'aesthetic historicism'.[75] Joining the 'aesthetic horizon' to historical perspective, Auerbach linked not only artistic value and historical understanding but also diachrony and synchrony. Parochialism or classicist prejudice prevented such an outlook, at once critical

---

71 'Wortwandel ist Kulturwandel', and 'Bedeutungswandel ist Kulturwandel' – *Linguistics*, 8; *World Harmony*, 77.
72 'Figura', trans. Ralph Manheim, *Scenes from the Drama of European Literature* (New York, 1959), 76. See Seth Lerer (ed.), *Literary History and the Challenge of Philology: The Legacy of Erich Auerbach* (Stanford, 1996).
73 *Literary Language and its Public in Late Latin Antiquity and in the Middle Ages*, trans. Ralph Manheim (New York, 1965).
74 Ibid., 6.
75 See *Scenes* and also *Gesammelte Aufsätze zur romanischen Philologie* (Bern, 1967), 222–74.

and panoramic. Aesthetic historicism as it emerged in the eighteenth century in reaction to classicism opened the way for 'general historicism', Auerbach believed, including the 'literary historicism' whose advent came with Stendhal and Balzac, as well as the sort of modern philological studies culminating in the work of modern scholars, such as Vossler, Spitzer, Ernst Curtius, and of course Auerbach, which finally historicized historicism itself.

The last in the great quartet of German philologists who practiced the history of ideas was Ernst Curtius, who began as a literary critic and only later, in reaction to Nazism, embarked on a massive project of reviewing the whole Latin heritage of Goethe's 'world-literature'.[76] For Curtius as for Vossler and Auerbach, Dante occupied the center of this tradition, summing up and fusing classical and Christian conventions which linked the Renaissance with antiquity. Indeed Curtius modelled his *European Literature and the Latin Middle Ages* on Dante's *Commedia*, following in a historical way the hierarchy of liberal arts, prescribed authors, and literary forms from classical originals to classicist imitations and transformations.

Unlike many of his contemporaries Curtius was not disturbed by a hostility between science and the humanities. For 'The concept of freedom is making its way into natural science, and science is once again open to the questionings of religion (Max Planck)', Curtius wrote, while 'History, for its part, turns its attention to the rise of culture' (*Kulturentstehung*).[77] For Curtius, in a perspective of six millennia of myth-making and with a new appreciation of the middle ages, 'a new completeness and coherence' will emerge from 'the crucible of historicism'. This is the end-product of a literature that began with Homer and a literary criticism that began with Friedrich Schlegel.

What now seems most striking about Curtius's work was his anticipation of the current revival of rhetoric as an alternative to philosophy and a vehicle of intellectual continuity within the canon of Latinate literature and its vernacular offshoots – the 'great chain of texts', as it has been called[78] – which Curtius celebrated and analyzed. Treating the western intellectual tradition in terms of textually observable themes – especially topoi and metaphors – and concrete issues such as the debates between self-styled 'moderns' and 'ancients' and questions of 'canon-formation', Curtius skirted the abstractions and obfuscations

---

[76] See E.R. Curtius', *European Literature and the Latin Middle Ages*, in *On Four Modern Humanists*, ed. Arthur R. Evans (Princeton, 1970) trans. Wellard R. Trask (Princeton, 1973), 85–145; and Ezio Raimondi, 'Curtius, l'Europa e l'utopia', *Intersezioni*, 17 (1997), 5–18.

[77] *European Literature*, 7.

[78] Daniel Stempel, 'History and Postmodern Literary Theory', in *Tracing Literary Theory*, ed. Joseph Natoli (Urbana, 1987), 96.

of *Geistesgeschichte*, which was the history not of literature but of Something Other than literature, and devoted himself to what he called a 'phenomenology of literature' and what he saw as 'the Europeanization of the historical picture'.

Within western tradition Curtius recognized deep divisions, and most especially the rivalry between German 'culture' and French 'civilization'. For German scholars since Humboldt, *Kultur* was the élitist perfecting of *Zivilisation*, which constituted the social base of intellectual progress, while for the French, culture was set below civilization, which represented the modern incarnation of the classical ideal.[79] Drawing strength from a tradition of centralization, Gallicanism, and classicism, the French regarded themselves as the caretakers of civilization and so of progress; and from this point of view Guizot, for one, envisioned European history. The primary expression of this view was French literature (corresponding to philosophy, art, science, and music in Germany). 'As the Latin Middle Ages is the crumbling Roman road from the antique to the modern world', so – here Curtius invokes the similar metaphor of Sainte-Beuve – the 'Humanist–literary tradition' in France was 'like the great Roman roads which are still visible at the present day, which spanned the whole Empire and led to the Eternal City'.[80] In general, while the historical experience of Germany was division and conflict, Curtius believed, that of France was unity and continuity – at least until the eye-opening débâcle of 1870.

Continuity – that nemesis of poststructuralism – was a central theme of Curtius's work. 'Continuity!' he apostrophized. 'We have met it in a hundred forms ... , from learning the rudiments to conscious and successful taking over of a heritage; from piecing together a cento to a mastery of Latin verse which equals antique models ... '[81] Continuity could be seen both in the survival of literary tradition in times of 'crisis', which was the condition of Curtius's own work, and in retrospective efforts of 'canon-formation'.[82] But it could be seen above all in the small rhetorical habits – the topoi – that authors shared throughout a tradition; for (the motto which Curtius liked to quote from Aby Warburg) 'God is in detail.'

From his *Topoiforschung* Curtius left a rich legacy for later scholars. Among the rhetorical 'places' that persisted over the centuries and across linguistic and cultural divides were commonplaces of beginnings and endings, of novelty and conclusion, or crisis and progress. 'I bring things never heard before,' declared authors from Aristophanes and Horace to Ariosto and

---

[79] *The Civilization of France: An Introduction*, trans. Olive Wyon (New York, 1932) from *Die Französische Kultur* (1930).
[80] *European Literature*, 19, and *The Civilization of France*, 111.
[81] *European Literature*, 392.
[82] Ibid., 256.

Milton, and the lament about the 'world turned upside-down' had a comparable life-span.[83] I finish my song, 'the game is over', was another theme that produced variations throughout world literature, as did the notion of the world as a book, or the mind as a blank page (*tabula rasa*).[84] More relevant to intellectual and cultural history were the themes of Ancients versus Moderns and the concurrence of Arms and Letters.[85] Like Spitzer, Curtius attached seminal importance to etymology, but as a 'category of thought' rather than a key to linguistic origins.[86]

The purpose of these latter-day *philologi*, although they were painfully aware of the disruptions and 'crisis' of their age, was to preserve the European scope of literature and its continuous life over two and a half millennia of western history. 'Amica philosophia, magis amica philologia,' Spitzer once remarked; and this might be taken as a motto for all of these latter-day philologists. Vossler, Spitzer, Auerbach, and Curtius sought not only literary but also historical understanding in, respectively, the 'spirit of language', in matters of style, in literary representation, and in rhetorical devices. What they also did was to suggest the primacy of linguistic and literary representation as an essential intermediary for, rather than a barrier to, the understanding of culture or a higher spiritual reality of pure ideas. The result has been that historians in particular have had to consider more carefully the role of linguistic, literary, and rhetorical convention as a constituent element in historical explanation and interpretation.

4.   Literature and Ideas

What does art have to do with ideas? More specifically, what does 'literature' have to do with intellectual history? Some critics look on literary works as philosophical surrogates and seek ideas – even, in Lovejoy's phrase, 'unit-ideas' – in novels, drama, and poetry. As Hans Robert Jauss put it, 'The history of ideas [*Geistesgeschichte*] strove secretly for a renewal of the history of philosophy in the mirror of literature.'[87] Others reject the philistine notion that literary art is a medium for formal conceptualization or can be reduced to propositional

---

[83] *European Literature*, 85, 94.
[84] Ibid., 89, 302.
[85] Ibid., 251, 178.
[86] Ibid., 495.
[87] *Toward an Aesthetic of Reception*, trans. T. Bahti (Minneapolis, 1982), 6; and see R. S. Crane, 'The History of Ideas and Literary Theory', *The Practice of Modern Scholarship* (Glenview, IL, 1954), 27–38.

statements, that poetry can drop its rhyme and rhythm and be converted into reasonable prose and intelligible messages. But intellectual history is not tied to unit-ideas, for it reaches out also to larger cultural formations, whether defined as spirit, structure, patterns, *Weltanschauung*, or mentality. These rubrics are often vague, but they do locate the common ground, including the semantic field and linguistic horizons, within which even the workings of genius are set. 'Poets, not otherwise than philosophers, painters, sculptors, and musicians are, in one sense, the creators, and, in another, the creations of their age', Shelley declared – and moreover, qualifying his vision of the Unbound Promethean poet, 'From this subjugation the loftiest do not escape' in any age.[88]

Devotees of literature have often hoped to protect their terrain from critical and scholarly interlopers, but the purity and autonomy of their special arena have been violated from many angles, while the countervailing interdisciplinary ventures of literary studies have made deep inroads into science, art, and the social sciences. So Marjorie Hope Nicolson showed the impact of the new optics – the telescope and the microscope as well as Newtonian theory – on poetic imagery; and so later scholars have revealed the counter-Newtonian impact of Goethe, in whose writing science and poetry were joined. So, too, Erwin Panofsky explored the relations between artistic form and perspective across the liberal arts, including poetry and history, illustrating the Renaissance incarnations of the classical formula *ut pictura poesis*, while Henry Peyre emphasized the role of generational patterns in literary creation, finding social patterns and periodicity over centuries of literary history.[89] Even while establishing autonomy, then, Literature – 'good letters' – could not avoid contact with many parts of that multi-disciplined encyclopedia from which it had emerged.

Despite the survival of world literature and the rise of comparative literature, literary scholarship continued to run mainly in the channels cut by the major national languages. Journals, professional associations, textbooks, courses of study, university departments, and other institutions reinforced this tendency, which invaded other areas of cultural study. Old conventions of national character not only intruded on aesthetics but were projected into a remote past, which became the target of rival historiographical claims, continuing Renaissance debates between Germanists, Romanists, and Celticists. These were modern counterparts of earlier imputations of implausible antiquity to peoples, which Vico had stigmatized as the 'conceit of scholars'.

---

[88] Preface to *Prometheus Unbound*; and see A.D. Harvey, *Literature into History* (New York, 1988), 13ff.
[89] *Les Générations littéraires* (Paris, 1948).

In France literary scholars investigated the construction of national history, especially by emphasizing the impact of books, printers, authors, and readers on historical change. Daniel Mornet began a massive inquest into the 'intellectual origins of the Revolution', opposing the narrowly based judgments of Taine and De Tocqueville, broadening the horizons of literary inquiry into ideas by 'multiplying documents', and seeking intellectual agency and 'influence' in the quotidian as well as the artistic and the erudite as reflected in printed texts.[90] Mornet uncovered many 'hidden' as well as famous masters of revolutionary disciples in the later eighteenth century, but his emphasis was always on the evolution of the 'intelligence' that underlay, even in its excesses, revolutionary change. Mornet's is a task that is still being pursued by Roger Chartier, Robert Darnton, and others, though in rather more sophisticated ways that go beyond the *c'est-la-faute-de-Voltaire* tendencies of earlier scholarship, whether celebratory, denunciatory, or merely analytical.

More broadly based still, in conception if not in vocabulary, is Paul Hazard's discriminating exploration of the 'crisis' of European consciousness, which traces links between the new philosophy and the skeptical anti-philosophy of the seventeenth century and the socializing and reformist efforts of the Enlightenment.[91] What Hazard sees is not an evolution of subversive notions, however, but a thrilling drama of ideas being disseminated by colorful intellectuals debating the most basic questions of belief and existence across all the disciplines throughout the Republic of Letters. Skeptics, critics, deists, rationalists, empiricists, atheists, and naturalists – these are the movers and shakers of the European conscience; and to depict the extraordinary transformation of the generation of *c.* 1700 Hazard invokes a profusion of metaphors: Europe in ferment, generations at war, the fabric of civilization torn, foundations demolished and rebuilt, men (few women) taking adventurous mental journeys, perspectives being changed, and always the question of historicists and anti-historicists alike: what is Europe? What has it been, and what has it become through ideas and values – and errors – generated during these pivotal decades?

Or, wondered other French scholars, did the ferment, the demolition, the war, and in short the Revolution, begin earlier? Henri Busson and René Pintard pursued two components of Hazard's thesis – rationalism and libertinism – back to earlier phases of subversive thought associated with

---

[90] *Les Origines intellectuelles de la révolution française 1715–1787* (Paris, 1954[5]); and see Lanson, 'Sur la notion de l'influence', in *Essais*, 95.

[91] *The European Mind 1680–1715*, trans. J. Lewis May (Cleveland, 1963), from *La Crise de la conscience européenne* (1935).

Renaissance scholarship; and they tried, in exaggerated ways, to incorporate their erudite findings into a Whiggish or triumphalist story of progressive and subversive secularization.[92] This story the historian of political thought Georges de Lagarde traced further back to the nominalist and Averroist schools of the fourteenth century.[93] Since the work of Lucien Febvre in particular such intellectual projects grounded in mainly literary or philosophical texts have been criticized and 'contextualized' in keeping with broader appreciations of historical and cultural environment.[94]

In Britain the discussion of literature was more measured and increasingly insular (and uncomparative). After Arnold, English literary criticism in Britain, as well as in France and Germany, was diverted increasingly into academic channels and became preoccupied with scholarship – 'philology' in a pejorative sense – without, however, being sure about the relevance of historical erudition to the appreciation of literary texts. Diverted by biographical details – 'Shakespeare's laundry lists' – some critics tended to lose sight of what René Wellek and Austin Warren called the 'intrinsic study of literature' and 'modes of existence of the literary work of art'.[95]

On the most elementary level the issue took the form of the 'personal heresy', as C. S. Lewis defined it, which assumed that a work of art such as a poem was above all an expression of the psychology of the poet and, conversely, that grasping the mental state of an author was the best way of understanding the work.[96] This was the issue debated by Lewis and E. M. W. Tillyard, which recapitulated the opposition between Proust and Sainte-Beuve about the uses of criticism. On the one hand were the neoclassical or formalist arguments for the autonomy, ahistoricity, and aesthetic transcendence of literary art, and on the other the fascination with gossip and scandal. An example involving Sainte-Beuve himself was his affair with Victor Hugo's wife, which may not have shed light on the literary practice of either but which was (as Irving Babbitt remarked) 'a delectable morsel for the ultra-biographical school'.[97]

---

[92] Pintard, *Le Libertinage érudit dans la première moitié du XVIIe siècle* (Paris, 1943), and Busson, *Le Rationalisme dans la littérature française de la Renaissance (1533–1601)* (Paris, 1971²).

[93] *La Naissance de l'esprit laïque au déclin du moyen-âge* (Paris, 1956–70³).

[94] *The Problem of Unbelief in the Sixteenth Century*, trans. Beatrice Gottlieb (Cambridge, MA, 1982).

[95] *Theory of Literature* (New York, 1949), 139.

[96] E. M. W. Tillyard and C. S. Lewis, *The Personal Heresy: A Controversy* (London, 1939).

[97] *The Masters of Modern French Criticism* (London, 1913).

On the cultural level the opposition was between formalism and another distraction from aesthetic focus, namely the notion of historical context. Here, by way of illustration, was another classic debate, this one between F. R. Leavis, posing as the 'Responsible Critic', and F. W. Bateson, responding as champion of scholarship and what he called 'the discipline of contextual reading' (such as practiced, for example, by Rosamond Tuve).[98] The notoriously opinionated Leavis demurred, arguing that the notion of placing a poem back into 'total context' was nonsense and that 'social context' was an illusion arising involuntarily 'out of one's personal living' in the twentieth century. In any case, Leavis added, 'social' was an invidious term which should not be allowed to contaminate the high art of Literature. 'I myself am firmly convinced', he declared, 'that literature must be judged as literature and not as something else.'[99] For Leavis such pretensions to scholarship suggested an inability to read poetry and to make the sort of aesthetic judgments which were really the office of the critic.

Yet English literary scholars continued to carry on their historical researches for the most part in the mode of Stephen and Lecky, keeping one eye on questions of religion, the threats thereto and the loss thereof. One such traditionalist was Basil Willey, who offered leisurely tours of the 'background' of English literature from Bacon to the Victorians and who indeed associated himself with the 'history of ideas' following the 'pioneering' efforts of Mark Pattison.[100] However, like Whitehead, Lovejoy, and Burtt (all of them cited), Willey was particularly sensitive to unconscious premises – 'doctrines felt as facts' and other aspects of the 'climates of opinions' of an age (the phrase of Joseph Glanvill which Willey helped to restore). Thus – invoking T. E. Hulme and T. S. Eliot on the value of such pursuits – Willey ranged through the fields of religion, science, and philosophy to gain an understanding of relevant 'world-views' and so a deeper appreciation of poetry.

Tillyard was another scholar who carried on the great tradition of literary history in an updated Stephensian style, still concerned with the Religious (if not the Social) Question – no longer, however, out of nostalgia or sense of loss but out of a desire to reconstruct the bygone 'world-picture', based on an older 'humanism', which modern secular scholars have forgotten how to understand. Tillyard's *Elizabethan World Picture* (1944) – 'a most glorious

---

[98] Repr. in *A Selection from Scrutiny*, ed. F. R. Leavis (Cambridge, 1968), II, 280ff.
[99] *Anna Karenina and other essays* (London, 1967), 195.
[100] *More Nineteenth Century Studies* (London, 1956), 137; also *Nineteenth Century Studies: Coleridge to Arnold* (London, 1949); *The Eighteenth Century Background: Studies on the Idea of Nature in the Thought of the Period* (London, 1940); and *The Seventeenth Century Background* (London, 1934).

book', in the opinion of Spitzer[101] – undertook just such a reconstruction not only of a climate of opinion but of an elaborate structure of beliefs, correspondences, and unconscious assumptions which constituted doctrines felt as facts. Tillyard has come under fire of late for the static and supposedly insensitive view of Elizabethan order, prejudice, and superstition which his work portrayed – although all Tillyard professed to do was provide material for a better understanding of Shakespeare, Milton, and other poets. For him criticism as well as history was subordinate to the literary 'work' itself. His main interest lay not in an alien climate of opinion but in literary creations that survived changes in the cultural environment and the loss of primary context.

The relationship between ideas and literature (and so literary criticism) has always been uneasy, analogous to that between literal and figurative kinds of interpretation. One may seek to extract ideas from poetry or, more easily, from a 'novel of ideas'; but such efforts suggest an act of desecration, or at least of muddling of genres. One may also attempt to construct narratives about literature as a cultural form with a definable history or even canon, but this transcends the world of authors and texts. The most persuasive, and most traditional, connection may be the belief that language, and therefore literature, reflects Being (in Heidegger's sense) in human terms.

This is a belief that began perhaps as an onomastic superstition – the Adamic power of naming – but it has ended up as conviction of the most cultivated modern intellectuals. One approach, which might be called the mystical, is exemplified by Walter Benjamin, who – alluding to Hamann and anticipating Heidegger – remarked that 'Language communicates the linguistic being of things'; and 'It is therefore the linguistic being of man to name things.'[102] A more historical view was taken by T. S. Eliot, who argued for linguistic and literary learning on the grounds that this optimized the power of an author in his own use of language. 'The essential of tradition is in this', he wrote; 'in getting as much as possible of the whole weight of history of the language behind the word.'[103] This historicist advice was for the poet and for the literary critic, but it might also be heeded by intellectual and cultural historians.

---

[101] *The Elizabethan World Picture: A Study of the Idea of Order in the Age of Shakespeare, Donne and Milton* (London, 1944); and see Spitzer, *World Harmony*, 196.

[102] 'On Languages as Such and on the Language of Man', in *Reflections*, ed. Peter Demetz (New York, 1979), 316.

[103] 'The Three Provincialities' (1922), cited by James Longenbach, *Modernist Poetics of History: Pound, Eliot, and the Sense of the Past* (Princeton, 1987), 236.

5. American Criticism

American literary history followed the national model developed by European scholars and was agitated by the same problems of the autonomy of literature versus the intrusions of reductionist history and stifling context. The poles of earlier American literary history were set by traditional–triumphalist stories in the style of Barrett Wendell and the later Van Wyck Brooks, and the radical alternative represented by Vernon L. Parrington and Granville Hicks.[104] Both approaches in the search for what Brooks called a 'usable past' preserved a conventional, largely doxographical narrative, though also contextual and differing in choice of aesthetic (and social and political) values and in the fixing of a national literary canon.

The old philology was still alive and was aesthetically as well as historically productive. John Livingston Lowes brought his Chaucerian training and exegetical care to Coleridge's poetry, subjecting it to a virtuoso display of *Quellenforschung*, passing 'through half the lands and all the seven seas of the globe' and revealing not only many of the images and conceits of 'The Ancient Mariner' and 'Kubla Khan' but also the plagiaristic methods by which Coleridge achieved his 'magical synthesis'. 'For the road to Xanadu, as we have traced it, is the road of the human spirit', Lowes concluded, 'and the imagination voyaging through chaos and reducing it to clarity and order is the symbol of all the quests which bring glory to our dust.'[105]

Irving Babbitt, though billing himself as a 'New humanist', is another example of the Old Historicism. Regarding history, biography, and science as the best preparation for the critic, Babbitt turned for instruction to the post-Romantic tradition, especially Sainte-Beuve, whose critical practice he saw as extending across concentric, psychological, and cultural horizons. 'The first relation [Sainte-Beuve] establishes in his network of relativity', Babbitt writes, 'is that between a work and its author; between the author in turn and his family, race, and age; and then between the age and the age and the preceding age, and so on in widening circles.'[106] Less deterministic than Taine, Sainte-Beuve was concerned not merely with material conditions and signs of 'fatality' but also with the 'spiritual climate' (*climat des esprits*) in studying literary creation in the successions of masters and disciples (or defectors). Not that Babbitt was satisfied with the parochialisms of literary scholarship; for he

---

[104] Wendell, *The Traditions of European Literature* (New York, 1920).
[105] *The Road to Xanadu: A Study in the Ways of the Imagination* (London, 1927), 3, 396.
[106] *Masters*, 151.

placed his own learning, controversially, in the service of a backward-looking doctrine of New Humanism which recapitulated the old Schlegelian antagonisms of Classical and Romantic, attributing to the latter all the literary and many of the intellectual ills of modernity.[107]

Arthur O. Lovejoy was a historian of literature as well as of philosophy, and he was even more discriminating historically than many literary scholars. He disapproved of Babbitt's study of Rousseau, with its attack on Romanticism; and he distinguished between a number of historical 'romanticisms'.[108] For Lovejoy 'Romanticism' stood for a whole complex of ideas 'rather than certain simpler, diversely combinable, intellectual and emotional components' of such a complex. He showed that, for Schlegel, 'romantic Poetry' was originally an ordinary historical term and only later, around 1797, acquired aesthetic and philosophical connotations of 'sentimentality', with its 'modern' and even revolutionary opposition to classicism. Yet Lovejoy often seemed to undervalue the aesthetic dimension of literature and the arts, arguing that literature was to be *studied*

> chiefly for its thought-content, and that the history of literature is largely as a record of the movement of ideas which have affected men's imagination and emotions and behavior.[109]

Here Lovejoy, whether deliberately or not, identified a central issue in the literary scholarship of his generation.

Philology kept its grip on conventional literary studies; but some younger critics, and especially academic critics, of the period between the wars did not want to be beholden to historical scholarship, whether traditionalist or radical, in their search for literary significance. The New Criticism (an old and indeed recurrent name for a novel program)[110] represented a shift to aesthetic and in some ways formalist standards which affirmed the integrity of the literary work – referring mainly to poems – as well as the autonomy of their own discipline, which for some approached the level of an independent science, though not in the sense of Germanic *Literaturwissenschaft*.

---

[107] *The New Laocoön: An Essay on the Confusion of the Arts* (Boston, 1910), and Irving Babbitt, *Rousseau and Romanticism* (Boston, 1919).

[108] 'The Meaning of "Romantic" in Early German Romanticism', 'Schiller and the Genesis of German Romanticism', and 'On the Discrimination of Romanticisms', in *Essays in the History of Ideas* (Baltimore, 1948), 183–253.

[109] *The Great Chain of Being: The Study of the History of an Idea* (Cambridge, MA, 1950), 16.

[110] See, for example, Joel Spingarn's manifesto of 1910 on 'the new criticism', drawing on the aesthetics of Croce.

Some of the poets whom they admired, notably Eliot and Pound, were themselves profoundly historical-minded, as James Longenbach has shown, in 'drawing many representations of the past into their work'.[111] Yet the main drift of the New Critics was anti-historical as well as anti-contextual – the confrontation being, as R. S. Crane put it, 'history versus criticism in the study of literature'.[112] Like Leavis and William Empson, New Critics like Allen Tate deplored the pedantry that buried art under bio-bibliography and historical trivia. They were uneasy with the notion that poetry was a vehicle for prosaic 'ideas' – and so subject to the judgments of historians thereof – and they took the old view that poetry, while employing human speech, might touch Being itself: 'A poem should not mean/But be', in MacLeish's prosaic and didactic formulation – a distant echo, perhaps, of Heidegger's 1930s turn to poetry (especially Romantic German poetry) as the next best thing to 'Being' itself.[113] As Terry Eagleton said, they 'converted the poem into a fetish'.[114]

After the Second World War criticism pursued still newer fashions and stranger gods, and yet scholarship and literary history continued to be defended and practiced by academic critics such as René Wellek, Harry Levin, Perry Miller, Walter Jackson Bate, and M. H. Abrams, to name just a few whose work preserved – though with new twists and critical judgment – connections with philology, the old historicism, cultural history, and, conditionally, the history of ideas as defined by Lovejoy.[115] Lovejoy's problem was that he was more a philosopher than a historian, according to Levin (who had been a student of Babbitt and Lowes at Harvard), and so was better at tracing single ideas than in 'placing a "thought-complex" against its age'.[116] Levin concluded that Lovejoy's method, the opposite of the Marxist approach, is best understood as 'philosophic intellectualism'. In his indulgent response Lovejoy promised to mend his hyper-intellectualist ways, though he continued to insist that his method was consistent with these contextualist recommendations.

The literary historian who remained closest to Lovejoy's views of the history of ideas was Perry Miller, whose studies of the New England mind

---

[111] *Modernist Poetics of History*, 11.

[112] *The Idea of the Humanities* (Chicago, 1967), II, 3–24.

[113] Frank Lentricchia, *After the New Criticism* (Chicago, 1974), 6.

[114] *Literary Theory: An Introduction* (Minneapolis, 1983), 49.

[115] Henri Peyre, *Writers and their Critics: A Study of Misunderstanding* (Ithaca, 1944), 269–313, held out hopes for a 'reconciliation of scholarship, criticism, and literature'. M. H. Abrams, *Doing Things with Texts* (New York, 1989), calls himself a 'cultural historian', who writes the history 'not of reality ... [but of] the overall form of the past, the present condition and future of the human race'.

[116] *Grounds for Comparison* (Cambridge, MA, 1972), 133–4.

revised the national perspectives of authors like Brooks and Parrington and revealed the significance and complexities of Puritan thought, with reference to Augustinian piety and Ramist 'method'. Following a topical method, Miller described the 'anatomy' of the Puritan mind, the 'architecture of intellect brought to America', according to a hierarchical arrangement (God, nature, man, society) not unlike the Great Chain of Being itself.[117] For Miller the function of 'ideas' was to provide a link between Puritanism and Primitive Christianity and to the secular society of the eighteenth century, when 'the greatness of man's dependence upon God' was increasingly shortened to simply the 'greatness of man'.[118]

Literary history and criticism in a conventional sense was chronicled and celebrated in René Wellek's comprehensive *History of Modern Criticism*, which began with a sketch of eighteenth-century classicism and the divergence between philosophical and literary *Kritik*, the latter following the methods of ancient and Renaissance 'grammar'. Then Wellek settled into the story of the 'great tradition', Schlegel and the Romantic school. In general Wellek preferred Lovejoy's concrete views to the vagueness of *Geistesgeschichte*. The history of literature is 'simply a branch of the history of ideas which is only in loose relationship with the literature produced at the time', he wrote; and 'Criticism is part of the history of culture in general and is then set in historical and social context.'[119] And 'ideas wander, migrate, blow about, are carried by winds of doctrine'.[120] Wellek also noted the 'new mythology' of the early nineteenth century as well as the 'new historicism' of that same period, and he remarked on Leslie Stephen's anticipation of Lovejoy's notion that 'ideas in literature are philosophical ideas in dilution'.[121]

In an essay of 1941 Wellek celebrated 'the rise of literary history', but a generation later, at the close of his eight-volume masterwork – he lamented its 'fall'.[122] For Wellek, pseudo-apocalyptic talk of the 'death of literature', the 'end of art', and the 'death of culture' signaled the demise, too, of the history of literature and perhaps of ideas. Wellek exaggerated, of course; a new age of criticism and theory was rising just as his own canonical narrative

---

[117] *The New England Mind: The Seventeenth Century* (Boston, 1939), 490; and see David Hollinger, 'Perry Miller and Philosophical History', *In the American Province: Studies in the History and Historiography of Ideas* (Baltimore, 1985), 152–66.
[118] *The New England Mind: From Colony to Province* (Boston, 1953), 485.
[119] *A History of Modern Criticism*, I, *The Later Eighteenth Century*, 7–8.
[120] Ibid., III, xv.
[121] Ibid., IV, 186; and on Lovejoy's 'influence', VI, 70, and (with Austin Warren), *Theory of Literature*, 111.
[122] *The Attack on Literature* (Chapel Hill, 1982), 64ff.

was brought to a close in the 1950s 'after the New Criticism'.[123] Frank Lentricchia portrays a panoramic scene of competing theories, beginning with Northrop Frye's turn to myth and rhetoric in his *Anatomy of Criticism* of 1957 and including an extraordinary influx of continental philosophy – phenomenology, existentialism, structuralism, and the chaotic poststructuralist ideas of derivative, Germanophile French criticism and theory. Belatedly, the influence of Heidegger and, at second hand, Nietzsche, transformed conventional ideas of a unified tradition of Literature (if not of Criticism) and Authorship – with attendant implications for intellectual and cultural history.

Frye himself understood the impermanence of literary theories. 'Whenever we construct a system of thought to unite earth with heaven, the story of the Tower of Babel recurs', he concluded: 'we discover that after all we can't quite make it, and that what we have in the meantime is a plurality of languages.'[124] It is under these conditions that philology rather than philosophy applies and that, in the formula of Friedrich Wolf, 'History speaks.'

6. Litero-Philosophy

In the past generation historians have seen not only the 'linguistic turn' but also the 'revenge of literature',[125] but both of these apparent novelties are more properly understood as extensions of earlier movements intended to broaden intellectual horizons. A literary text may serve as either a 'document' or a 'work' (according to Heidegger's distinction).[126] In the first form it offers a small piece of evidence for a writer's career or immediate intellectual context; in the second form it opens up larger disciplinary horizons. 'The repertory of a literary text does not consist solely of social and cultural norms', Wolfgang Iser writes; 'it also incorporates elements and, indeed, whole traditions of literature, that are made together with these norms.'[127] It

---

[123] *After the New Criticism*, 1ff., 81ff.

[124] *Anatomy of Criticism: Four Essays* (Princeton, 1957), 354.

[125] See Linda Orr, 'The Revenge of Literature: A History of History', in *Studies in Historical Change*, ed. Ralph Cohen (Charlottesville, 1992), 84–108; David Harlan, 'Intellectual History and the Return of Literature', *American Historical Review*, 94 (1989), 581–698.

[126] 'The Origin of the Work of Art', *Poetry, Language, Thought*, trans. Albert Hofstadter (New York, 1971), 15–87; and see Dominick LaCapra, *Rethinking Intellectual History* (Ithaca, 1983), 28ff.

[127] *The Art of Reading: A Theory of Aesthetic Response* (Baltimore, 1978), 79. Heidegger, 'Origin of the Work of Art', 15–87; and cf. Dominick LaCapra, 'Rethinking

has been the special aim of literary historians, critics, and theorists to explore such metatextual and metalinguistic phenomena and so, with the license of aesthetic and hermeneutical theory, to trespass on the territory of intellectual and cultural history.

If there was a 'fall of literary history' in the last part of the twentieth century, as Wellek lamented, it was accompanied by an even more spectacular rise of literary criticism and especially theory.[128] Not that success has brought consensus, for the generation or two since the demise of the New Criticism has seen an inundation of theories. Most of these critical movements have been, as Lentricchia remarked in his survey of literary criticism since Frye, 'scandalously short-lived';[129] and yet their interdisciplinary reach, if not always conceptual grasp, makes them worthy of some attention.

In its recent expansion literary theory has followed a familiar path of seeking first disciplinary independence and then interdisciplinary hegemony. From the 1950s literary critics followed philosophers, historians, and other scholars in seeking autonomy for their crafts; and the result has been a variety of approaches to criticism – phenomenological, structuralist, narratological, and semiotic. After this came encroachment not only on adjacent fields of the humanities but also on philosophy, history, science, and all kinds of 'cultural criticism'. The last step has been the implicit or explicit assertion of jurisdiction over older disciplines, on the grounds that philosophy, history, and even the sciences are all forms of literary discourse and textual performance and so, arguably, open to the professional judgment of literary critics.

The postwar turn to theory occurred in the name of novelty, and it has generally entailed rejection of the old philology, the old literary history, and what is pejoratively (and uncritically) called the 'old historicism'. The upshot has been that many of the premises of the history of ideas as conceived by Curtius, Auerbach, Collingwood, and Lovejoy, have been challenged or discarded. This reaction began with formalist criticism, which was based on the application of linguistics (structural rather than historical) to literature,

---

Intellectual History and Reading Texts', in *Modern European Intellectual History: Reappraisals and New Perspectives*, ed. Dominick LaCapra and Stephen L. Kaplan (Ithaca, 1982), 47–85.

[128] In a vast literature see *The Future of Literary Theory*, ed. Ralph Cohen (New York, 1989); Joseph Natoli (ed.), *Tracing Literary Theory* (Urbana, 1987); Terry Eagleton, *Literary Theory: An Introduction* (Minneapolis, 1983); Diane Macdonell, *Theories of Discourse: An Introduction* (Oxford, 1986); and Howard Felperin, *Beyond Deconstruction: The Uses and Abuses of Literary Theory* (Oxford, 1985).

[129] *After the New Criticism*, 65.

and then the New Criticism, which restored what Frye called 'the aesthetic view'.[130] Frye himself restored a certain historical perspective, but also in a formalist way that depended on a theory of literary modes and a neo-Romantic cyclical movement from myth to irony and back.

More recently, Frye's scheme was adapted by Hayden White for 'metahistorical' purposes, which in effect subsumed the study of history – or at least 'historical theory' – under literary theory and criticism.[131] This is also the drift of Paul Ricœur's analysis of time and narrative, which treats historical meaning apart from questions of extra-textual truth or heuristics, except for general considerations of enigmatic historical 'traces', which find meaning only in historical narrative.[132] The result is 'a philosophy of history for readers of history only'.[133]

The common ground of most schools of literary theory appears in the much-discussed 'linguistic turn' (which in the perspective of this book is rather a linguistic *return*), a phrase as polyvalent and problematic as language itself and referring to analytic and anti-historical as well as hermeneutical and historical views.[134] But whatever else this turn might suggest, conventional 'ideas' were not among them; preexistent, private, or mental language is rejected as beyond semantic analysis and historical inquiry; and indeed the recent turn is reminiscent of the 'metacritical' position of Herder, who likewise wanted to replace philosophy with literature and linguistics and to make cultural history the foundational science of humanity. In the twentieth century philosophy has again had to resist assimilation by literary scholars.

One manifestation of the recent linguistic turn was the appearance of the 'new rhetoric', reinforced by the work of Kenneth Burke and others and, like literary theory, displaying interdisciplinary and imperialist tendencies. But once again the new was followed by the shadow of the old. Since the sophists rhetoric had been a standing challenge to philosophy, replacing propositional argument with literary language and ideas with human discourse.[135] In contrast

---

[130] *Anatomy of Criticism*, 350.

[131] *The Content of the Form: Narrative Discourse and Historical Representation* (Baltimore, 1987), 26.

[132] *Temps et récit*, I (Paris, 1983), 137ff; III (Paris, 1985), 171ff.

[133] Leon Goldstein, *Historical Knowing* (Austin, 1976), 164.

[134] Richard M. Rorty (ed.), *The Linguistic Turn: Essays in Philosophical Method* (Chicago, 1992²); and Martin Jay, 'Should Intellectual History Take a Linguistic Turn?', in *Modern European Intellectual History*, ed. LaCapra and Kaplan, 86–110.

[135] Ch. Perelman and L. Olbrechts-Tyteca, *The New Rhetoric*, trans. J. Wilkinson and P. Weaver (Notre Dame, 1969); and Kenneth Burke, *A Rhetoric of Motives* (New York, 1950).

to philosophy, rhetoric introduces human colorings of persuasion, specificity, sociability, taste, and judgment as well as threats of relativism, historicism, and perhaps political subversion. As White and his followers have argued, historical narrative is a primary realm of rhetorical structures and performance; but what is more problematic, so are the primary documentary sources of historical inquiry and interpretation. There is, in effect, no level of discourse free of rhetorical structure, and intellectual and cultural history must operate within these constraints.

Insisting on the primacy of the rhetorical aspect of history has been the special project of White, LaCapra, and other sometime historians who have taken a literary turn.[136] They are aware that this project has roots in ancient literary theory, although they seem to claim originality in reasserting the simple truths that the past has no meaning other than what writers of history impose on it through narrative structures. The gains for intellectual history have been substantial, but the neglect of the heuristic aspects of history – privileging the 'work' above the 'document' – has brought a new aetheticism and a defection of many of these scholars from history to literary history and theory and, in that connection, a 'new philosophy of history'.[137]

One of the key devices of rhetoric is metaphor, but metaphor is also a condition of language and a vehicle of explanation employed by historians as well as philosophers and scientists.[138] Knowledge is represented as analogous to sight, for example, and the passage of time to the flow of a stream, while the complex notion of 'secularization' is drawn from the ecclesiastical law of property. Historical explanation often depends on metaphors of organic life, human measures of time, natural processes, technology, theater, sport, and music. Yet these analogies are worlds away from historical reality. As Alexander Demandt says,

---

[136] See Hayden White, *Topics of Discourse: Essays in Cultural Criticism* (Baltimore, 1978); Dominick LaCapra, 'Rhetoric and History', in *History and Criticism* (Ithaca, 1985), 15–44; and Frank Ankersmit, *Narrative Logic: A Semantic Analysis of the Historian's Language* (The Hague, 1983), and Hans Kellner, *Language and Historical Representation: Getting the Story Crooked* (Madison, 1989), among others. The remarkable, international following accumulated by White is suggested by the two issues of *Storia della storiografia*, 24 (1993) and 25 (1994), devoted to discussing his *Metahistory* twenty years after.

[137] Frank Ankersmit and Hans Kellner (eds), *A New Philosophy of History* (Chicago, 1995); see my review in *New Vico Studies*, 14 (1996), 101–10.

[138] See Mary Hesse, *Revolutions and Reconstructions in the Philosophy of Science* (Bloomington, 1980), 111–24, drawing especially on Max Black, *Models and Metaphors* (Ithaca, 1962); also Perelman and Olbrechts-Tyteca, *The New Rhetoric*; also Richard H. Brown, *A Poetic for Sociology: Toward a Logic of Discovery for the Human Sciences* (Cambridge, 1977).

> History is not a stream, not a road, and not a tragedy. History does not grow like a child or a tree. History does not 'move', and in history nothing moves either backwards or forwards, up or down, straight or in circles. History is not built like a house or woven like a carpet, nor is it played like a drama, a game of chess, or a symphony.[139]

But of course history in its written forms has been all these things and more.

The highest ambition of literary theory is indeed to pass judgments not merely on literary texts and traditions but also on the human predicament in the most global and existential sense; and the result has been what J. G. Merquior has called 'litero-philosophy'.[140] Here the first name is Nietzsche, who represents both a modernist point of departure and, in the guise of the 'new Nietzsche', a postmodernist ideal of philosophical and cultural criticism in a literary mode.[141] From Nietzsche, for example, Foucault derived many of his insights about questions of power and Derrida weapons in the struggle against logocentrism. Next to Nietzsche, Heidegger is arguably the major influence in contemporary criticism; and his privileging of poetry as the most direct expression of Being, notably in Rilke and Hölderlin, has further reinforced the prestige of literary theory as a way of foundational, litero-philosophical thinking.

As literary theory has invaded the terrain of philosophy, so it has intruded on the concerns of intellectual and cultural historians; and one result from the 1980s has been the self-styled New Historicism, which set itself in opposition not only to formalism in literature and criticism but also to a stereotypical old historicism, which allegedly rested on a naïvely developmental and élitist notion of historical change. Although not as overtly Marxist in inspiration as their British counterparts, the Cultural Materialists, the new historicists have also had a political agenda, which is to look for marginal groups, listen for suppressed voices detectable in literary texts, and find political/social referents for cultural symbols.

In the words of one advocate, the new historicism reveals both the historicity of the text and the textuality of history.[142] To read history out of a text or to

---

[139] *Metaphern für Geschichte: Sprachbilder und Gleichnisse im historisch–politischen Denken* (Munich, 1978), 453.
[140] J. G. Merquior, *Foucault* (Berkeley, 1985), 12.
[141] See, for example, Alan D. Schrift, *Nietzsche's French Legacy: A Genealogy of Poststructuralism* (New York, 1995), and David B. Allison (ed.), *The New Nietzsche* (Cambridge, MA, 1985); also Gianni Vattimo, *The End of Modernity*, trans. Jon R. Snyder (Baltimore, 1988), 164–5.
[142] Louis Montrose, 'Renaissance Literary Studies and the Subject of History', *English Literary Renaissance*, 16 (1986), 8. See also Brooks Thomas, *The New Historicism and Other Old-Fashioned Topics* (Princeton, 1991), and Carolyn Porter,

read history as a text: either way we are impelled to adopt a language-model rather than a science-model, according to which history is not a process to be explained but a field of bygone activity that can be represented only through the interpretation of traces, mainly linguistic traces, and often anecdotes. Literary theory has developed not only philosophical and historical ambitions, but also a political conscience that has opened the eyes of scholars to new, or at least overlooked, aspects of human experience. Although in some ways estranged from literature and aesthetics, literary criticism has expanded its intellectual horizons, especially through contact with the rich and riotous field of cultural studies and through interest in various forms of the Other – that is, 'alterity' and what might be called 'sub-alterity'.[143] This includes race, ethnicity, gender, sexuality, women's studies, and 'queer history'.

Women's history has produced important revisions of traditional history. To the question 'What is the place of feminist criticism in the history of ideas?' there is a growing list of responses.[144] The value of a gender perspective is not only to expand and to alter the literary canon founded on 'male ideology', but also to appreciate differences in quality and direction of thought – to understand that the mind indeed, despite philosophical prejudice, 'has sex'. What 'gynocriticism' has done is to find a language and rhetorical strategies to enlarge and to deepen the study of intellectual and cultural history.[145]

The fundamental questions historians must ask have always to do with meaning, and the 'meaning of meaning', and literary theorists have vastly complicated this ancient issue. This they have done by a three-pronged attack, which casts doubt, first, on the relevance of authorial intention, second, on the integrity of the text, and third, on the possibility ever of correct interpretation by readers. For intellectual and cultural historians this subversive line of criticism, inspired by the linguistic turn, has important, if unsettling, implications.

The problem of intentionalism (ungrammatically called the 'intentional fallacy') has been a feature of critical discussion ever since Wimsatt and

'History and Literature: "After the New Historicism"', in *History and* ... , ed. Ralph Cohen and Michael Roth (Charlottesville, 1995), 23–43.
143 See, for example, *Exoticism in the Enlightenment*, ed. G. S. Rousseau and Roy Porter (Manchester, 1990), and *Encountering the Other(s): Studies in Literature, History and Culture*, ed. Gisela Brinker-Gabler (Albany, 1995).
144 Posed by Sandra Gilbert and Susan Gubar, 'The Mirror and the Lamp: Reflections on Feminist Criticism', in *The Future of Literary Theory*, ed. Cohen, 144, and 'Sexual Linguistics: Gender, Language, Society', *New Literary History*, 16 (1984–85), 515ff.
145 See Rita Felski, *The Gender of Modernity* (Cambridge, MA, 1995).

Beardsley's famous paper of 1946.[146] This argument was offered originally
on aesthetic grounds, which fetishized the poem as a 'verbal icon' to be
judged in its own, post-authorial, terms. Yet it has other, more historical,
implications, associated especially with the 'speech-act' theory that credits
authorial ('illocutionary') initiative not only with intended communication
but also with social or political effects. Quentin Skinner in particular has
found the notion of intention essential for reconstructing authorial meaning,
determining contemporary context, and avoiding anachronism, which he
takes to be primary aims of intellectual history (though he has retreated a bit
from this narrowly intentionalist position).[147]

Whether or not it is ever effective, however, an author's control over
meaning ends once the text is established. Like birth, publication or merely
completion of a literary work entails an immediate severance of ties with the
parent, and hence with his or her 'conception', resulting in what Paul Ricoeur
has called the 'semantic autonomy of the text', which implies that texts can
never be restored to their original cultural environment, are always subject to
a process of interpretation carried on in different contexts, and so to some
degree must be open to misinterpretation.[148] This version of the rejection of
the 'intentional fallacy' again makes understanding, in Harold Bloom's terms,
a 'map of misreading' and applies to historical as well as literary
constructions.[149]

The problem of reading has attracted intellectual as well as social historians;
for books form a mental context no less immediate than the cultural
environment outside the study or the library.[150] In intellectual terms the
readerly shift restores an appreciation of the art of hermeneutics and brings
interpretation and 'dialogue' to the forefront, offering a valuable framework
for historians hoping to communicate with the dead. This necessarily creates
a risk of 'reading meaning into' a text, but how can meaning be found apart
from the reading thereof? 'Hermeneutics is', Odo Marquardt cynically
remarked, 'the art of getting out of a text what is not in it.'[151] Yet this is

---

[146] William K. Wimsatt and Monroe C. Beardsley, 'The Intentional Fallacy', *Sewanee
Review*, 54 (1946), 468–88, and *The Verbal Icon: Studies in the Meaning of Poetry*
(New York, 1954); also Northrop Frye, *Anatomy of Criticism*, 86.
[147] *Meaning and Context: Quentin Skinner and his Critics*, ed. James Tulley
(Princeton, 1988), 70–72, from 'Motives, Intentions, and the Interpretation of Texts',
New Literary History, 3 (1972), 392–408.
[148] *Interpretation Theory* (Fort Worth, 1976), 25.
[149] *A Map of Misreading* (New York, 1975); and on the 'intentional fallacy' see
William Wimsatt, *The Verbal Icon* (Louisville, 1954), 37.
[150] See above, Chapter 3 at note 45.
[151] *Farewell to Matters of Principle* (New York, 1989), 111.

precisely what contextual and retrospective interpretations may involve, since in a hermeneutical perspective, texts acquire new meanings and significance as contexts and readerships change.

In modern philosophical hermeneutics, as developed by Heidegger and Gadamer, aesthetics again has been a formative influence. Literary hermeneutics, however, situates texts in the realm of art, and so places them in the company of aesthetic values and conventions which have been accumulated over many centuries and which have complicated the task of the historian. There is an obvious incongruity between the aim of a historian to 'understand an author better than he understood himself' (the process of *Besserverstehen*)[152] and that of a literary scholar to find artistic meaning in the works of such an author; but both aims challenge the literalist assumptions of intentionalism, acknowledge differences in contexts, and reject simplistic ideas of literal and figurative meaning. These insights are also among the conditions of the contemporary study of intellectual history.

Another factor in determining meaning is the problem of canon-formation (and canon re-formation) and placing particular works in an intellectual tradition. Related to this is what some regard as a fallacy of prolepsis – prophecy, anticipation, prefiguration, and other forms of 'precursoritis' – which bestows new meaning by making precursors out of authors whose genius obviously could not extend to foreseeing doctrinal offspring or 'postcursors'. But it should not need saying that such judgments are based not on foolish imputations of impossible clairvoyance to earlier authors or scripturalist ideas of prophecy fulfilled.[153] Forerunnerhood is always a retrospective reward, a metaphorical way of designating relationships within a tradition, and a conventional way of writing intellectual history.

How far can textualist strategies and rhetoric take the historian and his inquiries? Every generation of theorists must distinguish itself from previous ones, and the result is not only a perennial recurrence of novelty – 'make it new', in the formula of Ezra Pound – but also the question of history-minded critics, 'But have we not heard something like this before?'[154] Susan Handelman finds signs of the rabbinic tradition in the works of Freud, Lacan, Derrida, and Harold Bloom.[155] In recent years the novelty of newness has worn off

---

152 See Wilhelm Dilthey, 'Schleiermacher's Hermeneutical System in Relation to Earlier Protestant Hermeneutics' (1860), *Hermeneutics and the Study of History*, in *Selected Works*, IV, ed. Rudolf Makkreel and Frithjof Rodi (Princeton, 1996), 147.

153 See Chapter 7 at note 62.

154 Lentricchia, *After the New Criticism*, 166.

155 *The Slayers of Moses: The Emergence of Rabbinic Interpretation in Modern Literary Theory* (Albany, 1982).

and has been replaced by a series of 'posts' – postmodern, poststructuralist, posthistorical, postcritical, posthuman, and so on. Such words are all shorthand for older assertions of the 'end' or 'death' of this phenomenon or that – the death of the novel or the end of history – the first being a judgment of literary criticism and the second that of philosophy. But who is it that pronounces the obituaries, and who will comment on the death of the obituary writers? And how will later generations distinguish themselves from post-ists, end-ists, and other proponents of neo-apocalyptic thought?[156] On these questions only history can speak, and then indistinctly.

In the wake of self-styled 'postmodern' criticism 'history' in the Hegelian–idealist (and Marxian–materialist) mode may well have come to an impasse, if not an end. Yet history in a different form has found a new life in the 'literary turn'. There are many stories to be told about the past, or rather many pasts that can be identified and interpreted from the standpoint of a changing present, whose 'presence' has itself been challenged – time will not have a stop. Nor, despite the constraints and complexities, will the writing of intellectual and cultural history.

---

[156] See Jean Baudrillard, *The Illusion of the End*, trans. Chris Turner (Stanford, 1994), and Norman Cohn, *Cosmos, Chaos and the World to Come: the Ancient Roots of Apocalyptic Faith* (New Haven, 1993).

Chapter 7

The History of Science

> There are in fact two versions of the history
> of science: the history of obsolete knowledge
> and the history of sanctioned knowledge.
> Georges Canguilhem

In the mid-eighteenth century J. F. Montucla deplored the huge disproportion between the libraries of books on wars and conflict and those devoted to the bright side of the human spirit and the benefactors of humanity.[1] His own monumental *History of Mathematics* was aimed at redressing this imbalance, and as such it became a model for the new field emerging in the wake of the Baconian program for the advancement of learning. Over the next two centuries many branches of natural science found not only their chroniclers but also their philosophical historians, including scholars such as Paul Tannery and Abel Rey, who aimed at producing a 'synthetic' history of all the sciences which would be at the same time a history of ideas and culture.[2] This enterprise occurred contemporaneously with the effort, pursued by many of the same scholars, to promote the history of science to the level of an independent academic discipline. The twofold development of intellectual expansion and specialization has resulted not only in institutional advancement but also in the emergence of bitterly warring disciplinary parties, which still seems to be the condition of the history of science at the beginning of the past century.

---

[1] *Histoire des mathematiques*, I (Paris, 1758), preface; and see Noel Swerdlow, 'Montucla's Legacy: The History of the Exact Sciences', *Journal of the History of Ideas*, 54 (1993), 315.

[2] In a vast literature see R. C. Olby et al. (eds), *Companion to the History of Modern Science* (London, 1990); A. C. Crombie, *Styles of Scientific Thinking in the European Tradition: The history of argument and explanation especially in the mathematical and biomedical sciences and arts* (3 vols; London, 1994), with a 589-page bibliography.

1. The Baconian Legacy

The concept and the phrase 'history of science' goes back at least to Bacon, whose idea of the advancement of learning was taken up in the Enlightenment, modernized and summarized in Diderot's *Encyclopédie* and revised and systematized in the 'Positive Philosophy' constructed by Condorcet, Comte, and others.[3] For Bacon knowledge was like a pyramid, 'whereof history is the base'; for D'Alembert (following Descartes and followed by Saint-Simon) knowledge formed a chain of particular 'filiated' sciences (Comte's and D'Alembert's term), isomorphic with the chain of reasoning which had produced them. So the history of science was a continuous construction, following the sequence of scientific discovery and the progress of the human spirit and culture.

But there was a difference between the sequence and the 'logic of scientific discovery', as earlier critics well knew.[4] Comte understood the difference between doctrinal and historical advance (*la marche dogmatique* and *la marche historique*), between the rational structure of theory and organized disciplines and the irregular pattern of history, following 'the progressive march of the human spirit'.[5] The former approach adhered to 'sanctioned knowledge', while the latter took into account trial and error. Yet somehow the history of science must do justice both to the disciplines it studies and to the human condition which contains and shapes them.[6]

Just as the history of art, literature, and philosophy begins with individuals and their works – with doxography – so the history of science begins with particular discoveries and not disciplines and social context; and the basic

---

[3] H. Florus Cohen, *The Scientific Revolution: A Historiographical Inquiry* (Chicago, 1994); I. Bernard Cohen, *Revolution in Science* (Cambridge, MA, 1985); *Revolution and Continuity: Essays in the History of Early Modern Science*, ed. Peter Barker and Roger Ariew (Washington, DC, 1991); Walter M. Simon, *European Positivism in the Nineteenth Century: An Essay in Intellectual History* (Ithaca, 1963); and *The Sciences in Enlightened Europe*, ed. William Clark, Jan Golinski, and Simon Schaffer (Chicago, 1999).

[4] Karl R. Popper, *The Logic of Scientific Discovery* (New York, 1961 [1934]).

[5] *Cours de philosophie positive*, ed. Ch. Le Verrier (Paris, n.d.), I, 123; also 'évolution intellectuelle', 'développement de l'esprit humain' (I, 10), 'révolution générale de l'esprit' (I, 12), and so on; and cf. A. A. Cournot, *Traité de l'enchaînement des idées dans les sciences et dans l'histoire*, in *Oeuvres complètes*, III, ed. Nelly Bruyère (Paris, 1982). Also J.-S. Sylvain, *Histoire de l'astronomie ancienne* (Paris, 1769), 143: 'une science est une somme de vérités … [m]ais la chaîne de ces vérités n'est pas l'ordre de leurs découvertes'.

[6] Jacques Roger, 'Pour une Histoire historienne des sciences', *Pour une histoire des sciences à part entière* (Paris, 1995), 45–73.

question, again posed by Bacon, was the role of the individual in scientific advance. Here English and French styles of philosophy (or their popular images) were opposed, the Baconian model of organized empirical research contrasting with the Cartesian ideal of the solitary genius working logically toward certainty: on the one hand gradual, piecemeal advance and on the other, 'Eureka!' – and a revolution. Evidence can be adduced to support either view. Like Descartes, Bacon could be represented as an initiator of a 'revolution in science' (terms employed by him),[7] while Descartes's largely unacknowledged debt to scholastic tradition, despite claims to originality, has been shown by Etienne Gilson and others.[8]

In contrast to historians of culture, who were inclined to gradualist and evolutionary interpretations, historians of philosophy have leaned toward a revolutionary, saltatory, and eurekan paradigm of scientific progress; and the concept of 'scientific revolution' was endorsed and given currency by Kant, who spoke of 'a revolution, brought about in one effort by the happy thought of one individual man' – such as the intellectual feats of Copernicus and Newton.[9] Despite his sociological orientation, Comte accepted the idea of a scientific revolution in the seventeenth century through the efforts of Bacon, Galileo, Newton, Descartes, and other Moderns who seemed to have won the old Quarrel with the Ancients. There was some disagreement, however, about the timing of the full emergence of modern science. For Diderot, 'We are on the verge of a great revolution in the sciences';[10] and such predictions continued in the nineteenth century, casting doubt on the idea of a single turning point. For Baconians the revolution was a continuing process, and for example William Whewell, devout Baconian that he was, saw scientific revolutions as general results of continuing movements from the 'colligation' of singular facts to the formation of general concepts.

For every revolution there is a counter-revolution, and here religion comes into view. The thesis of the emergence of modern science over the protests and malign resistance of organized religion was expressed in its most extreme and vulgar form by Andrew Dickson White, who also accepted the notion of

---

[7] Cohen, *Revolution in Science*, 500, citing Bacon's *Novum Organum*, aphorism lxxviii, on the three 'revolutions' in 'science'; John Schuster, 'The Scientific Revolution', in *Companion to the History of Modern Science*, ed. Olby et al., 217–42; and Stephen Gaukroger (ed.), *The Uses of Antiquity: The Scientific Revolution and the Classical Tradition* (Dordrecht, 1991).

[8] *Etudes sur le rôle de la pensée médiévale dans la formation du système cartésien* (Paris, 1975⁴), and *Index Scholastico-cartésien* (Paris, 1913); and Stephen Menn, *Descartes and Augustine* (Cambridge, 1998).

[9] And see Cohen, *Revolution in Science*, 244.

[10] Ibid., 219.

the scientific revolution of the seventeenth century, carried out by five evangelists – Copernicus, Kepler, Galileo, Descartes, and Newton, who 'had given a new divine revelation to the world'.[11] White's argument, based on a rehearsal of familiar evidence to demonstrate 'the dissolving away of traditional opinions', was cast in a simplistic 'from–to' pattern: from *mythos* to *logos*, from creation to evolution, from 'signs and wonders' to law, from Genesis to geology, from magic to chemistry and physics, from miracles to medicine, from fetish to hygiene, from 'demonical possession' to insanity, from Babel to comparative linguistics, from Dead Sea legends to comparative mythology, from Leviticus to political economy, from divine oracles to the higher criticism – from 'them' to 'us'. In these formulas White offered a grand narrative of linear progress in all areas of thought led by individual saints and martyrs defying the dead hand of Theology.

At the turn of the twentieth century capital-S Science was still in its 'classical' mode. It had experienced a number of 'revolutions', but for many practitioners and philosophers it was approaching apotheosis, a 'Laplacean spirit' (in the phrase of Cassirer) presiding over the disciplines of physical science and moving into the life and human sciences as well.[12] The most fundamental discoveries had been made, and laws had been established, needing at most adjustment and refinement; the mental world was divided, as Herbert Spencer taught, into the knowable and unknowable, and the second was rapidly being subjected to the first.[13] Science was dominated by stable concepts of reality and causality, a sense of secure philosophical foundations, and the assumption that, in Max Planck's words, (not just the Galilean 'what can be measured can be known' but the more arrogant) 'What can be measured exists.'[14]

This may be a simplistic summary, but it is perhaps not unfair as a characterization of the way in which the history of science was being written even as the foundations of this comfortable scientistic view were being shaken by Planck, Mach, Einstein, Poincaré, and other rebels against classical Science. This perspective on science was bound up, too, with ideas of evolution and progress which reached a high point in the early years of the twentieth century. Not that there were no doubts, even among celebrators of these ideas. 'In other words', J. B. Bury asked, 'does not Progress itself suggest that

---

[11] *A History of the Warfare of Science with Theology* (New York, 1907), I, 15; II, 393.

[12] *Determinism and Indeterminism in Modern Physics*, trans. O. Theodor Benfey (New Haven, 1956).

[13] Spencer, *First Principles* (London, 1864).

[14] Cassirer, *Substance and Function* and *Einstein's Theory of Relativity*, trans. William Curtis Swabey and Marie Collins Swabey (Chicago, 1923), 357.

its value is only relative, corresponding to a certain not very advanced stage of civilisation ... ?'[15] This is a question that has continued to trouble serious historians of science, if not scientists.

2. Continuity and Context

In France the history of science turned on the question of intellectual continuity. In the twentieth century this emergent discipline was the subject of debate between revolutionaries and traditionalists. On the one hand was a positivist doctrine tied to the progressive and cumulative advance of science, highlighted by stories of heroic men like Galileo, whose telescope, law of falling bodies, and legendary 'eppur si muove' symbolized the revolutionary character and triumphalist plot of scientific historiography. They were the counterparts of the creative geniuses dominating the parallel canons of philosophy, art, and literature. On the other hand was a story of gradual enlightenment begun by 'precursors' and continued by 'postcursors' within a tradition that preserved connections with religion.

Pierre Duhem was a distinguished physicist, classically trained scholar, and devout Catholic who opposed Dreyfus as well as Einstein's relativity. Duhem's task was to tell the story of the rise of modern physics (statics and dynamics) within the received framework, but a strange thing happened on his way to completing this history and his studies of Leonardo da Vinci: assuming that there were no important landmarks on the road from Archimedes to Leonardo and, via Cardano, Galileo, Descartes, and Newton, Duhem discovered the work of Jordanes of Nemor, Albert of Saxony, Nicholas Oresme, and other scholastic philosophers, which opened up a whole world – three centuries and more – of 'precursors', as he called them, of Leonardo and Galileo.

For Duhem this constituted an earlier, or pre-revolution, though to some critics it seemed more like a counter-revolution, of science; and he turned to a massive retelling of the story as a work of post-scholastic system-building – of which, indeed, his own work was a continuation. The result was his extraordinary researches into the scholastic background of Galilean science and attacks on those mired in 'ignorance of the history of human thought' or victims of the 'strange delusion' of early modern thinkers that the new science was entirely their own work.[16] For Duhem this was a delusion common

---

[15] *The Idea of Progress* (London, 1932), 352.
[16] See the selections in Duhem, *Medieval Cosmology: Theories of Infinity, Place, Time, Void, and the Plurality of Worlds*, trans. Roger Ariew (Chicago, 1985), and

to Moderns who, as so often before, ungratefully overlooked the bequests of the Ancients.

Revealing the work of a series of scientific forebears, Duhem and (in his wake) Anneliese Maier, Marshall Clagett, J. H. Randall, Jr, and William Wallace have stressed the continuity of physical science, between the middle ages and the seventeenth century, in the schools of Oxford, Paris, Padua, and Rome. For Duhem mechanics was 'not a creation' because 'Galileo and his emulators were the heirs of this Parisian tradition.' So modern science was not a revolutionary break but the climax of a long tradition extending back to the devout and unheroic scholastic philosophers of the fourteenth century – a process of enlightenment not unlike the new eclecticism envisioned by Thomasius, Sturm, and Brucker over two centuries earlier – not to mention Duhem's own Parisian precursor, Victor Cousin.

Duhem's exciting discoveries were reinforced by his orthodoxy and sometimes ill-concealed religiosity, and he welcomed the ammunition he could use against anti-clerical ideology underlying the educational establishment of the Third Republic. Yet he was careful to give scholarly legitimacy to his ideological line by presenting it as an objective history of ideas and a well-grounded theory of conceptual advance. 'Science does not know of spontaneous generation', he wrote in 1905. 'Not even the most unfamiliar discoveries have ever been made in all detail in the mind which generated them.'[17] According to this latter-day *lex continui*, Duhem explained,

> The science of mechanics and physics, of which modern times are so rightfully proud, derives in an uninterrupted sequence of hardly visible improvements from doctrines professed in medieval schools. The pretended intellectual revolutions were all too often but slow and long-prepared evolution. The so-called renaissances were often but unjust and sterile reactions. Respect for tradition is an essential condition of scientific progress.[18]

In this way Duhem – not unlike Louis Dutens in the eighteenth and Cousin in the nineteenth century – sought to reconcile modernism with the Christian past.

Duhem tried to tell his revisionist story in a rationalist and internalist fashion, attending to what amounted to clear and distinct ideas, such as momentum and free-fall, and an emphasis on pure theory – 'saving the

---

John E. Murdoch, 'Pierre Duhem and the History of Late Medieval Science and Philosophy in the Latin West', *Gli Studi di filosofia medievale fra otto e novecento* (Rome, 1991), 253–302.

[17] Duhem, *Les Origines de la statique* (Paris, 1905), I, 156.

[18] Ibid., 2.

phenomena', in the medieval formula.[19] 'To give the history of a physical principle', he argued, 'is at the same time to make a logical analysis.'[20] Yet despite this belief in reasoned history, Duhem also employed mythical devices, such as the claim for a first scientific revolution, which produced the medieval 'system of the world'. Thus:

> One of the principal aims of the present work is to justify the assertion that modern science was born, so to speak, on March 7, 1277, from the decree issued by Msgr. Etienne Tempier, bishop of Paris.[21]

This assault on naturalism – and declaration of independence from Aristotelian authority – liberated scholars from these limitations and opened the way to consideration of theses such as the 'plurality of worlds'. How, he asked, could a Parisian (a Catholic Parisian, at that) fail to be proud of this?

Though severely criticized by later scholars, Duhem's work was of enormous importance in establishing the disciplinary status of the history of science at the turn of the century; but he was not alone in his pioneering efforts. Paul Tannery wrote many articles and proposals devoted to the same cause. Although Tannery failed (for political reasons) to gain the chair of the history of science established at the Collège de France in 1892 (losing out to a little-known Comtean),[22] he worked tirelessly to plan courses and programs in the field. For Tannery the object of this discipline was not only (as for Duhem) the 'filiation of ideas and scientific discoveries' but also the 'synthesis of the histories of particular sciences'; and he praised the work of J. T. Merz for precisely this effort.[23] Tannery's campaigns, though they led into the recesses of ancient Greek astronomy and music, were quite consciously pursued in the spirit of the 'historical synthesis' that was being promoted contemporaneously by Henri Berr. In a volume in Berr's *Evolution de l'Humanité* series, Abel Rey celebrated Tannery as one who had 'renewed the history of sciences by

---

[19] *To Save the Phenomena: An Essay on the Idea of Physical Theory from Plato to Galileo*, trans. Edmund Doland and Chaninah Maschler (Chicago, 1969).

[20] *The Aim and Structure of Physical Theory*, trans. P. Wiener (Princeton, 1954), 269.

[21] *Le Système du monde*, VI (Paris, 1973 [1913]), 66.

[22] Forty years earlier Auguste Comte had urged Guizot to establish such a chair, according to Henry Guerlac, *Essays and Papers in the History of Modern Science* (Baltimore, 1977), 33.

[23] *Mémoires scientifiques*, ed. J.-L. Heiberg and H.-G. Zeuthen (17 vols; Paris, 1912–50), X, 179, 168; XII, 47. See E. Coumet, 'Paul Tannery: l'organisation de l'enseignement de l'histoire des sciences', *Revue de synthèse*, 102 (1981), 87–124, and Georges Gusdorf, *De l'histoire des sciences à l'histoire de la pensée* (Paris, 1966), 112–18.

treating their true history, linking it, as Comte had done, to the history of ideas and human thought'.[24]

Variations on Duhem's counter-revolutionary theme reemerged in the middle years of the century, with E. J. Dijksterhuis, Annliese Maier, A. C. Crombie, and Clagett finding unsuspected continuities and precedents underlying revolutionary formulations. Such historicizing scholars pursued, though more critically, Duhem's search for anticipations of mathematical science in the scholastic tradition. The grounds for this historicizing were explained by Clagett, who argued 'that the physical concepts of a Galileo or a Descartes, radical as they may seem, were conditioned in many ways by the ancient and modern learning that survived into the early modern period'.[25] Examining the concepts of an earlier period, Clagett continued, 'will give some insight into how a proto-scientific theory was criticized and emended until it was no longer a cogent whole ... [and] how the very points of criticism of the older system became points of departure for the new'. The history of Aristotelianism, its reception, criticism, apparent rejections, and survivals, offers a good illustration of this process and of the old historicism which tries to account for it. Continuing along this counter-revolutionary line, other scholars, such as Charles Schmitt, Charles Lohr, Eckhart Kessler, and Dennis Des Chene, have shown how Aristotelian philosophy not only survived in early modern times but has in many ways enjoyed a revival.[26]

Social history, with concealed roots in Marxist thought, has also reinforced ideas or assumptions of continuity in scientific thinking. As a 'cultural practice', science cannot do without authority, collective efforts, and a stable community, as Steven Shapin has argued in his 'social history of truth'.[27] Like Marcel

---

[24] *La Science dans l'antiquité: la jeunesse de la science grecque* (Paris, 1933), dedication.

[25] *The Science of Mechanics in the Middle Ages* (Madison, 1959), xix.

[26] Schmitt, *Aristotle and the Renaissance* (Cambridge, MA, 1983), among other works; see also Charles H. Lohr, 'The Sixteenth-Century Transformation of the Aristotelian Division of the Speculative Sciences', in *The Shapes of Knowledge from the Renaissance to the Enlightenment*, ed. D. R. Kelley and R. H. Popkin (Dordrecht, 1991), 49–58; Eckhard Kessler, 'The Transformation of Aristotle during the Renaissance', in *New Perspectives on Renaissance Thought*, ed. John Henry and Sarah Hutton (London, 1990), 137–47; Dennis Des Chene, *Physiologia: Natural Philosophy in Late Aristotelian and Cartesian Thought* (Ithaca, 1996), and *Atoms, Pneuma, and Tranquillity: Epicurean and Stoic Themes in European Thought*, ed. Margaret J. Osler (Cambridge, 1991), 135–54.

[27] *A Social History of Truth: Civility and Science in Seventeenth-Century England* (Chicago, 1994); see also Barbara J. Shapiro, *A Culture of Fact: England 1550–1720* (Ithaca, 2000), Mary Poovey, *A History of the Modern Fact: Problems of Knowledge in the Sciences of Wealth and Society* (Chicago, 1998), Peter Burke, *A Social History*

Detienne's 'masters of truth' in ancient Greece, Shapin's scientific gentlemen relied on consensus and a certain kind of tradition for acceptance of their science as beyond dispute (even as it was being disputed). Like history, which needed faith or trustworthiness (*fides historiae* is the formula), so natural science requires trust and credibility.[28] These are complex arguments which contain significant insights about the history of science as a collective enterprise – even if they do not quite warrant Shapin's more recent hyperbolic (though not unqualified) conclusion that 'There was no such thing as the Scientific Revolution ... '[29]

3. Revolution and Rupture

But of course the 'scientific revolution' was not a 'thing'; it was a perception and judgment which are the materials of intellectual and cultural history. For half a century Thomas Kuhn's *Structure of Scientific Revolutions* provided the conceptual framework for discussions of this question. This work gave focus to the theoretical debates in the history of science not only through the notions of paradigms and quasi-revolutionary 'paradigm-shifts', but also through the recognition of a social dimension.[30] This dimension had been explored by Robert Merton and Marxist scholars; it was a largely missing element in the mainstream discussion. The notion of 'paradigm' (originally a grammatical term)[31] is analogous to other efforts to map an intellectual field; namely, ideas of *Weltanschauung* and *mentalité*, yet more specific, being a way of demarcating the intellectual horizons not of a culture but of 'normal science'; of philosophical 'system', yet more open, being a way to formulate questions and set research agendas; and perhaps of a Foucauldian *episteme*, yet aimed not at cultural criticism but at defining disciplinary premises and limits.

'Paradigm-shift' is an idea for all seasons and situations, ranging from a eurekan flash of insight or political *coup* to seismic shifts in society and culture, and it raises the question of just what the historian of science wants

---

of *Knowledge: From Gutenberg to Diderot* (Cambridge, 2000), and Brendan Dooley, *The Social History of Skepticism: Experience and Doubt in Early Modern Culture* (Baltimore, 1999).

28 *The Masters of Truth in Archaic Greece*, trans. Janet Lloyd (New York, 1996).

29 *The Scientific Revolution* (Chicago, 1996), 1.

30 See especially *Paradigms and Revolutions: Applications and Appraisals of Thomas Kuhn's Philosophy of Science*, ed. Gary Gutting (Notre Dame, 1980), and Steve Fuller, *Thomas Kuhn: A Philosophical History for our Times* (Chicago, 2000), 318, on 'Paradigmitis'.

31 See Thomas Kuhn, *The Essential Tension* (Chicago, 1977), xix.

to explore or explain. Is it a particular scientific discovery or theory? The rise of a particular scientific practice or discipline? The reception of a particular idea or theory? The activities and debates of a scientific community? The larger resonances of scientific discovery and discussion in society as a whole? The transition from one view of the world to another over several generations? Of course historians of science must consider all of these questions and many others, but they cannot be accommodated within a simple theory of change.

After two generations of debate, what is interesting about the Kuhn thesis is its extraordinary impact on other disciplines as a way of characterizing – if not 'explaining' – transformations in research agendas and academic commitments. It would be a major research project itself to trace the reception of Kuhn's work in and between disciplines – the history of linguistics, archeology, anthropology, sociology, psychology, political theory, literary theory, legal studies, feminist and gender studies, art history, and of course intellectual and cultural history.[32] Some of these applications may seem to be travesties of Kuhn's original conception, but they are common in many fields where explanations for conceptual change are sought.

In the nineteenth century 'revolution' was much more, or less, than a red flag; it became also a metaphor for conspicuous change on many levels – political, social, cultural, industrial, and scientific. I. Bernard Cohen has examined this semantic field and the usages of the term 'revolution' by

---

[32] The extraordinary and even ubiquitous interdisciplinary influence of Thomas Kuhn's *The Structure of Scientific Revolutions* (Chicago, 1970²) beyond the philosophy of science may be suggested by a few random references: Gutting (ed.), *Paradigms and Revolutions*; H. G. Gadamer, *Reason in the Age of Science*, trans. Frederick G. Lawrence (Cambridge, MA, 1981), 164; Hans Blumenberg, *The Genesis of the Copernican World*, trans. Robert M. Wallace (Cambridge, MA, 1987), 512; Gary Gutting, *Michel Foucault's Archaeology of Scientific Reason* (Cambridge, 1989); Richard Rorty, J. B. Schneewind, and Quentin Skinner (eds), *Philosophy in History* (Cambridge, 1984), esp. 114ff. (Ian Hacking, 'Five Parables'); Shapin, *A Social History of Truth*, 315; Antonio Pérez-Ramos, *Francis Bacon's Idea of Science and the Maker's Knowledge Tradition* (Oxford, 1988), 32ff.; Mitchell Ash, *Gestalt Psychology in German Culture 1890–1967* (Cambridge, 1995), 193 ('gestalt switch'); J. G. A. Pocock, *Politics, Language, and Time* (New York, 1971), 13; Geoffrey Hawthorne, *Enlightenment and Despair* (Cambridge, 1987²), 4, 255; George W. Stocking, Jr, *Race, Culture, and Evolution* (Chicago, 1968), 5; Richard J. Bernstein, *The Restructuring of Social and Political Theory* (Philadelphia, 1978), 84ff.; Jeffrey C. Alexander, *Structure and Meaning* (New York, 1989), 17; Howard Felperin, *Beyond Deconstruction* (Oxford, 1985), 27; Michael Ann Holly, *Panofsky and the Foundations of Art History* (Ithaca, 1984), 55; D. R. Kelley, *Foundations of Modern Historical Scholarship* (New York, 1970), 9; and Horst Walter Blanke, *Historiographiegeschichte als Historik* (Stuttgart, 1991).

prominent figures (Kant, Goethe, Humboldt, Hegel, and Comte) and many less prominent ones, as well as areas of science to which the term was applied, or denied – especially the theories of Darwin, Einstein, and Planck, which have been seen as historical analogues to the original Copernican model. This was another quarrel of Ancients and Moderns, with Duhem looking back to an old legacy and Koyré and Burtt defending the revolutionary breakthroughs of Copernicus, Kepler, and Galileo.

In the history of science the leading proponent of the revolution approach was Alexandre Koyré, who followed the philosophical turn of Tannery and who owed debts to Boutroux, Durkheim, and Levy-Bruhl as well as to Cassirer, Husserl, and Heidegger. Koyré respected the achievement of Duhem but wanted to set the history of science into a broader context of ideas and religious thought. In his and E. A. Burtt's work a new battle of Platonists and Aristotelians, led by Duhem and later William Wallace, of cumulative and qualitative scholastic science versus sudden mathematical illumination, was initiated. Rejecting the continuity thesis, Koyré at the same time appreciated the light that Duhem had cast back into the middle ages and took as his own point of departure the Christian concept of infinity implied by a transcendent being but extended eventually to the creation of this omnipotent deity.[33] Central to Koyré's story of scientific development were the mathematical solutions to problems left unanswered by ancient physical science – solutions which could be provided only by individual ratiocination. Science was indeed a cooperative enterprise, Koyré recognized, but it turned not on empiricism or craft-mentality but on the achievements and eurekan breakthroughs of philosophical-minded thinkers like Galileo and Kepler; and in this connection Koyré became the leading proponent of a full-fledged scientific revolution.[34]

Koyré's was an idealist view stressing the centrality and continuity of the Platonic tradition (so neglecting Aristotelian survivals) and, in opposition to a Baconian or positivist notion of science without metaphysics, the 'influence of philosophy on science'.[35] He saw in the mind-expanding theology of St

---

[33] Koyré, *L'Idée de Dieu dans la philosophie de St. Anselme* (Paris, 1984 [1923]); *Etudes galiléennes* (Paris, 1966 [1939]); *De la Mystique à la science*, ed. Pietro Redondi (Paris, 1986); 'Science: The Renaissance of a History', *History and Technology*, 4 (1987).

[34] Alexandre Koyré, *From the Closed World to the Open Universe* (Baltimore, 1957), vii: 'during this period human, or at least European, minds underwent a deep revolution which has changed the very framework and patterns of our thinking ... ', Cohen, *Revolution in Science*, 396.

[35] 'De l'Influence des conceptions philosophiques sur l'évolution des théories scientifiques', *Etudes d'histoire de la pensée philosophique* (Paris, 1961), 253–69; 'Galileo and Plato', *Journal of the History of Ideas*, 4 (1943), 400–428.

Anselm, which tried to grasp and to demonstrate the existence of God, not only a continuation of Platonic influence but also a powerful and original creation, especially the ontological proof, which signaled a 'true revolution in thought'. Another example of this combination of philosophical tradition and revolution was the work of Galileo, who represented the two cornerstones of modern science, 'the geometrization of space' and the notion of an infinite universe.[36] Like Burtt, whose work he admired, Koyré rejected the naïve positivism; he emphasized the 'metaphysical foundations of modern science' and believed that the history of science had to be understood within such a conceptual framework.[37]

Koyré's picture of a great mental mutation, defended most comprehensively in his *Etudes galiléennes* of 1939, became a standard in the history of science, especially through the popular work of Herbert Butterfield and Thomas Kuhn, who defended this idea, within the conventional terms of 'revolution', in a theoretical form that had repercussions in many fields outside the history of science.[38] Koyré's was a story of secularization, or pantheism, in which the metaphysical attributes of God were passed on to the universe itself, though without the accompanying moral aspects of divinity.[39] So the stage was set for what Edmund Husserl, who also focussed on Galileo and his revolutionary 'mathematicization' of the world, called 'the crisis of the European sciences' in the twentieth century.[40]

For Husserl the crisis was the result of the determinism and dualism of classical physical science, but his criticisms were hardly surprising to historians of science; and Duhem's Divine Comedy of natural science was itself at odds with the philosophy of science of his time. Methodological doubts about the logical character and continuity of scientific discovery had already been expressed, for example, by Emile Boutroux, whose subversive thesis on the contingency of natural laws appeared in 1874. 'It is act that explains essence'

---

[36] *Etudes galiléennes*, 13.

[37] *The Metaphysical Foundations of Modern Science* (New York, 1954 [1924; rev. 1932]).

[38] Kuhn, *The Essential Tension*: 'The History of Science', 'The Relations between History and the History of Science', 'The Relations between the History and the Philosophy of Science', 'The Historical Structure of Scientific Discovery'. See David C. Lindberg, 'Concepts of the Scientific Revolution from Bacon to Butterfield: A Preliminary Sketch', in *Reappraisals of the Scientific Revolution*, ed. David C. Lindberg and Robert C. Westman (Cambridge, 1990), 17–19; and *Paradigms and Revolutions*, ed. Gutting, and see below, note 76.

[39] *From the Closed World to the Open Universe*, 276.

[40] *The Crisis of the European Sciences and Transcendental Phenomenology*, trans. David Carr (Evanston, 1970).

rather than vice versa, he argued in terms which to modern ears sound positively existentialist. 'It is not, then, the "nature of things" that should be the final object of our scientific investigations, it is their history.'[41] All the more so since, Boutroux remarked, 'he would be a bold man who would affirm that some particular conception had a future before it, while some other had had its day'.[42]

Boutroux's purpose was both to call scientific dogmatism into question and to reconcile modern science with religiously based ideas of human freedom, but he also opened the door to more fundamental criticisms of positivism, especially the notion of universal law. 'In explaining a phenomenon by a law', Emile Meyerson wrote, 'all we are doing is employing a synecdoche.'[43] Such doubts were reinforced by the work of Henri Poincaré, who stressed the hypothetical character of scientific thought, the role of imagination in discovery, the relativism implied by non-Euclidean geometry, and other ideas which were subverting classical physics. Whether or not God was dead, as Nietzsche scandalously suggested, his Creation seemed to be receding from the perceptions of human observers; and all the light brought by Newton could not bring it back into clear focus.

More upsetting to naïve positivism, realism, and associated histories of science was the shift from mechanical to what Mach called 'phenomenological physics'.[44] The epistemological result of this shift was to situate the observer in the natural process and make observation a factor in its analysis. A more remote consequence was that not only scientific ideas but also 'facts' were constructions of the observer – 'Everything significantly factual', Goethe remarked, 'is already theory.'[45] This is a modern version of that concept of

---

[41] *The Contingency of the Laws of Nature*, trans. Fred Rothwell (Chicago, 1916), 166; and see Richard Horner, 'A Pragmatist in Paris: Frédéric Rauh's "Task of Dissolution"', *Journal of the History of Ideas*, 58 (1997), 289–308.

[42] *Historical Studies in Philosophy*, trans. Fred Rothwell (Port Washington, NY, [1912]), 5.

[43] *Identité et réalité* (Paris, 1951⁵ [1907]), 'en expliquant un phénomène par une loi, nous ne faisons qu'user d'une synecdoche'.

[44] See Ernst Cassirer, *The Problem of Knowledge: Philosophy, Science, and History since Hegel*, trans. William H. Woglom and Charles W. Hendel (New Haven, 1950), 95, and Theodore M. Porter, 'The Death of the Object: *Fin de siècle* Philosophy of Physics', in *Modernist Impulses in the Human Sciences*, ed. Dorothy Ross (Baltimore, 1994), 128–51.

[45] Cited by Cassirer, *Determinism and Indeterminism*, 136; Ludwig Fleck, *Genesis and Development of a Scientific Fact*, trans. Fred Bradley and Thaddeus J. Trenn (Chicago, 1979 [1935]); Heinrich Rickert, *The Limits of Concept Formation in Natural Science*, trans. Guy Oakes (Cambridge, 1986); also Robert E. Butts and James Robert Brown (eds), *Constructivism and Science: Essays in Recent German Philosophy* (Dordrecht, 1989).

'maker's knowledge' that Bacon, Hobbes, Gassendi, Vico, and others had defended.[46] It is also an anticipation of Ludwig Fleck's notion of the temporal nature of scientific facts.[47] If this sort of constructivism and relativism were characteristic of modern natural science, how much more must they be for the history of science?

Other factors acted to dissolve the imperial visions of scientism. It is a commonplace that there cannot reasonably be a coherent history of science but only of sciences, and to this may be added an awareness that there is also no single method valid for all the sciences or even for one science at all times. Bachelard cites the opinion of the chemist Georges Urbain that 'not even the best of methods can last forever'. In his view, 'every method eventually loses its initial fecundity'.[48] Not only the laws of nature, it seems, but even the procedures of reason and 'method' have their basis in 'contingency' and so have their own histories.[49]

Underlying these problems is the old question of the nature of ideas, especially of complex ideas. The indelibly Whiggish nature of the history of science, deriving from the unavoidably prejudicial view of its object, leads to assumptions about the stability of concepts over long periods of time. Yet even ostensibly stable concepts do not keep their identity in the course of their history. Just as there are no simple phenomena, wrote Bachelard, so 'there is no such thing as a simple idea'.[50] Consider the concept of 'matter', which philosophers have discussed more or less unproblematically for centuries but which has gone through at least five stages, according to Bachelard: pre-scientific, operational (as in comparing weights), and the views entailed by the Newtonian system, relativity, and quantum mechanics. As Henri Poincaré dramatically put it, 'One of the most astonishing discoveries which has been announced by physical scientists in recent years is that matter does not exist', he wrote in 1902 – though history could

---

[46] See Perez-Ramos, *Francis Bacon's Idea of Science and the Maker's Knowledge Tradition*.

[47] *Genesis and Development of a Scientific Fact*.

[48] Bachelard, *The New Scientific Spirit*, trans. Arthur Goldhammer (Boston, 1984), 135.

[49] See Marcello Pera, *The Discourses of Science*, trans. Clarissa Botsford (Chicago, 1994); and Henry H. Bauer, *Scientific Literacy and the Myth of the Scientific Method* (Urbana, 1992).

[50] *The New Scientific Spirit*, 148; and cf. *Le Matérialisme rationnel* (Paris, 1953), 209, criticizing 'continuistes' like Duhem; Mary McAllester Jones, *Gaston Bachelard: Subversive Humanist* (Paris, 1981), Mary Tiles, *Bachelard: Science and Objectivity* (Cambridge, 1984), and Gutting, *Michel Foucault's Archaeology of Scientific Reason*; also Antonio Aliotta, *La reazione idealistica contro la scienza* (Naples, 1912).

change even this opinion, for 'I hasten to add that this discovery is not yet definitive.'[51]

The final humiliation to the ideal of a unified science founded on reason and experience was probably the efforts of humanists to demonstrate – similar to Taine's interpretation of literary and art history – that science, too, was affected by external factors, including national and social context as well as individual psychology. In 1873 Alphonse Candolle had published a *History of the Sciences and of Men of Learning*, which investigated, in terms of statistics and quantitative researches, many extra-scientific 'influences', including family background, religion, language, geography, gender, and especially heredity and natural selection, which were associated not with the 'logic of scientific discovery' (in Karl Popper's phrase) but rather with the historical and cultural conditions of discovery.[52] Soon these objects of research were to be further relativized – and 'historicized' – by association with the idea of 'mentality', first given currency by Lucien Levy-Bruhl and later adopted by younger historians of science such as Rey, Bachelard, and Koyré.

Contingency, constructivism, and context: these intellectual intrusions into scientific practice, theory, and culture have implications as well for the history of science, which, no less than conventional history, is subject to revisionism and which must begin by reconceptualizing, perhaps periodically, the object of its investigations and interpretations. There was nothing new in this sort of relativism, especially not in the continental tradition of scientific thought. Against Newtonian science Goethe had argued that the observer was always part of the process of investigation (the visual experience, for example, was part of the laws of optics).[53] For similar reasons, Goethe remarked (writing as a scientist rather than a poet),

> History must from time to time be rewritten, not because new facts have been discovered, but because new aspects come into view, because the participant in the

---

[51] *La Science et l'hypothèse* (Paris, 1902), 273. See also Ernan McMullin (ed.), *The Concept of Matter in Modern Philosophy* (Notre Dame, 1978[2]), and Stephen Toulmin and June Goodfield, *The Architecture of Matter: The Physics, Chemistry of Matter, Both Animate and Inanimate, As It Has Evolved since the Beginning of Science* (Chicago, 1926).

[52] Alphonse Candolle, *Histoire des sciences et des savants depuis deux siècles* (Paris, 1885 [1873]); and see *Puritanism and the Rise of Modern Science: the Merton Thesis*, I, ed. I. Bernard Cohen (New Brunswick, 1990), 145–50.

[53] R. H. Stephenson, *Goethe's Conception of Knowledge and Science* (Edinburgh, 1995); and Dennis L. Sepper, 'Goethe, Colour and the Science of Seeing', in *Romanticism and the Sciences*, ed. Andrew Cunningham and Nicholas Jardine (Cambridge, 1990), 189–98.

progress of an age is led to standpoints from which the past can be regarded and judged in a new manner.[54]

And this goes for the apparently most unproblematical of concepts: neither mathematics nor 'experience' is stable enough to provide constants transcending the process of history – or of historiographical inquiry.[55]

4.   The History of Scientific Ideas

In general the history of science may be pursued on various levels. It may be a chronicle of a particular discipline or, as Tannery hoped, 'a synthetic history' of all these particular histories or, as Tannery's disciple Abel Rey envisioned, it may be expanded to include the history of ideas more generally or extended still further, as Margaret Jacob has done, into areas of society, politics, and culture.[56] The more the history of science moves away from chronicle and particular disciplinary practices, the more it depends on conceptual aids and philosophy and the more it involves not science 'itself' but its philosophy and what Georges Canguilhem has called the 'ideology of science'.[57]

One unavoidable condition of the history of science is that, whatever consideration is given to collective efforts, climates of opinion, and intellectual tradition, scientific achievement must be studied through individual discoveries, breakthroughs, 'ruptures', and formulations. In the case of ostensibly clear and distinct ideas, such as the law of falling bodies or planetary motion, historians of science, like those of literature, have resorted to notions of intuition and genius. After all, some sixteenth-century scholars had read as

---

[54] J.T. Merz, *A History of European Thought in the Nineteenth Century* (4 vols, Edinburgh, 1904–12), I, 7; and see Heisenberg, 'Goethe's View of Nature and the World of Science and Technology', *Across the Frontiers*, trans. Peter Heath (New York, 1974), 122–41.

[55] Peter Dear, *Discipline and Experience: The Mathematical Way in the Scientific Revolution* (Chicago, 1995); and see Joan Scott, 'The Evidence of Experience', in *Questions of Evidence: Proof, Practice, and Persuasion across the Disciplines*, ed. James Chandler, Arnold Davidson, and Harry Harootunian (Chicago, 1994), 363–87.

[56] Tannery, *Mémoires scientifiques*, X, 168; Rey, *La Science dans l'antiquité* (Paris, 1933), dedicated to Tannery; and Jacob, *The Cultural Meaning of the Scientific Revolution* (Philadelphia, 1988).

[57] Canguilhem, *Ideology and Rationality in the History of the Life Sciences*, trans. Arthur Goldhammer (Cambridge, MA, 1988), 32; and see Patrick Tort, *La Pensée hiérarchique et l'évolution* (Paris, 1983), 19.

widely as Copernicus and even reflected on the aporias of Ptolemaic astronomy; yet as Koyré said, 'No one before Copernicus had his genius.'[58]

For historians of science trying to assess individual effort, three questions arise which belong mainly to internalist analysis: priority (originality), influence, and precursorship. The first two are accessible to historical study, while the status of forerunner (*précurseur, Vorläufer*) is a retrospective construction. For Goethe German literature could not have reached its current state without powerful 'precursors' (*Vorgänger*) like Herder and Klopstock.[59] He was skeptical of 'originality', since the world began to affect the mind from birth and only will, energy, and strength were original endowments. 'If I could give an account of all that I owe to great predecessors and contemporaries', he wrote, 'there would be but a small balance in my favour.'[60] In the history of science the importance of 'precursors' for the greatness of Galileo resided in the medieval calculators discovered by Duhem. Sometimes precursors run in groups, and in the 'growth' of calculus and evolutionism historians have found many 'forerunners'.[61]

'Precursoritis', as the conjectural assignment of intellectual ancestry has been called, has often been criticized.[62] 'The notion of "forerunner" is a very dangerous one for the historian', Koyré has written:

> It is no doubt true that ideas have a *quasi* independent development, that is to say, they are born in one mind, and reach maturity to bear fruit in another; consequently, the history of problems and their solutions can be traced. It is equally true that the historical importance of a doctrine is measured by its fruitfulness, and that later generations are not concerned with those that precede them except in so far as they see in them their 'ancestors' or 'forerunners.' It is quite obvious (or should be) that no-one has ever regarded himself as the 'forerunner' of someone else, nor been able to do so. Consequently, to regard anyone in this light is the best way of preventing oneself from understanding them.[63]

---

[58] *The Astronomical Revolution: Copernicus – Kepler – Borelli*, trans. R. E. W. Maddison (London, 1973), 42.

[59] J. P. Eckermann, *Gespräche mit Goethe in den letzten Jahren seines Lebens* (Berlin, 1982), 106; *Conversations with Goethe*, trans. J. Oxenford (London, 1946), 70.

[60] *Gespräche*, 138; *Conversations*, 115.

[61] Edna E. Kramer, *The Nature and Growth of Modern Mathematics* (Princeton, 1970), 172–6; Carl B. Boyer, *The History of the Calculus and its Conceptual Development* (New York, 1949); and Ernst Mayr, *The Growth of Biological Thought: Diversity, Evolution, and Inheritance* (Cambridge, MA, 1982), 343–93.

[62] Georges Canguilhem, *A Vital Rationalist*, ed. F. Delaporte and trans. A. Goldhammer (New York, 1994), 49; Ernest Nagel in *Critical Problems in the History of Science*, ed. Marshall Clagett (Madison, 1959); Gutting, *Michel Foucault's Archaeology of Scientific Reason*, 39.

[63] *The Astronomical Revolution*, 77.

But if this 'light' is of little use for a research agenda, it does permit the construction of an intellectual tradition, in which figures are recalled not for present use but 'only as "precursors"', as Scott Atram has put it, 'with regard to problems that currently agitate systematics'.[64] This is also the import of the famous scholastic–Newtonian conceit illuminated by Robert Merton, that is, the identification of the earlier giants on whose shoulders the dwarfs of modern times stand.[65]

A more specific version of this problem is the phenomenon of 'priority conflicts', the subject of what has been called the 'other Merton thesis'.[66] Such debates as that between Leibniz and Newton over the calculus are common in the past century and overlap with plagiarism. They are also analogous to the old question of literary property, traceable back at least to Seneca, for whom the truth could be the property of no man. Nor could there be 'property' in ideas. 'An exclusive property cannot be obtained in every Idea that we perceive, nor in every sentiment that occurs to us', wrote Bishop Warburton, 'because nature has framed us with similar Organs, so that the same Objects must necessarily make similar Impressions on us.'[67] Only in society was there property, and this 'Property of the First Taker' is where controversies over priority and historical judgment arose.

The question of 'influence', which arises in so many contexts, is more complex.[68] In the eighteenth century this medico-astrological term was applied uncritically to social, cultural, and political subjects; and it has become an unexamined convention of historical discourse.[69] Influence in scientific thinking can be as vague as that of Plato and Nicholas of Cusa, as pervasive as that of Aristotle or Euclid, as specific as that of Archimedes or Epicurus, as ineffable as Chaldean science or the hermetic philosophy. Influence can be positive, as that of Darwin on cultural historians, or negative, as that of Hegel on Marx. The forms that influence can take are endless; but the extremes may be

---

[64] *Cognitive Foundations of Natural History: Towards an Anthropology of Natural History* (Cambridge, 1990), 85.

[65] *On the Shoulders of Giants: A Shandean Postscript* (New York, 1965).

[66] Merton, 'Priorities in Scientific Discovery', *American Sociological Review*, 22 (1957), 635–59, and in *Puritanism and the Rise of Modern Science*, ed. Cohen, 343, and the literature there cited; and cf. Kuhn, *The Essential Tension*, 166.

[67] *An Enquiry into the nature and origin of Literary Property* (London, 1762), 3; and see above, Chapter 2, at note 56.

[68] Canguilhem, *Ideology and Rationality*, 9.

[69] See above, Chapter 2 at note 57. A search of the ARTFL database suggests that it is in the eighteenth century that the term came to be extended from the restricted physical denotation to broader, metaphorical meanings applied to social and cultural phenomena.

suggested by the cases of Descartes and Gassendi, the first claiming originality in the midst of unacknowledged debts to Thomas Aquinas, the second ostentatiously constructing a new system on the philosophy of Epicurus; and it is one job of historians to assess the weight of such influence.

5. The Outside and the Inside

The questions introduced by Alphonse Candolle over a century ago have, in recent years, reappeared in a debate dividing historians of science into two parties, the internalists and externalists, or intellectualists and contextualists.[70] The first of these corresponds in one sense to old-fashioned Whiggish history, which follows the 'march of ideas' (in Cournot's phrase) teleologically through individual exploits to the current state of science; the second expands the field of research to the scientific community and larger social and political contexts. 'External history is a matter of politics, economics, the funding of institutes, the circulation of journals, and all the social circumstances that are external to knowledge itself', Ian Hacking has said. 'Internal history is the history of individual items of knowledge, conjectures, experiments, refutations, perhaps.'[71]

This contrast also has an epistemological aspect, which is between 'maker's knowledge' and the cultural construction of knowledge. The first is the old view – going back to Vico, Hobbes, and Plato – that one is able to understand only what one has made and, perhaps, make possible a meeting of minds across the ages through ideas, theories, common sense, and other intellectual creations. The second is the belief that knowledge is shaped, influenced, or determined by the conditions – limits as well as possibilities – of social environment and power relations, class structure, and factors of gender, race,

---

[70] For recent discussions of this crypto-Marxist distinction, see Jan Golinski, *Making Natural Knowledge: Constructivism and the History of Science* (Cambridge, 1998); Vasiliki Betty Smocovitis, *Unifying Biology: The Evolutionary Synthesis and Evolutionary Biology* (Princeton, 1996), 73–96; Mary Hesse, *Revolutions and Reconstructions in the Philosophy of Science* (Bloomington, 1980), 27ff.; Robert E. Butts and James Robert Brown (eds), *Constructivism and Science* (Dordrecht, 1989); and Clifford Geertz, 'The Strange Estrangement: Taylor and the Natural Sciences', in *Philosophy in an Age of Pluralism: The Philosophy of Charles Taylor in Question*, ed. James Tully (Cambridge, 1994), 93.

[71] Ian Hacking, 'How Should We Do the History of Statistics?', in *The Foucault Effect*, ed. Graham Burchell, Colin Gordon, and Peter Miller (Chicago, 1991), 191, adding that 'We have no good account of the relationship between external and internal history.'

nationality, and so on. Put differently, the contrast is between a phenomenological view taking ideas on their own terms, as mental phenomena, and a
constructivist, or reductionist, view which treats them as in some way
Something Else.

The problem of how to write history between these poles leads to other
polarities: one, the microhistorical studies that deal with the endlessly surprising
record of unpredictable and perhaps incommensurable discoveries and
practices; and the other, the macrohistorical interpretations that draw these
discoveries and practices into a reasoned, perhaps Whiggish historical
narrative.[72] The other opposition is that pointed out by Canguilhem between
'the history of obsolete knowledge and the history of sanctioned knowledge',
which again brings up the question of Whig history.[73]

Taking the view from the outside, scientific inquiry is carried on in a wide
range of contexts, temporal and spatial, theoretical and practical, social and
political, which cast doubt on the ideal of science as an objective and purely
rational enterprise and introduce elements of relativism and historicism. There
are choices of scientific traditions and national styles, research agendas and
strategies, vehicles of scientific exchange and dissemination, professional
communities, public support and social utility, generational conflict and gender
considerations – all of which factors went into the making of the scientific
revolution. No less important have been the institutional contexts in which
research has been carried on – academies, universities,[74] societies, craft
organizations, the medium of print (scientific journals as well as books),[75]
and, more recently, the laboratory.[76] The modern scientific community is in
some ways a descendent of the old Republic of Letters, but it has formed
entangling alliances with many more ideological concerns and practical
interests; and historians of science have perforce to extend and diversify their
programs accordingly, going both beyond and below the aims of intellectual
history.

---

[72] See Ernst Mayr, 'The Idea of Teleology', *Journal of the History of Ideas*, 53
(1992), 117–35.

[73] *A Vital Rationalist*, 44.

[74] See the studies by David Lux and Mordecai Feingold in *Revolution and Continuity*,
ed. Barker and Ariew.

[75] See especially *Books and the Sciences in History*, ed. Maria Frasca Spada and
Nick Jardine (Cambridge, 2000), and Adrian Johns, *The Nature of the Book: Print
and Knowledge in the Making* (Chicago, 1998).

[76] See *Reappraisals of the Scientific Revolution*, ed. Lindberg and Westman, and B.
Latour and S. Woolgar, *Laboratory Life: The Social Construction of Scientific Facts*
(London, 1979); also Ian Hacking, *The Social Construction of What?* (Cambridge,
MA, 1999).

The larger conceptual field in which this debate has been carried on is the 'Sociology of Scientific Knowledge' (SSK in the trade), with all of its terminological and acronymical paraphernalia. This is not merely the Kuhnian sort of sociology that limits itself to the theory of paradigm-shifts, for it also descends into empirical and local questions of social context. The result has been to emphasize cultural and social factors, including gender, in the emergence and success of particular theories or practices and the myths about individual agency produced by publicity in the wake of such successes.[77] One example of this approach is the work of Bruno Latour, whose study of Pasteur has re-created the debates, cultural climate, and political environment of proto-bacteriology and the nineteenth-century hygiene movement and so has revealed the social and cultural origins and conditions of – and the minor role of individual human agency in – Pasteurism.[78] The larger aim of the book is to discredit the hagiographic and internalist form taken by classical and canonical history of science. In effect Latour's epic is an Odyssey without Odysseus. The internalist view can ostensibly be seen in its purest form in the history of an abstract field like mathematics, in which one can literally rethink the thoughts of, say, Euclid, in his construction of the sequence of propositions in plane geometry – or perhaps (as an older generation believed) rethink the thoughts of God himself.[79] Yet the work of scholars like David Lachterman and Joan Richards shows that mathematics, too, while dependent on individual ratiocination, has externalist dimensions associated with the exchanges of members of a community at a particular time.[80] The climate of

---

[77] In a vast and expanding literature see Ernan McMullin (ed.), *The Social Dimensions of Science* (Notre Dame, 1992); Andrew Pickering (ed.), *Science as Practice and Culture* (Chicago, 1992); Peter Gallison and David Stump (eds), *The Disunity of Science: Boundaries, Contexts and Power* (Stanford, 1996); Golinski, *Making Natural Knowledge*; and the anthology, Helga Nowotny and Klaus Taschwer, *The Sociology of the Sciences* (Cheltenham, 1996).

[78] *The Pasteurization of France*, trans. Alan Sheridan and John Law (Cambridge, MA, 1988).

[79] For example, Kant's contemporary Solomon Maimon: 'In this [mathematical construction] we are therefore similar to God', quoted by David Rapport Lachterman, *The Ethics of Geometry: A Genealogy of Modernity* (New York, 1989), ix.

[80] Lachterman, *Ethics*; Richards, *Mathematical Visions: The Pursuit of Geometry in Victorian England* (Boston, 1988), 61, on 'non-Euclidean geometry and mathematical truth'; Nicholas Jardine, 'Demonstration, Dialectic, and Rhetoric in Galileo's *Dialogue*', in *The Shapes of Knowledge from the Renaissance to the Enlightenment*, ed. Kelley and Popkin, 101–21; and see Phillip J. Davis, 'Rhetoric and Mathematics', in *The Rhetoric of the Human Sciences*, ed. J. Nelson, A. Megill, and D. McClosky (Madison, 1987), 53–68; also *Scientific Controversies: Philosophical and Historical Perspectives*, ed. Peter Machamer, Marcello Pera, and Aristides Baltas (New York, 2000).

opinion of the present time, it might be added, also discourages ideas that mathematics has a transcendent position with regard to universal truth.[81] As Euclidean geometry classically (and non-Euclidean geometry modernly) suggests, this branch of mathematics is more than nominally a human 'construction'.

In the twentieth century the externalist–internalist (E–I) debate has centered first on the pioneering work of Robert K. Merton, who, following Weber, found striking correlations between 'extrinsic factors' of Puritan belief and interest in science.[82] Merton has been criticized, as was Weber, for this imputed linkage; but in fact neither argued for a causal connection, only for, as Merton put it, 'compatibility'. The results of these forays into the sociology of science were reinforced by more dogmatic Marxist views of the role of material factors, and despite the decline of Marxist influence, what Mary Hesse calls the 'strong thesis' of the SSK has returned with a vengeance in recent works, emphasizing not merely contingency but 'messy contingencies', not only historicizing but also socializing 'truth'.[83]

In the wake of the SSK 'revolution' the E–I distinction may have fallen out of terminological fashion. Yet it is a polarity that is embedded deeply in western thought and languages – most obviously and most paradigmatically, perhaps, in Plato's distinction between the true (inner) world of ideas and the false (outer) world of appearances – and it was reinforced by Christian dualisms of body–soul and letter–spirit, as well as the Cartesian dualism of *res extensa* and *res cogitans* and the Freudian dualism of Ego and Id. Nor does either history or language allow us to escape this structure of thought, no matter what the external context. We are all limited by 'personal knowledge', as Polanyi argued in his call for a 'post-critical' strategy.[84]

In any case externalist approaches to important scientific achievements, despite their fidelity to historical understanding, tend to lose sight of what attracted their attention in the first place. The question put to the externalists is, in the words of David Bloor, 'Can the sociology of knowledge investigate and explain the very content and nature of scientific knowledge?' Jacques Derrida, for one, doubted it: '[E]xternal history or sociology … is powerless

---

[81] See the comparative discussion of Arkady Plotnitsky, *Complementarity: Anti-Epistemology after Bohr and Derrida* (Durham, 1994).

[82] Cohen (ed.), *Puritanism and the Rise of Modern Science*.

[83] Shapin, *A Social History of Truth*; Hesse, *Revolutions and Reconstructions*, 29; Andrew Pickering, *The Mangle of Practice: Time, Agency, and Science* (Chicago, 1995); and H. F. Cohen, *The Scientific Revolution*, 229.

[84] Michael Polanyi, *Personal Knowledge: Towards a Post-Critical Philosophy* (Chicago, 1958).

to take the measure of the philosophemes that it claims to explain.'[85] And this applies even more appropriately to the sciences, including the human sciences.

However, there may be one conceptual bridge between the E–I extremes. 'Contexts' require externalist history, but there are also contexts associated with internalist history, as indeed Shapin himself has recognized.[86] In particular there are not only synchronic contexts but also diachronic contexts. Questions not only of society, institutions, and politics but also of language, discourse, mentality, and associated traditions involve, in their own temporal and less tangible way, 'contexts' and what Gadamer has called the 'experience of tradition'.[87]

In one sense this may take us back to Burtt, Koyré, and the old-fashioned history of ideas, to the extent that early modern science drew, whether deliberately or not, on Platonism, Aristotelianism, Stoicism, Epicureanism, skepticism, and other philosophical schools. Lovejoy's much-criticized notion of 'unit-ideas' still finds a place in the study of traditions of commentary – diachronic contexts – on key themes, such as the seminal concept of form, which Nora Emerton has traced from Platonic and Aristotelian origins to modern chemistry and crystallography[88] (though not to its postmodern extension in chaos theory, which scholars are beginning to associate with humanist themes).[89]

But internalist interpretation need not limit itself to the 'sanctioned' science. Another element in the alleged revolution of modern science was the practice and theory of magic, which likewise sought to penetrate the secrets of, and to gain dominion over, nature, and which also figures in the forestructures and prejudices of early modern science. The thesis of Lynn Thorndike in the 1920s was given a fresh impulse by Frances Yates, who singled out the hermetic tradition as a formative influence in the mentality of the new science.[90] Exaggerations aside, Yates's work on occult traditions has become vital for understanding the curiosities and contradictions in the major figures

---

[85] *Points … Interviews, 1974–1994*, trans. Peggy Kamuf et al. (Stanford, 1995), 184.

[86] 'Social Uses of Science', *The Ferment of Knowledge*, ed. G.S. Rousseau and Roy Porter (New York, 1980), 105.

[87] *Truth and Method*, trans. Garrett Barden and John Cumming (New York, 1982), 310ff.

[88] *The Scientific Reinterpretation of Form* (Ithaca, 1984).

[89] N. Katherine Hayles, *Chaos Bound: Orderly Disorder in Contemporary Literature and Science* (Ithaca, 1990).

[90] Yates, *Giordano Bruno and the Hermetic Tradition* (London, 1964) and *The Occult Philosophy in the Elizabethan Age* (London, 1979).

of the new science, and a large literature has arisen in the wake of her books.[91] Her work has also drawn attention to the unstated premises, prejudices, and blind alleys of scientific inquiry, including magic, the occult, and particular styles of research.[92]

Many of the central figures in the 'scientific revolution' suggest reasons for denying the phenonomenon for which they have been given responsibility. The prime example is Newton, whose investigations extended into alchemy, chronology, mythology, antiquities, Egyptology, prophecy, and biblical scholarship. Nor, according to recent scholars, were these lines of inquiry mere pastimes or aberrations, for they had a creative role in Newton's larger agenda of seeking a universal principle of nature and a unified truth.[93] This view is also in line with the more general thesis, argued by Amos Funkenstein, which retains a formative role for theology in early modern science – in the sense both of God's transubstantial presence in the world of substance and his certification of the essential rationality of nature.[94]

Curiosity about these aspects of the forestructures of early modern science also suggests some of the reasons for the 'literary turn' taken by the history of science in recent years. In its classical form (and omitting the qualifications suggested by Yates and other historians of occult traditions) science was supposed to be separate from, or purified of, contingencies of language; but changes in scientific practices and philosophy always produce changes in rhetoric. The role of rhetoric is obvious in the tradition of empirical science – Bacon himself, for example, relied on conventions of Renaissance rhetoric in the formulation of his 'method' – but it cannot be divorced from other scientific programs, even mathematics.[95] Nor does this apply only to the persuasive aspects of scientific activity – the selling and reception of scientific

---

[91] Brian Vickers (ed.), *Occult and Scientific Mentalities in the Renaissance* (Cambridge, 1984); Ingrid Merkel and Allan G. Debus (eds), *Hermeticism and the Renaissance: Intellectual History and the Occult in Early Modern Europe* (Washington, DC, 1988), esp. 79–110, Brian Copenhaver, 'Hermes Trismegistus, Proclus, and the Question of a Philosophy of Magic in the Renaissance'; also Copenhaver, 'Natural Magic, Hermeticism, and Occultism in Early Modern Science', in *Reappraisals of the Scientific Revolution*, ed. Lindberg and Westman, 261–302.

[92] Crombie, *Styles of Scientific Thinking*.

[93] B. J. T. Dobbs, *The Janus Face of Genius: The Role of Alchemy in Newton's Thought* (Cambridge, 1991), and Frank Manuel, *Isaac Newton Historian* (Cambridge, MA, 1963).

[94] *Theology and the Scientific Imagination from the Middle Ages to the Seventeenth Century* (Princeton, 1986).

[95] Philip J. Davis and Reuben Hersh, 'Rhetoric and Mathematics', in *Rhetoric and the Human Sciences: Language and Argument in Scholarship and Public Affairs*, ed. John S. Nelson, Allan Megill, and Donald N. McClosky (Madison, 1987), 53–68.

ideas over official resistance or popular ignorance, as illustrated by the famous, and paradigmatic, cases of Copernicus, Galileo, Darwin, and Einstein. For, as recent scholars have begun to insist, it is inseparable from scientific thought and procedures and connected in particular to what has been called 'the final-form expression of scientific ideas'.[96]

The emergence of modern science was itself accompanied not only by a shift of terminology but also by a radically different view of language itself. The search for an original, God-given language inscribed in nature was given up; and attention turned instead to projects for improving and perfecting modern language, or even of devising an unambiguous 'universal characteristic' or 'calculus' on the level of mathematics. For Galileo nature could not be 'read', but it could be measured; and in modern science language was detached from things, from analogical thinking, and became instead an instrument for their decipherment and classification. Adam's work had to be done all over again, this time by modern science: this is what James Bono calls a shift from 'the word of God to the language of man'.[97]

The sharpest of literary turns have been made by scholars who seek to re-create pre-scientific mentality, in which metaphor, myth, and what Fernand Hallyn called a 'vertical', or qualitative (as distinguished from a 'horizontal', or empirical) meaning of phenomena, still functioned in natural philosophy.[98] In textualist and tropological terms Hallyn (like Burtt) shows the persistence of anthropomorphism in the analogical thinking (mathematical and musical thinking) of Copernicus, Kepler, and other founders of the new astronomy. With a similar literary orientation (and more particularly Derridean as well as Freudian inspiration), Timothy Reiss tries to move from the 'analytical-referential', the willful and authoritarian 'discourse of modernism', to the lost, enchanted, and in a sense pre-rational world at the other end of Galileo's

---

[96] Dudley Shapere, 'On Deciding What to Believe and How to Talk about Nature', in *Persuading Science: The Art of Scientific Rhetoric*, ed. Marcello Pera and William R. Shea (Canton, MA, 1991), 103; Pera, *The Discourses of Science*; Peter Dear (ed.), *The Literary Structure of Scientific Argument: Historical Studies* (Philadelphia, 1991); and see *History of the Human Sciences*, 3 (2) (1990), special issue on 'Rhetoric and Science'.

[97] *The Word of God and the Languages of Man: Interpreting Nature in Early Modern Science and Medicine*, I, *Ficino to Descartes* (Madison, 1995); see also Timothy Reiss, *The Discourse of Modernism* (Ithaca, 1982); Brian Vickers, 'Analogy versus Identity: the Rejection of Occult Symbolism, 1580–1680', in *Occult and Scientific Mentalities in the Renaissance*, ed. Vickers, 95–164, and 'On the Function of Analogy in the Occult', in *Hermeticism and the Renaissance*, ed. Merkel and Debus, 265–92.

[98] *The Poetic Structure of the World: Copernicus and Kepler*, trans. Donald M. Leslie (New York, 1990), 19ff.

magic tube.[99] This was the world of folkloric and common-sense science which, for Atram, could no longer accommodate the knowledge that had been accumulated by the seventeenth century and so turned to 'counter-intuitive' ideas.[100]

Hans Blumenberg has also ranged beyond the artificial terrain of pure and internal science in Copernicanism to the literary and philosophical traditions and contexts of human 'consciousness'.[101] For Blumenberg the mind-set of Copernicus was still anthropocentric – the world was still made 'for us' – but it was nevertheless revolutionary in its naturalistic implications, especially after Galileo's telescope offered visual evidence for the reformed world-system and Newton 'physicalized' the Copernican hypothesis. Copernicus became a protagonist of the new science not so much because he offered a better cosmology, argued Blumenberg, 'as because he established a new and absolutely universal claim to truth', and did so beyond the spiritual realm of Platonic ideas.[102] The autonomous Copernican science of astronomy was a key element in the emergence of 'modernity', whose career Blumenberg traced in his later works, and the chilling and unmaternal concept of 'mothership earth' moving alone in the cosmos that is not 'for us', even though we may seem to be unique. But of course all these speculations go beyond the horizons of ordinary and even vicariously historical experience, and return us to the old projects of conjectural history, on which historians still occasionally draw.

---

[99] *The Discourse of Modernism.*
[100] *Cognitive Foundations*, 167, 247, 265.
[101] *The Genesis of the Copernican World.*
[102] *The Legitimacy of the Modern Age*, trans. Robert M. Wallace (Cambridge, MA, 1983), 361.

Chapter 8

Human Sciences

> The first condition for the possibility
> of a human science lies in the
> consciousness that ... the one who
> examines history also makes history.
> Wilhelm Dilthey

Modern 'social science' emerged in the last decade of the eighteenth century at the juncture between the contradictory socializing and individualizing – socialist and liberal – turn taken in the wake of the Revolution, especially the efforts to create a science of society on the model of natural science. As the Revolution proposed to give history a new start, so Napoleon, in the name of this Revolution, hoped to control it through a rational system of government, including a national code, which would touch social life from cradle to grave and from the private to the public sphere.[1] This was the political context of modern social science in its first phase – the second phase being the emergence of a new discipline designed not only as a systematic science but also, in the form of positivism, as a secular religion and perhaps even a remedy for the 'social question', which neither the Revolution nor Napoleon was able to resolve. History might or might not have a role in all this, but in any case it had a number of new disciplines and new ideas to confront.[2]

---

[1] D. R. Kelley, *Historians and the Law in Postrevolutionary France* (Princeton, 1984), 45.

[2] See the survey of the modern period, with emphasis on the life sciences, by Roger Smith, *The Norton History of the Human Sciences* (New York, 1996), with comprehensive (English-language) bibliography, and see D. R. Kelley, 'Fortunes of Psyche: Reflections on Roger Smith's *History of the Human Sciences*', *History of the Human Sciences*, 14 (2001), 130–40. This chapter must be much more selective in treating the relation of just four 'human sciences' – neglecting economics, medicine, and other disciplines – in their special, ambivalent, and problematic relation to intellectual history.

1. Political Science

The 'noble science' of politics has an ancient heritage that has never been lost, going back to Plato and Aristotle, whose *Politics* has been the object of critical commentary ever since. 'Political science' (statecraft) and 'civil science' (forensic rhetoric and the law) were established terms by the sixteenth century. In the seventeenth century natural law gave political thought a more universal and scientific basis. By the next century political science had found a place in the German universities in the form of *Cameral-* and *Staatswissenschaft*.[3] The expansion of the discipline in the age of state-building and empire-seizing can be seen in three historiographical *summae* published after the mid-century: Robert von Mohl's massive handbook, an 'encyclopedia' of political science; Robert Blackey's pious and long-winded anthology of political literature, which had the merit of attending to literary sources, including drama and ballads; and Paul Janet's prize-winning history of political science, following, in doxographical fashion, the western canon down to Kant and his 'project for perpetual peace'.[4]

The history of political thought has been carried out in the shadows of the histories of philosophy, law, and to some extent literature; but it has developed its own conventions and canon of classical texts.[5] In the past two centuries the concept of the political has been set off from those of civil society, culture, and religion and has been given definition in terms of modern statism and nationalism and the macrohistorical problems associated with this condition of public life; and as such it is not the most refined way of understanding the historical process or the public sphere.[6] Yet despite this engagement in current problems and frequent indulgence in anachronism, it has, by following currently and betimes anachronistically relevant themes and issues back into the more remote past, made significant contributions to intellectual history.

---

[3] See David F. Lindenfeld, *The Practical Imagination: The German Science of State in the Nineteenth Century* (Chicago, 1997).

[4] Von Mohl, *Die Geschichte und Literatur der Staatswissenschaften in Monographien dargestellt* (3 vols; Erlangen, 1855–58); Blackey, *The History of Political Literature from the earliest times* (2 vols; London, 1855); Janet, *Histoire de la philosophie morale et politique dans l'antiquité et temps modernes* (2 vols; Paris, 1860); and see Angelo d'Orsi, *Guida della storia del pensiero politico* (Florence, 1995), 93ff.

[5] John Dunn, *The History of Political Theory and Other Essays* (Cambridge, 1996), 11–38, and Conal Condren, *The Status and Appraisal of Classic Texts: An Essay on Political Theory, its Inheritance, and the History of Ideas* (Princeton, 1985).

[6] See, for example, Carl Schmitt, *The Concept of the Political*, trans. George Schwab (Chicago, 1996), and Terence Ball, James Farr, and Russell L. Hansen (eds), *Political Innovation and Conceptual Change* (Cambridge, 1989).

The medieval period has attracted some of the most subtle and wide-ranging studies of political thinking in every national tradition of Europe. In the Anglophone world F. W. Maitland, A. J. and R. W. Carlyle, C. H. McIlwain, Walter Ullmann, and others have sought the origins of modern political and legal categories and problems in the most recondite and technical sources that reflect social behavior as well as assumptions and ideals of communal life, its organization and control. In Germany Otto von Gierke sought to trace the origins of communal life in even deeper and more structural terms, while Ernst Kantorowicz followed a similar interest through ideas of kingship, corporate forms, and political continuity found in the mysteries of 'political theology'; and in France Georges de Lagarde uncovered the foundations of modern secularism in the work of William of Ockham and Marsilius of Padua. In many ways the traditions of law and politics have carried fundamental ideas about the social and political forms of the human condition.[7]

With the Renaissance politics and its history become more focused and connected, apparently, with modern views. The various faces of Machiavelli have contributed powerfully to the shaping of modern 'political science' (itself a sixteenth-century coinage). The Machiavellian concept of 'reason of state' (*ragione di stato*; *Staatsräson*), which became European-wide from the later sixteenth century, was investigated by Friedrich Meinecke in a classic study of *Ideengeschichte* and pursued from the sixteenth century down to the times of Ranke and Bismarck.[8] A different aspect of Machiavellianism, that of the republican and 'civic humanism', was revealed and celebrated by Hans Baron, a thesis taken up by J. G. A. Pocock and others and projected through many contexts of European history from Renaissance Italy through Stuart England down, less plausibly, to the French Revolution.[9] Deeper background has been provided by studies of the earlier legal context and the parallel concept of 'civil humanism'.[10] Debates over Machiavelli, like those over Locke, Hobbes, Rousseau, and Hegel, illustrate the phenomenon of canon-

---

[7] In general Walter Ullmann, *Law and Politics in the Middle Ages* (Ithaca, 1975), and D. R. Kelley, *The Human Measure: Social Thought in the Western Legal Tradition* (Cambridge, MA, 1990).

[8] *Machiavellism*, trans. Douglas Scott (London, 1957).

[9] Pocock *The Machiavellian Moment: Florentine Political Thought and the Atlantic Republican Tradition* (Princeton, 1975).

[10] D. R. Kelley, 'Civil Science in the Renaissance: Jurisprudence Italian Style', *Historical Journal*, 22 (1979), 777–97, and 'Civil Science in the Renaissance: Jurisprudence in the French Manner', *History of European Ideas*, 2 (1981), 261–76; and Walter Ullmann, *Medieval Foundations of Renaissance Humanism* (London, 1977).

formation as well as the distorting effects of disciplinary history and its tendency to take 'tunnel views' through the intervening contexts of history. By contrast, consider the work of Felix Gilbert, which situates Machiavelli's language in the semantic field of his own time, particularly the vocabulary of Florentine politics at the turn of the sixteenth century.[11]

One of the important contributions of the 'Cambridge school' of the history of political thought, to which Pocock, John Dunn, and Quentin Skinner have been assigned, is the linguistic turn which each has made. In the Anglophone world there is good precedent for this, recalling the old-fashioned search for 'keywords' (from George Cornwall Lewis's *Remarks on the use and abuse of some political terms* of 1832 down to the work of Raymond Williams);[12] but Skinner and Pocock have brought more sensitive views of textual problems. The question of language in history is often posed in terms of the relationship between text and context, and it is usually Skinner's formulation of 1969 that is invoked – rejecting the ahistorical views of pure political science, counterpart of the formalism of the New Criticism of the postwar period, in favor of a historical method emphasizing the original intention of the author of a particular text in the context of his or her own time.[13]

Skinner's intentionalism, beneficial as it was in the late 1960s as a corrective to unproblematized 'dialogues with the dead', has needed modification, especially when joined to a propositional view of language and communication; and indeed more recently he has turned to the force of rhetoric undermining this original view.[14] Pocock has gone beyond intentionalism, too, by concentrating on a wide range of political (and 'paradigmatic') languages that need to be distinguished in examining texts and contexts.[15] Political discourse is a Babel of tongues, including Roman and common law, classical

---

[11] *Machiavelli and Guicciardini* (Princeton, 1965).

[12] Williams, *Keywords: A Vocabulary of Culture and Society* (London, 1983²); and see *Political Innovation and Conceptual Change*, ed. Ball, Farr, and Hansen.

[13] David Boucher, *Texts in Context: Revisionist Methods for Studying the History of Ideas* (Dordrecht, 1985); James Tully (ed.), *Meaning and Context: Quentin Skinner and his Critics* (Cambridge, 1988); Condren, *The Status and Appraisal of Classic Texts*; d'Orsi, *Guida della storia del pensiero politico*; and David Harlan, 'Intellectual History and the Return of Literature', *American Historical Review*, 94 (1989), 581–698, with comments by David Hollinger, Allan Megill, Theodore Hammerow, Gertrude Himmelfarb, Lawrence W. Levine, Joan Scott, and John Toews.

[14] *Reason and Rhetoric in the Philosophy of Hobbes* (Cambridge, 1996), 14.

[15] 'The Concept of a Language and the *Métier d'historien*: Some Considerations on Practice', in Anthony Pagden (ed.), *The Language of Political Theory in Early-Modern Europe* (Cambridge, 1987), 19–38.

republicanism, scholasticism, and political economy; and intellectual discourse more generally increases this confusion. He has also reminded us that texts are not only written but also read – and misread – since, as any teacher knows, the lesson taught is seldom (in principle perhaps never) the same as the lesson learned (if any). How much more is this the case when communication, translation, and reception are carried on across different languages and in different contexts? The point is that after the authorial act or 'text event', texts have as many meanings as they have contexts, which is to say readers who supply these contexts. Both Pocock and Skinner are concerned with historical 'meaning', though within the relatively narrow and contrived framework of political thought conceived in a Whiggish spirit and featuring authors not necessarily part of a single project or even on speaking terms with each other.

A parallel school of the history of political thought is *Begriffsgeschichte*, whose purpose is likewise hermeneutical – being, as Reinhard Koselleck writes, 'to translate the words of the past and their meanings into our present understanding'.[16] It is not a circular movement from word to thing and back, but a study of changing contexts as well as meanings. Focusing on the *Sattelzeit* (the pivotal period across the Revolutionary and Napoleonic hiatus), practitioners of *Begriffsgeschichte* trace the accumulated and layered meanings of keywords – state, society, constitution, class, and so on – over long periods of time and in different historical contexts. *Begriffsgeschichte* (a Hegelian coinage) preserves a certain mentalist orientation, but it does affect to offer a 'social history of ideas' joining semantic history with political and social context.

A broader agenda appears in recent work on 'political culture', where emphasis is shifted from power and action to discourse and practices.[17] The study of political culture, like *Begriffsgeschichte*, has been especially concerned with the Revolutionary period, because it was a period not only of violent change but also of efforts to control society and to create culture and ideas as well as institutions, and ultimately to politicize all aspects of human behavior. Historians of political culture do not search for causes, underlying or

---

[16] 'Begriffsgeschichte and Social History', *Futures Past: On the Semantics of Historical Time*, trans. Keith Tribe (Cambridge, MA, 1985), 80; see also Melvin Richter, *The History of Political and Social Concepts: A Critical Introduction* (Oxford, 1995), and *The Meaning of Historical Terms: New Studies on Begriffsgeschichte*, ed. Hartmut Lehmann and Melvin Richter (Washington, 1996).

[17] *The French Revolution and the Creation of Modern Political Culture*, I, *The Political Culture of the Old Regime*, ed. Keith Michael Baker (Oxford, 1987), introduction; and Baker, *Inventing the French Revolution: Essays on French Political Culture in the Eighteenth Century* (Cambridge, 1990).

immediate, of great social movements like the Revolution; rather they seek meaning in the symbols of political legitimacy and threats to this – in language, art, literature, theater, music, ceremonial, and other displays of élite and popular behavior accessible to the methods of intellectual and cultural history.

2. Sociology

Another creation of revolutionary hubris was the new science of society that took the name of 'sociology'. This new discipline, a product of both revolution and counter-revolution, had two main roots, one French and the other German. It was the last in the line of 'prophets of Paris', Auguste Comte (in the wake of Turgot, Condorcet, and Saint-Simon), who coined the term and set the agenda for this new discipline.[18] For Comte *la Sociologie* was not only a science and a remedy for the 'social question' of the early nineteenth century but also a religion that would bring harmony to the whole human community; and his vision of history was a product of this sociologizing vision. The ages of theology, metaphysics, and positivism formed the periodization of intellectual history and signaled the transformations of human mentality – metaphysics being 'the ghost of dead theologies' and the secular, if still spiritualist, forerunner of positivist science.

The German road to sociology led from Hegel to Marx and their followers and critics. Like Comte, Hegel rejected individualism and contractualism as a basis for civil society; and his conflation of the Ideal and the Real likewise assimilated history to a conceptual system, making it the expression of reason. A drop-out from the Hegelian school as well as the law school of the University of Berlin, Marx (like Saint-Simon) sought an understanding of the historical process in the material conditions of society and seemed to relegate intellectual phenomena – superstructure and class consciousness – to a derivative position.[19] As Hegel had tried to subsume the history of thought to a philosophical system, so Marx subordinated it to the social structures and interests which made up the historical context of intellectual practice, identifying philosophy with the 'false consciousness' of a socially determined 'ideology' in a pejorative sense. Marx sought a 'science' that went beyond not only philosophy but also

---

[18] See Frank E. Manuel, *The Prophets of Paris: Turgot, Condorcet, Saint-Simon, Fourier, Comte* (Cambridge, MA, 1962).

[19] D. R. Kelley, 'The Metaphysics of Law: An Essay on the Very Young Marx', *American Historical Review*, 83 (1978), 350–67, repr. in D.R. Kelley, *History, Law, and the Human Sciences* (London, 1984).

the historical process itself, and when he was disappointed by that process in the wake of the abortive revolutions of 1848, he shifted his trust to the vision of the future promised by his dialectical-materialist science. And Marxist history long continued to be written in the spirit of this vision and this disillusionment.[20]

German sociology was forged in the crucible of controversy over the legacy of the systems of Kant, Hegel, and Marx, especially issues of epistemology and a series of binary oppositions which were analogous to the medieval problem of universals but with a social and a historical twist. Idealism and materialism, mind (*Geist*) and nature, individual and society, subjectivity and objectivity, the concrete and the abstract, 'idiographic' and 'nomothetic' methods, value and value-freedom, history and theory (philosophy), master and slave – these were the terms of the dialectic which informed the historical process.[21] Reality, including the cultural dimension of this reality, is infinitely complex; and the task of Windelband, Rickert, Weber, and others caught in the Neo-Kantian (and Neo-Hegelian) problems of historical knowledge was to reconcile these polarities through the formation and manipulation of concepts. The bias of all these thinkers was generally toward theory and system, in which 'historicism' was a source of irrationality and 'crisis'.[22]

American sociology emerged from a German background, though it soon became naturalized. The leading figure in the Chicago school, Albion Small, headed the first American sociology department (1892) and was a founder both of the *American Journal of Sociology* (1895) and the American Sociological Society (1905). For Small sociology was 'not a comet, as popularly pictured, viz., a body coming from nowhere and bound nowhere'; for 'Its lineage is as old as man's efforts to understand the human lot.'[23] In particular the origins went back to the historical school of law of nineteenth-century Germany and more remotely to the cameral science of the eighteenth.[24] The later history of the Chicago school and its surrender to scientism illustrates

---

[20] See Dominick LaCapra, 'Reading Marx: The Case of *The Eighteenth Brumaire*', *Rethinking Intellectual History: Texts, Contexts, Language* (Ithaca, 1983), 268–90.

[21] See Guy Oakes, *Weber and Rickert: Concept Formation in the Cultural Sciences* (Cambridge, MA, 1988).

[22] For Georg Lukacs, *The Destruction of Reason*, trans. Peter Palmer (Atlantic Highlands, NJ, 1981), sociology forms part of his story of the development of irrationalism 'from Schelling to Hitler'.

[23] Small, *Origins of Sociology* (Chicago, 1924), 19, 41; and see Martin Bulmer, *The Chicago School of Sociology: Institutionalization, Diversity, and the Rise of Sociological Research* (Chicago, 1984), 33ff.

[24] D. R. Kelley, 'The Prehistory of Sociology: Montesquieu, Vico, and the Legal Tradition', *Journal of the History of the Behavioral Sciences*, 16 (1980), 133–44, repr. in *History, Law, and the Human Sciences*.

the thesis of Ernst Becker, who analyzed the 'failure of the science of man' – a failure which, he added significantly, can only be understood historically – and spoke in particular of 'the tragic paradox of Albion Small', whose own failure, and that of what Becker calls his 'paradigm tradition', was to reject the notion of a 'value-free' social science.[25]

Sociology has always been possessed by a sense of crisis, especially its own,[26] and a confused view of its past – torn as it has been between objective, 'value-free science' and the search for a 'good society'. Many taxonomies and canons have been proposed, projecting sociology into its pre-disciplinary past and integrating it with the history of thought. Robert Nisbet, for example, tried to define sociological tradition in terms of the theories of classic German and French practitioners of this craft.[27] In a modern version of conjectural history Nisbet steers a course between doxography and the history of intellectual systems, ignores questions of social and institutional context, and takes as the protagonists of his story the sociological equivalents of Lovejoy's 'unit-ideas' – in this case the ideas of community, authority, status, the sacred, and alienation – as viewed from the 'holy ground' of the present. Nisbet adopts an interdisciplinary point of view; but his account is carried on in a strictly disciplinary mode, seeking a 'usable past' or constructing or reinforcing a disciplinary canon, its conventions, its collectivities, and its language, similar to the procedures of histories of literature, science, and art.

Sociology has tried to transcend some of the complacent conventions of historical interpretation through attention to collective behavior. Though abstract, as Georg Simmel argued, it was not spiritualist, for it rejected notions of individual 'genius' as causes of 'the great contents of historical life – language, religion, the formation of states, material culture', and turned instead to the idea of 'the production of phenomena through social life'.[28] Durkheim, too, had a 'sociological theory of knowledge', which derived ideas and the human sciences from collective experience and which distinguished different civilizations according to differing systems of concepts:

> Collective representations are the result of an immense co-operation, which stretches not only into space but into time as well ... to make them, a multitude of minds have associated, united, and combined their ideas and sentiments ... [29]

---

[25] *The Lost Science of Man* (New York, 1971), ix.
[26] Alvin Gouldner, *The Coming Crisis of Western Sociology* (New York, 1970).
[27] *The Sociological Tradition* (New York, 1966).
[28] *The Sociology of Georg Simmel*, trans. Kurt H. Wolff (New York, 1950), 12–13.
[29] *The Elementary Forms of Religious Life*, trans. Joseph Ward Swain (New York, 1915), 29.

Such representations were not necessarily the product of reason, then, but rather of what Villefredo Pareto, contemporaneously with Durkheim, called 'non-logical conduct' and 'residues', which linked modern mentalities of man with the 'savage mind' and its 'symbolic interpretations' portrayed by Lucien Levy-Bruhl.[30]

This notion of the social construction of knowledge, potentially congenial to historical interpretation, appeared in the work of German sociologists like Weber and especially Ernst Troeltsch, who moved uneasily between *Religionsgeschichte* and *Geistesgeschichte* in his effort to provide a social dimension for intellectual history.[31] It was most apparent, however, in the subdiscipline known as the sociology of knowledge which Lovejoy admitted to his agenda for the history of ideas. Karl Mannheim, the leading promoter of *Wissensoziologie* in the twentieth century, was concerned to overcome the Marxist (and Lukacsian) view of ideology by finding a social-scientific method of linking consciousness and society in a historical way. 'Strictly speaking it is incorrect to say that the single mind thinks', he wrote. 'Rather it is more correct to insist that he participates in thinking further what other men have thought before him.'[32] For Mannheim this approach was the proper way to approach 'intellectual history'.[33] According to Mannheim's disciple Werner Stark, the goal of the sociology of knowledge was specifically 'a deeper understanding of the history of ideas'.[34]

This was also one of the aims of the 'critical theory' of the Frankfurt school and especially of its eclectic alumnus Jürgen Habermas, whose work *Knowledge and Human Interests* represents not only a project of 'unmasking' – a 'critique of ideology' – in a post-Marxist, metahistorical mode but also, says one expert, 'a history of ideas with systematic intent'.[35] Critical theory

---

[30] Pareto, *The Mind and Society*, trans. Arthur Livingston (New York, 1935), I, II; and Levy-Bruhl, *La Mentalité primitive* (Paris, 1922).

[31] Carol Antoni, *From History to Sociology*, trans. Hayden White (Detroit, 1959), 72, and Robert J. Rubanowice, *Crisis in Consciousness: The Thought of Ernst Troeltsch* (Tallahassee, 1982); also Ian Hacking, *The Social Construction of What?* (Cambridge, MA, 1999).

[32] *Ideology and Utopia*, trans. L. Wirth and E. Shils (New York, 1952), 3.

[33] Ibid., 93.

[34] The subtitle of his book, *The Sociology of Knowledge* (New Brunswick, 1991); and see Volker Meja and Nico Stehr (eds), *Knowledge and Politics: The Sociology of Knowledge Dispute* (London, 1990).

[35] Thomas McCarthy, *The Critical Theory of Jürgen Habermas* (Cambridge, MA, 1978), 110. According to Rolf Wiggershaus, *The Frankfurt School*, trans. Michael Robertson (Cambridge, MA, 1994), 111, before the break-up of the Institute in 1933 'a study group on Social History and the History of Ideas' was formed by Mannheim, Löwe, Bergstraesser, and Noack. See also Martin Jay, *The Dialectical Imagination: A*

emerged in the wake of Marxism and Freudianism (and their various revisionisms) and followed an agenda of systematic research. Its aim was philosophy with a social dimension; and while it opposed idealism, it made a pronounced cultural turn, moving into the broad fields of both high culture (with studies of literature, art, and music) and low, that is, mass or popular, culture. It was 'critical' in the sense that it proposed, in the spirit of Marx and Freud, to unmask the social and psychic worlds concealed by culture and ideology.

German sociology after Weber and Husserl has been concerned not only with reactive social behavior but also with purposeful action and its social meaning, objective as well as subjective, from which stems the idea of an 'interpretative social science' following a hermeneutical rather than a natural-science model of analysis.[36] This approach, in which emphasis is placed on language, rationality, and communication, reaches its most comprehensive expression in Habermas's theory of communicative action. The rationalism of this eclectic theory carries over also into Habermas's notion of the task of the intellectual historian, or interpreter, which is to establish meaning by analyzing a text in terms of the 'reasons' of an author within the horizons of his and his audience's life-world. But Habermas's universalist system leaves little place for the irrational, the unconscious, or mis-communication, except in terms of 'social pathologies'.[37] The life-worlds of the past remain largely unproblematized, and the future-oriented theory formulated within Habermas's own modernist life-world overshadows history.

In France, too, some scholars have clung to sociological analysis as the key to superstructural phenomena. Thus Pierre Bourdieu uses the analogy of 'fields' of forces and struggles to give social meaning to the work of artists and intellectuals operating in cultural, literary, and linguistic 'fields'. Yet Bourdieu denies regressing to 'economism', and he does consider implications for the history of ideas and of philosophy. For him these areas of study are 'impoverished and transformed in the direction of an empty humanism', which is intensified by the notion of philosophical activity as a summit conference between 'great philosophers'. But such intellectualization has little meaning without a broader external view which acknowledges that

---

History of the Frankfurt School and the Institute of Social Research 1923–1950 (Boston, 1973).

[36] See Alfred Schutz, *The Phenomenology of the Social World*, trans. George Walsh and Frederick Lehnert (Evanston, 1967).

[37] *The Theory of Communicative Action*, I, *Reason and the Rationalization of Society*, trans. Thomas McCarthy (Boston, 1981), 131ff.; in II, *Lifeworld and System*, 119, Habermas writes of 'the hermeneutical idealism of interpretive sociology'.

in fact what circulates between contemporary philosophers, or those of different epochs, are not only canonical texts, but a whole philosophical doxa carried along by intellectual rumor – labels of schools, truncated quotations, functioning as slogans in celebration or polemics – by academic routine and above all by school manuals, which perhaps do more than anything else to constitute the 'common sense' of an intellectual generation.[38]

3. Anthropology

In any case, before, during, and since the passing of Marxism, there has been a conspicuous turning from sociology to anthropology – from reductionist views of history to interest in many aspects of culture without privileging certain kinds of behavior and taking instead phenomenological or symbolic approaches to cultural history. Indeed Marx himself, through his reading of Maine, Tylor, Morgan, and others, made an extraordinary 'cultural turn' late in his life.[39] 'Culture', too, of course, partakes of a sort of holistic, or systematic, character (like Durkheimian 'society'), which detracts from the utility of such concepts as 'cultural construction'. Yet it is not tied to selective explanatory premises and is open to consideration of all aspects of human behavior – around the clock and from cradle to grave.

Anthropology is an old term, equivalent to 'psychology' in a philosophical sense, but as a discipline it is relatively new, being raised to the level of a science only after intersecting with the separate field of empirical ethnology.[40] In Germany the tradition of philosophical anthropology is over two centuries old, going back to eighteenth-century historians of culture and critics of philosophy such as Herder as well as to Kant and Hegel's 'Philosophie des Geistes'.[41] In the twentieth century Arnold Gehlen (and in a different way Martin Heidegger) carried on this tradition of seeking an interdisciplinary

---

[38] *The Field of Cultural Production*, ed. Randal Johnson (New York, 1993), 35, 33; also *Language and Symbolic Power*, trans. Gino Raymond and Matthew Adamson (Cambridge, MA, 1991).

[39] D. R. Kelley, 'The Science of Anthropology: An Essay on the Very Old Marx', *Journal of the History of Ideas*, 45 (1984), 245–62; in D. R. Kelley repr. *The Writing of History and the Study of Law* (Aldershot, 1997).

[40] On the first 'new anthropology' see Georges Gusdorf, *Les Sciences humaines et la pensée occidentale*, VII, *Naissance de la conscience romantique au siècle des lumières* (Paris, 1978). Cf. H. G. Gadamer and Paul Voglei (eds), *Neue Anthropologie* (4 vols; Stuttgart, 1972).

[41] See Michael Landmann, *Philosophical Anthropology*, trans. D. Parent (Philadelphia, 1974); and Odo Marquardt, 'Zur Geschichte des philosophischen Begriffs "Anthropologie" seit den Ende des 18. Jahrhunderts', *Collegium Philosophicum: Studien Joachim Ritter zum 60. Geburtstag* (Basel, 1965), 209–39.

view of human nature on the basis not of the philosophy of consciousness but a philosophy of life, not the rational subject but the acting being, not the *Cogito* but the *Dasein*. Anthropological understanding required consideration of forestructure, prejudice, and natural and cultural endowment as well as character and purposeful behavior; and the programs of both Foucault and Derrida are in keeping with this view of anthropology.[42]

Since the eighteenth century anthropology has had repeated contacts with the study of history, especially cultural history. There are fundamental methodological parallels between these two fields in the sense that like the anthropologist, the historian must confront the Other – heterology, radical alterity – and diversity.[43] For the historian 'the past is a foreign country', whose language, customs, and culture need to be translated in one way or another into currently intelligible terms, that is, written down in the language of the discipline. For the historian, too, and especially for the historian of popular culture, nothing is too trivial or marginal to be ignored as possible conveyors of cultural meaning. The main difference is that history normally proceeds in diachronic fashion, while anthropology is synchronic and indeed sometimes ignores the more distant past of societies, or relegates it to an undifferentiated background (though in practice cultural historians may also take synchronic views, though set in a particular period).

Like society, culture brings theory to historical inquiry, offering it a field of meaning, a tradition of interpretation, and a repository of concepts and terms to give shape to evidence. Like Dilthey, Clifford Geertz has spoken of 'cultural systems', such as religion, which are composed of the world-systems and symbols through which humans express and communicate meaning. Ideology is another cultural system which must be interpreted and deciphered by anthropologists, as perhaps are particular disciplines, since anthropologists are themselves locked into such a system; and indeed Geertz, in the way of 'interpretative anthropology', has treated colleagues (as well as himself) in just this way. Like writing history, writing anthropology requires a high degree of irony and self-consciousness.[44]

The intersections between anthropology and intellectual history have been especially evident in the study of religion and myth, where the methods were

---

[42] See Axel Honneth and Hans Joas, *Social Action and Human Nature*, trans. Raymond Meyer (Cambridge, 1988), 130ff.

[43] Tzvetan Todorov, *On Human Diversity: Nationalism, Racism, and Exoticism in French Thought*, trans. Catherine Porter (Cambridge, MA, 1993), and Bernard McGrane, *Beyond Anthropology: Society and the Other* (New York, 1989).

[44] *Works and Lives: The Anthropologist as Author* (Stanford, 1988) and *After the Fact: Two Countries, Four Decades, One Anthropologist* (Cambridge, MA, 1995).

those of philology and classical and biblical scholarship. This was the point of departure for scholars like Max Müller and James Frazer, whose approach (following Creuzer and Tylor) was 'intellectualist' or 'mentalist' and devoted to the deciphering of myth and linguistic roots as expressions of primitive reactions to nature or some primordial religious experience. Combined with universalist conceptions of human nature, such literary or linguistic anthropology also overlapped with psychological theories, as in the cases of Freud, Jung, and Kerenyi, and even with turn-of-the-century curiosity about spiritualist phenomena (which attracted Max Müller's nemesis Andrew Lang, among others).

Comparative methods in history as well as mythology seem to require some universalist (metahistorical or metamythical) basis, illustrated by the Indo-European quest pursued by Georges Dumezil and his admirers; but as a profession anthropology turned against the spiritualism of its founders and practitioners, which relied too much on linguistic and etymological speculation, on the old quest for origins, and, at least implicitly, on the old Christian framework updated by secular evolutionism. Like historians, anthropologists were anxious to have their discipline accepted as a science, not merely an art. Ethnography, social anthropology, archeology, the study of material culture, and emphasis on field research have made the philosophical bias of armchair scholars seem obsolete – and have certainly changed notions about what constitutes anthropological (or indeed historical) evidence.

Like other human sciences, anthropology has often heard, and given way to, the siren song of reductionism; but the study of religion and myth continues to resist assaults by naturism, animism, and other theories of the mechanics of human nature across centuries and cultures. No more than philosophy does any of the human sciences have the power to assimilate the whole process of human history – or indeed to make sense of every human creation. (Sometimes a cigar is only a cigar, and a ritual, as far as the uninitiated are concerned, a ritual.) This was admitted even by that philosopher's philosopher, Wittgenstein. Objecting to the explanatory efforts of Frazer's *Golden Bough*, Wittgenstein remarked, 'Here one can only describe and say: this is what human life is like.'[45] To be merely 'interesting' must suffice for phenomena occurring beyond one's horizons.

From the beginning, anthropology, like the informal ethnographical aspects of western historiography, encouraged a distrust of universals and absolutes associated with grand theory and faith. 'The only thing that links Freud,

---

[45] Wittgenstein, 'Remarks on Frazer's *Golden Bough*', in *Philosophical Occasions 1912–1951*, ed. James Klagge and Alfred Nordmann (Indianapolis, 1993), 121.

Piaget, von Neumann, and Chomsky (to say nothing of Jung and B. F. Skinner)', Geertz has written, 'is the conviction that the mechanics of human thinking is invariable across time, space, and circumstance, and that they know what it is.'[46] The implied relativism of Geertz's 'interpretative anthropology' cuts against the grain of religious, philosophical, and scientific conventions and in radical form – incommensurability – even of comparative methods. Along with skepticism, it represented, in extreme form, a sort of cognitive atheism which began by denying absolutes and ended by questioning both rationality and the possibility of scientific knowledge; and it has generated almost as much controversy as the denial of the existence of God, the original guarantor of such knowledge.

A paradigmatic example of this issue is the Whorf–Sapir thesis about the relativism of language – that every language implies a conceptual system and an associated world-view and therefore shaped reality, that is, human perceptions of reality, accordingly (a thesis that carries over into the history of gestures as well).[47] The classical philosophical example is the relationship between Aristotelian metaphysics and the linguistic structure of Greek from which it appears to be derived, but the same is true of Newton's ideas of space, time, and matter, which are also 'recepts from culture and language'.[48] Whorf's ideas are still in dispute, if not disrepute, in part because of the exaggerated arguments of his early formulations, which rashly proclaimed a 'new theory of relativity'. What counted against him even more was the prevailing rigidity of 'linguistic science' in the age of Chomsky, which resisted the idea that 'facts' were a function of language and which inferred linguistic determinism in Benjamin Whorf's linking of 'background linguistic systems' and conceptual systems. Whorf's views and the research agenda, they imply, will be rehabilitated in more sympathetic retrospect.

A fellow-traveler of relativism is the more modest cautionary attitude called historicism, which suggests that human understanding is time-, space-, and culture-bound and lacks, even in logic and mathematics, a metalanguage in which explanations and interpretations can be formulated. Everything appears in 'the river of Becoming', as Troeltsch put it.[49] Among the reasons why cultural theory and criticism often look with fear, if not loathing, on

----

[46] *Local Knowledge: Further Essays in Interpretive Anthropology* (New York, 1983), 150.

[47] Benjamin Lee Whorf, *Language, Thought, and Reality* (Cambridge, MA, 1956); and see Jan Bremmer and Herman Roodenburg, *A Cultural History of Gesture* (Ithaca, 1991).

[48] Ibid., 153.

[49] Cited by Rubanowice, *Troeltsch*, 50.

historical inquiry, are the risk of being overwhelmed by data, of being misled by the conceits and conventions of historical tradition, and of being enticed by the hyper-empirical belief that judgment must be deferred until the record is complete, if not surrendered entirely.

The history of anthropology as a discipline has made its appearance in the past generation, especially in the work of George Stocking and his colleagues.[50] Their focus has been on the classical period and the 'revolution' associated with Boas and Malinowski, as amateur and armchair anthropology was replaced by scientific attitudes and field work – which represents for anthropologists what the archives are for historians. 'Culture' shifted from ideas of system, organicism, and development to unhistorical notions of elements, patterns, and the material base emphasized by social anthropology and ethnographers like Morgan. The views of these scholars are generally, though critically and ironically, Baconian, 'culture' in the old humanistic sense given it by Arnold and Tylor being transformed into the basis of a scientific discipline that outgrew ethnography and distinguished itself from psychology and other human sciences.

While working cautiously with the Kuhnian conception of paradigms, Stocking has also been wary of 'presentism' in writing disciplinary history.[51] Historically, Stocking has encouraged exploration of institutional and political factors – for like political science and sociology, anthropology sought public functions as well as support and flourished in the wake of empire – but he has also been on the look-out for ideas characteristic of contemporary anthropology, notably the emergence of what R. H. Codrington (in 1863) called 'the native' view, which tried to separate the problem of the Other apart from comfortable ethnocentric and anachronistic views, and ideas of 'survivals' and 'residues', which define seemingly irrational practices whose functions have been forgotten but which are nonetheless defining features of a particular culture.[52] Like the histories of sociology and psychology, the history of anthropology has made efforts to incorporate larger aspects of the history of philosophy and of ideas, conscripting Aristotle into the anthropological canon, for example, because of

---

[50] See especially George Stocking, *Race, Culture, and Evolution: Essays in the History of Anthropology* (Chicago, 1982²); *The Ethnographer's Magic and Other Essays in the History of Anthropology* (Madison, 1992); *After Tylor: British Social Anthropology 1888–1952* (Madison, 1995); and the annual series, *History of Anthropology*, edited by him.

[51] 'Paradigmatic Traditions in the History of Anthropology', in *The Ethnographer's Magic*, 324–61; and 'On the Limits of "Presentism" and "Historicism" in the Historiography of the Behavioral Sciences', *Race, Culture, and Evolution*, 1–12.

[52] *After Tylor*, 42, 52, and so on.

his concept of a 'second [that is, a social] self' beyond the psyche and his efforts to find a broad definition of humanity.[53]

Gaining a history and establishing ties with literature and philosophy, anthropology seems to have lost much of its disciplinary rigor, while its central concept, 'culture', has largely lost its utility. Its original value was to open up to scientific investigation all aspects of human behavior – nothing too trivial to be irrelevant – but the question was, relevant to what? Culture has come to suggest a superorganic, spiritual field – 'webs of significance', Geertz calls them – coterminous with the whole horizon of existence. Cultural studies invite inquiry into literally everything and, with this, a hermeneutical virtuosity linking things to an undefinable field. The result is to make possible a limitless range of histories but no plausible story of culture, or cultures, in general. On the other hand the one concept that anthropology – as an interpretative if not a structuralist pursuit – cannot do without is that of the thinking and writing subject, since here it is that meaning takes up its first residence; and to this extent the old associations with psychology are still in place. This seems to be the case, too, with the study of intellectual and cultural history.

4. Psychology

The object of psychological study is the soul, or the mind, its mechanics and its creations, including ideas. In its earliest Greek stages the mind (*psyche*) had material foundations, at least as far as language and etymology can suggest – parts or functions of the body serving to designate the senses and bases of cognition.[54] In philosophical tradition, especially in commentaries on Aristotle's *De Anima*, the connection with the body was preserved, but mentalism predominated not only in Christian thought but also in more modern forms of spiritualism, including Cousin's 'psychological method', and the 'philosophy of mind'. Like anthropology, psychology claimed scientific status in the nineteenth century, when philosophical and empirical approaches to psychological phenomena intersected and produced national schools of psychological study – German scientists remaining in touch with philosophy,

---

[53] See Gregory Schrempp, 'Aristotle's Other Self: On the Boundless Subject of Anthropological Discourse', in *History of Anthropology*, ed. Stocking, VI, *Romantic Motives* (Madison, 1989), 10–43.

[54] See R. B. Onians, *The Origins of European Thought about the Body, the Mind, the Soul, the World, Time, and Fate* (Cambridge, 1952).

the British turning to physical causes, and the French becoming increasingly interested in pathological aspects.[55]

In philosophy, especially after Kant, the discussion of the soul focused on the 'category of the person' – the *Ego*, the *Ich*, the *Moi* – and the self-conscious subject in its various states, rational, irrational, socialized, and pathological, and across many centuries and many cultures.[56] Fichte's theory of the 'I' and the 'not-I' defined the issue of subjectivity down to the time of Husserl and Sartre.[57] The 'person' figures centrally in language, classically in the trinitarian form of subject, object, and verb, and also in the law, in the form of person (subject of the law), thing (potentially property), and action (as in action at law); and in this pattern has persisted in western thought in various ways, including the ego-psychology of Fichte and the dialectic of Hegel and Marx.[58] The self remained at the center of debate even as its integrity and even existence was being undermined by positivists like Ernst Mach.

Within the horizons of human life the person or self remains central, and psychology is a conceptual expression of this centrality. The Delphic directive, 'Know thyself', was received and extended in many ways, as psychology moved from the conscious to the unconscious and formed ties with other human sciences, especially *Völkerpsychologie* and anthropology.[59] As Carl Gustav Carus wrote in 1846, the unconscious life of the soul preceded and produced the mental characteristics which only later come to the surface.[60] The object of 'depth psychology' and psychoanalysis continued to be human meaning but no longer merely the apparent meaning displayed in rational discourse. As cultural historians had sought manifestations of reason in the earliest stages of history and prehistory, so modern psychologists, psychiatrists, and psychoanalysts sought layers of psychic life hidden beneath the socialized

---

[55] Graham Richards, *Mental Machinery: The Origins and Consequences of Psychological Ideas, 1600–1850* (Baltimore, 1992).

[56] See Marcel Mauss, 'A Category of the Human Mind: the Person; the Notion of Self', in *The Category of the Person: Anthropology, Philosophy, History*, ed. Michael Carrithers, Steven Collins, and Steven Lukes (Cambridge, 1985); and *Problèmes de la personne*, ed. Ignace Meyeron (Paris, 1973).

[57] See Frederick Neuhouser, *Fichte's Theory of Subjectivity* (Cambridge, 1990), 170.

[58] See D. R. Kelley, 'Gaius Noster: Substructures of Western Social Thought', in *American Historical Review*, 84 (1979), 619–48, repr. in *History, Law, and the Human Sciences*.

[59] *Psychoanalysis and Social Science*, ed. Hendrik M. Ruitenbeek (New York, 1962).

[60] *Psyche: On the Development of the Soul*, trans. Renata Welch (Dallas, 1989), 15.

behavior of humanity in its civilized adult forms. The turn to pathological aspects of psychic phenomena was also well established by the nineteenth century.[61]

The person and the self have also become targets of attack by philosophical critics of rationalism, ideological critics of liberal individualism, and psychoanalytic interrogators of the conscious subject. In its Husserlian form phenomenology began as an effort to preserve the integrity of the self and its ideas as well as philosophy itself by an epistemological maneuver joining subject and object in a single field of cognition; but despite the pre-given, limiting conditions of this field in relation to human 'intention', this was ultimately to evade the forces of the unconscious and self-destructive urges revealed by psychoanalysis beneath the surface of the free and knowing subject.

Recurring questions – dividing psychologists but giving coherence to the history of the discipline – were whether psychology was a natural or a human science, and whether one could achieve a 'science of mind' as well as a 'philosophy of mind'. Although there was no consensus about the epistemological status of psychology, it did, in the form of 'psychologism', impinge on other disciplines, including logic and philosophy (Husserl) and cultural history (Lamprecht, via Wundt); but the most direct challenge to the positivist and atomistic view was the ill-fated German school of *Gestalt* psychology – a term which invoked Goethe's morphological and holistic conceptions of science.[62] The formalism of Gestalt psychology offered a new basis for that 'consciousness' whose existence William James had put in question, and for new ties between psychology and other human disciplines, including philosophy, aesthetics, social thought, anthropology, and history.

For centuries psychology was part of philosophy and followed its method of self-analysis and introspection before entering its modern empirical and clinical stage; with Freud this tendency has been reversed.[63] In recent years Freudianism seems to have gone the way of Marxism – in the sense that while the orthodox doctrine is accepted by a few of the faithful, many of the major insights have been absorbed in intellectual and even popular culture. In a

---

[61] See J. B. Friedrich, *Versuch einer Literärgeschichte der Pathologie und Therapie der psychischen Krankheiten* (Würsburg, 1830).

[62] Mitchell Ash, *Gestalt Psychology in German Culture 1890–1967: Holism and the Quest for Objectivity* (Cambridge, 1995).

[63] See G. S. Rousseau, 'Psychology', in *The Ferment of Knowledge*, 143–210; *The Languages of Psyche: Mind and Body in Enlightenment Thought* (Berkeley, 1990); and *Enlightenment Borders: Pre- and Post-Modern Discourses, Medical, Scientific* (Manchester, 1991).

sense Freud anticipated the linguistic and literary turn, his psychoanalytical method being fundamentally hermeneutical and depending on the analysis of discourse. Freud's approach was, according to Paul Ricœur, a 'hermeneutics of suspicion' – a process of 'demystification' and 'reduction of illusion' – by deciphering the signs of the unconscious and its repressions.[64]

How to transfer an individual therapeutic operation to the reading of texts and analysis of their authors is a problem that not all historians believe is soluble, and yet it is impossible to avoid seeking 'unconscious' aspects of human behavior and thought even after doubts have been cast on the reality of the 'conscious'.[65] William James's old question (which also worried Lovejoy), 'Does Consciousness Exist?', finds an affirmative answer neither in psychology nor in the study of language. And in any case, who would be present to give this answer?

Psychoanalysis takes another tack than either phenomenology or natural science, proposing to find meaning not in the mechanics or motivational aspects but in the prehistory (*Vorzeit*) of consciousness. Beginning as a 'biologist of the mind',[66] Freud ended up as an archeologist, mythographer, and conjectural historian, for whom (as for revisionist followers like Lacan) the unconscious was in effect a language or symbol system to be deciphered according to a peculiar sort of logic in which each term contained its opposite. While founded on psychologism (or metapsychologism), Freudianism vastly expanded the field of inquiry, beginning with the Cartesian *Cogito* or Fichtean *Ich* – the bourgeois Ego, with its anguishes and hidden aspects (defined as Id and Superego), but extending into remote areas of history and culture. 'No, psychoanalysis is not a science of observation', as Paul Ricœur has argued; 'it is an interpretation, more comparable to history than to psychology.'[67]

Freudianism has had as many revisionist versions as Marxism, and the internecine debates have undermined its earlier universal pretensions, yet its philosophical effects have been notable. Psychoanalysis was an effort to restore, as well as analyzing and in a sense deconstructing, the thinking and unthinking subject. Trying to rescue Freudianism from behaviorist and medicalist reduction (and at the same time to radicalize it), Jacques Lacan took a linguistic turn, bringing together Hegel's and Heidegger's views of the

---

[64] Paul Ricœur, *Freud and Philosophy: An Essay on Interpretation*, trans. Denis Savage (New Haven, 1970), 27.

[65] See David Couzzens Hoy, 'A History of Consciousness: from Kant and Hegel to Derrida and Foucault', *History of the Human Sciences*, 4 (1991), 261–81.

[66] Frank J. Sulloway, *Freud, Biologist of the Mind: Beyond the Psychoanalytic Legend* (New York, 1979).

[67] *Freud and Philosophy*, 345.

subject and its 'caring' condition, though adding the Freudian unconscious according to his own structuralist interpretation and taking it beyond the Family Romance to a symbolic world created by language, in which the Ego (*Moi*) becomes the subject (*Je*) of speech.[68] In *Anti-Oedipus* Gilles Deleuze and Félix Guattari – with the help of Nietzsche as well as Marx and Freud – took psychoanalysis, or what they preferred to call schizoanalysis, further into the irrational field, the expanded *Dasein* as it were of late capitalist society.

Like Marx, Freud and his work have been not only adapted by followers and defectors but also dissolved in the common culture of intellectuals and assumptions about the duplicity of human behavior and 'unintended meanings'. But whatever its failings as a method of therapy, Freudianism in its non-doctrinaire forms has been applied to many parts of the human sciences. In his more adventurous speculations Freud had proposed to reevaluate culture itself, situating it between *eros* and *thanatos*, love and the death instinct – and this, too, has shaped the thinking of scholars in history and the human sciences.[69] In the form of psychohistory or psychobiography Freudian investigations have uncovered deeper structures and motives of public behavior, as in Erikson's biography of Luther, whose struggles against an authoritarian Church were linked to the familial and psychosexual problems which, on this reading, Luther shared with other evangelical-minded Christians and which he sublimated into a new form of religion.[70]

One recent employment of psychology of particular interest to intellectual and cultural historians is the problem of memory, which, in its collective form, may be regarded as a spiritual kind of history, not only for peoples without written culture but also for civilized nations occupied with 'commemorating' their pasts. Historical sources such as archives, libraries, museums, and (now) databases are also artificial 'memory institutions', which are subject to cultural and political construction as well as recollection.[71] In a

---

[68] *The Language of the Self: The Function of Language in Psychoanalysis*, trans. Anthony Wilden (New York, 1968); and see Ellie Ragland-Sullivan, *Jacques Lacan and the Philosophy of Psychoanalysis* (Urbana, 1986), and Elizabeth Roudinesco, *Jacques Lacan & Co.: A History of Psychoanalysis in France, 1925–1985*, trans. Jeffrey Mehlman (Chicago, 1990).

[69] Norman O. Brown, *Life against Death: The Psychoanalytical Meaning of History* (Middletown, 1959).

[70] *Young Man Luther: A Study in Psychoanalysis and History* (New York, 1958). And see Philip Pomper, *The Structure of the Mind in History* (New York, 1985), on Freud, Erikson, Marcuse, Brown, and Lifton.

[71] Patrick Hutton, *History and the Art of Memory* (Hanover, VT, 1993), and Jacques Le Goff, *History and Memory*, trans. Steven Rendell and Elizabeth Claman

sense contemporary studies in cultural memory and 'places of memory' represent a form of cultural history with a new sort of historical awareness that focuses on the ways in which humanity attempts to preserve, reconstruct, or imagine the past to give it present meaning.

Yet memory is even less secure than the subject which it presumably informs. This receives striking confirmation in the phenomenon of multiple personality disorder, which Ian Hacking has recently analyzed and associated with the peculiarly western ideas of the soul. For Hacking these ideas are 'part of an oppressive, perhaps even patriarchal system' and also associated with what, on analogy with Foucault's 'anatomo-politics' and 'bio-politics', he calls 'memoropolitics', referring to the cultural construction and misconstruction of memory, collective as well as 'personal'.[72] This has serious implications not only for intention, consciousness, the mind, and 'ideas', but also for current wisdom about history as a form of memory and, at the same time, an expression of verifiable and extra-psychological truth.

Psychology, too, even in its most scientific forms, is a discipline practiced within a 'domain of constructions'; and psychological investigation, experimentation, and discovery are themselves all social processes. Its history, as Kurt Danziger argues, 'is neither a series of narratives about famous psychologists nor an enumeration of their successive "findings"', since the historians must consider also the shifting 'constructive schemes' which produce and regulate the interpretation of data.[73] Nor can these schemes be separated from life outside the laboratory or clinic – that is, from political, economic, and social forces which bear on psychological research and which are part of the history of psychology. Whether conscripted by political or commercial institutions or placed in the service of human emancipation (such as women's liberation), psychology remains problematic for intellectual and cultural as well as disciplinary historians.[74]

(New York, 1992); also Jan Assmann, *Moses the Egyptian: The Memory of Egypt in Western Monotheism* (Cambridge, MA, 1997), George S. Shrimpton, *History and Memory in Ancient Greece* (Montreal, 1997), Patrick Geary, *Phantoms of Remembrance: Memory and Oblivion at the End of the First Millennium* (Princeton, 1994), and William Engel, *Mapping Mortality: The Persistence of Melancholy and Memory in Early Modern England* (Amherst, 1995).

[72] *Rewriting the Soul: Multiple Personality Disorder and the Sciences of Memory* (Princeton, 1995), citing Jean Comaroff, 'Aristotle Re-membered', in *Questions of Evidence: Proof, Practice, and Persuasion across the Disciplines*, ed. James Chandler et al. (Chicago, 1994), 463–9.

[73] *Constructing the Subject: Historical Origins of Psychological Research* (Cambridge, 1990), 3.

[74] See Ellen Herman, *The Romance of American Psychology: Political Culture in an Age of Experts* (Berkeley, 1995).

5. Disciplinary History

Human knowledge in its modern itinerary has progressively been divided into disciplines and subdisciplines, and intellectual history cannot avoid the structural and terminological results of this process. Classically, 'discipline' designates the order given to fields of knowledge for pedagogical purposes, especially transmission from master to disciple in formal academic traditions; and in this sense it is part of the very structure of intellectual history.[75] Philosophy, literature, science, and their subdivisions are all branches of learning with long and problematic genealogies; but they all emerged in 'modern' and recognizably disciplinary forms in the wake of the 'renaissance of letters', the associated public culture created by the new medium of print, and the appearance of specialized departments in universities. They found more specific scientific definition and direction in the quest for an effective method and a rigorous science, and they have also spawned countless subdisciplines and '-ologies', which often go on to seek their own independence.

Disciplines serve particular needs; adopt formal language, methods, agendas, and organization; find a consensus, an institutional base, and ways of preserving intellectual continuity through a master–disciple connection; and finally, fashion their self-image and legitimacy through construction of their histories. The process invites anthropological as well as historical study, for disciplines are cultural constructions in which 'disciples' seem to behave like the natives of ethnographic study. According to one observer of disciplinary behavior, 'Each tribe has a name and a territory, settles its own affairs, goes to war with others, has a distinct language and a variety of ways of demonstrating its apartness.'[76]

Reaching the status of a 'rigorous science' in the late eighteenth century, philosophy was still claiming this position a century later in the work of Husserl and his disciples. Even when modestly construed as a 'practice', philosophy has a distinctive and professional history, with all the usual canonical names, through the efforts of academic practitioners.[77] Less set in

---

[75] See D. R. Kelley (ed.), *History and the Disciplines: The Reclassification of Knowledge in Early Modern Europe* (Rochester, 1997) and with R. H. Popkin (eds), *The Shapes of Knowledge* (Dordrecht, 1991); Loren Graham and Wolf Lepenies (eds), *Functions and Uses of Disciplinary Histories* (Cambridge, MA, 1983); and Ellen Messer-Davidov, David R. Shumway, and David J. Sylvan (eds), *Knowledges: Historical and Critical Studies in Disciplinarity* (Charlottesville, 1993).

[76] Tony Becher, *Academic Tribes and Territories: Intellectual Enquiry and the Culture of Disciplines* (Bristol, PA, 1989), citing F. G. Bailey, *Morality and Expediency* (Oxford, 1979), 12.

[77] D. W. Hamlyn, *Being a Philosopher: The History of a Practice* (London, 1992).

its habits, literature and its history are the subject of a constantly changing canon and critical approaches; but they likewise enjoy academic continuity and disciplinary status even as literary scholars try to rewrite or even to deny their history. And the natural sciences have produced even more structured and Whiggish histories, dependent on the current paradigms of disciplinary specialties and sub-specialties – as have the human sciences treated in this chapter.

Viewed historically, disciplines locate arenas in which communications are established over generations, across cultural and linguistic barriers, and between ideological antagonists; and they develop hermeneutical practices in which 'dialogues with the dead' become an essential part of their method. The histories of political science, sociology, anthropology, and psychology all project their disciplinary lineage back at least to Plato and Aristotle. These are all histories *ante litteram*, though each of them (except for the miscegenated, Latin–Greek 'sociology') has terminological roots in Aristotelian philosophy; and they constitute prime examples of fabricated Whiggish history.

Psychology, emerging from its position as introspective philosophy, asserted claims to be first scientific, then clinical and therapeutic – and then, perhaps, in the form of 'psychologism' and endless debates over the 'mind–body problem', philosophy again.[78] Psychology is by definition limited to individual thought and action, even in projecting this study toward collective behavior. The history of psychology is in a particular state of confusion these days, with the decline of behaviorism, Gestalt psychology, and Freudianism as accepted paradigms of research and therapy. Yet each of these movements has left its imprint on the discipline; and Freudianism in particular continues, at least marginally, to be employed by historians, anthropologists, and other investigators of the human condition. The interest in 'self-fashioning', introduced by Stephen Greenblatt and others associated with the new historicism, suggests the continuing force of a rather conventional ego-psychology in cultural history.[79] So, perhaps, does feminist theory, which introduces gender considerations into the later fortunes of the Cartesian *Cogito* and Freud's Œdipal psyche.[80]

Like psychology (with which, indeed, it was once virtually identified), anthropology emerged from a general philosophical status to become, with

---

[78] See not only *The Languages of Psyche*, ed. Rousseau, but also Robert M. Young, 'The Mind–Body Problem', in *Companion to the History of Modern Science*, ed. R. C. Olby et al. (London, 1990), 702–11.

[79] *Renaissance Self-Fashioning from More to Shakespeare* (Chicago, 1980).

[80] See, for example, Andrea Nye, *Feminist Theory and the Philosophies of Man* (New York, 1988).

the help of ethnography and ethnology, a practical and theoretical science and an academic discipline. In Germany, and to some extent France, anthropology retained its associations with philosophy, while in the Anglophone world it has been split into empirical and interpretative varieties, the latter maintaining some ties with philosophical and literary studies. The history of anthropology remains torn between the philosophical and empirical traditions even as it reaches out beyond its disciplinary frontiers in the form of cultural criticism.[81] While no longer making the sort of universal claims that evolutionary theory encourages, anthropologists have employed small-scale investigations to reinforce contemporary notions of the parochialism and diversity of human nature as conditions of the sciences of humanity. And anthropologists, with renewed awareness of the literary aspects of their trade, have turned their own ethnographic methods on themselves.[82]

Sociologists have done the same, and likewise, in part, as one of the tactics of intellectual imperialism. Writing still in the shadow of Parsons, Robert Friedrichs has recalled the priestly and prophetic pretensions of classical sociology and has argued that the former position (which casts others in the role of laypersons) must be surrendered. However, he clings to the prophetic tradition in the sense of the discipline's utopian function of holding out social ideals beyond the reality of contemporary society.[83] Yet as the central, if not foundational, science of humanity, sociology has been overshadowed by anthropology and has itself, after generations of universalist aspirations, turned to 'interpretative' methods to bring itself up to date. At the same time, perhaps as a byproduct of decline, sociologists have shown an intensified interest in the history of their discipline and the classical authors of their canon. Sociology's past does indeed seem more glorious than, at present, its future.

Political science retains its disciplinary power, but less for its intellectual ambitions or achievements than for its alliance with institutions of the public sphere, beginning and ending with the state. More than other human sciences, political theory is bound by what Conal Condren calls 'issue orthodoxy', an assumption comparable to the belief in perennial questions in philosophy.[84] Questions of the state, democracy, citizenship, and revolution have been treated in many contexts and periods;[85] but they tend to be

---

[81] George E. Marcus and Michael M.J. Fischer, *Anthropology as Cultural Critique: An Experimental Moment in the Human Sciences* (Chicago, 1986).

[82] See especially Geertz, *Works and Lives*.

[83] Robert W. Friedrichs, *A Sociology of Sociology* (New York, 1970).

[84] *The Status and Appraisal of Classic Texts*, 44ff.

[85] For example, *Political Innovation and Conceptual Change*, ed. Ball, Farr, and Hansen.

flattened out unhistorically within the tradition of political science, with ancient and modern authors holding imaginary dialogues with little consideration for the disparity between the texts of today and yesteryear, for the distorting effects of the 'classic' status of texts,[86] and for the lost questions of bygone ages. Sensitivity to the changes in political language has alleviated these problems, although the political 'We' is often extended, by disciplinary courtesy, to authors of the most remote ages as if political behavior, structures, and language remain constant over the ages. Yet only recently has the masculine bias, embedded especially in Aristotelian tradition, been fundamentally challenged through attention to women's place outside the home.[87]

It should be added that 'discipline', with its connotations of rigidity and (thanks to Foucault, at least in translation) associations with 'punish', has lost some of its attraction in modern times. We no longer share the authoritarian notions of the structure of knowledge tied to the old encyclopedia. Many scholars prefer to work in the interstices of the disciplines or to reject the notion of discipline altogether; and some, with Paul Feyerabend, may rage against the imperialism of capital-M Method that subordinates disciplinary practices to a unitary Reason.[88] Yet we cannot entirely escape the premises of this disciplinary perspective, if only because of the conventions of academic language and argument. Knowledge is a culturally constructed phenomenon, and particular disciplines represent the cultural forms in which this knowledge has been preserved, transmitted, and transformed throughout history.

In any case the history of ideas has found new fields of exploration in the histories of particular disciplines. Once again the approaches have been of two sorts. One starts with the self-image of a discipline at a particular, usually 'presentist', point of view, accepting the special conventions and terminology as they have been accepted by the disciplinary community.[89] The other takes disciplines as cultural constructions to be understood and judged more generally from the standpoint and according to the values of the host society. Either way disciplinary histories form a significant part of contemporary intellectual history. And as for the fashionable concept of

---

[86] See Condren, *The Status and Appraisal of Classic Texts*.

[87] See, for example, *Women in Western Political Philosophy*, ed. Ellen Kennedy and Susan Mendus (New York, 1987).

[88] *Farewell to Reason* (London, 1987).

[89] Much of Jeremy L. Tobey, *The History of Ideas: A Bibliographical Introduction*, II, *Medieval and Early Modern Europe* (Santa Barbara, 1977), is organized along disciplinary lines.

'interdisciplinarity', this only reinforces the significance of disciplines and their significance for intellectual and cultural history.[90]

6. Post-Human Sciences

In recent years the 'human sciences' and their culturalist terminology have been replacing the old concept of the 'social sciences', as scholars become dissatisfied with narrowness and reductionism in socioeconomic explanations of human behavior.[91] Traditional sociology (Marxist, Weberian, Parsonian, Bourdieuian) addresses collective human behavior through universalizing scientific categories; and partly for this reason, after an impressive cycle of imperial expansion, the discipline has entered into decline. 'Sociology has gone astray', Steven Seidman writes, because of its scientism, quest for foundations, and pretensions to a privileged status.[92] So sociology has been in many ways superseded by anthropology, with its emphasis on cultural specificity, 'thick description', and human difference.

Anthropology, which itself passed through a universalist and evolutionist stage, has been transformed by an interdisciplinary 'blurring of genres' (in Geertz's phrase) and in particular interactions with literary theory, facilitated by the fact that ethnography is itself 'a semi-literary genre of anthropological discourse'.[93] One result has been to represent culture not as a process to be analyzed but as a text to be read or translated. Another has been to emphasize the question of 'alterity', which is entailed by a hermeneutical approach. As literary theory shifts attention from author to reader, so anthropology shifts attention from the observer to the observed – to the Other, who is at once the subject of inquiry and interpretation and, as anthropologists followed the course of empire, the object of European oppression. Politically, anthropology has entered a postcolonial phase and admits on equal terms the culture of marginal groups both inside and outside of western civilization, while historical scholars have followed this

---

[90] For Jean Piaget, *Main Trends in Inter-Disciplinary Research* (New York, 1970), this approach involves collaborations between the disciplines, scientific and humanistic. See also, for example, Jürgen Kocha (ed.), *Interdiziplinarität* (Frankfurt, 1987).

[91] See Steven Seidman, 'The End of Sociological Theory', in *The Postmodern Turn: New Perspectives on Social Theory*, ed. Seidman (Cambridge, 1994), 119–39.

[92] Ibid.

[93] Marcus and Fischer, *Anthropology as Cultural Critique,* 5; and see Geertz, 'Blurred Genres: The Refiguration of Social Thought', in *Local Knowledge* (New York, 1983), 19–35.

lead into earlier periods and even prehistory.[94] Parallel with this is the critique of the masculinist bias of anthropology, which feminism has brought through a new sensitivity to gender relations.[95]

The life sciences, too, have been admitted to the human sciences, as the body, biological inheritance, and the biosphere are included within the horizons of cultural studies, especially under the impact of feminist theory. History has always been more of a presence in these fields than in hard sciences, as Jacques Roger remarked, and this presence was magnified by Darwinism and its revisionist offspring.[96] In the works of Roger, Georges Canguilhem, G. S. Rousseau, Betty Smocovitis, Scott Atram, Londa Schiebinger, and others, the life sciences have also been introduced to the linguistic and literary (as well as gender and sexual) turns and so are brought more directly in touch with intellectual and cultural history.[97]

In contrast with economic and social history, the 'new' as well as the old, intellectual and cultural historians, moved by such extra-disciplinary examples, confront all aspects of human life, individual as well as collective behavior, body as well as mind, play as well as work, madness as well as reason, and other dimensions of experience accommodated by the humanizing (and, for Marxists like Lukacs, irrational) notion of *Lebensphilosophie*. With Terence and Montaigne, nothing human is foreign to them, and they turn their attention not only to what can be explained but also to what is merely, inexplicably, 'interesting'.

Yet this humanist and humane thrust has its own drawbacks, as post-structuralist practitioners of the human sciences like Foucault have shown;

---

[94] See, for example, *Exoticism in the Enlightenment*, ed. G. S. Rousseau and Roy Porter (Manchester, 1990); *Encountering the Other(s): Studies in Literature, History, and Culture*, ed. Gisela Brinker-Gabler (Albany, 1995); Roger Célestin, *From Cannibals to Radicals: Figures and Limits of Exoticism* (Minneapolis, 1996); and Richard Waswo, *The Founding Legend of Western Civilization: From Virgil to Vietnam* (Hanover, 1997).

[95] See Henrietta L. Moore, *Feminism and Anthropology* (Minneapolis, 1988).

[96] Roger, *Les Sciences de la vie dans la pensée française du XVIIIe siècle* (Paris, 1987 [1963]).

[97] Rousseau, *Enlightenment Borders*; and see *Inventing Human Science: Eighteenth-Century Domains*, ed. Christopher Fox, Roy Porter, and Robert Wokler (Berkeley, 1995); Canguilhem, *Ideology and Rationality in the History of the Life Sciences*, trans. Arthur Goldhammer (Cambridge, MA, 1988); Smocovitis, *Unifying Biology: The Evolutionary Synthesis and Evolutionary Biology* (Princeton, 1996); Atram, *Cognitive Foundations of Natural History: Towards an Anthropology of Science* (Cambridge, 1990); and Schiebinger, 'Gender in Early Modern Science', in *History and the Disciplines: The Reclassification of Knowledge in Early Modern Europe*, ed. D. R. Kelley (Rochester, 1997), 319–35.

and criticism of subjectivity and reason has sometimes, under the influence of Nietzsche and Heidegger, given an anti-humanist impulse to these disciplines, shifting attention to external conditions and factors beyond the control of human will and perhaps the grasp of the human intellect. The result has been to challenge the orthodoxies not only of the human sciences but also of the normal science of history, including ideas of agency, reason, meaning, and truth.[98]

The assault on human agency is an old story, going back to the skeptical and deterministic theories of antiquity and, in modern times, to Marxist critiques of ideology and Freudian critiques of ego-psychology. The result was not only to reject the 'Great Man' theory of history (vulgar Anglophone offspring of Hegel's world-historical individual) but also to proclaim the death of man and the conscious subject and the illusory character of presence. Good intentions are the hallmark of humanism, and from the point of view of postmodern criticism, they have not lived up to the bright expectations created by modern natural and social science. In any case the so-called subject is not so much a willful or effective actor as (somehow or other) a construction of language, culture, and history, as indeed are all the values, ideals, and prejudices associated with this subject, beginning with the defining intellectual quality of enlightened humanity.

The critique of reason begun by Kant has entered a radical phase, as reason has been demoted from a universal and objective to a localized and temporalized condition. Weberian criticism of modernization, social planning, and bureaucratic management has reinforced suspicions of value-free rationality, reconceptualized as another form of domination – a 'repressive ideology', according to Christopher Norris – which evades some of its own constitutive elements, including not only class but also race and gender.[99] Disillusionment with Enlightenment views of reason has likewise infected discussions of scientific method, which has also been reduced, relativized, aestheticized, and denied universal status.

What about the question of meaning? '[T]he meaning of a word is its use in the language,'[100] writes Wittgenstein (though admitting exceptions). But in

---

[98] Among several summaries, see Pauline Marie Rosenau, *Postmodernism and the Social Sciences: Insights, Inroads, and Intrusions* (Princeton, 1992).

[99] See the volumes edited by Maryanne Cline Horowitz from the *Journal of the History of Ideas: Race, Gender, and Rank: Early Modern Ideas of Humanity* (Rochester, 1992) and *Race, Class and Gender in 19th-Century Culture* (Rochester, 1991).

[100] *Philosophical Investigations*, trans. G. E. M. Anscombe (Oxford, 1963²), para. 43.

whose experience and judgment, and what if the interpreters disagree? Having been divorced from authorial intention and textual dwelling, meaning has been delivered over to readers and critics and thus rendered radically unstable, since there is no privileged vantage point or standard of judgment. 'The interpretative character of all that happens' is the Nietzschean message which, expanded by Heidegger, Gadamer, and others into hermeneutics, has found a postmodern audience, especially among literary critics and theorists and even intellectual historians.[101] The aim of knowledge was not causal explanation (for centuries the very definition of 'science') but interpretation, with translation as the fundamental model. This suggests a view that recognizes the creative role of imagination in social thought and that, no longer aspiring to rigorous explanation, turns instead to 'interpretative social science' – if not a 'poetic' of sociology, as Richard Brown has suggested – opening the door to subversive views that reject the methods, categories, and generalities of old-fashioned sociology.[102]

The upshot for history is that it must be regarded not as a record of truth or reality but, at least in its larger goals, only 'our myth'.[103] It is a groundless narrative disguising the pluralist, fragmentary, chaotic, and ruptured character of past 'experience' (which itself is a fiction). Though it pretends to tell of the past, the study of history is carried on in an eternal present (that immediately becomes a past). We remain in the clutches of the tense structure of our language; only through this and rhetorical devices can we express such pastness. Nor can there be historical 'explanation', which is a matter of assigning causes and in a strict sense is identical with prediction except for the positioning of time's arrow.[104] As Isaiah Berlin and Paul Veyne argue, all the historian can attempt is *retrodiction* and some sort of reductionism or a selecting of causal factors, which is tied to a particular point of view that seems to be inconsistent with an explanatory ideal.[105]

---

[101] *Nietzsche as Postmodernist: Essays Pro and Contra*, ed. Clayton Koelb (Albany, 1990).

[102] Geertz, *The Interpretation of Culture* (New York, 1973), and Taylor, 'Interpretation and the Sciences of Man', in *Philosophy and the Human Sciences, Philosophical Papers*, II (Cambridge, 1985), 15–57; and Richard H. Brown, *A Poetic for Sociology* (Cambridge, 1977); cf. Robert Nisbet, *Sociology as Art Form* (Oxford, 1976).

[103] Michel de Certeau, *The Writing of History*, trans. Tom Conley (New York, 1988), 21.

[104] Alan Garfinkel, *Forms of Explanation: Rethinking the Questions in Social Theory* (New Haven, 1981).

[105] Berlin, 'The Concept of Scientific History', in *Philosophical Analysis and History*, ed. William Dray (New York, 1966), 13, and Veyne, *Comment on écrit l'histoire* (Paris, 1971), 182.

Finally, is there a political subtext to these skeptical – these post- or end-of-history – attitudes? Habermas thinks that such views conceal political conservatism, and he subsumes them under the rubric of 'postmodernism'.[106] These challenges subvert not only the comforting metanarrative of western liberal history but also, paradoxically, the sort of cultural criticism which, with Habermas, envisages liberation from the burdens of modernism; viewed historically, however, these 'postmodern' attitudes all have precedents in western intellectual tradition and indeed seem to be extensions or radicalizations of modernist ideas, available to ideologists of both right and left. What have postmodernists wrought, for example, that was not imagined by Dadaists? One may not be able to write postmodernistically of such an abstraction as postmodernism, but one may say of it (more easily than of history), that 'this, too, shall pass' – and shall, despite its own best efforts, be historicized.

Nevertheless, self-designated postmodern perspectives, whatever their conceptual value, have called attention to areas of experience which have often been neglected by both classical and modernist social science. The marginal, the irrational, the subjugated, the subaltern, the oppressed, the silenced, and the deferred are all received into the plural narratives of a world fearing that an end to history (as we know it) has come and turning to chaos and complexity theories to yield new sorts of meaning. The failing of the Kantian critique of reason, which was to turn criticism on reason itself, has been realized with a vengeance by postmodern human science. Postmodern perspectives also suggest a more pluralistic conception of justice, with more sensitive concern for the Others and attendant injustices against the totalizing vision of modern rational order.[107] Postmodern and deconstructionist ideologues, or anti-ideologues, have in many ways filled the vacuum left by the Old and the New Left and also discredited the old spectral positioning.

The postmodern predicament, or at least its rhetoric, posits an end to subject-centered rationality, a decentering of language, the illusory character of presence, and a radical indeterminacy of meaning. Research is relativized, as for example feminism seeks its own methodologies in the human sciences.[108] For cultural study and local knowledge ambiguity seems to find, in contrast to computer-designed univocality, a new value; and the suggestive theories of

---

[106] *The New Conservatism: Cultural Criticism and the Historians' Debate*, trans. Shierry Weber Nicholson (Cambridge, MA, 1989); and see Richard Rorty, 'Habermas and Lyotard on Postmodernity', in *Habermas and Modernity*, ed. Richard Bernstein (Cambridge, MA, 1985), 161–76.

[107] See Stephen K. White, *Political Theory and Postmodernism* (Cambridge, 1991).

[108] *Feminist Methods in Social Research*, ed. Shulamit Reinharz (New York, 1992).

chaos and complexity seem to reinforce these skeptical lines of thought.[109] It may be too much to expect intellectual and cultural historians to draw specifically on these notions, which inform the present climate (whether or not 'postmodern') of opinion, but they cannot avoid taking them into account in the opening years of the new millennium, when so many of the old gods have failed and so many of the old ideas have been discredited.

---

[109] See N. Katherine Hayles, *Chaos Bound: Orderly Disorder in Contemporary Literature and Science* (Ithaca, 1990), and Donald N. Levine, *The Flight from Ambiguity: Essays in Social and Cultural Theory* (Chicago, 1985); and cf. Andrew Pickering, *The Mangle of Practice: Time, Agency, and Science* (Chicago, 1995), 24.

Chapter 9

The History of Philosophy

> The passing of the past is ...
> the gathering of what endures ... ,
> which needs us as messengers.
> Martin Heidegger

Since the Enlightenment, philosophy seemed to repudiate its encyclopedic past in the search for purity, scientific status, and professional preeminence – the Kantian view of 'pure thought', at least in its extreme form, as Trendelenberg wrote, 'demands that it be purified of all content'.[1] Yet philosophy preserved some ties with the history of thought and culture. The grounds for this included not only Cousin's eclecticism but also German 'neocriticism', following the idealist systems of Kant and Hegel and turning back in various ways to historical, linguistic, and cultural dimensions of thought.[2] These were evident in the continuing pursuit of British 'conjectural history' and especially Scottish philosophy, which emphasized the social character and progressive trajectory of human intelligence and culture and which has been a premise of intellectual history down to the present.

1. Dilthey and the Critique of Historical Reason

In the later nineteenth century the call for a move 'back to Kant' and the high priority given to the problem of knowledge were of special interest for the natural and human sciences in general and for intellectual history in particular.[3] According to the received story, Kant had set the agenda for continental philosophy, while Hegel had set about resolving remaining questions through a hybrid dialectic joining the ideal and the real. Positivist and materialist

---

[1] Cited by Klaus Christian Köhnke, *The Rise of Neo-Kantianism: German Academic Philosophy between Idealism and Positivism* (Cambridge, 1991), 29.

[2] See Gianna Giolotta (ed.), *Il neocritismo tedesco* (Turin, 1983).

[3] Thomas E. Willey, *Back to Kant: The Revival of Kantianism in German Social and Historical Thought, 1860–1914* (Detroit, 1978).

reactions to these formalistic approaches to 'spirit' seemed at first to undermine such speculative philosophy,[4] as Neo-Kantianism had to take into account new forms of experience and conceptions of science, both human and natural. The insights of the historical schools and sociology led to historical and anthropological 'turns' in philosophical thinking crucial for continuing efforts to chronicle and to conceptualize the history of the human spirit.

As in the eighteenth century, the issue was how to explore and to understand the phenomenon of 'spirit' (*Geist*). As Georg Simmel insisted, historical knowledge depended on the knowing subject, whose main object of study was other knowing subjects. He opposed the sort of 'historicism' that denied this position. 'If history is not a mere puppet show, then it must be the history of mental processes ... ', Simmel wrote.[5] 'The various attempts to reconstruct the physical conditions responsible for the peculiarities of historical events does [*sic*] not alter this fact.' For Simmel history was a form of 'applied psychology'.

There was a growing belief, however, that, while psychology might hold the key to this question, inner reflection was not sufficient, and attention had to be paid, too, to social and cultural conditions. Wilhelm Dilthey spoke of spirit and the sciences thereof (*Geisteswissenschaften*), but not in an idealistic sense. 'Spirit [*Geist*] has the same meaning as Montesquieu's spirit of the laws, Hegel's objective spirit, and Ihering's spirit of Roman law.'[6] This was what in the eighteenth century was called the 'moral sciences', which defined the whole arena of what can be apprehended, since – German idealism's version of 'maker's knowledge' and Vico's *verum-factum* principle – 'The spirit understands only that which it has created.'[7] The first condition for history as a human science, Dilthey wrote, 'lies in the consciousness that I am myself a historical creature, that the one who examines history also makes history'.[8]

The Kantian revolution involved a turn away from the substance of cultural history; Neo-Kantianism represented, in the work of Dilthey, Windelband,

---

[4] See Frederick Albert Lange, *The History of Materialism* (1873[2]), trans. Ernest Chester Thomas (New York, 1925).

[5] *The Problems of the Philosophy of History: An Epistemological Essay*, trans. Guy Oakes (New York, 1977), 39.

[6] *Der Aufbau der geschichtlichen Welt in den Geisteswissenschaften*, in *Gesammelte Schriften* (Leipzig, 1927), VII, 86; English trans. by Patricia Van Tuyl in *Selected Works*, IV, *Hermeneutics and the Study of History*, ed. Rudolf Makkreel and Frithjof Rodi (Princeton, 1996), 325–86; and see Theodore Plantinga, *Historical Understanding in the Thought of Wilhelm Dilthey* (Toronto, 1980), 40ff., and Charles R. Babbach, *Heidegger, Dilthey, and the Crisis of Historicism* (Ithaca, 1995).

[7] Ibid., 148.

[8] *Gesammelte Schriften*, VII, 278, cited by Makkreel, 25.

Rickert, Cassirer, and others, a return to such concerns. In other words, the Kantian trinity of critiques (pure and practical reason and judgment) were inadequate for the understanding of historical experience – the problem arising from the Kantian notion that 'reason has the sources of knowledge in itself, not in the objects and their observation'.[9] What was required was a revised view of experience and, in the famous phrase of Dilthey, a 'critique of historical reason' (and also a historical critique of reason). This was the impulse underlying the efforts of post-Kantian and post-Hegelian philosophers to construct a science of the human spirit (*Geisteswissenschaft*) that acknowledged the historicity of mind (*Geschichtlichkeit des Seelenlebens*) and accommodated practical life as well as pure reason. In contrast to Kant's intellectualism, Dilthey 'came from history' to philosophy and never lost his appreciation of positive knowledge,[10] believing that 'We need analysis of special domains' (*Einzelanalysen*).[11] He also recognized that poetic insight and imagination were no less important for the human sciences than the philosophical critique of reason. Together they prepared the way for a larger synthesis of 'life philosophy' (*Lebensphilosophie*), a term used by the disciples of Dilthey, and, in the union of human and scientific knowledge that provided meaning, a 'world-view' (*Weltanschauung*), a term taken from his teacher Trendelenberg.[12]

As in the eighteenth century, too, there were scholars who distrusted the antiquated vocabulary of idealism; Heinrich Rickert, for one, preferred to speak (as Dilthey sometimes spoke) not of 'spirit' but rather of 'culture' – not *Geisteswissenschaft* but *Kulturwissenschaft* – distinguishing the latter by its 'idiographic' (individualizing) method and concern for values as contrasted to the 'nomothetic' (generalizing and law-giving) character of natural science. Elaborating on this argument by Windelband, Rickert nevertheless sought a 'science of individuals' as understood in particular values and contexts, from particular perspectives, and with the help of modern geography, economic materialism, and 'cultural history'.[13] Rickert distinguished historical from

---

[9] *Prolegomena to Any Future Metaphysics*, trans. L. W. Beck (New York, 1950), Preamble.

[10] *Gesammelte Schriften*, V, 10, cf. VIII, 175ff.

[11] *Introduction to the Human Sciences*, ed. Rudolf Makkreel and Frithjof Rodi (Princeton, 1989), 117.

[12] See Carlo Antoni, *From History to Sociology*, trans. Hayden White (Detroit, 1959), 3, and Fritz Ringer, *The Decline of the German Mandarins* (Cambridge, MA, 1969), 336.

[13] Windelband, 'Geschichte und Naturwissenschaft' (1894), *Präludien* (Tübingen, 1915), 136–60, and Rickert, *The Limits of Concept Formation in Natural Science: A Logical Introduction to the Historical Sciences*, trans. Guy Oakes (Cambridge, 1986)

philosophical significance, although in so doing he raised the hermeneutical issue of 're-creative understanding', that is, how 'to re-create the real mental life of another person' – 'how does one psyche see the *reality* of another, and not merely the nonreal [scientific or representational] meaning that both have in common?'[14] We may understand the words and yet not the person. Dilthey continued to regard psychology as central to the human sciences, since it was in the individual that nature and culture intersected.[15] Yet the individual was not defined merely through introspection, and Dilthey emphasized historical biography and autobiography as a way of gaining access to the human science of psychology, an insight followed up by his editor and son-in-law Georg Misch.[16]

Unlike the Neo-Kantians of the Baden school, Dilthey still regarded history as fundamental to the human sciences. 'A human being is allotted only a small portion of time', he wrote; 'how can he make the past present?'[17] Much of the preparatory work for his unfinished system was pursued in areas of intellectual history (*Geistesgeschichte*), which – in a way superior to the crude positivism, sociology, and 'philosophy of history' of the nineteenth century – investigated the practical foundations of the human sciences. From the time of the ancient poets, wrote Dilthey, historical facts were preserved, and in general 'The interest of a later time, together with historical coincidence, serves to select which of these facts will reach us.'[18] Whence the fundamental importance of philology and hermeneutics, which had been developed by the nineteenth-century historical school in opposition to the hyper-philosophical views of the Enlightenment, in order to reconstruct this process of selection and to recover this collective memory which had been lost in the shift of historical 'interests'.

For Dilthey the fundamental method of the human sciences was the art of hermeneutics, which emerged from philology to achieve general philosophical status in the work of Schleiermacher.[19] Hermeneutics, which Dilthey defines as

---

– but rejecting (184) the nomothetic *Kulturgeschichte* of Karl Lamprecht. See also Guy Oakes, *Weber and Rickert: Concept Formation in the Cultural Sciences* (Cambridge, MA, 1988).

[14] Ibid., 167.

[15] *Introduction*, 101.

[16] *Geschichte der Autobiographie* (Leipzig, 1907).

[17] 'On Understanding and Hermeneutics: Student Lecture Notes' (1867–68), in *Selected Works*, IV, *Hermeneutics and the Study of History*, in ed. Makkreel and Rodi, 233.

[18] *Introduction*, 76.

[19] 'The Rise of Hermeneutics', trans. Frederic Jameson and Rudolf A. Makkreel, in *Hermeneutics and the Study of History*, 235–58.

'the methodology of the interpretation of written records', allows the critic to reconstruct the essential meaning of texts using historical exegesis and context and thereby, in the famous and presumptuous formula of *Besserverstehen*, 'to understand the author better than he understood himself'.[20] Such understanding is of course subjective, since we are all locked within our own consciousness, our thought escaping only in words or equivalents; and the best we can achieve is, in another famous formula, 'a rediscovery of the I in the Thou'.[21] Such is the basis of historical understanding and the 'human sciences' more generally. Dilthey operated in the tradition of idealist philosophy in pursuit of a 'system', and most of the commentary on Dilthey concerns this unrealized philosophical vision. Yet much of his published work was devoted to intellectual and cultural history before, and underlying the philosophical structures of, Kant and Hegel. His central theme was the transformation of 'world-views' from religious to secular forms, as illustrated by the rise of natural law, pantheism, the 'new anthropology' of the seventeenth century, philosophical hermeneutics, and the historical view associated with the Göttingen school of the eighteenth century – the familiar secularizing story told by modern intellectual historians.[22]

2. Cassirer and the Critique of Culture

Another Neo-Kantian drawn to intellectual history as a way of carrying on the critique of reason was Ernst Cassirer, in whose own systematic effort, the philosophy of symbolic forms, 'The critique of reason becomes the critique of culture.'[23] Cassirer had an interest in both the natural and the human sciences (*Geisteswissenschaften*), which shaped the prehistory of this project (*Vorgeschichte der Vernunftkritik*). Like Dilthey, Cassirer combined history

---

[20] *Selected Writings*, trans. H. P. Rickman (Cambridge, 1976), 259–60 (*Gesammelte Schriften*, V, 331).

[21] 'Construction of the Historical World', in ibid., 208 (*Gesammelte Schriften*, VII, 191).

[22] See, for example, *Gesammelte Schriften*, II, *Auffassung und Analyse des Menschen im 15. und 16. Jahrhundert*, III, 'Leibniz und sein Zeitalter' and 'Friedrich der Grosse und die deutsche Aufklärung'; IV, 'Die Jugendgeschichte Hegels'; VIII, 'Das geschichtliche Bewusstsein und die Weltanschauungen', and so on.

[23] *The Philosophy of Symbolic Forms*, trans. Ralph Manheim (New Haven, 1953–57), I, 80. See John Michael Krois, *Cassirer: Symbolic Forms and History* (New Haven, 1987); Thora Ilin Bayer, *Cassirer's Metaphysics of Symbolic Forms* (New Haven, 2001); S. G. Lofts, *Ernst Cassirer: A 'Repetition' of Modernity* (Albany, 2000); and Carl H. Hamburg, *Symbol and Reality: Studies in the Philosophy of Ernst Cassirer* (The Hague, 1956); also Heinz Paetzold, *Ernst Cassirer: Von Marburg nach New York* (Darmstadt, 1995).

and system and in particular 'the development of the systems of the human sciences'.[24] He always tried, he said, 'to avoid any cleavage between the systematic and historical considerations and have striven for a close fusion between the two'.[25] For Cassirer every epoch had its own basic system (*Grundsystem*), which was described in the work of philosophers – especially the precursors and postcursors of Kant.[26] But philosophy was only part of the story of spiritual culture (*der geistige Kultur*); and the modern phase began with the Renaissance according not only to Dilthey but also to historians of philosophy like Brucker and Cousin and to cultural historians like Michelet and Burckhardt, who likewise saw the rise of a distinctive 'Renaissance Philosophy'.[27]

European thought was like a fugue, according to Goethe, in which parts were successively taken up by different European nations. So, Cassirer wrote, 'The writings of Valla, Vives, and Ramus define three different stages in which the gradual reception of humanism was accomplished through three great cultural nations' (*Kulturvölker*).[28] What Renaissance humanism brought was a 'new theory of thought' derived from its ideas of language.[29] The result was a kind of self-consciousness that underlay the more formalized subjectivity (the *Ichbegriff*) that furnished the premise of Cartesian and critical philosophy (and that made possible the 'Copernican revolution' of Kant), which, for Cassirer, resolved the 'subject–object problem' by positing an 'idealistic idea of truth'. It also brought, in the form of skepticism and the philosophy of history, an awareness of the limitations of dogmatic philosophy and the special problems of the human sciences. In the last, much-delayed volume of his *Problem of Knowledge*, Cassirer, like Dilthey, shifted from the familiar canon of philosophy to particular modes of knowledge, especially mathematical, biological, and historical. 'For philosophy is gradually losing its leadership in this domain that it had held and treasured for centuries', he wrote. 'The individual sciences will no longer delegate their authority but mean to see and judge for themselves.'[30]

---

[24] *Leibniz' System in seinen wissenschaftlichen Grundlagens* (Marburg, 1902), xi, xii.

[25] *Philosophy of Symbolic Forms*, III, *Phenomenology of Knowledge*, xvi.

[26] *Das Erkenntnisproblem in der neueren Geschichte* (Berlin, 1922³), I, v.

[27] Ibid., I, 145.

[28] Ibid., I, 135.

[29] *Philosophy of Symbolic Forms*, I, 127; and see John Herman Randall, Jr, 'Cassirer's Theory of History, as Illustrated in His Treatment of Renaissance Thought', in *The Philosophy of Ernst Cassirer*, ed. Paul Arthur Schilp (New York, 1958), 689–728.

[30] *The Problem of Knowledge: Philosophy, Science, and History since Hegel*, trans. William H. Woglom and Charles W. Hendel (New Haven, 1950), 10.

For Cassirer intellectual history was associated at first with natural science, beginning with Descartes and Leibniz and involving not merely empirical and mathematical philosophy but also the problem of the individual and consciousness.[31] From the time of Nicholas of Cusa, indeed, epistemology had come to take precedence over metaphysics, thus preparing the way for Kant's conceptual revolution and establishing the conditions of modernity. Descartes had played a central part in this transition to modernity, but in his philosophy there was no place for the human sciences, so that 'both ethics and history remained alien to his plan and his construction'.[32] Kant had begun to fill this void with his critique of practical reason, that is, moral philosophy, and he recognized the force of imagination in his critique of judgment treating aesthetics, that 'secondary epistemology' (*Gnoseologia inferior*);[33] but it remained for his followers, such as Dilthey, Rickert, and Cassirer, to complete the project by acknowledging the historical dimension which prevailed in Cassirer's time, when 'Historicism found being no longer in God or in the Absolute Idea and wanted to hold fast to it in the human mind and the totality of humanity.'[34]

In general Cassirer saw no division between the Neo-Kantian program and that of natural science, and he rejected Rickert's distinction between natural and cultural sciences; for there was a fusion between Inner and Outer – 'a continuous oscillation between experience and the concept'. The unity of thought was based not on the notorious *Ding an sich* but rather on intellectual construction. Cassirer found this unity expressed in all forms of human thought, including language, art, and myth as well as scientific conceptualizing; and he extended the Kantian aesthetic by turning to the literary tradition to supplement philosophy. This new direction appeared in *Freiheit und Form*, published in 1916, in which, referring to Winckelmann, Herder, Goethe, Hölderlin, and Schiller (all of them the progeny of Leibniz), he argued that 'human culture [*Bildung*] is attained not in the logical but in the aesthetic'.[35] To sense, reason, and understanding must be joined *Phantasie*; and the true, in the Neoplatonic–Romantic adage, is also the beautiful.

Already before his encounter with the Warburg library (after his appointment at the University of Hamburg in 1920) Cassirer had made this literary turn, though he still followed Kant rather than Herder, who had failed (he thought)

---

31 See Massimo Ferrari, *Il giovane Cassirer e la scuola di Marburgo* (Milan, 1988).
32 *Das Erkenntnisproblem*, I, 587.
33 *Freiheit und Form: Studien zur deutschen Geistesgeschichte* (Berlin, 1916), 119.
34 *Problem of Knowledge*, 325.
35 *Freiheit und Form*, 124.

to rise to the critical perspective.[36] The new horizons of imagination were apparent in Cassirer's studies in language and myth, which were part of his philosophy of symbolic forms.[37] Building on the work not only of Kant (the Kant of imagination rather than of reason) but also of Humboldt and Schelling as well as modern linguistics, mythology, and anthropology, Cassirer continued his aesthetico-philosophical search for the 'morphology of the spirit' found in language, myth, and art.[38] These modes of symbolic expression were 'the primary subjective sources, the original attitudes and formative modes of consciousness', whose exploration was essential if one hoped to go beyond the Kantian trichotomy of the purely logical, ethical, and aesthetic categories.[39] They were pre-scientific but nevertheless unified 'configurations *towards* being'.[40]

Language is the first and most fundamental of these forms, being grounded on perception as well as reflection and so exemplifying the Aristotelian formula repeated several times by Cassirer: 'nothing is in the intellect that was not previously in the senses'. Language made its foundational contribution to the philosophical union of experience and concept in a primordial and mimetic form of 'concept-formation' which Cassirer calls 'the concrescence of name and thing'.[41] Extending humanist philology, eighteenth-century scholars went beyond philosophical speculation about language in general through an 'increasing interest in *individuality*, the spiritual specificity of the *particular* languages'.[42] This was further developed by nineteenth-century studies in historical and comparative philology, which (as in the work of Karl Vossler) took into account both the inventiveness of speakers and the inertial force of languages in development.[43]

---

[36] *Kant's Life and Thought*, trans. James Haden (New Haven, 1981), 229.

[37] See Krois, *Cassirer: Symbolic Forms and History*; Silvia Beretti, *Cassirer, Panofsky, and Warburg*, trans. Richard Pierce (New Haven, 1989); and Ivan Strenski, *Four Theories of Myth in Twentieth Century History: Cassirer, Eliade, Lévi-Strauss and Malinowski* (Iowa City, 1987).

[38] 'Der Begriff der symbolischen Formen in Aufbau der Geisteswissenschaften' (1921–22), in *Wesen und Wirkung des Symbolbegriffes* (Darmstadt, 1956), 174: 'die Sprache als Ganzes, der Mythos als Ganzes, die Kunst als Ganzes'. See also his 'Davos Discussion' in Heidegger, *Kant and the Problem of Metaphysics*, trans. Richard Taft (Bloomington, 1990), 172; and Michael Friedman, *A Parting of the Ways: Carnap, Cassirer, and Heidegger* (Chicago, 2000).

[39] *Philosophy of Symbolic Forms*, III, 57.

[40] Ibid., I, 107.

[41] Ibid., II, 25. And see Annabella d'Atri, *Cultura, creatività e regole fra Kant e Cassirer* (Cosenza, 1990).

[42] *Philosophy of Symbolic Forms*, I, 139.

[43] Ibid., I, 169, referring to Vossler's *Sprach als Schöpfung und Entwicklung* (1905), on which see *Carteggio Croce–Vossler 1899–1949* (Bari, 1951), 76ff.

This development Cassirer saw, rather abstractly (if not in imitation of Hegel or Comte), as threefold. At the stage of imitation language was bound to a primitive copy-theory (which some modern thinkers still accepted). At the stage of analogy it moves from efforts of designation to those of signification, consciously separating phonetic conventions from their referents. At the symbolical stage language is able finally to operate in terms of pure relation and so of abstract reason and science, as projected, perhaps, by Leibniz's 'universal characteristic' and by Herder's pioneering efforts to join subject and object in a unified conception of language in particular and culture in general – a line of argument which represented, according to Cassirer, 'a turning point not only in psychology but also in the whole development of the human sciences'.[44] To this extent, at least, Herder's work supported the critical philosophy of Kant and his followers, in which the Inner and the Outer – the subject and the object – also achieve a higher 'spiritual' synthesis.[45]

Another 'formative mode of consciousness' was myth, and this reflects another 'odyssey of the spirit', which has its own morphology but which moves through the same three stages as does language: the mimetic, in which real and ideal are fused; the analogical, in which, as in religion, a separation is made between sign and meaning; and the symbolical, which represents the philosophy of religion.[46] Nevertheless, as Schelling had urged in the previous century, myth demands to be explored on its own terms and not merely for what might objectively lie behind it, as Creuzer and others had wanted to do. In myth subject and object merge, so that there is no 'fixed dividing line between mere "representation" and "real" perception, between wish and fulfillment, between image and thing'.[47] Nor indeed because of the common originating structure is there a fixed dividing line between language and myth, both being interposed between humanity and nature, and both entirely reconcilable with the relativistic and indeterministic implications of twentieth-century science, which Cassirer was also following closely.[48]

Science – 'the phenomenology of knowledge' – completes both this trinity and the Kantian critique which Cassirer self-consciously set out to revise. Thus 'Philosophical Knowledge must first free itself from the constraints of

---

[44] *Philosophy of Symbolic Forms*, III, 33.

[45] Ibid., I, 190–97.

[46] Ibid., II, 237.

[47] Ibid., II, 36.

[48] Elaborated on in Cassirer's related works on Einstein's theory of relativity and on determinism and indeterminism in modern physics; and see Seymour W. Itzkoff, *Ernst Cassirer: Scientific Knowledge and the Concept of Man* (Notre Dame, 1971).

language and myth; it must, as it were, thrust out these witnesses of human inadequacy, before it can rise to the pure ether of thought.'[49] Here, following the trail blazed by Galileo, Leibniz, and, more recently, Einstein, Cassirer sees the culmination of the turn from ideas of imitation or analogy to understanding based on 'purely symbolic relations'. This was the full story of the problem of 'concept-formation' discussed so aridly and abstractly even by Kantians like Rickert; and on this historical and phenomenological basis, Cassirer returns to the old Kantian questions of space, time, and modern scientific knowledge.

But the drive to surpass Kant remains primary, as is clear from the last (fourth and unfinished) volume of the *Philosophy of Symbolic Forms*, in which Cassirer turns to 'life-philosophy' (the term shared by Dilthey and Simmel and rejected by Heidegger) and insists that his goal is 'philosophical anthropology'.[50] 'Modern' life was characterized not only by a sense of history and of crisis but also a 'sense of culture'. For Cassirer the duality of life and spirit (*Geist*) is inherent in the philosophy of life and accounts for the contemporary 'turn to idea' and the 'transition from the realm of "nature" to that of "freedom"'.[51] Again in opposition to Heidegger (the famous 'Davos' confrontation almost contemporaneous with this volume), Cassirer joined his philosophy of symbolic forms not to a Nietzschean 'will to power' but to a Goethean 'will to formation'.

This suggests the conceptual framework for Cassirer's impressive and influential contributions to intellectual history, which range from primitive culture to quantum physics, from ancient ideas to modern politics and ethics, and from systematic philosophy to detailed historical investigations, though always within the framework of the canon of post-Kantian philosophy.

3.   Croce, Collingwood, and Absolute Historicism

It was in the life-work of Benedetto Croce that historicism reached its fullest expression: 'Historicism ... is the affirmation that life and reality are history and history alone.'[52] Although Croce served an apprenticeship in philology and history, his main goal was a 'philosophy of spirit', conceived in Hegelian fashion but aimed at practical philosophy – 'the primacy of active life' – and

---

[49] *Philosophy of Symbolic Forms*, III, 16.
[50] Ibid., IV, *The Metaphysics of Symbolic Forms*, trans. John Michael Krois (New Haven, 1996), 34, 8, 19.
[51] Ibid., IV, 111.
[52] *History as the Story of Liberty*, trans. S. Sprigge (New York, 1941), 65.

concrete knowledge. Croce was led back to Hegel through an early encounter with Marx, but fruitful as this conjunction was, he rejected the groundless idealism of the one and the mindless materialism of the other. Hegelianism was hyper-rationalism, Marxism was pseudo-science, and Croce preferred the historicist fusion of philology and philosophy which he found in his fellow Neapolitan, Vico, whom he tried to draw into the philosophical canon. For Croce knowledge was not only logical but also intuitive – not only science but also art. As logic was joined to intellect, relationships, and general concepts, so intuition implied imagination, individual things, and images: such was the reason for the foundational role of history and aesthetics – 'the source of intuitive or expressive knowledge' – in Croce's system.

Although Croce put in time as a practicing historian, his calling, and the primary source of his conception of history, was philosophy, especially Hegelian philosophy and its imperialist thrust over other fields of study. '[T]he history of philosophy has several times tried to devour the history of poetry and art ... ', Croce wrote, 'and also ... the history of *practice*, that of politics and ethics, or "social history".'[53] This was done, he added, by reducing history to a history of 'ideas', in the sense not merely of intellectual formations but of practical acts, sentiments, dispositions, customs, and institutions, all of which (Croce noted) belong in the field that German scholars called 'cultural history' and the French 'history of civilization'.

It was Vico even more than Hegel who set Croce on the path away from metaphysics to a philosophy of 'absolute historicism' – which for Croce (unlike Weber, Troeltsch, and others) marked not the intellectual 'crisis' of the new century but the solution to this crisis. 'All judgment is historical judgment', Croce concluded, 'and all knowledge is historical knowledge.' 'The new historicism', he wrote, 'accepts, extends, deepens, and applies Vico's principle that men know only what they do (and so all they know is their own history which they made themselves).'[54] For Croce such knowledge was situated in that 'science of intuitive or expressive knowledge' which was called *Esthetica* and which, as he and Vossler discussed at length, was identified with history.[55] According to a seminal essay of Croce, history was 'subsumed under the general concept of art' – while philosophy, in its turn, was to be subsumed under the general concept of history.

Croce's philosophical itinerary (he rejected the idea of 'system') culminated in a vision of history which was identified with the history of thought and

---

[53] *History: Its Theory and Practice*, trans. Douglas Ainslie (New York, 1960), 147.
[54] *Philosophy, Poetry, History*, trans. C. Sprigge (Oxford, 1966), 615.
[55] *Carteggio Croce–Vossler*, 65ff.

thus was fundamentally 'humanistic'.[56] For Croce history gives life to chronicle and dissociates itself from pseudo-historical and pseudo-scientific operations, and does so by cleaving to the Vichian principles of *verum factum convertuntur* and the production of the *verum* out of the *certum* through science. As Croce explained,

> For it is in our breasts alone that is to be found that crucible in which the *certain* is converted into the *true*, and *philology*, joining with *philosophy*, produces *history*. If chronicle expressed merely will, history expresses thought; and to achieve this conceptual level we must supersede – that is to say, transform – values of *sentiment* with values of *thought*.

This means both choosing and criticizing documentary sources and linking facts into explanatory patterns.

In all of his works Croce was indeed a historian – but specifically not a chronicler – of thought, which meant applying criticism to the record of past actions and thoughts. To study a philosopher required not merely exposition of a series of works but rather to determine, for example, 'what is living and what is dead in the philosophy of Hegel'. What was living was the casting of philosophy in a historical form (Hegel being, for Croce, the father of the history of philosophy); what was dead was the 'abuse of the dialectic' that identified the real with the rational. Thus Croce carried on the old eclectic method which examined both truth and error in the pursuit of wisdom and took what was best in all schools. Was Croce a Hegelian? Yes and no:

> I am, and believe it necessary to be, an Hegelian; but in the same sense in which anyone who has a philosophical spirit and philosophical culture in our time, is and feels himself to be at once: *Eleatic, Heraclitean, Socratic, Platonic, Aristotelian, Stoic, Sceptic, Neoplatonic, Christian, Buddhist, Cartesian, Spinozist, Leibnizian, Vichian, Kantian*; and so on.[57]

This was Vico updated, except that for Croce Christianity was included among the other schools, for it was part of Croce's historicist extrapolation from Vico that, in the progress of the spirit, religion was displaced by philosophy as well as history.

R. G. Collingwood was a disciple of Croce, and neither recent efforts to establish his originality nor Collingwood's own marginal criticisms can obscure his basic debts to Croce's way of thinking about art, language, and

---

[56] *History: In Theory and Practice*, 94.
[57] *What is Living and What is Dead in the Philosophy of Hegel?*, trans. Douglas Ainslie (London, 1915), 216.

history.[58] In his early work, *Speculum Mentis*, Collingwood's inclination toward historicism and a dialectical view of knowledge was already apparent. In this theoretical restructuring of the encyclopedia Collingwood gave a temporalized form to his Crocean 'pentateuch' (as Louis Mink calls it), so that art, religion, science, and history move, progressively and dialectically, toward the self-awareness of philosophy. Each of the first four of these 'concrete forms of experience' was 'implicit philosophy' that is not only dogmatic but, being 'at the mercy of abstraction and prejudice', wrong. Unphilosophically, Art separates emotion from thought, Religion confuses metaphor with reality, Science mistakes abstraction for reality, and History mistakes concrete fact for reality (thus falling into the error of positivism).

For this 'map of knowledge' Collingwood proposed a view of intellectual history consonant not only with Croce's and Hegel's but also with the old eclectic theory. What he suggested is a 'table of errors' conceived either as a history of thought or as a critical (and dialectical) review of philosophical systems. 'In its actual course', Collingwood explained,

> thinking moves by the dialectical criticism of errors – the criticism of an error by itself, its break-up under the stress of its internal contradictions – to their denial: this denial is a truth … , but generally falling into a new and opposite error by an exaggerated fear of the old … , [which] if thinking goes vigorously forward, initiates a new dialectical criticism and the process will be repeated on a higher plane.[59]

The intellectualism of Collingwood's view of history appears in several works down to the posthumously published *Idea of History* – which is actually, it should be noted, a history of philosophy.

Like Croce, Collingwood believed that history is not 'the study of successive events lying in a dead past' but the imaginative 're-enactment of past experience', the forms of such experience being the overlapping fields of art, religion, science, history, and philosophy. History was dialogical, and truth itself was a property not of propositions but of 'a complex consisting of questions and answers'.[60] Like Croce, too, Collingwood took the purpose of history to be essentially the same as philosophy in its youth, when Socrates gave rational form to the motto of the Delphic oracle: self-knowledge and the

---

[58] See Lionel Rubinoff, 'The Relation between Philosophy and History in the Thought of Benedetto Croce and R. G. Collingwood', in *Collingwood Studies*, ed. David Boucher and Bruce Haddock, 3 (1996), 137–72.

[59] *Speculum Mentis* (Oxford, 1924), 289.

[60] *Autobiography* (Oxford, 1939), 37; and see William H. Dray, *History as Re-Enactment: R. G. Collingwood's Idea of History* (Oxford, 1995).

path to a 'science of human nature' which philosophy in a traditional, unhistorical form could not (according to many critics) yield.

What Collingwood and Croce, following Vico, added to the injunction of 'know thyself' was the insight that the condition of this self-knowledge was the historical process of self-making. Art and language are keys for both Collingwood and Croce because they are archetypically models of human creation, and targets of human re-creation, according to the notion of maker's knowledge and the conditions of intellectual and cultural history. Ideas and language, as the common products of human interactions, allow modern thinkers to understand the thoughts of ancients, or even perhaps aliens, and so to reconstruct their history.

Collingwood's view of philosophy and history was not only idealist (as unsympathetic British colleagues complained), but also hermeneutical. His assumption, in other words, was that history was not a natural process to be analyzed from dead and bygone facts, but a living presence which had to be re-created in the historian's mind. For Collingwood, Vico and Herder were the first to glimpse this insight; and Neo-Kantians like Windelband, Rickert, and Dilthey went further, although because of lingering positivist prejudice they fell short of a proper understanding of the 'peculiarity of historical thought'.[61] What they failed to see, as Collingwood remarked of Rickert, was

> the way in which the historian's mind, as the mind of the present day, apprehends the process by which this mind has come into existence through the mental development of the past ... , and that what gives value to past facts is the fact that they are not mere past facts, they are not a dead past but a living past, a heritage of past thoughts which by the work of his historical consciousness the historian makes his own.[62]

Croce came closer still to the proper understanding of history (he was the culminating figure in the historiographical part of Collingwood's *Idea of History* – which itself follows the design of Croce's *History: Its Theory and Practice*), but it remained for Collingwood himself to give the final, philosophical formulation, summarized most strikingly and simplistically in the famous Crocean aphorism, that 'all history is the history of thought'.

Such expressions of radical historicism – modern offsprings of eclecticism – were received also into the common wisdom of professional historians. As that most quotable of historians, Lord Acton, put it:

---

[61] *The Idea of History* (Oxford, 1993²), 63, 88.
[62] Ibid., 169–70.

It is an old story now that the true history of philosophy is the true evolution of philosophy ... and that when we have eliminated whatever has been damaged ... by subsequent advance ... , we shall find in our possession not only a record of growth but the full grown fruit itself.[63]

This is a virtual paraphrase of the lesson taught by the German and French eclectics a century and more earlier. There were important implications for the study of the history of ideas, too; for as Acton wrote elsewhere, 'What chiefly distinguishes the modern historical art from that of the ancients is that the history of ideas is now understood in its bearings on the history of events ... ' Moreover, as he wrote in 1859, 'To exhibit the course of ideas in their parallel progress and their action on each other, is a principal function of the modern historian.'[64]

4.   Lovejoy and the History of Ideas

There can be little doubt that the study of the history of ideas was pursued largely in the shadow of the history of philosophy; for in this field, according to Arthur O. Lovejoy, 'is to be found the common seed-plot, the *locus* of initial manifestation in writing, of the greater number of the more fundamental and pervasive ideas, and especially of the ruling preconceptions, which manifest themselves in other regions of intellectual history'.[65] Lovejoy did aspire to make the history of ideas an interdisciplinary enterprise, but he never himself broke entirely with the preconceptions of the discipline in which he fashioned his career, thought, and writing.

Lovejoy was the founder of the 'history of ideas' in this country, but the phrase itself was older, having been applied, for example, to a series of volumes published by the philosophy department of Columbia University between 1918 and 1935, which were devoted to 'a field ... in which it appears that ideas have a history and that their history is influenced by contact with lines of experience not commonly called philosophical'.[66] Lovejoy

---

[63] Review of Flint's *Historical Philosophy* in *Selected Writings*, ed. J. Rufus Fears, II, *Essays in the Study and Writing of History* (Indianapolis, 1985), 498.

[64] Herbert Butterfield, 'Acton: His Training and Intellectual System', *Studies in Diplomatic History and Historical Geography in Honour of G. P. Gooch* (London, 1961), 189.

[65] *Essays in the History of Ideas* (Baltimore, 1948), 8. Lovejoy's first usage of the phrase 'history of ideas' occurred in 1919 (*Modern Language Notes*, 34, 305), according to Gladys Gordon-Bournique, *Arthur O. Lovejoy et l'histoire des idées* (Ph.D. dissertation, Paris, 1974).

[66] *Studies in the History of Ideas*, ed. the Department of Philosophy of Columbia

was more deliberate in applying the phrase to what he regarded as a new discipline, or interdisciplinary area, distinct from the history of philosophy and intellectual history as practiced by scholars such as James Harvey Robinson and his followers.[67] 'The History of Ideas Club' at the Johns Hopkins University, which began meeting from 1923, was the scene of papers given by many distinguished scholars.[68]

In the first of his famous William James Lectures given at Harvard in 1933 and published three years later as *The Great Chain of Being*, Lovejoy gave theoretical form to the practices of the history of ideas and elaborated on his views in later publications.[69] But he had for a long time been concerned with the conceptual problems produced by the intersection of philosophy and history – the secular form of that between 'religion and the time-process' (the title of an article of 1902) – beginning with the turn-of-the-century fascination with Neo-Darwinian 'emergent evolution', Bergsonian vitalism, and the old problem of time and transcendence. These concerns included also the questions provoked by William James about the existence of consciousness and, more specifically, the 'existence of ideas'.[70] Lovejoy never doubted this and wrote in 1914, in opposition to both behaviorists and 'new realists', that consciousness, although not observable, was 'not a groundless and functionless philosophical superstition, but a natural product of human reflection upon certain common human experiences'; and so were the ideas which are known

---

University (3 vols; New York, 1918, 1925, 1935), prefatory note, including contributions by John Dewey, Frederick Woodbridge, John Hermann Randall, Richard McKeon, Sidney Hook, Herbert Schneider, and Ernest Nagel.

[67] See *Essays in Intellectual History, dedicated to James Harvey Robinson by his former seminar students* (New York, 1929), including contributions by James Shotwell, Carlton Hayes, Preserved Smith, Harry Elmer Barnes, Joseph Ward Swain, Lynn Thorndike, and others.

[68] These included, besides Lovejoy himself, George Boas, Harold Cherniss, Ludwig Edelstein, Leo Spitzer, Gilbert Chinard, Philip Wiener, Dorothy Stimson, and Erich Auerbach, Carl Becker, Charles Beard, Niels Bohr, John von Neumann, Hans Baron, Owen Lattimore, Lionel Venturi, Samuel E. Morison, Americo Castro, Charles Singleton, Hajo Holborn, Don Cameron Allen, Basel Willey, Alexandre Koyré, and Eric Vogelin. See Boas et al., *Studies in Intellectual History* (Baltimore, 1953), 200–217.

[69] See the contributions of Daniel J. Wilson, Edward P. Mahoney, and Francis Oakley to 'Lovejoy, *The Great Chain*, and the History of Ideas', *Journal of the History of Ideas*, 48 (1987), 187–263, repr. in D. R. Kelley (ed.), *The History of Ideas: Canon and Variations* (Rochester, 1990); also Mahoney, 'The Great Chain of Being in Early Modern Philosophy and the Medieval Background', in *Meeting of the Minds: The Relations between Medieval and Classical Modern European Philosophy*, ed. Stephen F. Brown (Turnhout, 1998).

[70] 'On the Existence of Ideas', *The Johns Hopkins University Circular*, 33 (1914), 178–235.

to this consciousness. This was the argument he pursued in *The Revolt against Dualism* in 1929, and it was the grounds for the notion of 'unit-ideas' underlying the agenda for the history of ideas which he set down in 1933. The key was derived, he admitted, from his reading of Windelband's *History of Philosophy*, which (as Gadamer remarked) 'was based upon the assumption of a constancy of problems from which, depending upon the changing historical situation, varying answers followed'.[71]

William James had posed the question 'Does consciousness exist?' and so seemed to deny the existence of ideas as well.[72] 'Pragmatism itself ... was primarily epistemological temporalism', Lovejoy complained in 1911. 'It proposes to define "meaning" and "truth" in terms of intertemporal relations between successive phases of experience.'[73] Lovejoy rejected such pragmatist anti-intellectualism, arguing that 'man is an epistemological animal'. Yet he was also critical of Kant, who seemed to ignore historical change and temporal perspective.[74] Epistemologically, the problem for Lovejoy was how to render present something that was absent, and his answer was originally 'representative ideas', which guaranteed an intellectual connection and continuity with the past. It was for this reason, too, that he defended a philosophical dualism that distinguished, in a Neo-Lockean way, between things and the intellectual signs which did not depend on direct and present apprehension but which could summon images or signs of things out of the past through the medium of memory.

The 'unit-idea' surveyed in *The Great Chain of Being* was a principle elaborated on by Plato and a succession of authors, literary and philosophical, across many centuries, cultures, and disciplines, and so an ideal target for the history of ideas as Lovejoy conceived of this field.[75] The 'scale of forms' had accumulated a tradition of commentary by pagans, Christians, and modern 'creative' evolutionists which allowed scholars in the here and now to think back into a there and then for ever beyond ordinary experience. From hierarchy to natural process, from plenitude to the infinite universe, this idea attracted inquiry, speculation, and criticism that formed an intellectual continuum

---

[71] Gadamer, *Heidegger's Ways*, trans. John W. Stanley (Albany, 1994), 154; and see Wilson, *Arthur O. Lovejoy and the Quest for Intelligibility* (Chapel Hill, 1980), 230.

[72] *The Thirteen Pragmatisms and Other Essays* (Baltimore, 1963), 113–32.

[73] Ibid., 108 (first published in the *International Journal of Ethics*, 21 [1911]).

[74] See Lewis White Beck, *Essays on Kant and Hume* (New Haven, 1978), 61–79 (originally in *Journal of the History of Ideas*, 33 [1972], 471–84).

[75] See Thomas Bredsdorff, 'Lovejoy's Idea of "Idea"', *New Literary History*, 8 (1977), 195–211; and Frank E. Manuel, 'Lovejoy Revisited', *Daedalus*, 17 (1987), 125–47.

recoverable through a judicious selection and interpretation of texts. And the same could be done with such polyvalent concepts as 'nature', 'romanticism', and 'primitivism'.[76]

Lovejoy's colleague George Boas expanded on the idealist implications of his methods. For Boas ideas are essentially meanings which lie behind – and which evolve independently of – words. 'The history of ideas is not confined to historical semantics', he wrote, and 'a dictionary aims only to give the meaning of words, not of ideas, and sometimes a single idea may have two names'.[77] Yet these are assumptions which cannot be expressed or communicated except through words and historical semantics – a paradox which neither Lovejoy nor Boas resolved, or chose to confront. As they acknowledged, 'The history of any idea, or complex of ideas, is best presented through the citation of the *ipsissima verba* of the writers who have expressed it.'[78]

In connection with his dualism Lovejoy accepted the philosophy of consciousness and authorial intention, with ideas separable and distinguishable from their social environment. His was, in one sense, a Neoplatonic project in which ideas represented a permanent aspect of the human condition, which was, to all appearances, a chaos of contingent events and conflicts. At the same time nor did Lovejoy propose to limit himself to the recognized canonical figures of philosophy and literature; and indeed, by taking ideas rather than thinkers as his protagonists, he was able to reach beyond the formal tradition of philosophy to the realm of opinion, especially 'public opinion', which he no longer used in a pejorative sense. Great masters may have a better sense of past and future, but 'inferior geniuses' more accurately reflect the life and problems of their time.

Nor were Lovejoy's unit-ideas limited to formal and intellectualized concepts, for he also wanted to accommodate less conscious and intellectual 'mental units'. These included 'implicit or incompletely explicit *assumptions* or more or less *unconscious mental habits*, operating in the thought of an individual or a generation'; 'dialectical motives', or methodological assumptions (nominalist or 'organismic', for example) also inexpressible in propositions; metaphysical pathos, which awakened particular moods (love of the obscure or esoteric, for example); and ideas associated with particular sacred words and phrases intelligible through semantic analysis.[79] It should be added that

---

[76] Lovejoy and Boas, *Primitivism and Related Ideas in Antiquity* (Baltimore, 1935), and Boas, *Primitivism and Related Ideas in the Middle Ages* (Baltimore, 1948).

[77] *The History of Ideas* (New York, 1969), 11.

[78] *Primitivism and Related Ideas in Antiquity*, viii.

[79] *The Great Chain of Being: A Study of the History of an Idea* (Cambridge, MA, 1936), 7ff.

all of these 'ideas', which were regarded as the expression of whole groups and ages, were illustrated and interpreted by mainly literary texts, especially poetry, from several national traditions, in keeping with the international and interdisciplinary thrust of Lovejoy's agenda.

Lovejoy's concern was always concepts, especially '-isms', but in some ways he anticipated the 'linguistic turn' of the later years of the last century, pointing out in particular 'the role of semantic shifts, ambiguities, and confusions, in the history of thought and taste', and remarking that 'nearly all of the great catchwords have been equivocal – or rather, multivocal'.[80] If ideas could be given stable definitions, they were nonetheless often, in the context of language, in conflict, even in the mind of a single thinker, for such was the 'anomaly of knowledge'.[81] For this reason Lovejoy took pains to distinguish the various meanings behind catchwords such as 'nature', 'perfectibility', 'romanticism', 'progress', and 'pragmatism', not to mention more inflammatory terms of ideological debate.

What the stability of ideas, despite the variability of their linguistic expression, guaranteed was conceptual continuity, so that the historian could identify 'precursors', antecedents, and doctrines held *ante litteram*. Lovejoy was deeply concerned with human values, but as a scholar he did not take philosophical truth as his main goal, and indeed even as a philosopher he mistrusted invidious judgments, such as Kant's self-serving distinction between 'critical' and 'dogmatic' thinking, based on an unhistorical under-appreciation of earlier thinkers. Lovejoy noted, and in a way celebrated, the 'obsolescence of the eternal', as Kant was outdated by Darwinism. Nor, for Lovejoy, was the history of ideas a conjectural process linked by reason and logic. It relied on old devices from the history of philosophy and literature, including notions of 'emergence', 'influence', and 'climates of opinion'. Despite his philosophical calling, Lovejoy was a thoroughgoing 'historicist' in his scholarly efforts; and this has been the case with his epigones ever since.

It is characteristic of disciplines on the rise – for example, law in the later middle ages, philosophy in the later eighteenth century, biology in the nineteenth century – to attempt to establish hegemony over other intellectual areas, or anyway to subsume them in a new classification of knowledge. In Lovejoy's program the history of ideas, too, extended its sway over no less than twelve fields of study, beginning with the history of philosophy and including the history of science, religion, the arts, language, literature, ('what is unhappily called', as he fastidiously put it) comparative literature, folklore,

---

[80] *Essays in the History of Ideas*, xii, xiii.
[81] *Thirteen Pragmatisms*, 236.

economic, political, and social history, and sociology (the new field of sociology of knowledge).[82] These fields were all traditions in themselves, claiming disciplinary status; the novelty was to treat them in an interdisciplinary and synthetic way.

While Lovejoy, unlike Cousin and earlier eclectics, surrendered the hope of achieving metahistorical truth through the critical study of the thought of earlier ages, he did not give up the notion that some measure of wisdom might be gained, and as usual in the classical form of self-knowledge. For him the history of ideas was the major repository of such knowledge and concern for the human condition, including what (writing in the dark year, 1940, in the first issue of the journal founded to realize his agenda) he regarded as 'the gravest and most fundamental of our problems', namely 'the question, "What's the matter with man?"'[83] It is a question surely still worth asking, especially since the demons and threats of Lovejoy's day have been replaced by shadows and hostile forces even more impenetrable to historical inquiry.

5. In the Wake of Crisis

Lovejoy published his *Great Chain of Being* in 1936, and with it his agenda for the new field, 'history of ideas'. He was involved in many public and philosophical issues, including academic freedom. As a scholar he was familiar with writings in several European languages, and as an informed reader he followed work in many adjacent areas in the humanities and science, including Einsteinian relativity. Yet he did not seem to be much concerned with various developments and modernist debates which were changing intellectual life and the conditions of the history of ideas. Among contemporary philosophers he tended to invoke the names of older French, English, and American thinkers, such as Bergson, Whitehead, and James; but he largely ignored the likes of Dilthey, Cassirer, Husserl, and Heidegger – not to mention the 'extravagant' views of Freud, whom he mentioned only once.[84] If Lovejoy's project was conceived in interdisciplinary terms, it remained, for him and many followers, innocent of some of the deeper and darker visions of western history.

---

[82] *Essays in the History of Ideas*, 1–2; and see D. R. Kelley, 'What is Happening to the History of Ideas?', *Journal of the History of Ideas*, 51 (1990), 3–25.

[83] 'Reflections on the History of Ideas', *Journal of the History of Ideas*, 1 (1940), 9, repr. in *The History of Ideas*, ed. Kelley.

[84] Wilson, *Arthur O. Lovejoy*, 173.

During and after the First World War European thought entered a period of self-conscious 'crisis' – a crisis of history, values, and reason itself.[85] One of the criticisms of the 'New Sorbonne' made by 'Agathon' in 1910 (recalling Hegel's scorn for 'pedantry') was that it 'reduced philosophy to the history of philosophical doctrines, or else to sociology'.[86] In lectures given in 1925 Heidegger noted the 'despair and helplessness' expressed even by Max Weber in this connection.[87] In the 1930s the crisis was intensified by the Great Depression, the rise of Nazism, Stalinism, and the specter of an even more destructive international disaster. Contemporary with Lovejoy's classic, forward-looking work were Husserl's *Crisis of the European Sciences*; the self-correcting 'turns' of Wittgenstein (away from analytical philosophy) and Heidegger (away from phenomenology) and the latter's lectures on Nietzsche; Kojève's equally influential lectures on Hegel; the revelation of the 'humanist Marx'; the critical theory of the Frankfurt school; the last years of Freud and the popularizing and revising of his ideas; and the growing movement of European *émigré* intellectuals who gave further currency to these ideas and helped to reshape the theory and practice of intellectual and cultural history.[88]

The past century, and millennium, has seen a resurgence of philosophical sects contending for intellectual supremacy and challenging historians to understand their significance. Neo-positivism and historicism, phenomenology and existentialism, Marxism and critical theory, Freudianism and Neo-Freudianism, structuralism and poststructuralism, analytical philosophy and philosophical hermeneutics, as well as offshoots, revisionisms, and emigrations led by Bachelard, Merleau-Ponty, Ricœur, Foucault, Derrida, Barthes, and Gusdorf, drawing often – very much in the manner of Cousin a century earlier – on German sources (though the influence operated in the opposite

[85] See Karl Heussi, *Die Krisis der Historismus* (Tübingen, 1932), and Babbach, *Heidegger, Dilthey, and the Crisis of Historicism*.

[86] Fritz Ringer, *Fields of Knowledge: French Academic Culture in Comparative Perspective, 1890–1920* (Cambridge, 1992), 250.

[87] *History of the Concept of Time*, trans. Theodore Kisiel (Bloomington, 1985), 2.

[88] Older studies include H. Stuart Hughes, *Consciousness and Society: The Reconstruction of European Social Thought 1890–1930* (New York, 1958); Gerhard Masur, *Prophets of Yesterday: Studies in European Culture 1890–1914* (New York, 1961); Frederick W. Grunefeld, *Prophets without Honor: A Background to Freud, Kafka, Einstein and their World* (New York, 1979); Robert Wohl, *The Generation of 1914* (Cambridge, MA, 1979); Gianni Vattino, *The End of Modernity*, trans. Jon R. Snyder (Baltimore, 1988); also see Jürgen Habermas, *The Philosophical Discourse of Modernity*, trans. Frederick Lawrence (Cambridge, MA, 1990); and Manfred Frank, *What Is Neostructuralism?*, trans. Sabine Wilke and Richard Gray (Minneapolis, 1990).

direction, too, as suggested by German 'Francolatry').[89] There were also many eclectic creations combining to form a kaleidoscopic climate of opinion which historians must perforce experience as well as examine critically.

In the conceptual confusion of the twentieth century philosophy has continued to seek a ground of (or beyond) history[90] – or, as with analytical philosophy, to beg the question and take propositional logic – and what might be called 'thin description' – as a basis. The quest for this ground has involved, successively, religion, reason, subjectivity, 'intersubjectivity', and various modes of 'being', from 'being-there' (Heidegger's *Dasein* is among other things a 'state of mind'), to Being 'itself' – together with its purely theoretical history (*Seinsgeschichte*). The deeper background to these discussions involves the drive of philosophy to imperial status among the disciplines. Like K. L. Reinhold over a century before, Husserl had early in his career envisioned philosophy as a 'rigorous science' and foundational to other disciplines; and phenomenology was a way of subsuming the historical world under philosophical reflection, although in the name not of an abstract 'experience' but of a (theoretically) concrete 'life-philosophy'.[91] This was taken a step further by Merleau-Ponty, who gave phenomenology a sort of carnal turn by emphasizing the corporeal basis of the subject – the body, which was neglected by idealist philosophy, including Husserl's.[92]

This had been the effect, too, of Kant's 'apriori history of philosophy' and of Hegel's dialectic, designed to join together philosophy and history – Being and Becoming, logic and language, presence and history, the Real and the Rational. In this Hegel's lead was also followed by Heidegger, whose philosophical approach involved 'the assimilation of history' into his conception of Being.[93] This allowed Heidegger to return to philosophy to restore what Habermas has called 'its lost plenitude of power'.[94] Though

---

[89] See Frank, *What is Neostructuralism?*; Habermas, *The New Conservatism: Cultural Criticism and the Historians' Debate*, trans. Shierry Weber Nicholson (Cambridge, MA, 1989); and Wolfgang Welsch, 'Lacancan et Derridada: Über Frankolatrie in der Kulturwissenschaften', *Unsere postmoderne Moderne* (Weinheim, 1987).

[90] Michael Allen Gillespie, *Hegel, Heidegger, and the Ground of History* (Chicago, 1984).

[91] *The Crisis of the European Sciences and Transcendental Phenomenology*, trans. David Carr (Evanston, 1970), 103; and see Herbert Spiegelberg, *The Phenomenological Movement: A Historical Introduction* (The Hague, 1982³).

[92] *Phenomenology of Perception*, trans. Colin Smith (London, 1962), 67ff.

[93] *Heidegger's Ways*, 71.

[94] *The Philosophical Discourse of Modernity*, 131–2. See *The Cambridge Companion to Heidegger*, ed. Charles B. Guignon (Cambridge, 1993).

founded on interior reflection, Heidegger's philosophical goal was not merely consciousness (the ground of phenomenology) or nature (the ground of positivism) but a higher synthesis joining subject and object in an overarching, and underpinning, idea of Being. That this ambitious program also found an analogy in Heidegger's political involvements was his personal tragedy.[95]

Nevertheless, Heidegger's thinking about being, time, and history still casts its shadow at the beginning of the millennium (both directly and through such errant followers as Gadamer, Sartre, Ricœur, Derrida, and Rorty); and we cannot think ourselves back to the conceptual and historical innocence in which Lovejoy's program was born. Intellectual history has been at least an indirect beneficiary of this spiritual legacy, based on a philosophy of consciousness, according to which ideas and systems of thought were significant parts of, if not a moving force in, the process of history.

'Being – Spirit – God': these three words lie at the roots of metaphysics, says Gadamer, and they have continued to haunt the post-Nietzschean world of phenomenology, existentialism, structuralism, and even poststructuralism. Although ostensibly secularized, philosophy in the twentieth century, and especially the philosophy of consciousness, preserved its concern with the Holy in its modern forms. For Karl Löwith, a primary reason for Heidegger's extraordinary impact – like that of Fichte and Schelling (and Hegel) a century earlier – is that 'the force of his philosophical thinking is bound to a religious motive'.[96] God might be 'dead', and 'spirit' and metaphysics along with him, but in the work of mandarin intellectuals like Husserl and Heidegger, the secular priesthood of philosophy still lives.

For Heidegger, however, the object of this post-religious motive is not the transcendent Other of conventional theology but an existential house of his own building. In a godless and post-metaphysical world in which 'God is dead' (in the Nietzschean formula adoped and expanded by Heidegger), where could sovereignty lie but in the Being which, though already present, needed to be reduced to philosophy and so – the old Hegelian dream – mastered. I say 'building' because, while Being is primordial, it needs language for expression ('Language is the house of Being') and because this language is no longer that of holy texts but rather a thought-world formulated in neologisms devised by a conceptual Humpty Dumpty, a new 'beginning [and, I would add, 'begetting'] philosopher' (like Descartes, Kant, and Husserl) –

---

[95] See *The Heidegger Controversy: A Critical Reader*, ed. Richard Wolin (New York, 1991).
[96] *Martin Heidegger and European Nihilism*, trans. Gary Steiner (New York, 1995), 96.

playing, as Karl Löwith put it, a sort of 'glass bead game with words'.[97] Moreover, commented Derrida, it was a game that, with all of Heidegger's various twists, turns, and terminological virtuosity, 'still remains within the grammar and lexicon of metaphysics'.[98]

Even Heidegger played disciple for a time to masters. His points of departure were scholastic philosophy and Husserl's phenomenology, which places philosophy in a field, a 'life-world', encompassing consciousness and things appearing within the horizons of this consciousness, whose analogue is always vision and what Martin Jay calls ocularcentrism.[99] What Husserl's phenomenology seemed to miss, however, was the linguistic turn being followed by Wittgenstein, Heidegger, and other contemporary thinkers. In phenomenology, then, commented Heidegger's student Gadamer, 'the same abysmal forgetfulness of language, so characteristic of transcendental idealism, was repeated, thus appearing to confirm, albeit belatedly, Herder's ill-fated criticism of the Kantian transcendental turn'.[100]

For similar reasons Heidegger soon declared his independence and his own mastery. Unlike Husserl, he claimed to 'overcome' consciousness and penetrate to Being 'itself', which resided in language. He accomplished this in part, it should be added, with the help of Presocratics like Heraclitus and Parmenides – the Greek language being for him even closer to Being than German. The point is that Heidegger's revelations had to take place inside the 'House of Being' which is language – but then, as he asks elsewhere, 'What kind of Being does language have, if there can be such a thing as a "dead" language?' Perhaps language is an 'abyss', as Hamann suggested to Herder.[101] Hamann himself sought an 'Angel language', and perhaps this was Heidegger's own model – or perhaps it was only his scholastic habits of mind.[102]

'Language speaks', says Heidegger, the philosopher, more than once; 'History speaks', says F. A. Wolf, the philologist, more than once; but of course they speak in different tongues. Does history speak for Heidegger? The short answer is yes, but not with the clarity of Being or Time. Heidegger has a

---

[97] Ibid., 41; and on 'beginning philosophers' see Wolf Lepenies in *Philosophy in History*, ed. Richard Rorty et al. (Cambridge, 1984), 151.

[98] *Margins of Philosophy*, trans. Alan Bass (Chicago, 1982), 63.

[99] *Downcast Eyes: The Denigration of Vision in Twentieth-Century French Thought* (Berkeley, 1993), 265ff.

[100] '*Destruktion* and Deconstruction', trans. Geoff Waite and Richard Palmer, in *Dialogue and Deconstruction: The Gadamer–Derrida Encounter*, ed. Diane P. Michelfelder and Richard Palmer (Albany, 1989), 102.

[101] Cited by Heidegger, 'Language' (1959), *Poetry, Language, Thought*, trans. Albert Hofstadter (New York, 1971), 191.

[102] See above, Chapter 4.

hypostatized, or existentialized, idea of history (*Geschichte*) as the past (*Vergangenheit*), as distinguished from 'historiology' (his translators' rendering of *Historie*). Like philology, historiology, the study of history, is confined in an interpretative circle and is 'derivative', so that it does not qualify as a 'rigorous science'.[103] In the tradition of German idealism since Kant, Heidegger consigns erudition of all sorts, including the history of philosophy (though not etymology), not only to a subordinate position but in effect to conceptual irrelevance. Unlike the *Cogito*, *Dasein* has historicity and memory, but it has quite as little use for learning, except perhaps as part of the undefined 'forestructure' and the 'vicious circle' of interpretation.

History, in the general sense which philosophers usually employ, defines the limits of the human condition. Heidegger's *Dasein* is located within spatial horizons – the arena of 'life-philosophy', or the lighted 'clearing' which *Dasein* occupies, according to the special terminology of Heidegger – and is subjected to 'forestructures' not of its own choosing. In its acknowledged 'historicity', however, it occupies a temporal continuum in which 'presence' defines experience and expression. It is this limitation that leads philosophers as well as historians to speak of the 'beginning' or 'end' of this or that human creation – of philosophy, history, the novel, and so on – of ever-present 'crises', crises of modernity,[104] postmodernity, and whatever comes later to be present to mind and to distinguish that present from bygone presents, and presences. And the 'history of ideas', too, is subject to the parochiality and present-ness of this horizon-structure of human existence.

So history, like skepticism, remains a threat to the quest for being as it had been to revealed religion, pure reason, and other foundational givens or constructs. 'Historicism' is a term coined in the later eighteenth century to suggest the historical character of human knowledge in contrast to philosophy – the historical schools of the Romantic Age versus the philosophical school of the Enlightenment. The word was appropriated by philosophers, especially in relation to Hegel, to designate a doctrine in its own right. Rudolf Haym spoke of 'illusory historicism' and Rudolf Eucken of 'enervating historicism' – in contrast to 'true historicity' (*wirkliche Geschichtlichkeit*).[105] The result was that by the early twentieth century, along with other new '-isms'

---

[103] *Being and Time*, trans. John Marguarrie and Eduard Robinson (New York, 1962), 152.

[104] Edward W. Said, *Beginnings: Intention and Method* (Baltimore, 1975).

[105] Haym, *Hegel und seine Zeit* (Hildesheim, 1857), 467; Eucken, *Main Currents of Modern Thought*, trans. M. Booth (New York, 1912), 316; and see Gunter Scholtz, *'Historismus' als spekulative Geschichtstheologie: Christlieb Julius Braniss (1792–1873)* (Frankfurt, 1973).

(psychologism, naturalism, relativism, and modernism in general), historicism provoked a 'crisis' of foundational values of all sorts, especially in theology, science, and liberal economics; and it was rejected by critics ranging from Troeltsch and Weber to Husserl and Heidegger.[106]

For many philosophers not only is their enterprise above and beyond historical inquiry but so are some of the figures of their canon. As Aristotelians had regarded Aristotle, Thomists St Thomas, and Cartesians Descartes, so Kantians regarded Kant and Heideggerians Heidegger; the 'master' of the Pythagorean *magister dixit* still lived. Kant rejected 'mere anthropology', and for Heidegger 'to search for dependence and influence between thinkers is a misunderstanding of thought'.[107] He refers to Nietzsche, but he meant that he, too, was dependent not on historical circumstance or tradition but 'on the call of Being'. This was the old German 'liberty of philosophizing' (*libertas philosophandi*) and 'freedom of thought' in an existential mode.

For historians and biographers this is unsatisfactory. As Pierre Bourdieu argued, 'There are doubtless few intellectual systems more profoundly rooted in their times than what Croce called the "pure philosophy" of Heidegger.'[108] One would like to apply the terms 'influence', 'humanism', 'metaphysics', 'anthropocentrism', 'historicism', and so on to Heidegger's own 'way of thought', but this is impossible as long as one takes at face value his insistence on systematic neologism. 'The limits of my language mean the limits of my world,' wrote Wittgenstein;[109] but Heidegger takes this limitation as an invitation to create new linguistic formulations that claim to reveal Being itself. 'Language', Gadamer says, 'has no words for the unthinkability of Being';[110] but Heidegger's language strives to supply this lack. Is he, like Being (and, formerly, Truth), beyond the grasp of historical inquiry? Historicizing holy men has always been a hazardous undertaking, but the twists and turns of Heidegger's ways would seem to demand such historicist efforts.

In any case history remains a presence, and indeed – in its hypostatized and philosophized form – has continued to challenge philosophy for hegemony. By inverting the Hegelian formulation Marx may have brought about the 'end of philosophy', but the new sovereign turned out, after 1848, to be no

---

[106] Babbach, *Heidegger, Dilthey, and the Crisis of Historicism*.

[107] Cited by Jeffrey Andrew Barash, *Martin Heidegger and the Problem of Historical Meaning* (Dordrecht, 1988), 241, 284.

[108] *The Political Ontology of Martin Heidegger*, trans. Peter Collier (Stanford, 1991), 1.

[109] *Tractatus*, 5, 6.

[110] *Heidegger's Ways*, 27.

less disappointing than the old one.[111] Such was the experience, too, of Heidegger, whose hubris, no less grandiose than that of Marx, led him to identify his philosophy with the historical process in Germany at a time when neither reason nor philosophy could promise survival, let alone national salvation. Of course Husserl, in facing up to and tracing the history of the twentieth-century 'crisis' of the sciences, gave up the 'dream' of 'philosophy as a rigorous science',[112] but Heidegger turned to another poetic and (for a time) political dream altogether that would transcend philosophy itself – and perhaps return to history. Like Hegel, Heidegger tried to assimilate history to philosophy; yet in his quest for Being, his 'turns' and his 'ways' have provoked further questions about the former. Perhaps this is the best service philosophy can perform for intellectual and cultural history, whose business has more to do with questions than with final answers.

---

[111] Martin Heidegger, 'The End of Philosophy and the Task of Thinking', in *Basic Writings*, trans. David Farrell Krell (New York, 1977), 243ff.; and see Karl Löwith, *From Hegel to Nietzsche: The Revolution of Nineteenth-Century Thought*, trans. David E. Green (New York, 1964), 71.

[112] *The Crisis*, 389.

Chapter 10

After the New Histories

> For, behold, I create new heavens and a
> new earth, and the former shall not be
> remembered, nor come into mind.
> Isaiah 65:17

As 'what actually happened' in the past, history is old, but as an account or interpretation thereof, it is always new – or so historians have often liked to boast. The 'new histories' of the early twentieth century found novelty above all in shifting emphasis from politics and war to intellectual and cultural matters, although such an agenda was far from being a novelty and indeed was implicit from the beginning in Herodotean inquiry, not to mention what Carl Becker called the 'new history' of the Enlightenment.[1] But it was at the turn of the last century that proclamations of historiographical novelty became most insistent, and the history of ideas, or intellectual history, was perhaps the primary beneficiary of this innovationism.

1. Between the Old and the New

The best starting-point is perhaps Karl Lamprecht's *Kulturgeschichte*, which (despite his bow to Herder and other earlier cultural historians) was first denounced and then praised as 'new history' and which emphasized factors of 'spirit' and 'consciousness', individual as well as national.[2] Even earlier his supporter Eberhard Gothein, a historian of Italian culture, defended cultural history against the charges of materialism and went so far as to declare that 'in its pure form cultural history is the history of ideas'.[3] In France Henri

---

[1] *The Heavenly City of the Eighteenth-Century Philosophers* (New Haven, 1932), 71.

[2] *Deutsche Geschichte* (Berlin, 1920; 6th edn, unaltered), I, 'Einleitung. Geschichte der Formen des Nationalbewusstseins'.

[3] *Die Aufgaben der Kulturgeschichte* (Leipzig, 1889), 50: 'Kulturgeschichte in ihrer reinen Form ist Ideengeschichte.' And see Georg von Below, *Die deutsche Geschichte-schreibung von der Befreiungskriegen bis zu unsern Tagen* (Munich, 1924), 31ff.

Berr, working out his concept of 'synthetic history', employed the terminology of 'history of ideas' (*l'histoire des idées*) from the first issue of the *Revue de Synthèse*; and out of his ambitious program came the 'new history' in France associated later with his younger colleagues of the *Annales* school, Lucien Febvre and Marc Bloch.[4]

In the United States, too, in the wake of the discussions of Lamprecht and Berr, another innovationist history made its appearance, as James Harvey Robinson of Columbia University, a pioneering intellectual historian, proclaimed in 1912 his own version of the 'new history', which attracted many disciples, including Carl Becker, Charles Beard, and Harry Elmer Barnes.[5] For Barnes this new history reached its 'triumph' in the work of (among others) Berr, Lamprecht, Robinson, Becker, Beard, Toynbee (!), and Barnes himself, but 'in the light of twentieth-century knowledge and methods'. Another still more recent *histoire nouvelle* has taken Lamprecht, Berr, and Robinson as 'precursors', though the main figures kept their innovative claims uncontaminated by the older new history.[6] These were the major examples of a more general tendency of historians, in keeping with the commercial spirit of the past two centuries, to claim novelty for their ancient calling.[7]

Some intellectual historians, of course, have carried on with less flourish. The subject was pursued by American scholars in a progressivist and historicist mode that was often not far removed from the history of religion. Henry Osborn Taylor, for example, had a brief flirtation with skepticism, but as a student of the 'intellectually preposterous' middle ages he became 'a believing

---

[4] *La Synthèse de connaissance et l'histoire* (Paris, 1898), followed by another manifesto, *La Synthèse en histoire* (Paris, 1911), 217, citing Lamprecht; and see Martin Siegel, 'Henri Berr's *Revue de Synthèse historique*', *History and Theory*, 9 (1970), 322–34; and *Henri Berr et la culture du XXe siècle*, ed. Agnès Biard, Dominique Bourel, and Eric Brian (Paris, 1997); also, on the *Annaliste* school, Jacques Le Goff, Jacques Revel and Roger Chartier (eds), *La Nouvelle Histoire* (Paris, 1978); François Dosse, *New History in France: The Triumph of the Annales*, trans. Peter V. Conroy, Jr (Urbana, 1994); Philippe Carrard, *Poetics of the New History: French Historical Discourse from Braudel to Chartier* (Baltimore, 1992); Peter Burke, 'The French Historical Revolution': The Annales School 1929–89 (Stanford, 1990); and Roger Chartier, 'Intellectual History and the History of *Mentalités*', *Cultural History*, trans. Lydia G. Cochrane (Ithaca, 1988), 19–52.

[5] *The New History: Essays Illustrating the Modern Historical Outlook* (New York, 1912), first version 1900.

[6] Théophile Obenga, *Pour une Histoire Nouvelle* (Paris, 1980), 11, calling for a global and indeed cosmic perspective not unlike the vision of Herder.

[7] Hervé Contau-Begarie, *Le Phenomène 'nouvelle histoire'* (Paris, 1983), and Ignacio Olábarri Gortázar, '"New" New History: A *Longue Durée* Structure', *History and Theory*, 34 (1995); also Jacques Le Goff, 'Antique (Ancient) Modern', *History and Memory*, trans. Steven Rendell and Elizabeth Claman (New York, 1992), 21–50.

Christian', his belief being, however, that the mutual operation of 'the human faculty constitutes progress [and] the increase of well being'.[8] His major works traced the development of western consciousness from the appearance of 'ancient ideals' through the sixteenth century – and always in terms of continuity, approaching not only classical ideals but even 'medieval thought as man meets man, and seeking in it what still may be valid'[9] rather than its 'foolishness' and the 'rottenness and ordure' with which the past was strewn.[10] 'Each age stands on the shoulders of the past', he concluded, 'though sometimes its feet slip painfully' (for the giants as well as the dwarfs?).[11] Taylor's work was cast in the old mold of Victorian secularized piety, and he apparently remained innocent of Marx, Freud, and other subverters of the idea of progress. However, this sort of gentlemanly complacence (Taylor was never a professional historian) could not survive the stress of the postwar period, even among progressivists.

Among American intellectual historians Carl Becker, who was associated with Robinson's sort of 'new history', is the prime example of a loss of faith in an evolutionary, progressivist view of western tradition. The experience of war and the intellectual solvent of pragmatism (rather than extensive reading in philosophy)[12] led Becker to question not only the idea of progress but also the foundations of historical epistemology. Taylor had written a book called *Fact, the Romance of Mind*, but not to question the accessibility of the 'mind' of the past; by contrast Becker came to deny the reality of 'facts' and to accept a sort of historical uncertainty principle (similar to that of the 'new physics' of the 1920s), and this attitude was reinforced by his belated acquaintance with European ideas, especially those of Croce. American debates over skepticism, relativism, and historicism were quite derivative, however, and largely innocent of the continental philosophical tradition in which the work of Weber, Mannheim, Troeltsch, Heussi, and Meinecke were rooted, although Charles Beard came to appreciate this tradition.[13]

In France the leading intellectual historian was Lucien Febvre, who began his career as a social historian but who, under the influence of Henri Berr,

---

[8] *Freedom of the Mind in History* (London, 1923), 16.

[9] *The Medieval Mind* (London, 1911), I, 285.

[10] 'The Phi Beta Kappa ideal', *Rice Institute Pamphlet*, 16 (1929), 117.

[11] *Freedom of the Mind*, 117.

[12] Though he did report influence from Freud, Vaihinger, Croce, Whitehead, and Dewey in the *New Republic* (7 December 1938), in Michael Kammen (ed.), *'What is the Use of History?' Selected Letters of Carl Becker, 1900–1945* (Ithaca, 1973), 264.

[13] Peter Novick, *That Noble Dream: The 'Objectivity Question' and the American Historical Profession* (Cambridge, 1988).

moved on to what he called 'an entirely different history' (*l'histoire à part entière*).[14] Following his work on geography Febvre turned first to the criticism of the 'strange thesis' of Abel Lefranc concerning Rabelais as a pioneering free-thinker and atheist, and then to Luther. 'But how difficult it is!', Febvre wrote to Berr: 'intellectual history, the history of ideas and beliefs, and as impassioned as it is difficult to write'.[15] His revisionist study of 'the problem of unbelief' centering on Rabelais (1939) was a virtuoso exploration not only of the 'climate of opinion', in the phrase of Joseph Glanvill that Becker revived, but also of the horizons of thought and belief of the sixteenth century.[16] Although Febvre's view of atheism (and its virtual impossibility in that age) has been challenged, his investigations reached beyond the sort of intellectual history being practiced in either Germany or the Anglophone world, including the 'history of ideas' being formulated contemporaneously by Lovejoy, to the extent that French scholars, under the influence of the social sciences, addressed questions of collective thought.

As German scholars employed ideas of *Weltanschauung* and *Geist*, so French historians wrote of collective *mentalité*, borrowed from Lucien Levy-Bruhl's work on 'primitive mentality', an early version of the 'Other'. For Levy-Bruhl the mentality of 'societies inferior to ours' included invisible, mystical, and 'pre-logical' elements remote from the 'positive spirit' of European culture.[17] Bloch was ahead of Febvre in his interest in questions of *mentalité*, and indeed asked Levy-Bruhl to review his pioneering book on the thaumaturgic kings. Conceived before the First World War, *The Royal Touch* took up the old question that troubled historians – that of miracles, and specifically the royal power to heal scrofula – and the conflict between common sense and the need to accept recorded testimony. Bloch's solution was to save rationality by recourse to the anthropological notion of miracles as 'collective error', but nonetheless a mighty presence in history and the history of ideas in particular.[18]

---

[14] *Pour une histoire à part entière* (Paris, 1962); trans. in part as *A New Kind of History*, trans. Peter Burke (London, 1973).

[15] Lucien Febire, *De la Revue de synthése aux annales: Lettres à Henri Berr 1911–1954* (Paris, 1997), 125 (August 1926).

[16] *The Problem of Unbelief in the Sixteenth Century: The Religion of Rabelais*, trans. Beatrice Gottlieb (Cambridge, MA, 1982); and see Guy Massicote, *L'Histoire-problème: la méthode de Lucien Febvre* (Paris, 1981).

[17] *La Mentalité primitive* (Paris, 1925[4]), 47. Cf. Wolfgang Köhler, *The Mentality of Apes* (English trans. 1925), and in general Jacques Le Goff, 'Les Mentalités: une histoire ambiguë', in *Faire de l'histoire*, ed. Le Goff and Pierre Nora (Paris, 1974), III, 76–94.

[18] *The Royal Touch: Sacred Monarchy and Scrofula in England and France*, trans. J. E. Anderson (London, 1973), 243.

The *Annales* school moved increasingly away from intellectual to social and economic history, but the history of ideas continued to be practiced, especially in connection with the history of science. Since the 1960s Georges Gusdorf has been a major scholarly (if not political) presence, especially through his thirteen-volume history of the human sciences (1966–88), which also offered an innovative vision of intellectual history.[19] Gusdorf based his interpretation of the history of science, physical and human, on the phenomenology of Husserl and Merleau-Ponty. Gusdorf's intellectual horizons coincided with the life-world (*Lebenswelt*; *monde vécu*), and his work traced the changing configurations of mental, cultural, and spiritual 'space-time' from antiquity down to the present. For Gusdorf the story turns first on the 'Galilean revolution', which was based on the 'panmathematization' of Descartes and Newton, and then on the second, 'non-Galilean revolution',[20] which produced the whole range of modern human and life sciences, especially anthropology and the 'plurality of epistemologies which it employs'; and it culminated in Romantic and post-Romantic hermeneutics, which, like historicism, was a methodology of sympathy, and which sought to find meaning in mental spaces foreign to it.[21]

Rejecting Foucauldian 'archeology' and totalizing history *à la Paris-Match* or Disneyland, Gusdorf emphasized continuities in intellectual history which no conceptual effort could escape:

> We are not masters of words; they come to us from the depth of ages charged with resonances and harmonies, with significations which continue to be enriched in usage by encounters, agreements, and disagreements with other words, whence arise unpredictable surges across mental space.[22]

So 'History is not a palimpsest', Gusdorf argued; 'it is the living recapitulation of the legacy of humanity.'[23] He was far removed from what he called the 'philosophies of frenzy' prevailing in his life-world, largely indifferent to the siren calls of criticism, and content to visit vicariously the places of cultural memory. No wonder that if Gusdorf was a major scholarly presence, he has been mainly an ideological absence, especially because of his rejection of the values of what he called the 'phoney war' of 1968 and because, as an author, he was quite eclipsed by the spectacular rise of Lévi-Strauss, Althusser, and especially Foucault.

---

[19] *Les Sciences humaines et la pensée occidentale* (Paris, 1966–88); and see my 'Gusdorfiad', *History of the Human Sciences*, 3 (1990), 123–40.
[20] *Les Sciences humaines*, VII, 37.
[21] Ibid., XIII.
[22] Ibid., X, 413.
[23] Ibid., XIII, 251.

The rhetoric of novelty persists. Talk about a 'new historicism' goes back at least to 1942, when Croce wrote that 'The New Historicism accepts, extends, and applies Vico's principle that men know only what they do.'[24] Forty years later another 'new historicism' was inaugurated. This new 'new historicism' (especially in its British form of 'cultural materialism') preserved some of the old hopes of unmasking, but in this effort turned, as Vico had done, to cultural forms, especially literature and art, to reveal underlying interests and power structures and to penetrate to inarticulate levels and marginal groups of society. This new historicism was part of the linguistic and textualist turn taken by history and the human sciences, including philosophy, in the past generation; and so was the closely allied innovationist movements which call themselves 'the new cultural history' and 'a new philosophy of history' (NPH).[25]

The latter refers to a claim made by a number of recent literary scholars who have made the literary turn and have embraced rhetoric as the primary condition of historical understanding.[26] One feature of the NPH is the emphasis on irony – by which they mean, however, the restoration of the subject, the '"I" foregrounded', in the words of Philippe Carrard, referring to ego- (or *nous-*) centered rhetoric of the *Annales* school.[27] The NPH rejects what Robert Berkhofer calls 'hegemonic viewpoints' and denies that there can any longer be a 'great story' that overlooks the losers or victims of western history.[28] The solution to the relativism implied by such criticism lies somehow, Berkhofer thinks, in representing polyvocality, that is, dialogism and multiple viewpoint – a *Rashomon* or Joycean model of historical narrative – to satisfy the postmodern pressures of multiculturalism and voices clamoring to be heard above the din of official history. Yet as one contributor asks, 'Is there anything new here?' As Goethe's Mephistopheles put it,

> Wer kann was Dummes, was Kluges denken,
> Das nicht die Vorwelt schon gedacht?

It is a question that historians are always obliged to ask.

---

[24] *Philosophy, Poetry, History*, trans. C. Sprigge (Oxford, 1966), 615.
[25] Lynn Hunt (ed.), *The New Cultural History* (Berkeley, 1989), and Frank Ankersmit and Hans Kellner (eds), *A New Philosophy of History* (Chicago, 1995).
[26] *A New Philosophy of History*.
[27] See also his *Poetics of the New History*.
[28] *Beyond the Great Story: History as Text and Discourse* (Cambridge, MA, 1995).

2. After the New

The conditions of writing intellectual history have been sharply problematized in the past generation or two, and there is a vast literature on challenges from literary theory, history of science, and philosophy. Compare this predicament with the program set forth by Lovejoy over a half-century ago and that of Michel Foucault a generation later. In the essay prefacing the first volume of the *Journal of the History of Ideas*, Lovejoy set down four goals of the new field as he conceived it:[29]

1   The influence of modern thought and of European tradition and American literature, arts, philosophy, and social movements.
2   The influence of philosophical ideas in literature, the arts, religion, and social thought.
3   The influence of scientific discoveries and theories in the same provinces of thought.
4   The history of the development and effects of individual pervasive and widely ramifying ideas or doctrines such as evolution, progress, primitivism, diverse theories of human motivation ... (and so on).

This ambitious agenda reflects not only the interdisciplinary orientation of Lovejoy but also the fallacies, fashions, totems, and taboos of intellectual history in its earlier state of methodological innocence.

Compare this with the assault on conventional intellectual history mounted by Michel Foucault, with the help of Nietzsche's notion of power and in the name of an 'archeology of knowledge'. One major contribution of Foucault to the history of ideas is the project of unveiling these power relations concealed by ideology, of getting behind the back of language, by examining 'cultural practices'. Like 'experience', however, 'practice' (offspring of Marxian *Praxis*) is itself a theoretical and often unproblematized concept that needs further refinement and specification. One way of doing this is to introduce a deeper evolutionary perspective suggesting (as does Maxine Sheets-Johnstone, in order to 'flesh out' Foucauldian analysis) that the body, especially the male body, 'is already inscribed and potent' and so, as inferred from posture, gesture, expression, and sexual approaches, is '*accessible* to power relations'.[30] So the 'animate form' of the human body already possesses 'the conceptual basis of power'.

---

[29] 'Reflections on the History of Ideas', *Journal of the History of Ideas*, 1 (1940), 7.
[30] *The Roots of Power: Animated Form and Gendered Bodies* (Chicago, 1994), 16, 14.

Foucault himself, like Nietzsche, Freud, and Merleau-Ponty, sought insights on a pre- or sub-rational level. His *Birth of the Clinic* claimed to transcend the ordinary history of ideas through a more critical 'archeology of scientific reason'.[31] Parallel to the bourgeois consciousness of the French Revolution, according to Foucault, was a new 'medical consciousness' and scientific profession that expressed its expert monopoly through control over technical language and division of the life-world of humans into the healthy and the diseased or, as in his earlier work, the normal (reason) and pathological (madness). As medical doctors sought to establish their hegemony through a new form of discourse, so Foucault sought a kind of linguistic (or metalinguistic) analysis that would expose their closed enterprise and the concealed political complicities and the power relations on which it was based. Yet despite Foucault's emphasis on practice, his criticism often seems to be a process of renaming, so that in the course of his work he shifts from ideas to 'discourse', from history to 'archeology', to the 'archive', then to Nietzschean 'genealogy', from memory to 'counter-memory', from development to 'rupture', and from spirit or mentality to 'episteme'.[32] His purpose is to dismantle the history of ideas, to introduce the genealogist as the 'new historian', and to produce not merely a discourse but a metadiscourse that can unmask the ideological surface of past and present culture – and ultimately, in post-Marxian terms, not merely to understand but to change history.

Tradition, influence, development and evolution, spirit, pre-given unities and links, familiar divisions and groups, the *œuvre*, the 'origin' and the 'already-said': these unreflective rubrics (to which should certainly be added 'idea') are the themes to be avoided in a critical history of ideas.[33] They constitute, Foucault says, 'unities of discourse', for whose conceptual value it is impossible to mount much of a defense, at least when they are divorced from the historical materials that might give them meaning. In what Allan Megill calls a parody of Cartesian method, Foucault proposes, through his own sort of methodological doubt, to eliminate the 'prejudices' of earlier

---

[31] *The Birth of the Clinic: An Archeology of Medical Perception*, trans. A. M. Sheridan Smith (New York, 1975); see also Gary Gutting, *Michel Foucault's Archaeology of Scientific Reason* (Cambridge, 1989), and G. S. Rousseau, *Enlightenment Borders: Pre- and Post-Modern Discourses, Medical, Scientific* (Manchester, 1991), 15ff.

[32] See *Language, Counter-Memory, Practice: Selected Essays and Interviews*, trans. Donald F. Bouchard and Sherry Simon (Ithaca, 1977).

[33] *The Archeology of Knowledge*, trans. A. M. Sheridan Smith (New York, 1972), 21–5. See Philip Barker, *Michel Foucault: Subversions of the Subject* (New York, 1993), 58ff., and David Couzens Hoy (ed.), *Foucault: A Critical Reader* (Oxford, 1986), and 'Foucault: Modern or Postmodern?', in *After Foucault*, ed. Jonathan Arac (New Brunswick, 1988), 12–41.

authors and to place the human sciences as well as their historiographical underpinning on critical grounds.[34]

'Tradition' is a sort of universal solvent that reduces difference to sameness, establishes false continuities, and leads to the endless and fruitless search for 'origins', which Foucault deplores. 'Influence' is an astrologico-medical term which, substituting obscurely for causation, also suggests spurious connections. The terms 'development' and 'evolution', with their biological associations, are rather more respectable metaphors; but they also produce false linkages and project them into an imagined past. The 'origin' and the 'already-said' – the inaccessible first in an intellectual series and the alleged source of an idea – are both byproducts of this retrospective historicizing; and so are presumed unities such as genres and disciplines, which claim both legitimacy and authority on this basis.

A target related to historical continuity was the notion of the self-conscious agent, the 'sovereign subject', the 'beginning knower', which was essential to notions of tradition and spirit. Subjectivity, the most fundamental of the 'discursive unities' put in question by Foucault, is obviously engrained in language, as Benveniste has shown; but the 'subject of a sentence' is not to be identified with its author and does not carry over into history.[35] The notion of a unified authorial *œuvre* is no more acceptable.[36] Nor does Foucault tolerate the conventional anthropology or humanistic philosophies based on such premises. The attack on the integrity of the subject defined by the Cartesian *Cogito* has a long history beginning with Hume (if not mystical theology) and including Marx, Nietzsche, and Freud; and like them Foucault regards subjectivism – 'subject-centered reason', Habermas has called it – as a barrier to intellectual history and to a critical science of humanity. In the last lines of *Les Mots et les choses* Foucault suggests, whether as a lament or a prediction, that with the criticism associated with his archeology of knowledge, the bourgeois concept of Man might 'be erased, like a face drawn in sand at the edge of the sea'.[37]

Yet as the speaker and writer fade from view, speech and writing, language and discourse, gather importance. Recently it has been the linguistic turn that

---

[34] *The Prophets of Extremity: Nietzsche, Heidegger, Foucault, Derrida* (Berkeley, 1985), 228; and see Manfred Frank, *What is Neostructuralism?*, trans. Sabine Wilke and Richard Gray (Minneapolis, 1989), 166.

[35] 'De la Subjectivité dans le langage', *Problèmes de linguistique générale*, I (Paris, 1966), 258–66.

[36] *Archeology of Knowledge*, 21ff.

[37] *The Order of Things: An Archeology of the Human Sciences* (New York, 1970), 387.37.22105.

has attracted the attention of historians.[38] The phrase is Gustav Bergman's but the phenomenon is far from unprecedented. Nietzsche's positing of 'the infinite interpretability of all things'[39] is an analogy drawn from language; and a century earlier there was what Gadamer called 'Herder's ill-fated criticism of the Kantian transcendental turn' – and Jacques Derrida also recalled this 'metacriticism'.[40] Renaissance humanism, too, was in part a linguistic – both a philological and a rhetorical – protest against the abstractive excesses of scholasticism, following the lead of the ancient sophists. In Stefan George's phrase, repeatedly cited by Heidegger, 'Where word breaks off no thing may be.'[41]

The 'linguistic turn' has been made by most philosophical movements by now, even analytical and Marxist philosophy, and as usual in the search for foundations and a universal standpoint from which to pass judgments on the human condition. Linguistic criticism certainly undercuts the spiritual world of ideas; but 'language', when divorced from the particularities of different linguistic traditions, can also be 'reified' and made into a philosophical fetish. Heidegger speaks of language but in practice regards German and Greek (rather than, say, Sanskrit or Chinese) as closer to Being than any other. His former pupil Gadamer (while regarding hermeneutics as universal) is more self-critical, speaking of 'trying to draw out of one's mother tongue new ways of thinking'.[42] The implication is not only that there is no *Ding an sich* but also no *Geist an sich*; and moreover, 'there is no meaning where expression fails'. Language is the ocean in which we all swim – and whatever our dreams of rigorous science, we are fishes, not oceanographers.

The linguistic turn was apparent in other connections, for example in the 'new rhetoric' of the past generation, which draws attention to the habits and conventions of language, like Foucault calling into question the control of speakers and writers over their own discourse. The arts of speaking and

---

[38] Richard Rorty (ed.), *The Linguistic Turn* (Chicago, 1967); Martin Jay, 'Should Intellectual History Take a Linguistic Turn?', in *Modern European Intellectual History: Reappraisals and New Perspectives*, ed. Dominick LaCapra and Steven Kaplan (Ithaca, 1982), from a conference originally called 'The future of intellectual history'.

[39] Ernst Behler, *Confrontations: Derrida, Heidegger, Nietzsche*, trans. Steven Taubenbeck (Stanford, 1991), 89; and see Alan D. Schrift, *Nietzsche and the Question of Interpretation: Between Hermeneutics and Deconstruction* (New York, 1990).

[40] *Dialogue and Deconstruction: The Gadamer–Derrida Encounter*, ed. Diane P. Michelfelder and Richard E. Palmer (Albany, 1989), 102; Derrida, *Edmund Husserl's Origins of Geometry*, trans. John P. Leavey (Stony Brook, 1978), 70.

[41] 'The Nature of Language', *On the Way to Language*, trans. Peter D. Hertz (San Francisco, 1982), 57–108.

[42] *Dialogue and Deconstruction*, 93.

writing are both based on conscious imitation, but every literate person is moving in linguistic channels carved by predecessors, deposited in the memory, and repeated in different contexts. Particular languages produce semantic fields which make possible communication and dialogue; and linguistic usage – particular topoi and word-combinations – has its own inertial force which acquires meaning apart from the intentions of users. This is one reason for being wary of the 'intentional fallacy' in interpreting texts.

One of the most impressive vistas opened up by the linguistic turn is the modern philosophy of hermeneutics in the form given by Gadamer, who, following Heidegger, extended the line of thought in the direction suggested not by Nietzsche (as did Heidegger and Derrida), but rather by Dilthey.[43] Rejecting revolutionary ruptures as a condition of understanding, Gadamer preserved belief in a kind of continuity making communication and 'dialogue' possible not only between speakers but also over time. There are no absolute beginnings, no understanding without prejudice, without 'forestructures of understanding' provided by language and the 'life-world'. Pursuing the old quest for 'the I in the Thou', Gadamer accepts the horizon-structure of experience but doubles it to accommodate the contexts of the past as well as the inquiring present. Language is a continuum making interpretation possible, but it does not permit the sort of retrospective mind-reading assumed by the 'empathy' of Romantic hermeneutics. That meaning must always be constructed in the present is the hermeneutical condition of Gadamer's kind of historicism. To understand, in short, is always to understand *differently*.

An important offshoot of hermeneutics is reception theory, or reception history (*Rezeptionsgeschichte*), which follows Gadamer's line by shifting attention from writing to reading. In fact intellectual history is more concerned with the original intention of authors and meaning of their texts than with their 'fortune' in later contexts. What Paul Ricœur calls the 'semantic autonomy' of texts is the condition of the interpretations and misinterpretations which accompany the reception of writings.[44] For Ricœur the poles of interpretation are the hermeneutics of tradition and the hermeneutics of suspicion, the first locating the position of Gadamer (and of Lovejoy), who seeks an experience of tradition, the second that of Foucault, who is devoted to the critique of ideology.[45] For Gadamer 'tradition' and continuity make possible the common ground of understanding and communication which,

---

[43] Ibid., 25.
[44] *Interpretation Theory* (Fort Worth, 1976), 25.
[45] *Hermeneutics and the Human Sciences*, trans. John B. Thompson (Cambridge, 1981), 63–100.

via ideas, connects present and past (the western past); for Foucault they
mean entrapment in or complicity with ideology and a denial of the ruptures
between the successive *epistemes* which represent decipherable codes (critically
fabricated *Weltanschauungen*) of culture and patterns of underlying power
relations.

The linguistic turn prompted another and more severe tactic, which was
the textualist turn. In this literary/philosophical game of one-upmanship
Derrida substituted the transcendent phenomenon of language by the visible
presence of 'writing', through which – or rather through the hyper-textualist
device of 'traces' – he attempts not only to operate in the 'margins' of texts
but also to speak in the realm of the unspeakable and in effect to 'get behind
the back of language' (in Gadamer's terms) and of philosophical discourse.
Taking writing as the condition of knowledge is itself a traditional move, as
illustrated in the Renaissance preoccupation with *littera* (*litteratura*) and
scriptura and, more conspicuously, in the tradition of rabbinical (but also of
Protestant) scholarship.[46]

In this and other metalinguistic maneuvers of deconstruction Derrida
surpasses even Heidegger in claiming to be a 'beginning thinker' – in the goal
of transcending criticism or even, as in the notorious (non-)confrontation
with Gadamer, dialogue.[47] The very idea of situating Derrida's own writing
in the history of philosophical thought, declares one devotee, 'would amount
to defusing its alterity [*sic*] and explosive potential'.[48] To be effective, it
seems, cultural criticism, like philosophy, must be beyond the horizons of
historical inquiry. Breaking with tradition is itself traditional in philosophical
thought, as this Derridean adds, though without suggesting that the break
and the 'alterity' occur in the medium of rhetoric, or writing, rather than a
transcendent tradition of thinking (in Derridean terms a transcendental state
of *différence*, *née* difference) – or an anti-tradition of deconstruction – which
is itself set beyond language, criticism, and perhaps even history.

Foucault, too, sought to transcend language and 'the history of historians',
hoping, with the help of his *episteme*, to uncover the structures of society and
relations of power underlying social practice and discourse, but historians
have questioned the methods and especially his attitude toward historical

---

[46] Susan A. Handelman, *The Slayers of Moses: The Emergence of Rabbinic
Interpretation in Modern Literary Theory* (Albany, 1982); and see Christopher Norris,
Derrida (Cambridge, MA, 1987).

[47] See *Dialogue and Deconstruction* and Fred Dallmayr, *Critical Encounters: Between
Philosophy and Politics* (Notre Dame, 1987), 130–58.

[48] Rodolphe Gasché, *Inventions of Difference: On Jacques Derrida* (Cambridge,
MA, 1994), 58.

evidence.[49] For Foucault, learning does not enjoy high priority; and whether or not he himself was, by intention or vocation, a historian, his opinion was that history was too important to leave to such.[50] Foucault had more important things on his agenda. Criticisms of the concept of *episteme* (and of 'practice' and 'discourse') must be of the same order as criticisms of other such collective abstractions as spirit (*Welt-* or *Volksgeist*), *Weltanschauung*, *mentalité*, and other shorthand devices for grouping apparent homologies in various areas of behavior within a particular cultural horizon. Like Marxism, Freudianism, and critical theory, including the work of Habermas, it is another effort of getting 'behind the back of language', which had for centuries been the dream of 'philosophy as a rigorous science'.

This is also to some extent the noble dream of the German approach to intellectual history that succeeded old-fashioned *Geistes-* or *Ideengeschichte*. Like the French 'mentalities', German 'history of concepts' (*Begriffsgeschichte*) is an effort to reconstruct an intellectual field through the history of terms and families of terms similar to the English study of 'keywords'.[51] In fact *Begriffsgeschichte* is a species of cultural history focusing on semantic change and the social and political context of ideas, and its program depends on metahistorical considerations to determine the meanings behind the keywords being analysed. This enterprise began thirty years ago, before databases like Proteus and ARTFL made possible a much more extensive searching of semantic fields, but it has nonetheless greatly enriched the practices of conventional intellectual and social history.[52]

A last new frontier of intellectual history at the end of the twentieth century was the effort to understand cultures not only past but also alien.

---

[49] See J. G. Merquior, *Foucault* (Berkeley, 1985), 62ff.

[50] Against the opinion of two historians (Allan Megill and Jan Goldstein) the philosopher Gary Gutting (ed.), *The Cambridge Companion to Foucault* (Cambridge, 1994), 65, judges him to qualify as such – although not one historian appears among the twelve contributions to this volume. On Gutting's own theory of history see *Michel Foucault's Archaeology of Scientific Reason*, 175. And see Jan Goldstein (ed.), *Foucault and the Writing of History* (Oxford, 1994).

[51] See H.-G. Gadamer, 'Die Begriffsgeschichte und die Sprache der Philosophie', *Arbeitsgemeinschaft für Forschung des Landes Nordhein-Westfalen*, 170 (1971); Reinhard Koselleck, *Futures Past: On the Semantics of Historical Time*, trans. Keith Tribe (Cambridge, MA, 1985); and Melvin Richter, *The History of Political and Social Concepts: A Critical Introduction* (Oxford, 1995), offering a sympathetic exposition of the collective work, *Geschichtliche Grundbegriffe* and the *Handbuch politisch-sozialer Grundbegriffe*. Cf. Raymond Williams, *Keywords: A Vocabulary of Culture and Society* (London, 1976).

[52] 'French Research on the Treasury of French Language', a database at the University of Chicago.

Philosophy has not been much concerned with alterity, what Michel de Certeau calls 'heterology', which has been faced by historians, anthropologists, archeologists, mythographers, and other outward- and backward-looking scholars.[53] 'The course of history does not show us the Becoming of things foreign to us', argued Hegel, 'but the Becoming of ourselves and of our knowledge.'[54] But the hermeneutical philosophy of his contemporary Friedrich Schleiermacher sought the Thou as well as the I – the Other as well as the We – and this aim has been carried on and intensified by more recent followers; and it is here that the methods of 'anthropology', which have been found suspect by Kant and Foucault alike, again become relevant.

3. Post Time

'We have a duty to think of the dead,' said Novalis – having just commented that 'The human being continues to live and be active only in the realm of ideas.'[55] The simplest distinction in historical thinking has been that between the living We of the present and the dead They of the past. This is the grounds for that much-debated condition called Modernity, classically and modernly set apart from Antiquity. This idea defines the modern We who are literally and etymologically *à la mode* (and the 'outmoded' They) – though whether we have surpassed our forebears, or will be surpassed by our 'afterbears', remains a question. Since the middle ages the *via antiqua* was the way of the fathers, while the *via moderna* of the sons – and daughters – has always promised a way into the future.[56] The famous seventeenth-century 'Quarrel between the Ancients and the Moderns' had its roots in antiquity, and we still hear its echoes.[57] The words are different, but the music sounds the same. Today the parties are redefined as Moderns and Postmoderns, but the anxiety to escape obsolescence (being 'history' in a pejorative sense) remains.

---

[53] *Heterologies: Discourse on the Other*, trans. Brian Massumi (Minneapolis, 1986).
[54] *Lectures on the History of Philosophy*, trans. E. S. Haldane and Frances H. Simon (London, 1892), I, 4.
[55] *Philosophical Writings*, trans. Margaret Mahoney Stoljar (Albany, 1997), 29.
[56] See 'Ancients and Moderns: A Symposium', *Journal of the History of Ideas*, 48 (1987), 3–50, with essays by William J. Courtenay, Charles Trinkaus, Heiko A. Oberman, and Niel W. Gilbert.
[57] See Joseph M. Levine, *The Battle of the Books: History and Literature in the Augustan Age* (Ithaca, 1991) and *Between the Ancients and the Moderns: Baroque Culture in Restoration England* (New Haven, 1999).

Modernity was defined by the changing horizons – problems, interests, and assumptions – of the present, and so the changing views of the past. Originally defined as a generational pattern in contrast to a more or less generalized Antiquity, Modernity has in the twentieth century been reduced to a doctrine, that is, Modernism, torn between the bright future of limitless Progress and descent into a new barbarism of hyper-rationality.[58] Modernism, along with its ugly sibling, 'modernization', has shaped and disfigured much of the past century, in the name, always, of the new. Modernism in art and literature has been a joy to behold, or to recall; its social, economic, and political aspects have been less edifying, as Max Weber saw a century ago. What has defined modernism above all is the 'demon of progress in the arts' (in Wyndham Lewis's words) – and a tyranny of the avant-garde that seems to grow even as Modernism itself disappears.[59] As Harry Levin asked forty years ago, 'What was Modernism?'[60]

Like modernism and modernization, modernity has come in for more serious criticism, especially with the failures of the Enlightenment's project of rational and moral progress; and of these the most searching has been Hans Blumenberg's critique of the process of 'secularization' (another face of modernism).[61] For Blumenberg neither beginnings nor endings are accessible to us. Beginnings are lost in myth, and there is no first myth perceivable to modern historians.[62] Ends are out of sight, too, and the Enlightenment hope for an 'end to myth' (through reason) is itself myth. Modernity can do no more than furnish us with new forms of myth, which we can never recognize as such until it is too late. (Perhaps this is what Vico meant to say about 'wisdom', which for him ends, as it begins, in barbarism and myth.)

But modernism is over; Ezra Pound's motto was 'Make it new!', but what happens when novelty – or the novelty of novelty – wears off and when the young want to escape the 'tradition of the new'?[63] One response may be to proclaim the death of some cultural phenomenon or other – 'the end of cultural history' (after 1918),[64] 'the end of art history', or even of Art itself.[65]

---

[58] David Kolb, *The Critique of Pure Modernity: Hegel, Heidegger, and After* (Chicago, 1986).

[59] Peter Bürger, *Theory of the Avant-Garde*, trans. M. Shaw (Minneapolis, 1984).

[60] *Massachusetts Review*, 1 (1960), 609–30.

[61] *The Legitimacy of the Modern Age*, trans. Robert M. Wallace (Cambridge, MA, 1983).

[62] *Work on Myth*, trans. Robert M. Wallace (Cambridge, MA, 1985).

[63] Harold Rosenberg, *The Tradition of the New* (Chicago, 1959).

[64] Stefan Haas, 'Historische Kulturforschung' in *Deutschland 1880–1930* (Cologne, 1994), 268.

[65] Hervé Fischer, *L'Histoire de l'art est terminée* (Mayenne, 1981).

But as another scholar has remarked, 'Art is not dead. What is finished is its history as a progress toward the new.'[66] And yet the 'new always returns' in some guise. After death we move on again, and what else could this new novelty – divested of innovationist rhetoric – be called except 'postmodernism' (on the analogy of Neoplatonism and *Nachkantianer*).[67]

Postmodernism is a beginning, as it were, that is defined as an ending, a historical category that affects to deny history. It is a sort of life of the mind after the death of the subject and the demise of the comforting metanarratives which used to give stable meaning to human life. 'The word "postmodern"', remarked a German critic, 'belongs to a network of "postist" concepts and ways of thinking' and hence a new species of '-isms' for the young to throw in the face of the old, or (at least in earlier times) the Left in the face of the Right. Even before the post-millennium we lived in a depressing climate of 'posts': post-industrialist, post-Marxist, post-feminist, post-historical, post-western, post-human, post-etcetera.[68] 'What are we calling postmodernity?', Foucault asked. 'I'm not up to date.'[69] (Or soon, or even already, perhaps, 'What was Postmodernism?')

It would be unwise in the present state of confusion to attempt a definition of the postmodern. In general postmodernism is a product of the excesses of modernism, and it is difficult to draw a line between the two, especially as 'postmodernism' resists definitions and the sort of historicizing judgment made in the first part of this sentence. Chronology becomes irrelevant: for Lyotard 'the essay (Montaigne) is postmodern, and the fragment (the *Athenaeum*) is modern'.[70] Postmodernism suggests the collapse of rational structures and metanarratives – but then so did modernism in some of its forms.

Yet the term has its own history, which, not surprisingly, begins in the heyday of modernism. During the First World War a German work on

---

[66] Hans Belting, *The End of the History of Art?*, trans. Christopher S. Wood (Chicago, 1987), 4; and in general see Germain Bazin, *Histoire de l'histoire de l'art de Vasari à nos jours* (Paris, 1986).

[67] Georg Iggers, *Historiography in the Twentieth Century: From Scientific Objectivity to the Postmodernist Challenge* (Hanover, NH, 1997); Manfred Frank, *Was ist Neo-Strukturalismus?* (Frankfurt, 1984); Derek Attridge, Geoff Bennington, and Robert Young (eds), *Post-Structuralism and the Question of History* (Cambridge, 1987).

[68] Most of these terms do not appear in the *OED*, which devotes eight columns to 'post-' words.

[69] 'Structuralism and Poststructuralism', *Telos*, 55 (1983), 204, cited by Alex Callinicos, *Against Postmodernism* (New York, 1990), 5; and see Thomas Flynn, 'Foucault's Mapping of History', in *Cambridge Companion to Foucault*, ed. Gutting, 42–4.

[70] Jean François Lyotard, *The Postmodern Explained* (Minneapolis, 1992), 15.

nihilism, decadence, and 'the crisis of European culture' applied it to the Nietzschean *Übermensch*.[71] Since then the term has had a colorful career in the arts and literature (though science has not been immune from its influence) but has retained its ties with Nietzscheanism. For Fredric Jameson postmodernism is an 'inverted millennarianism ... in which premonitions of the future have been replaced by senses of the end of this or that'; and there are already many indications of the end of postmodernism itself.[72]

The political aspect of postmodernism is debatable, but it seems undeniable that ethnicity, feminism, 'queer history', and various areas in cultural studies have reinforced the targets of postmodernist (as in many cases modernist) criticism, beginning with universal (male, bourgeois) reason, common (declassed, ungendered) language, conceptions of unified and hierarchical knowledge, general (often sociological) theories, and 'master narratives' of the development of western civilization.[73] To these one may also add the notion of 'experience', which has also enjoyed a general sort of legitimacy that belies its fragmented character[74] – and if 'experience', why not 'practice'? Notions of deconstruction, decentering, local knowledge, and non-linear history have called all the above into question – including even, perhaps, the idea of a foundational criticism that can perform the rational project of 'calling into question'.

If the Modern is a culmination of western culture, the Postmodern may be located not only after but also outside the confines of this self-constructed tradition.[75] The point of view of the 'Other', not only blacks and women

---

[71] Rudolf Pannwitz, *Die Krisis der europäischen Kultur* (Nürnberg, 1917), 674, 'postmodernen Menschen'.

[72] To judge from the titles of two books published already in the 1980s on *Farewell to (Post-) Modernism?* and *Life after Postmodernism*. For an old-fashioned empiricist attack on such newfangled notions see Kenneth Windschuttle, *The Killing of History: How a Discipline is Being Murdered by Literary Critics and Literary Theorists* (Sydney, 1994); a more muted (but also more superficial) criticism in Joyce Appleby, Lynn Hunt, and Margaret Jacob, *Telling the Truth about History* (New York, 1994).

[73] Donna J. Haraway, *Simians, Cyborgs, and Women: The Reinvention of Nature* (New York, 1991), 194; and see Joan Scott, *Gender and the Politics of History* (New York, 1988), Bonnie G. Smith, *The Gender of History: Men, Women, and Historical Practice* (Cambridge, 1998); and the two volumes of articles from the *Journal of the History of Ideas* edited by Maryanne Cline Horowitz, *Race, Gender, and Rank: Early Modern Ideas of Humanity* (Rochester, 1992) and *Race, Class, and Gender in 19th-Century Culture* (Rochester, 1991).

[74] See Joan W. Scott, 'The Evidence of Experience', in *Questions of Evidence: Proof, Practice, and Persuasion across the Disciplines*, ed. James Chandler, Arnold I. Davidson, and Harry Harootunian (Chicago, 1994), 363–87.

[75] See Robert Young, *Writing History and the West* (London, 1990), and Tzvetan Todorov, *On Human Diversity: Nationalism, Racism, and Exoticism in French Thought*, trans. Catherine Porter (Cambridge, MA, 1993).

excluded from male cultural monopolies but also colonial victims of the expansionist spirit of the western powers, can only be inferred from the outside – the eternal dilemma of anthropology – but this effort makes possible a critical stance with respect to the entrenched and collusive interests of academic learning, including the writing of history. For some critics the 'alterior' and the subaltern suggest a stance that is not only postmodern but also postwestern and posthistorical – and of course posthistoricist.[76]

Like the Postmodern, 'Posthistory' is (among other things) pretension, hyperbole, and mystification; yet one can appreciate the attempt to find a term equal to the new wave of shattering experiences of this generation.[77] The old Eurocentric story-lines of Hegel, Marx, and their dialectical progeny do not, in recent retrospect, make sense; Enlightened 'metanarratives' of Reason, Toleration, and Humanity (which Lovejoy would probably accept) and western civilization moving toward a glorious brotherly (and sisterly) future do not hold up under the scrutiny of experience or history. Yet there were premonitions of this collapse long before the catastrophes of the twentieth century – and Nietzsche's formula, 'God is Dead', is just one conceit that suggests the collapse of the 'Enlightenment project' and the rational and scientistic foundations on which it rested.

Yet there is little new in these views except the extent of their dissemination. To historians postmodernism is a process of unbuilding, undermining foundations, or denial of metanarratives; and as such, in this millennialist climate of opinion, it may claim some historical associations with such radical extensions of modernist and anti-foundationalist thought as Heidegger's destruction of metaphysics, Bohr's principle of complementarity, Heisenberg's indeterminism, Vaihinger's philosophy of 'as if', Gödel's critique of metalogic, and new ventures in chaos and complexity theory.[78] From this general perspective postmodernism may indeed be seen as a continuation of the negative aspect of the 'Enlightenment project' – and what a modern philosopher has called the 'modern project to rigor' from Descartes to Nietzsche (and the

[76] Megill, *Prophets of Extremity*, 151.

[77] Lutz Niethammer, *Posthistoire: Has History Come to an End?*, trans. Patrick Camiller (London, 1992), and Francis Fukuyama, *The End of History and the Last Man* (New York, 1992), and 'The End of History, Five Years Later', *History and Theory*, 34 (1995, Theme Issue), 27–43; also Gianni Vattimo, *The End of Modernity*, trans. Jon R. Snyder (Baltimore, 1988), 77.

[78] For example, Arkady Plotnitsky, *Complementarity: Anti-Epistemology after Bohr and Derrida* (Durham, 1994); and N. Katherine Hayles, *Chaos Bound: Orderly Disorder in Contemporary Literature and Science* (Ithaca, 1990), and *How We Became Posthuman* (Chicago, 1999).

'new Nietzsche') – that is, skepticism, criticism, and metacriticism, which each generation seems to take up afresh.[79] Reason completed, the turn is to imagination, or history; memory and emotions exhausted, it is to science; positivism ineffective, to the human sciences; modernism spent, to postmodernism – and so what next? Every generation has its turning, or returning, and its turning against, or overturning; and this must shape the writing of intellectual and cultural history.

This study has been about the 'backgrounds' of intellectual history; it offers no prescriptions but only suggestions and warnings about the conditions and possibilities of inquiry. Intellectual history is still linked to philosophy, but in its current state, including the postmodern eruptions, to the extent that they can be salvaged for purposes of historical inquiry. This means bypassing the old circular debates about Truth, Reality, Objectivity, and other absolutes, theological anxieties, and staples of metanarratives. There are many disciplinary paths to be followed, insights to be gained, connections to be made, many stories to be told, many methods to be considered from various arts and sciences – but no single method to be imposed. There are also still idols to be avoided. Academic fashions come and go; careers are made and unmade; the one constant is the need for extra-disciplinary criticism and historical questioning.

This may mean reconsidering some of the old taboos of historical scholarship. Continuity is a symptom of conservatism if not reaction, and yet it 'continues' on various levels of human existence, verbal and non-verbal – sometimes the words stay the same though the music changes and sometimes vice versa. 'We have never been modern', Bruno Latour argues – and so how can we be 'postmodern'?[80] Obituaries have been written for the Subject, the Author, and even the Book; but sentences continue to be uttered and written (whatever the consciousness and will behind them), and books continue to be produced. Anachronism has been one of the deadly sins of historians, and yet in view of the hermeneutical predicament revealed by philosophers, what else is interpretation but methodological anachronism? Situated within our own cultural horizons, we are all, like it or not, Whigs.

If we have got beyond the noble dreams of philosophy and older forms of history, we have not escaped our own myths and pretensions. Among these are the ever-renewed claims to novelty; the notion of a conceptual map that neatly defines our particular cultural horizons; the assumption of a coherent past about which a single consistent narrative can be fashioned; and the belief in a

---

[79] Patric Madigan, *The Modern Project to Rigor: Descartes to Nietzsche* (Lanham, MD, 1986).

[80] *We Have Never Been Modern*, trans. Catherine Porter (Cambridge, MA, 1993).

spiritual world of ideas which allows us direct and univocal communication. Now there is a sense, no doubt a philosophical sense, in which these claims may be defended; but they are not premises which make possible critical historical inquiry. Rather they are themselves creations of culture and of history and part of the background of intellectual history inviting investigation.

These are some of the terms, ideas, forms of discourse, and practices that arose in the last years of the past century, and millennium, and that inform the current climate of opinion in which intellectual and cultural history must be written, read, and discussed. Modern (and postmodern) conditions of intellectual inquiry cannot be ignored; nor can we return to a state of innocence, before the revelations and disillusions of twentieth-century experience. No business-as-usual sociology or analytical philosophy can nullify the insights and criticisms suggested by, among others, Heidegger, Foucault, and Blumenberg; and intellectual history cannot be written under the assumptions of simple rationality and belief in unfettered human agency. Hume's rule continues to apply and so deserves repeating: 'This sceptical doubt, both with respect to reason and the senses, is a malady which can never be radically cured, but must return upon us in every moment, however we may chase it away.'

4. New Intellectual History?

The idea of a 'new intellectual history' may seem to go against the premise of these studies, which have focused largely on the old – on the continuities which still underlie the apparent and highly publicized ruptures of modern and postmodern culture. Yet there are indeed new conditions which, provoked by recurrent visitations of skepticism, cannot be ignored. No more than philosophers can intellectual historians continue their work as if Heidegger, Gadamer, or Foucault had never written; and these novel results of an old skeptical line of questioning require rethinking the tasks and tactics of contemporary intellectual history.

In the first place it seems clear that the old-fashioned history of ideas has seen its best days, as have old-fashioned social, economic, and political history and crypto-Marxist or liberal efforts to connect the ideal and the real in any reductionist or simplistically 'reflective' way.[81] Nor, as François Simiand pointed

---

[81] Asks Jacques Le Goff, 'Peut-on encore parler d'une Histoire des Idées aujourd'hui?', in *Storia delle idee: problemi e perspective*, ed. Massimo L. Bianchi (Rome, 1989), 69.

out a century ago, is tracing ideas back to other ideas through 'influence' satisfactory, for 'In truth what has one explained?'[82] The problem is that, as far as historians are concerned, neither ideas nor social or political structures have any determinable – definable or historicizable – existence apart from the sources and the linguistic medium which shape and define historical inquiry.

Second, what confronts the historian and his or her devices are textual traces or other cultural surrogates which call for informed interpretation. It may be assumed that there are authorial or other creative intentions and ideas behind these traces and that inferences may be made about these intentions, ideas, and questions of human agency; but it is the tradition of interpretation, which is also to say misinterpretation, that constitutes the substance of intellectual history. What lies beyond are spiritual mysteries that can only be taken on faith.

Third, the texts in question require a setting in context, but such a context is not something merely to be appropriated at second hand from available historiographical conventions; rather it is to be drawn out of other textual materials within the same semantic horizons, whether defined by the language of the age or by intellectual traditions that apparently inform the texts.

Fourth, questions of meaning remain despite the decentering effects of interpretations which must at once consider authoritative, textual, and readerly assignations. So historians, no less than literary scholars, should consider inherent, implied, and potential as well as inferrably original meanings. There are human wills behind texts, but also texts – *ad infinitum* – behind wills.

As always, intellectual historians need help from other disciplines, but alliances have changed. What has happened to Marx and Freud? Of course devotees of these founding thinkers remain in practice – Fredric Jameson, for example, and Peter Gay[83] – but more recently Nietzsche, Heidegger, Gadamer, Habermas, Foucault, Kuhn, and Geertz have been much more in evidence (for the time being, anyway).[84] What happened to Marx, Freud, and the others is that, while their ideas lose their followings, it is because they have in part been absorbed in the more general culture.

One of the large intellectual shifts in the past generation has been the breakdown of the notion that history is an objective process that can be made

---

[82] *Méthode historique et sciences sociales*, ed. Marina Cedrono (Paris, 1987), 171 ('A propos de l'histoire des idées' [1903]).

[83] Gay, *Freud for Historians* (New York, 1985) and *The Bourgeois Experience* (New York, 1984–96); and Jameson, *The Ideologies of Theory* (Minneapolis, 1988) and *Postmodernism, or, the Contradictions of Late Capitalism* (Durham, 1994).

[84] *Why We are Not Nietzscheans*, ed. Luc Ferry and Alain Renaut and trans. Robert de Loaiza (Chicago, 1997 [1991]).

the target of a quantifying and, as it were, computerizable science.[85] Now some aspects of historical experience can surely be measured and plotted, but this is remote from any holistic conception of history as an analyzable mechanism or organism. This dream, whether or not noble, is an offspring of sociologism, if not of La Place's demon.

History is whatever can be recalled from memory or inferred from extant sources; and on such foundations an infinite number of stories can be told and retold, interpreted and reinterpreted. This is the case not only of the public sphere, classical forum for western historians, but also the private sphere, opened up by cultural history and postmodern 'cultural studies'. This suggests that the primary auxiliary to historical inquiry is heuristics – the art of selecting, criticizing, and deploying source materials in response to certain questions.

Efforts to resist this line of criticism, whether made out of fears or relativism or hopes of shoring up older values of historical explanation, are recurrent. Frequently, however, as in the case of a recent book of historiographical prescriptions, these well-intended efforts depend on misrepresentations, evasions, or ignorance of what Nietzsche and Heidegger, for example, were about or on what level the discussion is set.[86] Like Beauty and Virtue, Truth is a value that has a history, a rhetorical tradition, and many linguistic conditions: it is not an article of a metahistorical creed or of an unproblematized political agenda; but it remains an object of inquiry, at least for historians. In any case history in none of its forms can 'speak' except through human ventriloquism, and there can be no big story, or final myth, except perhaps for theology or poetry, that can capture the nature and destiny of man–humanity.

In a way the trajectory suggested in this study parallels the story told by Nietzsche, and after him Heidegger, about western philosophy, following humanity's alienation from being – analogous to the departure from Plato's cave or the expulsion from Paradise – and long journey down the false path of metaphysics. The trouble, as Nietzsche saw it, had begun with Plato, who 'severed the instincts from the *polis*' and made what was imaginary 'real' by placing his followers under the 'yoke of the "idea"' and by reducing ideas to objects of dialectic; and the process was continued in the canon of formal philosophy, especially by scholasticism, Cartesianism, and German idealism, which all sought 'reality' as well as truth, beauty, and justice in the world of

---

[85] See Alberto Gianquinto, *Storia e scienza* (Milan, 1985).
[86] Appleby, Hunt, and Jacob, *Telling the Truth about History*, and for background Novick, *That Noble Dream*.

'ideas'.[87] But reality, taught Nietzsche, was in the world of appearances – in the Platonic cave – and not in the fictional and logically manipulated forms of the philosophers. (Zarathustra, too, left his cave, but to enter the world not of supernatural enlightenment but of struggling humanity.) This was the argument sustaining Nietzsche's infamous maxim, 'God is dead', meaning, in Heidegger's paraphrase, that 'God as the supersensory ground and goal of all reality is dead.'[88] 'Great Pan is dead', indeed all the gods are dead, including little demi-gods like St Thomas, Descartes, Kant, and Hegel, who would think God's thoughts after (and even improve on) him. Historians, if not philosophers, cannot help being atheists.

This critical line of argument I follow not to justify the prophetic mode assumed by Nietzsche or the world-mastering dreams of Heidegger – alternative paths to secular salvation – but only to justify the conjectural account of the 'descent of ideas' and give some warrant to the projects of intellectual and cultural history. Released from the yoke of ideas, intellectual history can be regrounded in the temporal world – not the ontological world of Heidegger's Being and Time likewise oriented toward the future, but the world of limited horizons and particular points of view which both constrain and liberate historical inquiry. In this post-Nietzschean, post-Heideggerian age, historians cannot hope to ascend to the sphere of ideas, nor to discover solutions to questions of destiny, salvation, or even Lovejoy's query, 'What's the matter with man?' But they can pursue the original task of inquiry set by Herodotus and the historical alternative as a way to the common goal of human wisdom and self-knowledge. 'For', according to one of Heidegger's more modest aphorisms, 'questioning is the piety of thought.'[89]

The 'descent of ideas' is a graphic and perhaps hyperbolic way of referring to the direction, if not goal, of the study of the intellectual and cultural past. We have 'a duty to think of the dead', according to Novalis, but we do so without their complicity, in our own thoughts, which we express in the language of our place in time and space. We carry on 'dialogues with the dead', but the responses to our questions come mainly through texts which we can only interpret in our own words. *Ideas*, with their spiritualist baggage and the leap of faith they require for human exchange, are still alive in the

---

[87] *The Will to Power*, trans. Walter Kaufmann and R. J. Hollingdale (New York, 1967), 235, 282; and see Karl Löwith, *Martin Heidegger and European Nihilism*, trans. Gary Steiner (New York, 1995), 82.

[88] 'The Word of Nietzsche: "God is Dead"', in *The Question of Technology and other Essays*, trans. William Lovitt (New York, 1971), 61, referring to Nietzsche's *Gay Science* (1882), 125.

[89] *The Question of Technology*, 35.

history of philosophy, perhaps in the history of science, not much in the history of literature, in the human sciences hardly at all. As Whitehead put it, 'Ideas won't keep.'[90] This is the result not of nihilism but of a post-Humean return of skepticism, or criticism, which forbids a reversion to an innocent faith in ideas except as unexamined shorthand for deeper questions of language, discourse, interpretation, and communication imposed on historians. It is in this sense, and in this intellectual context, that we have seen the descent of ideas into the sublunar sphere of historical understanding.

---

[90] *The Dialogues of Alfred North Whitehead* (New York, 1953), 100.

Index